Free To Think

Why Scientific Integrity Matters

By Caroline Crocker, MSc, PhD

LEAFCUTTER PRESS

Leafcutter Press, Publisher

Leafcutter Press, PO Box 102, Southworth, WA 98386. Published in the United States of America

No portion of this book may be reproduced or transmitted in any form or by any means electronic or mechanical including photocopying, reprinting, or any information storage or retrieval system without a legitimately obtained license or permission in writing from Leafcutter Press, LLC.

Library Catalog Data

Author: I. Caroline Crocker (1958 –)

ISBN 978-0-9818734-4-2 (paperback)

1. Discrimination – United States
2. Education and science – United States
3. Law and legislation – United States
4. Religion and science – United States
5. Evolution (Biology)
6. Intelligent Design
7. Academic freedom – United States

Book cover photography by Jonathan Crocker
Book cover design by Mario A. Lopez and Kevin Wirth
Typography by Lori A. McKee

Acknowledgements & Dedication

This book is dedicated to my family, who have supported me through this adventure—

My wonderful husband Richard, who patiently listened to my dreams and disappointments and cheered me on throughout;

My amazing parents Frits and Meta, the only people in the world who act like they think I'm perfect;

My precious children, Catherine, Jonathan, James, and Stan, who know that I'm not, but love me anyway;

And of course my beautiful grandbaby, Megan Abigail.

I would also like to thank—

The people who have prayed for me, encouraged me, and given me practical help;

The community of scientists and professionals who have given me invaluable advice, especially Kevin Wirth my publisher, Mario Lopez my illustrator, Sig Swanstrom, Jim Hooker, Michael Behe, Art Chadwick, Tim Standish, Bill Dembski, Robert Marks, John Calvert, Norm Geisler, Annmarie Geddes-Lipold, and innumerable others;

The team of people who patiently reviewed this book, checking for accuracy and clarity, Judith Greisinger, Carolyn Burns, Kathy Gatewood, Bill Middlesworth, Jann Dunlap, Ed Sisson, James Crocker, Frits and Meta Evenbly and more;

And last, but not least, my students, whose determination to succeed, sometimes against all odds, will always be an inspiration to me.

About the Author

Caroline Crocker is the President of the American Institute for Technology and Science Education (AITSE), a nonprofit organization with the mission of increasing scientific understanding and integrity. Dr. Crocker taught various biology courses for five years at George Mason University (GMU) and Northern  Virginia Community College. While at GMU, she won three grants, including one from the Center for Teaching Excellence, received commendations for high student ratings and wrote a cell biology workbook. Dr. Crocker did post-doctoral studies in fluorescence resonance energy transfer analysis of interactions between proteins of the T-cell receptor/NF-κB signal transduction pathway at the Uniformed Services University of the Health Sciences in Bethesda, MD. While working on a Ph.D. in immunopharmacology (The Modulation of Phosphodiesterase Activity in Human T-Lymphocytes) as an external student at Southampton University, U.K., she was employed at Creighton University as a research associate, bringing in numerous grants, conducting basic immunology research, and publishing extensively. She received an M.Sc. from Birmingham University, a B.Sc. from Warwick University, and an A.A. from Des Moines Area Community College, having graduated from high school at the age of 16. Dr. Crocker now lives with her husband in California. They have four adult children (two married) and one grandchild.

Table of Contents

Foreword by Ben Stein

It would be lovely to believe that while all kinds of groups think vilification, libels, and superstition rule the worlds of daily life, inside the university the search for *truth* is paramount. It would be sweet to believe that once inside the gates of academic Eden, man throws aside all party affiliation and ideology and proceeds only on the basis of what is true, shows sound thinking and can be proved.

Alas, it would be nice to think so, but it's a total myth. The academic world, as far as I can tell, is largely, though not entirely, ruled by party politics, the prevailing academic fashion, and loyalty to the most powerful faction within the academy. I saw this myself many years ago when I, a fan of then President Richard Nixon, was a teacher at the University of California at Santa Cruz and was treated like a freak from outer space.

Within the last four years, when I set out with the persons at Premise Media to make a movie about academic suppression in the arena of biology, life origins, cell biology, and the social effects of Darwinism, I was dismayed to see that the situation had become far worse than what it had been in 1972.

Despite lack of clear evidence that Darwinism explains everything it purports to, no one is allowed to question that the evidence had to be "Darwinist", that is, accidental. Despite the truth that no life could exist without the basic laws of gravity and physics and thermodynamics, and despite the absence of any evidence that these laws came into being accidentally, one cannot question that they must have come about by chance.

Despite the fact of the incredible, mind boggling complexity of the cell, despite the truth that no one has ever been able to explain how a cell could have hundreds of thousands of interlocking parts that repair and reproduce themselves, no one is allowed to question that the cell happened by accident.

But a few brave people did question the unquestionable. A few brave people stood up to academic suppression and witch hunts. One of those people was Prof. Caroline Crocker. She dared to just suggest the possibility that there might have been an Intelligent Designer of the Universe and the cell. For this, she was tormented and thrown from the parapets of the academy.

But she did not die. She came back swinging hard, and she is still fighting.

She's really fighting for you, because if you picked up this book, you are probably at least a bit angry at the academic suppression of persons who suggest that there might be an Intelligent Designer. You are probably on the side of free speech about evolution vs. Intelligent Design--as Charles Darwin was himself.

Keep reading. This is a brave woman and her fight is your fight. It is our fight.

Preface by Edward Sisson

I consider it a privilege to be writing the preface to *Free to Think: Why Scientific Integrity Matters* because I believe this narrative has application to any professor who may find him or herself in a dispute with their university. It was also an honor to represent Professor Crocker in her specific complaint against George Mason University (GMU), which involved her academic freedom to dissent from majority scientific opinion on a matter of great public interest. I am grateful for the generosity of my law firm, Arnold & Porter (A&P), because they allowed me to work pro bono for her.

However, the events in this case are still quite troubling to me. It appears that the university where Dr. Crocker was a professor (GMU) infringed her rights of academic freedom, despite being a state institution bound by the First Amendment. Then, when GMU found out that one of my partners at A&P was interested in representing the university in an entirely separate commercial (not pro bono) legal matter, GMU used the possibility of that business as leverage to get A&P to order me to stop representing Professor Crocker. It is important to note that standard practice among large institutions is to waive such potential conflicts of interest.

To explain, in a world of large institutions and large law firms, it often happens that an institution that is being sued by one lawyer in a large firm will want to hire a different lawyer in the same firm in some other dispute, or in non-litigation matters. On its face, this can look like a conflict of interest: how can one partner in a law firm be suing a party when another partner is representing that same party? The rules of legal ethics anticipate this and allow that party to choose to accept that situation by "waiving" the conflict-of-interest; large law firms have standard procedures to "firewall" communications between the two lawyers, as does A&P. The waiver rules are intended to permit law firms to be both in favor of and adverse to the same party at the same time — so long as this does not amount to the same law firm representing both sides in the very same lawsuit.

But here, it appears to me that after receiving my initial letter asserting Dr. Crocker's claims and stating that I was representing her, GMU learned that a different partner in A&P was interested in representing the university in a commercial business transaction. This case was entirely unrelated to Professor Crocker's claim against GMU, but GMU realized that they could take advantage of the opportunity by knocking out Professor Crocker's lawyer (me) by refusing to make the standard waiver. It appears that GMU told my partner that they would not consider hiring him unless A&P promised to first discharge Professor Crocker as a client. I say "appears" because my firm did not alert me to any of this until after making the decision to accept GMU's condition and contacting Dr. Crocker. Thus I can only infer what must have happened. However, I hasten to add that this is based on my 14-year career at Arnold and Porter and knowing the customary practices of large law firms and large institutional clients.

It should be obvious to all professors — even those who oppose Professor Crocker on the merits of her case — that GMU should not have used this tactic to deprive Professor Crocker of her lawyer. Professors may find themselves in disputes with their universities and colleges for a wide variety of reasons, including cases that the professors believe strike at the very core of their academic freedom and constitutional rights. No professor should run the risk that his or her lawyer would be tempted away by their university dangling lucrative legal business in front of their law firm on condition that the firm drops the professor as a client. The chilling effect on academic freedom should be obvious, and frightening, to every professor.

Thus I believe it should be a general policy for all American universities that they will not condition their openness to offer legal business to any lawyer on requirement that the lawyer's firm stop representing one of the university's own professors in a dispute against their university. Instead, in order to maintain desirable ethical standards and to protect the academic freedom of its professors, the university should agree to "waive" every legal conflict of interest with the professor's law firm within the limits of the law. Furthermore, in order to avoid discouraging law firms from offering to represent professors, the universities should put this policy in writing and publicize it to the professors and the general public.

This rule is one that all professors ought to support. Universities must not take actions that will deprive their professors of legal representation. My hope is that *Free to Think* will ignite a storm of protest so that all universities that are interested in ethical treatment of professors will institute a policy to waive legal conflicts of interest, and academic freedom will once again be protected in our country.

Publisher's note: You can read Mr. Sisson's 7-page letter to GMU's then-president Alan Merton on Caroline Crocker's behalf, found in Appendix VI. You can also view an excellent 6-part video presentation with Ed Sisson by going to YouTube at: http://www.youtube.com/watch?v=6lCe5ICSKI0

Introduction by Caroline Crocker

Dear Reader,

Many times during the writing of this book I asked myself if it was really necessary to put myself through recollecting this painful time of my life. I came to the conclusion that it was. The story is just too important not to be told. If what happened to me was an isolated incident or if there were no strong indications of worse to come, then it would have been better to just move on with my life. But the sad fact is that many scientists, educators, and students are finding that expressing unpopular viewpoints about science has led to loss of research grants, jobs, and even careers.

Not so long ago, President Obama said that promoting science isn't just about providing resources but is about "letting scientists … do their jobs, free from manipulation or coercion, and listening to what they tell us, even when it's inconvenient— especially when it's inconvenient. It is about ensuring that scientific data is never distorted or concealed to serve a political agenda— and that we make scientific decisions based on facts, not ideology." I agree. Ideology, politics and finances should not distort science. But, I am very aware that they do. Brilliant young people tell me that they are not seeking degrees in science because those with political or ideological agendas control education and the students do not want to suffer persecution or be denied advancement because they are people of faith.

Here in the United States of America the U.S. Constitution and Bill of Rights were written to guarantee each of us the freedom to speak and write without fear of reprisal. But, the exercise of freedom requires one to have choices. These have been taken away by "consensus science," the idea that only those scientific ideas that are agreed, or are claimed to have been agreed upon, by a majority of scientists can be considered, published and taught. Of course, conformity (having no options) does not require, or allow, freedom.

One reason this book was written is to draw attention to the powerful suppression of truth that is active in academia and our scientific institutions. Freedom of speech, religion, and even thought are under attack; dissent is often stamped out. The consensus views are typically held to be more important than the scientific process itself. The result is that scientific integrity is compromised as new findings and evidence are forced to fit into existing theories. Consensus-driven science can also have a negative impact in other ways. For example, the ClimateGate controversy has brought to light the fact that scientific data challenging the anthropogenic nature of global warming, and indeed whether it is occurring at all, were being hidden.[1] The jury is still out on whether the scientific evidence actually supports manmade climate change,[2] but it is obvious that all the evidence should be heard and considered before serious decisions with costly consequences for taxpayers and even the status of our national sovereignty are made. Consensus-driven "science" causes thinking and questioning to become restricted and inaccurate, resulting in stifling of the scientific and technological innovation for which the USA is famous in the global marketplace. Restricting or eliminating the right to consider all the evidence is threatening the robust health, economic success and religious freedom that our nation enjoys. We desperately need a return to good science, based on evidence instead of consensus.

That is not the only reason why I persevered in bringing this project to completion. During my teaching career I had the privilege of being invited, even if only in a small way, into countless students' lives. As a result, I have celebrated, grieved, been uplifted, been frustrated, in-short— been made alive with hope for the positive change that is possible. I came to greatly admire and even love my students, many of whom overcame huge obstacles in their pursuit of an education. The future is not just bleak; because of them it is also hopeful. Therefore, several of their stories have joyfully been included in this book. Of course, to respect their privacy and protect them from potential adverse consequences, names, genders, nationalities, and even the courses they were taking have been changed. In some more sensitive instances, the story of more than one student has been blended, but in all cases I have endeavored to remain true to what really happened. Therefore, it may be that some of my students will find and recognize themselves in the pages of this book, even if they are at the "wrong" college.

Another reason for completing this project is to attempt to set the record straight about my own personal story. In the past few years, there has been lots of "noise" on the Internet from people who purport to know the details of my story, but most accounts are grossly inaccurate. Frankly, for a season, I was frightened into silence and did not reveal any of the details about my experiences for fear of additional reprisals. However, due to the habits formed by a lifetime in science, I kept careful records and much supporting documentation. These are supplied in the appendices so that the reader can separate fact from fiction for him or herself. The minutiae of dialogue did of course have to come from my memory of various conversations, but all the core details are supported by this revealing documentation.

---

1   BBC News. 20 November 2009. "Hackers Target Leading Climate Research Unit." http://news.bbc.co.uk/2/hi/science/nature/8370282.stm
2   Taranto, James. 2009. "Settled Science? Computer Hackers Reveal Corruption Behind the Global-warming 'Consensus'." http://online.wsj.com/article/best_of_the_web_today.html#printMode

The final reason for this book comes from my observation that as the evolution/intelligent design/creation controversy becomes increasingly public, there is an unfortunate tendency for some to become more firmly entrenched in their positions. I would like to make a plea for a different and more rational (and scientific) course of action: listening to those who have additional evidence or viewpoints to present and making some attempt at impartial evaluation of their claims.

In the fall of 2008 students taking Animal Biology, Genetics, Ecology and General Biology at George Mason University, a state school in Virginia, reported fascinating classroom incidents to me that clearly demonstrate this entrenchment. First, the Peppered Moth story, an "icon of evolution" challenged by writer and scientist Jonathan Wells (PhD, Molecular and Cellular Biology, Berkeley), has now been replaced by the evolution of "hypothetical deer mice." Similarly, the "evolution" of *E. coli*, which was a favorite example for evolutionists but has stubbornly remained the same species despite over 100 years of experimentation, has now been replaced by evolution of the Human Immunodeficiency Virus (HIV). Of course, the fact that HIV is a virus and that there is much discussion about whether viruses even qualify as being alive, was not mentioned. Then again, the definition of life also seems to have changed somewhat so that it too bows to evolutionary dogma: it is now "a self-replicating system of organic molecules *that can evolve*"! Only a few years prior life was more accurately defined by its characteristics and actions: cellular basis, reproduction, growth, usage and transformation of energy, responsiveness to the environment, etc.

The college textbooks have also responded to the controversy in an unhelpful manner—by reinforcing the prevailing consensus. Many books now include a section on Intelligent Design (ID), immediately discrediting this emerging theory by claiming that it is not science. Interestingly, the question of whether ID might be *true* or *supported* by science does not come up. Even the Campbell Biology Testbank v. 6.0 (standard biology test questions) has been altered to guarantee the students are properly indoctrinated. There are questions on micro and macroevolution, making sure that students agree that they are the same thing really, when it is obvious that they are not. (*Micro*evolution is change within a species over time such as occurs in the breeding of dogs. It is agreed by all and is demonstrable. On the other hand, *macro*evolution is more controversial, encompassing transition of one type of organism to another, requiring brand new information, such as would be required for the evolution of people from a bacterial common ancestor.) Other questions one-sidedly address irreducible complexity, the origin of life, and even religion. Since these tests use multiple-choice questions, if a student fails to answer with wholehearted agreement with the theory of naturalistic evolution, their answers are marked wrong. The popular Campbell and Reece's *Biology* is used in high schools as well as colleges, thereby making textbook-supported enforcement of consensus science easy.

Teachers and professors are also adversely affected by consensus science; this is not always due to their possible political or anti-religious motives. Educators can end up teaching inaccurately as a result of being too busy, not checking their sources, and teaching outside of their own field of expertise. One cannot judge these individuals too harshly. After all, many of us have likewise been forced to teach on a wide variety of subjects where we cannot possibly do all the background research necessary. However, the intentional suppression of information about controversial science issues by the consensus science chorus line compounds the challenges for busy teachers. This debate can, however, have a positive and honing effect on us all. For me, I have become much more careful to check my scientific sources. Although progress is slow, I have noticed other educators also becoming concerned about this same issue, no longer taking the textbooks as gospel, and doing their own research. We can bring this same positive effect to today's students if we not only teach them about the exciting controversies within science, but also equip them with the critical-thinking skills necessary to identify bad science and expose poor scholarship.

Another unfortunate effect of many scientific debates has been that many of those involved refuse to think objectively or listen to the other side. Some scientists, professors, and columnists even go as far as to resort to name-calling, threats, and abuse in order to buttress their position. Therefore, we need to insist on a more collegial academic atmosphere. For example, when I asked a student about how the scientific theory of Intelligent Design is addressed in class, he responded, "It isn't, except in the form of cheap shots." When pressed for details, he told me that, "ID is referred to as a *hilarious* theory believed by those who *do not understand* science. No challenge to the theory of evolution is permitted." This is a sad occurrence because we all know that understanding is facilitated and retention increases when we have the opportunity to listen to others who do not fully agree with the prevailing theory. This is especially true with the standard evolutionary orthodoxy that has dominated academia for so many years. Contrary to what the consensus science bandwagon would claim, teaching about the controversy and encouraging students to think about the issues is intellectually healthy and advances science education.

In fact, the best scenario would be for all those interested in good evidence-based science to have a seat at the table, honestly discussing the pros and cons of their position, and together working towards elucidation of the truth. Therefore, as I encounter those with viewpoints different from my own, my goal is to establish a mutually respectful relationship where open conversation on topics of importance is made possible. I currently enjoy friendships with atheist or agnostic Darwinists, theistic evolutionists, intelligent design advocates, and creationists. When asked about their views concerning the evolution issue, I have found that most individuals have some points I would consider to be valid, many of which have given me food for thought. Unfortunately, the viewpoints of those who are being persecuted are usually not given the opportunity of being honestly considered and assessed by others.

It is essential that we enter a new era of science education, one that is respectful of other viewpoints while insisting on rigorous scholarship. Scientists, possibly above all others, need to welcome challenges to conventional thinking when presented with evidence or reasoned argument. Scientists, professors, teachers, research organizations, and academic institutions all need to embrace a new standard of respect and commitment to scientific integrity. Perhaps statements endorsing evidence-based science and respectful collegiality need to be posted in schools and institutions as reminders and signatures agreeing to these standards obtained as a condition of employment. In a manner similar to the current workplace enforcement of equal opportunity or appropriate sexual behavior, we also should provide in-service training on scientific integrity.

As reported by National Public Radio's Barbara Bradley-Hagerty, a Darwin-doubting scientist she interviewed refused to be named because, "it would be a kiss of death for my career." This environment of abuse must stop. My own story, as told in this book, indicates that this scientist's fears were far from groundless. I was punished for attempting to teach evolution objectively, with scientific integrity. Unfortunately, this modern-day persecution is quite common. Many would prefer not to believe it, but the fact is that professors and students alike are afraid to publicly admit that modern scientific discovery and research challenges several aspects of Darwin's theory of evolution.

If the United States is to compete in this modern and technologically advanced era, science cannot afford to be narrow-minded or controlled by financial, political or religious motives. The public must have accurate information and scientists must have the freedom to consider all options, no matter the philosophical implications. Science must be based on evidence, not consensus. My hope is that this book will be useful to anyone who is interested in intellectual honesty and that together we will pursue a new era of scientific discovery in which we search for the truth, scientific or otherwise. Together we can nurture an atmosphere of healthy change, helping us usher in a new era of sound scientific discovery, and an environment in which honesty, integrity and serious inquiry are encouraged. We need once again to be *free to think*.

Chapter 1: In the Beginning

I signed in with the security guard in the luxurious foyer of the tall professional building in Washington D.C., took an elevator to the ninth floor, located the suite number, and entered the room through elegant glass doors. Immediately, my senses were assaulted by the smell of wine and cheese, the sight of men and women in business suits, and the buzz of eminent scientists and politicians discussing important issues. Not wearing a business suit and having just lost my job, I felt inferior and inadequate, despite being a trained scientist myself. Spotting a familiar face from Discovery Institute, I made my way across the room. Logan Gages's face lit up and he led me to a bearded scientist and author of several books, Dr. Jonathan Wells. I'd heard him speak several times, and on every occasion had been impressed by his gentle attitude and sharp mind. He was always amazingly gracious, and this time was no different.

"Caroline, I'm so glad to see you again. I've heard a little of what's been happening to you. I'm so sorry."

I took his offered hand and said, "It's good to see you, too. I've been reading some more of your books and learning so much."

"Thanks," he deflected my praise and paused to help himself to some cheese, "So, what are you doing these days?"

Oh dear, what should I say? I tried to elevate myself in his (and my) eyes; being unemployed makes one feel so worthless. "Well, I'm having trouble getting another teaching position, but am applying for jobs doing post-doctoral research. I have a couple of strong possibilities there. Then, I hope to get a tenure track position and be able to do what I love: teach and do research."

Jonathan smiled encouragingly, but his eyes showed concern. "I wish you success." Here he hesitated before he gently broke the bad news. "You do realize, don't you, that you'll probably never get tenure, whether or not you do a post-doc."

Shocked, I became defensive, "What do you mean? I had a good track record in research, publishing, and getting grants even before I got my Ph.D., so why couldn't I have a career as a prof?" I was finding it hard to believe what I was hearing.

Meanwhile another gentleman who overheard us stepped over and joined in our conversation, "A person who has publically admitted to questioning neo-Darwinian evolution typically doesn't get tenure. I know of scientists who try and try, but get nowhere. Graduate students also should not speak out about this issue; I know one Darwin-doubter who still hasn't had a chance to defend his dissertation, even though he completed his work years ago.[3] People are even denied entrance to medical school or post-graduate study programs."

Jonathan nodded in agreement, "You'll find that most people who publicly challenge Darwinism[4] do it after they already have tenure. Even then, it can lead to disaster. There are over 700 scientists who have openly admitted to having doubts about some aspects of evolution,[5] but there are many others who keep it secret so they don't jeopardize their careers."[6]

My heart sank as I finally began to realize that the future I had looked forward to for so long might no longer be possible. "You mean that, because I'm known to have questioned evolution, I'll never work as a professor?" I'd dreamed of doing this all my adult life. Having children and moving several times had interrupted my plans, but I had never stopped pursuing my goal. For me, it was the ideal career, allowing me to do the three things I enjoy and do best: research, teaching, and writing.

Jonathan did not mince his words, "Probably not. You might find a position in a Christian university, but not in another. Nowadays employers run a "Google" search on their prospective employees. You're too well known on the web. I have a friend who kept being rejected for tenure-track positions and finally asked a possible employer why. This employer was honest and admitted that my friend's notoriety on the web was the only problem, even though he is more than eminently qualified."[7]

Wow! When I started objectively teaching students about the state of our scientific knowledge concerning neo-Darwinian evolution, being very careful to not to promote any religion and not divulging my own opinions, I never expected I was going to end up in this kind of mess. I chided myself for being naïve. I had believed that intellectual honesty was possible, and that teaching students to be critical thinkers would even be viewed as a good thing. After all, I am a citizen of a country where freedom and creativity is prized. But now, it looked like I had blown my entire future career, first by teaching evolution objectively, and then by agreeing to be interviewed about the resultant job loss. I felt dizzy and my face and hands grew clammy, so I excused myself to go and sit down. It was difficult to hold back the tears. I had been working towards a goal for what seemed to be my whole life, only to have it snatched away because of my belief in scientific objectivity and intellectual honesty.

---

3 Bergin, 2005, p. 23.
4 Definitions can be found in Appendix I.
5 http://www.dissentfromdarwin.org/
6 Things Considered with Barbara Bradley-Hagerty, November 10, 2005 on National Public Radio.
7 Interview of Jonathan Wells by Caroline Crocker, August, 2005.

I love teaching and research, and once thought that it was what I was born to do, but today I have reluctantly accepted that there is little chance that I will ever again hold a teaching position or obtain a tenure-track position in a so-called "secular" university.

* * * *

Shortly after I finished my doctorate, my family moved to Northern Virginia for my husband's job. I was offered a post-doctoral fellowship at the National Institute of Allergy and Infectious Disease at the National Institutes of Health (NIH), but decided that a part time job in something a bit less all absorbing than research would be a good idea for a year. After all, I needed to help the family settle into new jobs, schools, and a house. Then, I heard that a local community college was looking for part time faculty. This appeared to be just what was needed, so I sent in an application to Northern Virginia Community College (NVCC) and was hired within a week.

At the new faculty orientation we were furnished with lots of practical information: the need for a syllabus and what it should contain, where to get free parking passes, when to withdraw a non-attending student from the class, what to do about cheating and how to get into and navigate around the college web system (a huge challenge). I was impressed by the emphasis on being honest and straightforward with students. The syllabus was to be considered a contract, where the student would know exactly what he or she could expect before the semester began. We were also told that cheating, stealing, or lying were not to be tolerated. Students were expected to be as honest with us as we were with them. This emphasis on honesty and integrity resonated with my own value system and I was excited about the prospect of working in such an environment.

All the new teachers were teamed up with a full time faculty member who was to be our mentor. I was assigned to Dr. Robert Buckley, a tall, bearded man with a wry smile. Dr. Buckley had been teaching for many years, was wise to the ways of students, patient with new teachers, and combined it all with a keen sense of humor. I was to make much use of him and, for all that we laughed about our relationship as mentor-mentee, I still think that this was the most valuable part of the orientation. Years later, it was to be extremely hurtful when Dr. Buckley put an announcement on his faculty website anonymously denouncing me for teaching the scientific (he referred to them as "non-scientific") problems with the evidence for macroevolution,[8] but refused to answer my requests that we meet to talk about it. Why should honest dialogue about both sides of an issue be so threatening as to destroy a friendship developed over a period of years?

---

8   http://www.nvcc.edu/home/rgorham/Sites/Home/Documents/Intelligent%20Design.html

The first course I was assigned at NVCC was introductory biology or Bio 101. This course started with basic chemistry, progressed to the molecular building blocks of cells, covered cells and cellular processes, touched on genetics and ended with an overview of evolution. Well, with a bachelor's degree in microbiology and virology, a master's in medical microbiology, and a doctorate in immunopharmacology, this should have been easy, right? Wrong! I had not obtained my degrees in the USA and didn't know at what level to pitch an American university course. The assigned text, Campbell's *Biology*,[9] was extremely complex and I wondered how relevant this material was to non-biology majors. Was this really what freshman were expected to learn? Not wanting to look like a beginning college teacher (which, of course, I was), I didn't ask, but assumed it was and dived in, reading and taking notes on the relevant chapters. I also made sure to emphasize anything that would help the students relate the information to their everyday lives. My teaching philosophy then and now was to encourage students not just to memorize but to understand, apply, and even be able to critique what they learn in an intellectually honest manner. After all, being able to understand and assess scientific information is critical to making good choices about one's health, nutrition, lifestyle, and even religion or worldview.

Another challenge I faced was that my post-graduate education had neither included courses nor practice in teaching, so I had no idea how to fulfill this aim. My past teaching experience was varied: trying to herd unruly preschoolers into an educational activity, leading a youth group for underprivileged adolescents, helping abused youth to learn vital life skills, teaching Bible studies for women, and training international pediatricians wanting to become allergists— but this was different. I thought back to my undergraduate university days in England and remembered that lecturers who wrote on a blackboard as they talked taught most of my courses. The students would take notes and the assessment came from one comprehensive exam, which was given at the end of the year.

Since that was years ago, I requested syllabi from a few of my full time faculty colleagues to see how they structured their courses. It appeared that things had not changed too much: the students were expected to take notes on lectures and be assessed by three or four exams. A quarter of the grade came from the lab and professors varied in how that was assessed. Therefore, I prepared by writing lecture notes and exams, decided how to assess the labs, and waited anxiously for the semester to start.

My first lecture was to fifty undergraduates who may have been as nervous as I was, but had less interest in hiding it. They were all ages and all races;

---

9   Campbell and Reece, 2002.

the roll call was complicated by the fact that less than a quarter of the names were in a language familiar to me. I took a deep breath, "Hi, I'm Dr. Crocker and you're in Biology 101. If that's not where you thought you were, I suggest you leave quietly while nobody is looking." A couple of sheepish students exited the room to nervous titters of laughter.

"If you didn't pick up a syllabus on the way in, please get it now." I waited for the hubbub of students coming to pick them up to die down. "We'll be going through it briefly, but remember that you should also read it. It is the course contract." I quickly went through the syllabus, explaining the structure of the course, how they would be graded, and what my expectations were with regard to tardiness, absences, and doing their own work. We then dived into the material of the first chapter, as I tried to ignore the continual stream of latecomers. The number of students who just sat and looked at me with blank expressions, not taking notes at all, amazed me. Others put their heads on their desks and went to sleep. Why would young people be so tired? This wasn't what I remembered from my days at university. Of course, then, most of the students did nothing but attend school; Mom and Dad paid for their educations. I also considered the fact that while I was at college I only had a part time job on Friday and Saturday nights. Many of these students were older and I suspected were working full time just to survive.

On the positive side, I noticed many students paying rapt attention and furiously taking notes. In particular, there was a petite, shabbily-dressed blond girl sitting in the front row, nodding as she understood, frowning when confused, and carefully writing down anything I emphasized. I quickly learned to watch her to know how well I was communicating. She would always smile or shake her head or give some other indication, which was extremely helpful. After the lecture she came forward.

Looking too young for college, she said, "Umm, Dr. Crocker?"

I nodded encouragingly.

"I...I'm Claire. I wanted to introduce myself because I'm going to be talking to you a lot this semester." Here she took a big breath, steeling herself for the next statement. "I'm learning disabled. See this form...you need to sign it. Also, I'm still in high school." Here she hung her head in shame. "It's an alternative one. I don't know if I can pass this course, but I'm going to try." Claire looked at me uncertainly, as if half-expecting instant rejection.

My heart went out to her and I assured her that I would do whatever was needed to help her succeed. I pointed out my office hours and home phone number listed on the syllabus. Although I hadn't anticipated that as a college lecturer I would be a coach as well as an educator, I was happy to do it. During the course of the semester, Claire did require extra help -- mostly in the form of encouraging words. She was a good student and attended faithfully, reading ahead and taking careful notes, checking with me about anything she didn't understand. Her lab reports were a delight, carefully documenting all she observed with beautiful illustrations; she was obviously a very talented artist. Claire's exam scores reflected her hard work. As she added success to success during the course, I saw her confidence increase; she laughed and interacted with her classmates, stealing glances at me to see if I approved. I made sure to always smile encouragingly. Claire and I stayed in contact after she completed my class and I even hired her to do brochure design work for some of my volunteer projects. Seeing this under-confident young woman blossom into a successful artist was a pleasure, the memory of which still brings me joy today. It was a privilege to be able to do what I believe a teacher should do: not just fill students with facts, but also help instill them with the ability and confidence to explore widely, think fearlessly, and joyfully be all they can be.

The first lab was an equally interesting experience. Here the goal was to teach students the basics of safe lab practice and introduce them to a few fundamental techniques. The full sum of the training I received for this responsibility was to be given a lab manual, told that the cart with supplies would be at the front of the room, and instructed that all lab materials must be returned to the cart at the end of class. It was left for me to discover what the things on the cart were! Checking the room number and grasping the list of students as I entered, I was surprised to find a young man with stringy dark hair dressed in the school uniform of ripped jeans and a T-shirt sitting at the teacher's desk.

He beamed at me, revealing a chipped tooth, and announced, "Hi! I'm your teacher's aide!"

Pretending that nothing was amiss, I excused myself, went to the biology office, and asked if I'd been given an aide. The departmental administrator assured me with a smile that this person was merely a mischievous student.

I returned and put on a mock frown. "Get out of my chair! I don't need any help for this lab." He meekly slunk to his chair and I turned to the class.

"Okay, please get out your lab books. If you don't have one, share with someone else. You'll need to get one by next week..." And so, I went on to explain what we would be doing that day, which basically consisted of becoming familiar with the lab and the equipment.

"Aww, Dr. Crocker," came a wail from the back of the class, "my friend said that her lab teacher let them out without doing the first lab. Why are you making us do it? It's not fair!"

And I thought that children outgrew the "it's not fair" syndrome. Unruffled because I had teenagers at home, I replied, "Be happy. I'm making sure you get everything you paid for."

During the lab session I walked from table to table, began to get to know the students and found them to be an eclectic and likeable group. They were all shapes and sizes from emaciated to overweight. There were amazing hairstyles, some short and standing on end, some long and silky, others multi-colored. There were pierced eyebrows, noses, tongues, tattoos of all kinds and in all places. The dress was equally diverse from sweatshirts and jeans to burkas, from office-suitable outfits to muscle shirts, micro-miniskirts, incredibly low-cut tops and even lower-cut bottoms with a thong peeking out. Some students were bright-eyed and eager to learn, others were half-asleep and smelling of alcohol (even at 9 am), and still others just looked bored and impatient to leave.

One young man, Carlos, appeared very tense, and as the semester went on I noticed that he frequently became extremely agitated with his lab partners. During one particularly challenging lab when the students were expected to put different chemicals in a series of test tubes, I heard, "That's the wrong way to do it! We are just wasting *$&#% time and I'm fed up with it! I'm not doing this anymore! *&%$ #%*" His voice rose steadily over the hum of students talking.

I casually walked over to his table. His lab partners looked nervous, expecting a blow up. "Carlos, would you like to leave and do this lab another time when you feel better?" I said, endeavoring to sound matter of fact.

Carlos looked at me gratefully, his temper gone. "Would that be okay… you wouldn't take points off? It's just that I have to prove to my old lady that I can do this. If I don't, she'll kick me out." Here he cast a venomous look at his partners, "And with these *#*^& freaks…"

I assured him that I would not penalize him and he left. Carlos' girlfriend then told me that Carlos was an ex-convict with some anger management problems and had been in significant trouble because of it. He was being given a last chance and had to go to college, get a job, and succeed in both. It was therefore gratifying to me when, with a bit of patience and support, Carlos finished the semester with a "B", despite his conviction that he was incapable of doing well. Again it seemed as if being a teacher was as much about encouraging as it was about educating. I hoped that Carlos would continue down the same right path now that he had succeeded at a college course known for its difficulty. Last I heard he was doing well and had graduated from college.

Soon it was time for the first exam. I was very concerned about this because so many of the students did not take notes and I thought that it might be because the material was much too easy for them. Carefully, I included questions suggested by the textbook, making sure to cover every lecture equally. I decided to go with multiple choice and true-false, so instructed the students to bring Scantron[10] standardized testing answer sheets to class. On the day of the exam, I arrived in the lecture hall to see most of the class furiously reviewing their notes and leafing through their books.

"Okay, please sit in every other seat, put away your books, and get out your Scantron." There was no movement except the continued review of their notes or books.

I raised my voice a bit, "If you don't know the material by now, another five minutes won't help. Put your things away."

"Uh, Dr. Crocker? You didn't tell us we needed a Scantron," claimed a student who may have missed the announcement due to his tendency to sleep through most classes.

The other students quickly put this assertion to rights.

"Mohammed, are you telling me that you forgot to bring one? Okay, I have extras, but you'll need to give me one back when you have them."

"Dr. Crocker, I forgot a pencil. Can I fill it out in pen?"

"No Tina, you'll need to borrow a pencil from someone."

After resolving these and numerous other problems, I handed out the exam. During the test I walked around the classroom, answering legitimate questions, watching for cheating, and encouraging those who seemed overcome by panic. To my surprise, I noticed one young man, a traffic warden who often appeared tired, had actually fallen asleep. I bent down and spoke to him quietly. "Joe, would you rather take the exam when you're not so tired?"

"No, I'm okay. It won't help anyway. I just worked all night."

My fear that the test was just too boring or easy was confirmed in my mind by the steady stream of students putting their completed exam on my desk and leaving early. After the exam was finished, I collected the Scantron sheets and proceeded to the grading machine. As the exams went through, I glanced at them to see how the class had done. To my dismay, most Scantron sheets had a LOT of red on them. Dr. Buckley, who happened to be passing, commented that the sound of the machine marking numerous errors was one familiar to him. It was still a great shock to me to find that fully 50% of the students had failed the exam and only one had achieved a grade of over 90%. Now I had a problem. The university had assigned the text and specified what should be covered. But, the students were not doing well. According to Dr. Buckley, this was normal for Bio 101 and I should shrug it off, but I determined to see if I could

---

10   Definitions can be found in Appendix I.

fix the problem with my class. I would curve this test, but clearly, other changes had to be made. I did not want to compromise and just lower the standard; after all, students come to university to be educated. But, right now they were not even learning the facts, let alone fulfilling my goal that they also be enabled to understand, apply and critique the knowledge they gained.

I sat down in the adjunct faculty lounge with a cup of coffee and began to ponder what I could do to help the students learn. First, I remembered that many students didn't take notes, and now I was sure that this wasn't because they knew the material already. Therefore, I decided to put my lectures onto PowerPoint slides in the future. This way I figured the students would have outlines that would help in taking notes. I also instituted extra credit, which merely consisted of turning in your hand-written lecture notes on exam day, an effort to encourage note-taking and review. Finally, I tried to make the next exam easier, making sure that at least one answer in every multiple-choice question was clearly wrong. Many students told me that the slides helped, but, to my dismay, only 60% of students passed the second exam. Better, but still not good enough. Since only half the class took the extra credit opportunity, I knew this was not entirely my fault, but nonetheless wanted to find ways to improve further in motivating the students to learn biology.

What should I do? Perhaps the students were not finding the lecture situation conducive to learning. Doing some reading on teaching and talking with other teachers, I remembered that different people have different styles of learning. It was clear that it would be necessary to cater to these if I was to be successful in my quest to improve student understanding and performance. Diagrams and pictures on the PowerPoint slides might help the visual learners, but what about those who had a tactile or an interactive learning style? I began to offer study groups at my home where I helped students master material by hands-on exercises and competitions. It was great fun to join with them in making DNA[11] out of toothpicks and marshmallows or in acting out protein synthesis with people, pillows, cardboard, and tape. I found that, with a bit of brainstorming, much of the course material could be illustrated or made into a learning game in some way or another. It also gave me an opportunity to encourage thinking about and application of facts gained.

These study sessions gave me a valuable opportunity to get to know the students on a much less formal basis and I found it instructive as they began to share their lives. Only a minority of the young people were living in circumstances similar to what I experienced while in college: at home with both parents

---

11   Definition can be found in Appendix I.

and working part time. Many of the students were working full time, as well as going to school, getting less than three hours of sleep a night. Several had children and a lot of these were single. Others had huge personal issues that made any type of concentration on school almost miraculous. I grew to respect and admire those I taught.

Sadie, a young person who stood out because of her many piercings, dyed hair, and tendency to dress entirely in black, would always arrive early because she needed to walk to a bus stop, take a bus and then walk to my house to attend the study groups. I commented on her determination to do well in the class and she replied wryly, "I've learned that any success requires hard work. My mother's real sick, so I've lived in over seven foster homes. Now, because I'm 18, the state has declared me independent. It's kind of scary, but at least now my future only depends on me." That seemed preferable and certainly safer to her. Sadie often arrived hungry and her emaciated frame told me that this was not an unusual state for her. After watching her devour the cookies on offer at the study groups, I began to save dinner for her, as well. With a family of six, cooking a bit extra was no trouble. Thus, Sadie soon learned to arrive even earlier! Sadie was determined to become a nurse. Despite continuing difficulties with her birth mother and brother, she passed my class and, when I last heard, was in her final year of nursing school. I then realized that, besides giving out facts and encouragement, teachers also need to give out food.

Another regular attendee, Thiang, was bubbly, tiny, very attractive, and made an impact everywhere she went. She certainly made an impression on my neighbors. After having attended one study group, Thiang figured she knew the way to my house. Arriving a bit early, she headed for a house with the front door standing ajar and the lights on. She was a bit confused by the fact that I was not there and wine bottles were standing ready, but figured that I'd decided to make this group really special and would come soon. Thiang helped herself to some wine, made herself comfortable on the couch, and waited. Soon a strange man entered the room and asked what she was doing in his house.

Thiang sprang up, "I...I...I...Where is Dr. Crocker?"

The neighbor laughed. "You have the wrong house. Go down three houses and you'll find her."

When Thiang arrived and told us the entire story, none of us were surprised. After all, it was Thiang.

As the term went by many of the less able students dropped the class. Dr. Buckley assured me that this was a normal state of affairs. In fact, he said this was preferable to a student getting a bad grade, so I was told to encourage it.

By the third exam, the class was doing well. Whether this was because many had dropped the course, the material was more interesting, the study groups were helping, or a combination of these, it was a great relief to me. This came to be my favorite time in every semester, when I began to know the students, and the lectures and labs became more enjoyable.

One of the most popular lab exercises was the one on genetics. This started with counting kernels of corn (not so exciting), progressed through analysis of the shape of your lab partner's ear lobe, the consistency of his or her ear wax, tests on color blindness and the ability to taste certain chemicals, and culminated in the students testing their own blood type. No one looked at the clock during this lab exercise.

"Okay, please take out your lab books. It's very important you listen carefully to what I'm saying because….Andrew, what are you doing?" Andrew had come to the front of the lab and was busily helping himself to the items he thought he needed for the experiment.

"Uh, I'm getting the stuff we need," explained the red-haired young man.

"What did I *tell* you to do?"

Andrew was silent as I watched the color rise in his face. Finally, one of his classmates rescued him by shouting out, "She said to sit and listen!"

I suppressed a smile. Andrew sat down and I resumed my instructions, "You must have read the entire section of the lab and have all your supplies at hand before starting. Whatever you do, do not prick your finger and then start wandering around the lab looking for supplies." I mimed a person looking through the tray of supplies while dripping blood on the floor and the students laughed.

I then went through all the instructions, especially the safety precautions, and told the class they could begin. Gloria was one of the first to get up. She obviously had not spent time to read the instructions, but collected the alcohol wipe, the lancet and a Band-Aid. She then sat down and began to prepare to prick her finger.

I hurried over. "Gloria, stop! What are you doing?"

"I was just going to prick myself."

"I can see that. Where are the slides and reagents you need for this experiment?"

"Oh…. I guess I forgot them."

Once again, I called for silence and reminded the class to have *everything* ready before they began. Eventually, they were ready and the bloodletting started. Again there was a range of responses. Some students had no problem sticking themselves; others were afraid to apply enough pressure and had to try several times before getting blood.

"Dr. Crocker, it's not working. I'm not getting any blood," complained Andrew.

"The lancets do work. You just didn't prick hard enough."

"Will it hurt?" asked Thiang.

"Probably." I answered encouragingly.

"Do I have to?"

"Well, you can use fake blood, but then you won't know your blood type."

Others had not listened to my instructions about using their middle finger and were trying to get blood out of the back of their hand or their arm and still others did not dare to stick themselves and requested the artificial blood that the college provided. Chaos reigned. Then came the excitement and questions as the students began to get results.

"Dr. Crocker, what do these dots on the slide mean?" asked Demitri

I walked over to see the slide and pointed to the board, where that result was detailed, "Well, look up there. It means that you are blood type AB."

"Is that good? What type is he?" Demitri asked, indicating his lab partner.

I looked at the partner's slide, "He's type O because there are no dots in his blood. Remember the dots mean that the antibodies in the reagent you put on the slide are attaching to the antigens on the surface of your blood cells and sticking them together into globs that you can see."

Demitri puffed up his chest, "That means mine is better than his, doesn't it?"

I restrained myself from laughing, "Not really. It just means you have different antigens on your red cells. But, it does mean that you can accept blood from anyone. He can only donate."

This seemed to satisfy Demitri, so I moved on to the next table. I knew that I would never grow bored of teaching—or students!

REFERENCES

Bergin, Mark. 2005. "Mad Scientists." *World*, August 20, p. 23.

Bradley-Hagerty, Barbara. 2005. "Intelligent Design and Academic Freedom." *All Things Considered*. National Public Radio. November 10. http://www. npr.org/templates/story/story.php?storyId=5007508 (as of 03/30/09).

"Buckley, Robert." "Statement on Intelligent Design." Faculty website. http:// www.nvcc.edu/home/rgorham/Sites/Home/Documents/Intelligent%20 Design.html (as of 03/30/09).

Campbell, Neil A., Jane B. Reece. 2002. *Biology*. 6th Edition. San Francisco, CA: Benjamin Cummings.

Wells, Jonathan. 2005. Interview of Jonathan Wells by Caroline Crocker, August.

Chapter 2: Teaching and Evolution

Some parts of this book are more scientifically complex than others. In most cases they are less than a paragraph in length, but in Chapter 2 this was not always possible.

When I first read the textbook assigned for the Bio 101 course at NVCC, it was glaringly obvious that the theory of evolution was being used to undergird and explain most of the concepts and information presented. I pondered the idea that those who compare Darwinian narratives to Rudyard Kipling's "Just So" stories may have a point.[12] Up until this time in teaching the course I hadn't made mention of evolution, but just concentrated on the pure science. For example, instead of teaching that the DNA code was the same for all living creatures because DNA evolved early in life's history, I separated the scientific facts—that the DNA code is the same (or similar) for all of life, how the code works, and what DNA is made of—from the inference: DNA evolved early. I found that it wasn't necessary or helpful for student understanding to coat the facts with a veneer of evolutionary theory, so--I didn't. It just did not add to their understanding of the topic. I was also very aware that students trust that what they are being taught is "the truth, the whole truth, and nothing but the truth." I did not want to betray that trust, inasmuch as that is possible.

My personal views on neo-Darwinian evolution had undergone a relatively recent evolution of their own. This particular journey didn't even start until nearly 20 years after I became a committed Christian, so had nothing to do with my religious beliefs. However, a preacher *did* influence me. As a teenager I heard a sermon with an oft-repeated message that riveted me to my seat. "Think about it. Don't just believe what I say; think about it. If it is true, you can think about it and it will still be true. If it isn't, then it's not worth believing."[13] This approach to faith and, indeed, to any idea, became a mantra in my life.

Encouraged by the idea that thinking and intellectual honesty about faith was not only allright, but to be commended, I listened carefully, read books and investigated, and eventually decided that for me, the most sensible and intellectually fulfilling option was to believe Jesus was who He claimed to be. I was an undergraduate at the time and the head of my department was an eminent scientist, Professor Derek Burke, who was one of the first to clone the human interferon gene.[14] Dr. Burke was also a man of faith, but had no problem with interpreting *Genesis* as having occurred by the processes of evolution, as do many

---

12   Gould, 1982.
13   Sermon by Donald Humphries at the University of Warwick, Coventry, England, October, 1975.
14   http://www.st-edmunds.cam.ac.uk/faraday/Biography.php?ID=94

of the authors of the book he edited.[15] Since I admired him greatly, I took his views as my own and never experienced a conflict between my faith and my views on evolution. I obviously had not yet fully embraced the instruction to "think about it," but that was to come.

My issues with the theory of neo-Darwinian evolution started as a result of a conflict, not between science and religion, but between science and science. That is, I began to question the sufficiency of the theory of neo-Darwinian evolution to provide a comprehensive explanation for all that we observe in biology. Evolution is said to proceed as a result of two processes. 1) Random mutations in DNA sequence result in changes or variations in the organism. 2) Those organisms that express mutations that increase their competitive edge in their environment leave more offspring; they are naturally selected.[16] But, for a number of reasons, this simple mechanism did not appear sufficient to account for the biological systems I was observing.

While working towards my doctorate, I spent much time reading about the basics of the immune system. I was particularly intrigued with helper T-cells,[17] which are the "directors" of the immune response. They recognize the "enemy" that is invading the body and decide its type, i.e., if it is a huge parasite, a bacterium, or a tiny virus that lives inside of cells. They tell the rest of the immune system what to do, whether to release an arsenal of chemicals to attack the parasite, generate antibodies to make the bacteria tasty for the immune cells that eat invaders, or cause a chain reaction of chemicals that would result in blowing up the body cells that are harboring a virus (Figure 1).

I was excited not just by the complexity, but also by the precision of it all, and began to think, "How could these intricate and specific interactions have happened by a gradual, random process of evolution?" As philosopher of science, Dr. Stephen Meyer later said, "...advances in the field of molecular biology made clear that the digital information in DNA was only part of a complex information-processing system, an advanced form of nanotechnology that mirrors and exceeds our own in its complexity, storage density, and logic of design."[18]

---

15   Burke, 1985, p. 172.
16   This explanation has been simplified for the sake of clarity.
17   Definitions can be found in Appendix I.
18   Meyer, 2009, p. 14.

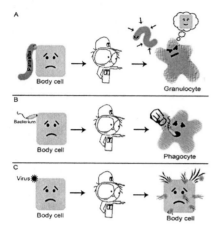

Figure 1 *The figure diagrams some actions of the T-helper cell in directing the immune response. On the left is a body cell being attacked by a parasite like a tapeworm (A), or a bacterium like Strep (B) or a virus like a cold (C). Since the three attackers are very different, the T cell needs to tailor the immune system's response. In the case of the parasite (line A), the T cell tells the granulocytes to kill the parasite by releasing chemical weapons. In the case of the bacterium (line B), the T cells tell the B cells to make antibodies that stick to the bacterium making it tasty to a type of granulocyte. Finally, since viruses live inside of cells hijacking their machinery to make more viruses, the cell cannot be saved. So, in line C the T cell directs that the hijacked cell should be blown up so no more virus can be made.[19]*

My particular project was to study glucocorticoid modulation of an enzyme called phosphodiesterase (PDE), which was thought to have an important role in asthma and allergic disease. In asthma, the airways become inflamed, swell, and become filled with mucus, making it difficult for the patient to breathe. The most common treatment for occasional episodes is administration of an inhaler with a chemical that causes the airways to relax and open. On a cellular level, the chemical causes an intracellular molecule, cyclic AMP (cAMP), to increase in concentration and this is what instructs smooth muscle to relax. PDE, put simply, is an enzyme that breaks down cAMP and it was thought that this enzyme was elevated in asthmatics. This would cause a reduction in cAMP in the muscles of their airways and the bronchi would constrict. If it were possible to inhibit the PDE or stop it from working (as is done by caffeine, an old-time remedy for asthma), then hypothetically one could keep asthmatics breathing more easily for a longer period of time (Figure 2).

The problem is, however, that PDE is not only found in cells in the airways, but is also located in most other tissues, including the heart and brain. This is why caffeine not only helps asthmatics to breathe; it also makes people nervous and shaky and can make their heart race. But, there is a potential answer to this problem. It seems that the PDE found in the lung smooth muscle and the immune system (both cause problems in asthmatics) is a different type from that found in the brain and the heart. So one could theoretically make a PDE inhibitor that would only target the brain or the heart or the immune system or some

---

19   For any immunologist reading this, I am aware that this is vastly over-simplified, but this is not a science textbook, nor is it meant to be one.

other tissue. PDE inhibitors specific for lung muscle and immune cells have recently been released for use by asthmatics, although vomiting is a troubling side-effect. Viagra is a PDE inhibitor that is targeted to still another area of the body. But my question was, how could this specialization of the various PDE's to the various tissue types have happened by survival of the fittest organism? After all, the tissues of the body are not in competition with each other and all the PDE's perform the same basic function. Evolution is said to work by selecting the fittest individuals; it cannot select genes or even traits. The only thing that is passed from generation to generation is a sperm and an egg (gametes), so a beneficial mutation would need to originate in a gamete. The entire genome is found in all the cells of the body; the various tissues types just express different genes. But why would it increase fitness for PDE IV to dominate in the immune cells, PDE III in the heart, and PDE I in the brain? And which control would be selected first? Control mechanisms in cells are like intricate circuit boards; how could something like this evolve through random mutation?

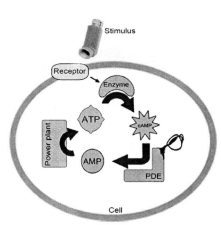

Figure 2 *This figure shows how, when an asthmatic person inhales their rescue medication, receptors on the surface of cells in their bronchi are stimulated. This activates an enzyme (turns on a machine) that makes cAMP from its high energy precursor, ATP (the molecule that is like fuel to the cell). cAMP causes the airways to open and the heart to speed up, giving the normal reactions to an inhaler—ability to breathe and a racing heart. PDE converts the cAMP to low energy AMP, so more medicine may be needed in only hours. AMP is then converted back to ATP by a cellular Power Plant using energy from food. Caffeine stops PDE from working properly, so that cAMP levels remain high. For this reason, strong coffee is sometimes used as a home remedy for asthma.*

This was a puzzle for me and I knew I needed some help in figuring it out.

Being a graduate student I was used to asking questions, so I asked those around me...my fellow students and my supervisors. It was frustrating to find that nobody had a satisfactory answer and it did not appear that they had even given the matter much thought. Many shrugged their shoulders and mumbled something about it taking a long time. I quickly got the message that these were questions I should not be asking. I didn't find this intellectually satisfying, but soon found the rigors of graduate school absorbed my attention and the question of just how evolution worked in that context was put aside. Evolution simply did not have much, if any, impact on my research. Instead, I needed to focus on figuring out the intricacies of PDE and its control in the T-cell.

The next chance I had to think about the issue was in 1999, shortly after finishing my doctorate, when I began to write the lectures on basic biology in preparation for teaching. Again, the apparent design of cellular processes hit me. Protein synthesis is a good example of such a marvelous and mystifying process. Cells can be compared to factories filled with lots of complex machines; many of these machines are made of several interacting parts.

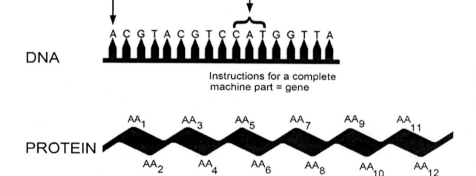

Figure 3 *This figure illustrates how DNA codes for proteins. DNA is a sequence of nucleotides (letters); three nucleotides (word) code for one amino acid (nut, bolt, etc.). A gene (blueprint) codes for the specific sequence of amino acids that are used to make one part of a protein machine.*[20]

These machines are made of proteins, but may also include other bio-molecules like RNA. The blueprint for how the protein machines are made and work is written in a code made of DNA (Figure 3). The DNA code consists of four types of molecular "letters" arranged into three letter "words," each of which specifies a tiny part of a machine (like a nut or bolt, but much smaller). These tiny parts are called amino acids. Proteins are made of specific sequences of amino acids joined together in long chains that are typically hundreds of amino acids long. In DNA terms, a sentence that specifies instructions for the

---

20　The latest definition of a gene is not this simple, including DNA sequences with regulatory functions, DNA that only seems to code for RNA, and more. In addition, some DNA sequences only code for polypeptides, which are parts of proteins. A detailed explanation of these complexities is beyond the scope of this book.

sequence of amino acids in part of a protein machine is a gene. When lots of these protein machines are working together, they may cause a characteristic.[21]

Since the blueprint (DNA) for the factory (cell) is important, DNA does not leave the "head office" or the nucleus of the cell (Figure 4). This is a problem, however, since the protein machines are made on the factory floor. There needs to be a go-between and this is messenger RNA (mRNA), a molecule traditionally thought to take a copy of the code for one protein to the ribosome (protein or "machine" assembly unit). We now know the mRNA can be edited by splicing together different parts to code for different proteins, giving many levels of complexity and specificity. The process of copying a gene into mRNA is called transcription. Enzymes and other proteins guide which DNA gene is copied.[22] In our example, this would be equivalent to a messenger telling head office which machine needs to be made. Then, because there are chemicals outside of the nucleus that destroy unprotected mRNA, the mRNA go-between is processed and "do not destroy" labels are added. This would be like laminating the blueprints because conditions on the factory floor are too harsh for mere paper instructions to survive.[23] The mRNA leaves the nucleus (head office) through elaborate door-like pores, where it is checked for accuracy and more (Figure 4).

Once the mRNA is on the factory floor, the cell faces another issue, which is the equivalent of the workers speaking a different language from the people in head office. That is, three of the mRNA letters or nucleotides make a "word" that codes for one of the twenty possible amino acids (a subunit of a protein, Figure 3). One of the ends of the mRNA even codes for an address label that tells the cell where the resultant protein will belong. But, how can the cell read the nucleotide words and translate them into amino acid words? It does not happen by magic. There are transfer RNA (tRNA) molecules that carry nucleotides on one end matching the ones on the mRNA while carrying the "matching" amino acid on the other side of the tRNA (Figure 5).

---

21 Characteristics are not only the product of genetics, but also of environment, making them notoriously difficult to predict or study. In fact, recent work even shows that inheritance is influenced by whether the gene came from your mother or your father.

22 An animation and explanation of some of these processes may be found at Dolan DNA Learning Center, http://www.dnai.org/text/mediashowcase/index2.html?id=585

23 An animation and explanation of some of these processes may be found at ndsu Virtual Cell Animations Project animation mRNA processing, www.youtube.com/watch?V=YjWuVrzvZYA

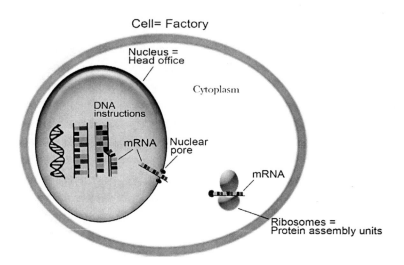

Cell= Factory

Nucleus =
Head office

Cytoplasm

DNA
instructions

mRNA   Nuclear
pore

mRNA

Ribosomes =
Protein assembly units

Figure 4 *This figure shows how the nucleus or head office of the cell contains the DNA instructions. The part of the instructions for how to make a particular machine is transcribed into mRNA. The mRNA is then edited and "laminated" so that it will survive outside of the nucleus.[24] After this, it is checked at the nuclear pore and released to the cytoplasm of the cell (factory floor). Finally, the proteins are made by ribosomes according to the mRNA instructions.*

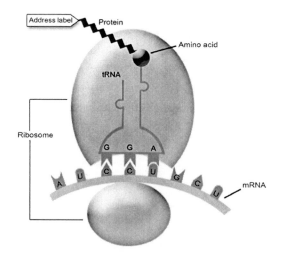

Address label   Protein

Amino acid

tRNA

Ribosome

G   G   A

mRNA

Figure 5 *This figure depicts translation of the code contained in the mRNA into the "language" of proteins (amino acids). The tRNA acts as a translator, having the complement to the mRNA code at one end and an amino acid at the other. The ribosome (protein assembly machine) sticks the amino acids together, making a protein. The first part of the protein made is an address label that tells the cell where that protein should go.[25]*

---

24 The mRNA in a eukaryotic cell is modified by removal of the introns (inserts that are not needed for a particular protein) and addition of a modified guanine cap and a poly-adenosine tail.
25 Again, the actual process is far more sophisticated, where some proteins are interwoven with membranes, others are destined for export, some are destined for specific organelles in the cell, and others for the cytoplasm. The cell distinguishes between these and deals with all of them in a different manner.

One could more meaningfully call these "translator" instead of transfer RNAs, since translation is what they do. Instructions for making the machines that assemble these tRNAs and the tRNAs themselves are also found in the head office blueprint (DNA). The tRNAs line up according to the mRNA instructions and protein assembly units (ribosomes) put the amino acids together, making a protein.[26] Some protein machines are complexes of many separate protein components and some even include parts made of RNA. Whether or not they are components of large multiprotein machines, many proteins are very intricately folded. This microscopic molecular origami is no more magical than the process of joining amino acids together in the correct sequence to make a protein. Some of the folding occurs automatically because of molecular attractions, but much of it requires help from chaperone proteins or chaperonins. These minute garbage-can-shaped proteins are also encoded in the DNA and made in the same general way as other proteins (Figure 6).

Figure 6

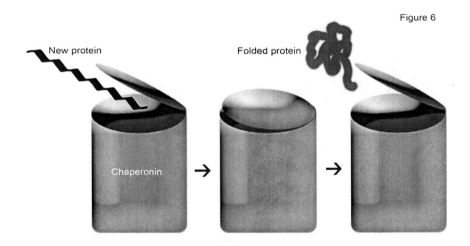

New protein

Folded protein

Chaperonin →   →

Figure 6 *The folding of proteins into a working machine is often done with the assistance of chaperonins (also proteins). The chaperonins take in unfolded proteins and release them after they are folded and functional.*

The unfolded protein gets put in the can, the lid is closed, and it comes out folded. If a magician was to put a shirt in a garbage can and pull it out folded, we would be impressed. Protein folding is MUCH more complicated than folding a shirt. If a protein is not folded correctly, it is labeled "recycle" and a proteosome "incinerator" usually destroys it.

---

26   An explanation and animation of translation can be found at www.youtube.com/watch?v=B606uRbID38NR=1

Now we encounter another problem. In any factory, especially a HUGE one that has many functions, the parts of complex machines not only need to be assembled; they need to be in the right place on the production line. In a cell, the first part of the protein made tells the cell where the protein will be needed. Some are made and assembled in situ. Other proteins are meant to be interwoven with membranes and so are made as part of that membrane. The signals for when to weave are also incorporated in the mRNA that codes for the protein. Still other proteins are meant for export and are loaded into vesicles (like maglevs), which are put onto microtubules (tracks) and carried to the right place by transport proteins that actually walk down the tracks using ATP "gasoline." Of course, the vesicles also have address labels so they go to the right place (Figure 7).[27]

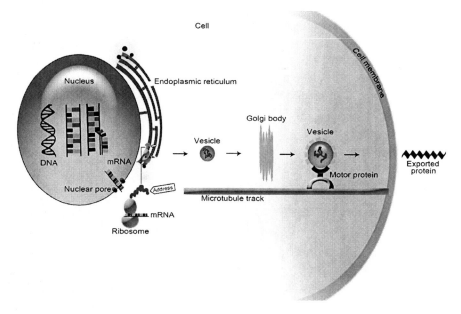

Figure 7 *This figure illustrates the manufacturing process for a protein destined for export from the cell. The instructions for making the protein are encoded in the DNA (set of 100's of encyclopedias of information). The specific part of the DNA that is applicable is transcribed into mRNA. The mRNA leaves the nucleus and picks up a ribosome, which begins to make the protein with the help of the tRNA translators. The first part of the protein made is an address label that causes the ribosome to sit on the endoplasmic reticulum while making the protein. The protein is modified in various ways as it passes through the endoplasmic reticulum and Golgi apparatus (processing plants). Since this protein is destined for export, it is fortified for the harsh conditions outside of the cell by adding sugar residues and cross-linking the structure. The protein is released from the Golgi enclosed in a vesicle (also bearing an address label). The vesicle is carried by a transport protein on microtubule tracks to the outer membrane of the cell. When it is time for the protein to be released, the vesicle fuses with the membrane and the protein is released.*

---

27   A nice animation of vesicle transport can be found at BioVisions, 1.18 minutes through the video at: http://www.youtube.com/watch?v=BVvvx5HGpLg

Any cell biologist would agree that this description of protein production is grossly over-simplified and that we are only beginning to scratch the surface of how a cell works. However, I suspect this is enough to show the complexity and apparent design of protein synthesis.[28] According to Dr. Bill Dembski, who holds doctorates in both mathematics and philosophy, the probability of the nucleic acid bases being arranged in an order that codes for the amino acids in a protein by chance is beyond the universal probability limit (1 in 10^{150}).[29] As I was reading in preparation for teaching, I found that I did not have enough faith to believe that this could happen by DNA mutation, even if it was paired with natural selection. After all, if a mutation did happen to produce a new and better protein, 1) why would the cell's checking mechanisms not catch the deviation and destroy the mistake, 2) how would the protein reach its new destination without a new address label, 3) how would the cell know which "machine" to add it to, and 4) since making proteins is a very energy consuming process, why would the cell make a protein that doesn't have a current purpose and, and, and...?

Again, I asked my colleagues, now fellow faculty members at NVCC. Once more, I got the same answer, "It took a long, long time," and encountered the same unwillingness to think any further about the matter. It almost seemed that questioning this scientific theory was threatening to them. But, at that point, I had not even reached the stage of doubting evolution. I assumed that it didn't make sense to me because I did not understand it and would have been open to any thoughtful and supported explanation.

I decided to do some reading and see if I could find other scientists who had noticed the apparent design in nature and addressed the questions it raises in a straightforward manner. I was unimpressed by those who just dogmatically stated that the design is only an illusion.[30, 31] This was definitely not a scientific statement. It was at this point that I first came across the writings of three scholars who have been studying this issue: Jonathan Wells, William Dembski, and Michael Behe. I was appalled to read that much of what is presented to students as incontrovertible evidence for evolution is scientifically problematic.[32] I was gratified to see Dembski's careful work dissecting the process whereby we instinctively decide whether something occurred as a result of intelligence and how this process can be applied to other branches of science.[33] I was enthralled by the way Behe's journey towards questioning the mechanism of evolution

---

28 For a more complete explanation, see Meyer, 2009.
29 Dembski, 2004.
30 Crick, 1988.
31 Dawkins, 1996, p. 4.
32 Wells, 2000.
33 Dembski, 1999.

closely paralleled mine because of the complexity he found inside cells.[34] I wondered why this was not more widely known within the scientific community and decided that being a good teacher required giving my students enough unbiased science-based information to enable them to form their own educated opinions about this issue.

My goal was to make sure that my students were equipped with both the scientific knowledge and the courage to be independent thinkers. There exists a pervasive myth that scientists and doctors are the bearers of truth and are absolutely trustworthy. I felt that the abuse of this trust was not only wrong, but could be dangerous. Claims that most people are not intelligent or educated enough to make their own decisions about what to believe about science abound, resulting in the formation of groups like the Coalition on the Public Understanding of Science.[35] Worse, I have often read claims that anyone who even questions evolution is uneducated or worse. According to evolutionary biologist Ernst Mayr writing in *Scientific American*, "No educated person any longer questions the validity of the so-called theory of evolution, which we now know to be a simple fact."[36] But, according to Einstein, who did not believe in a personal God but was educated and certainly considered intelligent, any serious scientist will be aware that there exists design in the laws of the universe that must have been produced by an intelligence vastly greater than ours.[37] Einstein also enthuses that, "A scientist's religious feeling takes the form of a rapturous amazement at the harmony of natural law, which reveals an intelligence of such superiority that, compared with it, all the systematic thinking and acting of human beings is an utterly insignificant reflection."[38]

Students need to be taught that experts do disagree and that they are not infallible. I felt it was important to help my students to become free and critical thinkers, able and willing to assess what they hear. I'd seen far too many people just believe what they hear the "experts" say and get duped into buying super-

---

34 Behe, 1996.
35 http://www.copusproject.org
36 Mayr, 2000.
37 Letter from Albert Einstein to Phyllis Wright, 1936. January 24.
"Scientific research is based on the assumption that all events, including the actions of mankind, are determined by the laws of nature. Therefore, a research scientist will hardly be inclined to believe that events could be influenced by a prayer, that is, by a wish addressed to a supernatural Being. However, we have to admit that our actual knowledge of these laws is only an incomplete piece of work (unvollkommenes Stückwerk), so that ultimately the belief in the existence of fundamental all-embracing laws also rests on a sort of faith. All the same, this faith has been largely justified by the success of science. On the other hand, however, **every one who is seriously engaged in the pursuit of science becomes convinced that the laws of nature manifest the existence of a spirit vastly superior to that of men**, and one in the face of which we with our modest powers must feel humble. The pursuit of science leads therefore to a religious feeling of a special kind, which differs essentially from the religiosity of more naïve people." (Emphasis added.)
38 Einstein, 1999, in *The World as I See It*.

fluous products, taking unneeded medicines, and fearing unfounded threats. Therefore, I wanted to teach evolution in a way that would provide students with the facts, help them understand the science, encourage them to think logically about what parts of the current controversy are based on science and which parts have their origin in philosophy, and to use this section of the course to teach them some critical scientific analysis skills.

After all, according to Paul Kurtz, "Science requires an open mind, free inquiry, critical thinking, the willingness to question assumptions, and peer review. The test of a theory or hypothesis is independent (at least one would hope) of bias, prejudice, faith, or tradition; and it is justified by the evidence, logical consistency, and mathematical coherence."[39]

In my introduction to the two lectures on evolution, I reminded my students of the definition of science given in the first lecture of the course. That is, science is an open-minded systematic study of the natural world based on experiments, observations, and measurements. Science describes the natural world, but cannot say anything about the supernatural; neither its nature nor whether it exists. I went over the origin of the theory of evolution and Darwin's observations, defining natural selection and survival of the fittest, using the assigned textbook as my source. I then outlined two parts of the theory as it stands today: 1) natural selection leading to minor variations within a type of organism like longer legs or antibiotic resistance (microevolution) and 2) evolution of a new type of organism with a new body plan, requiring major changes in morphology such as the development of lungs or legs (macroevolution). These two very different processes were not distinguished in the text used at that time (they are outlined in the next version), but I felt it important to do so for the sake of clarity.

"Okay, so let's review. Who can give me an example of microevolution?" Hands waved all over the room. "What do you think, Janice?"

"Microevolution is evolution of little things, like bacteria."

"Okay, that's a good guess, but not quite right. Anyone else?"

At this point, David, a young man who had managed an "A" on every test to date, spoke up. "It's *not evolution of little things, but things changing a little* because of environmental pressure or natural selection. Like, maybe if an animal that lives in the North Pole has a mutation so that its fur is white instead of brown, predators will not see it. Then, white animals will have a chance to mate and produce more young than the brown animal who was eaten early in its life.

---

39   Kurtz, 2003, p. 13

Eventually, the population will have more white than brown members, and this is microevolution."

I summed up, "Right, microevolution gives rise to small changes within a species or type of organism and is accepted by virtually all scientists because it can be seen in nature and has been observed in the lab. People throughout history have made microevolution occur by selective breeding. What then is macroevolution?"

Again, hands were raised. Omar, a very polite and friendly Egyptian student, answered, "Dr. Crocker, is it the part of evolution that makes big changes, like fish becoming amphibians?"

"Yes, the theory of macroevolution suggests that numerous, random mutations in the DNA of the sperm or egg cells of a species occur and some will cause a small increase in the "fitness" of the organism, so that those organisms will be at an advantage. They are selected for by natural selection. When lots and lots of these small changes are added up, eventually a new type of organism with a different morphology or shape is formed. This is the part of the theory of evolution that's now at the center of so much debate. Macroevolution certainly has not been achieved by people; despite breeding animals for centuries, dogs remain dogs and horses remain horses."

Here I took the opportunity to encourage my students to think and not just believe everything they are told. For example, there are claims that all scientists agree on the truth of evolution. However, experience shows that it is very hard to find *any* group of people that agree completely about *any* subject and scientists are people. Therefore, it is highly unlikely that all scientists agree about anything.[40]

"How many of you learned about evolution in high school?" Most of the class raised their hands. "Okay, how many of you learned that there are scientific questions about the theory?" Only one or two students responded. "Well, in the next two lectures, we're going to look at the evidence presented for evolution in the textbook, but also at why some scientists say this evidence is insufficient or even erroneous. We also are going to look briefly at the evidence some have suggested supports an alternative scientific view: Intelligent Design." A murmur of interest swept around the room and several leaned forward in their desks. Students love a controversy.

"My goal is for you to think about both sides of this argument, dissecting the science from religion and philosophy. Remember, science is an open-minded inquiry about nature, whereas religion is a set of beliefs about the cause, nature and purpose of life. Philosophy is similar in that it describes a system of beliefs,

---

40   Crichton, 2008.

values and tenets. If you choose to answer the final exam question on evolution you will need to present the scientific evidence for evolution and the problems with that evidence.[41] You will need to come up with an opinion based not on feelings or on what you have always believed, but on rational scientific thinking. I don't expect you to agree with me. In fact, I'm not going to tell you what I believe, but if you choose to answer that question I will expect you to support, with scientific facts, whatever conclusion you reach."

Next, continuing with the history of the theory of evolution, I discussed how Darwin came up with his theory, how he had to publish in a hurry because Alfred Wallace had the same idea, and how the theory has changed since Darwin published his findings in 1859.[42] Interestingly, although Darwin observed that organisms vary and that favorable variations lead to increased survival and reproduction, he did not know how these variations originated or were passed to the next generation. Gregor Mendel, a monk who lived at the same time as Darwin, published his groundbreaking research on genetics, but Darwin had not read Mendel's papers. The significance of Mendel's work was not fully appreciated until after the turn of the 20th century. In fact, Darwin's observations preceded the acceptance of DNA as the genetic material by about 100 years, so his conclusions could not have been based on the idea of DNA mutation leading to variation. The synthesis of Mendelian genetics, Darwinian ideas, and molecular biology that led to our current understanding of evolution did not occur until well into the 20th century.

I then pointed out that all theories do need to undergo occasional review to be sure that they are still the best explanation of the facts. For example, we now know that disease is not caused by an imbalance of the "humors," even though this was believed to be true for over 1300 years. Similarly, it may be that our recent understanding of cells, the complexity of the molecules and specificity of the systems inside them, and the apparent order in nature might challenge some aspects of the theory of evolution. After all, in Darwin's day cells were thought to be little more than bags of protoplasm or jelly.

"Can any of you think about any scientific theories that were overturned by new evidence?" I asked, hoping to stimulate thought.

Kaljit raised his hand, "What about people finding out that the Earth is not flat?" Some of his classmates giggled.

---

41   For the final exam students were allowed to choose to answer three out of a selection of six drawn from a total of ten essay questions to which they would have had access for the entire semester. There was NO requirement to answer the exam question on evolution. All exam questions were graded according to an unbiased and pre-existing rubric.
42   Darwin, 1859.

"Yes, but that has not been widely believed since the third Century.[43] How about any more recent discoveries?"

Again David answered, "For a long time doctors thought that stomach ulcers were caused by overproduction of stomach acid, but now we know that they're often caused by an infection."

"That's right. And, in fact, the scientist who proposed *Helicobacter pylori* as the cause of ulcers was not believed until he drank a flask of the bacteria and got ulcers himself."[44]

"Oooo, that's gross! I wouldn't have done that, even if people were making fun of me!" exclaimed Kaljit.

Janice chimed in, "Lots of scientists experiment on themselves or their families. What about the vaccine for small pox? The guy who discovered that tested it on his own son."

I smiled, "Unfortunately, you're right. And the scientist who first showed that it was possible to pass a tube from a blood vessel in the armpit into the heart, did it to himself, walked up several flights of stairs, and took an X-ray so he could prove it.[45] Nowadays we have groups assigned to evaluate the ethics of experiments before they're approved…not that scientist don't do things without telling others. I actually had a boss who frequently tested drugs on himself…" I trailed off, "But, let's get back to the lecture."

My students groaned. It's always such fun to get the teacher off subject.

"There are many examples of well-accepted scientific theories being over-turned or modified by new discoveries. If you think about it, that's the nature of true science—it is a search for facts about nature that builds on what has gone before."

We then turned to the experiments and evidence cited by the textbook as supporting evolution. For example, one of the first was Kettlewell's famous experiment showing that the peppered moth population in England changed from predominantly light-colored before the industrial revolution to predominantly black during it.[46] The hypothesis was that while resting on pollution darkened tree trunks the light moths were too visible to predators. Consequently, they were eaten before they could reproduce. The darker moths blended in with the pollution and survived to reproduce. This sounds like a very plausible explanation and would be evidence in favor of microevolution (which is not doubted anyway). Obviously the moths did not change into a different organism, so it

---

43   Russell, 1997.
44   Marshall and Warren, 1984.
45   Forssmann, 1931.
46   Kettlewell, 1955.

would be irrelevant as an example of macroevolution. My students nodded and some indicated that they had read about this in their textbook.

I explained that *textbooks do not have to be peer-reviewed*. That is, unlike published scientific articles in reputable journals that must be reviewed by other scientists who are experts in that field, it is not required that chapters in a textbook are screened by anyone but an editor. For this reason, there can be, and often are, mistakes in textbooks that can be passed from version to version. In the case of the peppered moth experiment, even though peer review has shown that this work has some critical problems, it continues to be taught in textbooks without mentioning them.[47]

In response to student questions, I then went on to explain the problems with this particular experiment. First, the work was conducted under conditions that were not true-to-life. The moths were released in the daytime and their behavior monitored at that time. But, peppered moths are nocturnal. The observation that sleepy moths blundering around in the sunshine get eaten is not terribly germane to whether they would have survived if it had been dark.

Second, the investigators assumed that moths rest on the exposed pollution-darkened lichen on trees, but were wrong. In fact, they didn't manage to find the real resting places of the moths. So, for the purposes of publication, they fraudulently glued the moths to trees in order to photograph them. This, in itself if it had been known at the time should have ensured rejection of the study for publication. Third, the assumption that the results showed that the pollution had led to evolution of the moths because they were no longer camouflaged may have been wrong. Evolution is related to genetic change, but no genetic change was shown, and indeed, could not be because the experiment was done before it was possible to do DNA analyses. Therefore, this was a premature conclusion. It is also entirely possible that the chemicals in the pollutants, not a genetic change in the population, actually caused the temporary black coloration. Therefore, many scientists agree that the experiment is inconclusive. It is possible that microevolution did occur, but it is equally possible that it didn't.[48]

"Dr. Crocker, why has no one ever told us this before?" asked a rather indignant Isaac, putting into words what I could see many students were thinking.

"Yeah, and how come the book includes this experiment as evidence, but doesn't tell us the other side of the story?" agreed his friend.

I did not know how to answer. Students tend to trust that they are being taught the truth and the betrayal a person feels when discovering this is not the case is understandable. I was careful to be as honest as possible, "I don't know...

---

47   Wells, 2000.
48   It is telling that as of 2009 many current biology textbooks no longer reference this experiment.

maybe those who taught you before only read the textbook and didn't do any further research. They probably didn't know about the problems with the experiment. As for why the experiment is in the book at all, it is possible that the publishers did not know about the issues either—or perhaps they included it because it illustrates a principle.[49] Of course, this is not real science. Real science should be interested in facts and where they lead."

I then went on to the other lines of evidence given in the textbook (fossil record, Miller-Urey experiments, Galapagos Finches, *etc.*), highlighting whether micro- or macroevolution was supported and also pointing out any scientific problems with the observations, experiments, or conclusions. At no time did I give any non-scientific objections nor did I divulge what I personally believed.

For example, the development of antibiotic resistance in bacteria is often cited as evidence for evolution. But this is, at best, microevolution. It would be invalid to extrapolate the results to claim they prove macroevolution. Here I quoted bacteriologist Alan Linton, who pointed out that a species of bacteria called *E. coli* has undergone 150 years of intensive culture and experimentation, including being genetically engineered.[50] Since bacteria grow very quickly, multiplying from one to millions in a day, it could be expected that evolution into a different form would be evident. Dr. R. Lenski grew this bacterium for 20,000 generations and did not find even *one* new molecular machine. All the mutations decreased cellular information.[51] As biologist Michael Behe pointed out, even though he had produced more bacteria than the sum total of all the chimpanzee to human primates on earth,[52] *E. coli* is still *E. coli* and not another species of bacteria, much less something besides a bacterium.

At the end of the lecture, I was flooded with students interested in the material and wanting to know more. This was one of the few lectures where students obviously did not want our time to end. I answered their questions as best I could and then put away my materials, preparing to leave. As I was going, I looked up to see a young man slouched despondently in his chair. I went over to him.

"What's the matter, Ramy?"

"Nothing…you've just ruined my life," he answered dejectedly.

"What? What do you mean?" This was an accusation I had not heard before.

He pillowed his head on his hand, "I thought I had it all figured out. If life is the result of random chance and nothing besides atoms and energy exists, then life is essentially meaningless, so I don't need to think about why things happen.

---

49   Wells, 2000, p. 233.
50   Linton, 2001.
51   Lenski, 2004.
52   Behe, 2007, p. 141.

But, now…well, if the evidence for evolution is so shaky, maybe God did it and then maybe He exists."

I pondered this for a while. "Well, that could be one explanation of how the world and life came to be, but why would that be so terrible?"

"I used to believe in God and then, a year ago, my dad died of cancer. He was really cool and didn't deserve that. It all seemed so meaningless, so I decided that I would stop believing in God and now…now you've screwed all that up."

"Ramy, I'm so sorry about your dad. I can imagine it's very confusing and I wish I could help you. But I can tell you that running from the questions won't help. If God is real, then you need to deal with Him; if not, you need to cope with that. But, if He exists, being angry with Him likely won't make Him go away." Although outside of class the constitution provides us with the freedom to openly express our faith, I did not want to abuse my position as a teacher, so was careful to be as impartial as possible.

"Yeah, that's what my mom says….it's just so hard. I feel so…." I could see him struggling to hold back tears. Ramy glumly packed his things and made his escape before they overflowed. "Anyway, see you Wednesday."

Ramy chose to answer the question on evolution on the final exam (students were free to choose which questions to answer) and gave a highly thoughtful and complete answer that I have kept to this day.

The following lecture came around quickly and I prepared to explain the scientific evidence said to directly challenge the theory of macroevolution and why it does. I also wanted to briefly introduce my students to the new theory of Intelligent Design.

"Okay, remember how I told you that science is the study of the natural world and cannot tell us about the supernatural?"

Omar responded, "Yeah, it can't tell us if it exists or if it doesn't."

"That's right. The same applies to any scientific theory, including the one I am about to talk about: Intelligent Design (ID)."

A hand waved, "I heard about that from Dr. Green. It's just creationism in disguise; it's not science." With that, the student sat back in his seat with a satisfied smirk.

I did not want to contradict my mentor, but also wanted to help my students to really analyze issues for themselves. I did not want them to unthinkingly accept a professor's word, whether it was me explaining a theory or Dr. Green dismissing a challenging theory by calling it by what would commonly be considered a derogatory "name."

"Well, let's think about that. Can intelligence be measured? Can the action of an intelligent being be detected? Can we do this using scientific methodology?"

"Of course, we do it in psychology and in archaeology," answered David.

"Okay, so we can detect intelligence. Now, when we detect the operation of intelligence in, let's say, a pig sty containing a spider's web with words written in it, do we assume God is speaking through the pig?"[53]

My students laughed.

I continued, "Not necessarily, but it would be normal to acknowledge that the words did not come about as a result of random chances in the way the spider happened to spin, especially if the message changed from day to day. Then, we would seek the source of that intelligence: the pig, the spider, the farmer, or even God. This may, or may not, take us outside the realm of science. In the case of *Charlotte's Web*, it takes us into fantasy."

"Well, ID in biology or physics is where the rules that we use to detect the actions of an intelligent being in other disciplines, like forensics or the Search for Extraterrestrial Intelligence (SETI), are applied to additional branches of science. Here we will consider biology. These rules have been called an explanatory filter."

I then went through the logic behind Dr. William Dembski's explanatory filter system.[54] Although we all use this system on a daily basis, we rarely articulate or even think about the process. For example, most of us, upon finding a cheese sandwich on our front porch would assume that someone, an "intelligence," put it there. If we found a leaf or a paint chip on the porch, we would probably not think this, although it is possible that someone did it. How do we make these decisions about whether a particular phenomenon was caused by intelligent intervention?

Dembski suggested that for every phenomenon there are three possible causes (they can occur in combination): necessity (natural law), chance, or design (intelligence). So, I adapted an example given by Dembski that would allow my students to engage in the discussion.

"Okay, say you are going for a nice walk in the forest. The air smells fresh, the sun is filtering through the leaves, and you feel a slight breeze on your face. Suddenly, your eye is caught by something white in the bushes. You walk over and find a man. He is dead. What might have happened? First, what are some natural laws that might have contributed to his death?"

"He might have been drunk and tripped over a branch, hit his head and died," volunteered a young man who looked as if he might have experience in this area.

"Or maybe he was hit by lightening!" suggested another student.

53 White, 1952.
54 Dembski, 2002.

"Good, those explanations might have been right and would point to natural law or random chance, except for something I forgot to tell you."

My students groaned.

"Yes, the man had an arrow in his chest. Does this mean someone murdered him?"

"Well, no," pondered the policeman in the class. "It might be that a hunter shot him accidentally and never even knew it."

"Or," giggled a pre-nursing student, "maybe he was wearing a pacemaker and the arrow was magnetic."

"Hmm, that's a bit of a stretch, but if true, the death would be a result of an accident, chance and natural law. But, what about if he had five arrows in his chest and his T-shirt had a bull's eye imprinted on it?"

"Then, we would need to start looking for the murderer," asserted the policeman, narrowing his eyes.

"Right, but how do you know that?"

My students looked puzzled, "We just do," answered one.

"It does seem like we make those decisions instinctively. But, Dr. Dembski, who has a Ph.D. in math, a Ph.D. in philosophy, and three other degrees, wrote out the process we all go through without realizing it. He said that, if the probability of an event happening is high, one can put it down to necessity (gravity contributing to a fall). If the probability is low, even extremely, extremely low, it might be chance (a stray arrow). If the probability is extremely low *and* there is specificity, like hitting a target that was there preceding several arrows hitting it, then Dembski suggested it is probably the result of the operation of an intelligent being."[55]

"So, let's look at three different series of letters." I wrote the following on the board.

Aslfkhgv orisc nksfalsjas salfnsngsg

as, an, it, up

My professor is the greatest.

"The first one is complex. That is, if I was to show it to you, take it away, and ask you to reproduce it, it would be difficult. The second is specified. The words, although short, mean something, but they aren't complex. You could memorize them in seconds. The first two lines could be produced by random chance or natural law. The last line is an example of specified complexity. It is

---

55   Dembski, 2002.

complex, in that there is a very low probability that the letters would fall into that pattern by accident, but it's also specified, in that it conforms to a pre-existing pattern; it means something. In our experience of the world so far, specified complexity only happens as the result of the intervention of an intelligent agent," I explained.

A hand waved, "Dr. Crocker, in my geology class we're learning about crystals and rock formations. Some of those are very specific, but they form naturally."

I nodded in understanding, "That's true. They're even elegant, but the patterns are also very simple and there is no specified *complexity*. Now, if we were to take a lump of granite, would that exhibit specificity or a pattern?"

"No, I guess not," Guillermo responded, showing that he was beginning to understand this quite difficult concept.

"Right, granite has a complex structure but no pattern so it does not exhibit *specified* complexity either."

We then went on to consider some of the biological data. My students had already learned about DNA and knew that it is a complex code, which, according to Bill Gates, puts our most complex computer programs to shame.[56] Since intelligence is the only source of code that we know of, many question whether this most complex and specific of codes originated by a series of accidents. There are no known natural laws that would cause the four "letters" of DNA (the nucleotide bases) to connect in a way that would make meaningful coding structures.

"Oh," said Thiang, "I get it! DNA is very complex and the chances of the bases just happening to arrange themselves into a certain order are very small, but that's not enough for us to assume design. But, the DNA coding for something makes it specific, as well. That makes it likely that the code contained in DNA was designed by an intelligent being."

In fact, here Thiang came very close to Dr. Meyer's claim that explanations of biological origins must address three features of life: "the origin of the system for storing and encoding digital information [DNA],…the functionally specified information in DNA,…the origin of the integrated complexity—the functional interdependence of parts—of the cell's information processing system."[57] Since the only source of digital code, functionally specified information, and integrated complexity that we know of is intelligence, it is logical to contemplate that DNA may have been designed by a thinking being.

---

56 Gates, 1995, p. 188.
57 Meyer, 2009, p. 135.

Please note that this does not necessarily mean that the being is a god. In fact, one of the discoverers of the DNA code believes that it probably was a result of directed panspermia (aliens).[58] Finding evidence that an intelligent being might have designed something tells us little about the nature of that being, just like seeing a painting only tells us a limited amount about the artist. This is consistent with what I said at the beginning my course: science can tell us a lot about how and what, but little about who or why.

Next, I introduced my students to the idea of irreducible complexity as published by Michael Behe.[59] I explained that evolution, by definition, is a result of small mutations that lead to an organism that is better-adapted to its environment.[60] Therefore, the only type of complexity that can occur by evolution would be cumulative, since nature cannot select a system that is not yet working. That is, there is a small change that would render the organism more "fit" for the environment and it would out-compete those that did not have that change. Then, there would be another small change, and on, so that changes would occur in a cumulative fashion. Since Charles Darwin lived during a time when scientists believed that cells were little more than bags of protoplasm, he cannot be blamed for proposing a theory that would only describe cumulative complexity. In fact, in the *Origin of Species*, he wrote that, "If it could be demonstrated that any complex organ existed which could not possibly have been formed by numerous, successive, slight modifications, my theory would absolutely break down."[61]

"But now we've found many biological systems that appear to display irreducible complexity.[62] That is, you cannot take away a part of the system and still have a functional system." My students had learned about some of these while studying the amazing complexities of the inner life of the cell, but I thought I would stimulate them to think about the question on a bigger scale, especially since their next biology course would investigate animals and plants.

---

58   Crick, 1973.
59   Behe, 1996.
60   The National Center for Science Education (NCSE) recommends the PBS website for information about evolution. There, evolution is defined as, "…the cumulative changes that occur in a population over time. These changes are produced at the genetic level as organisms' genes mutate and/or recombine in different ways during reproduction and are passed on to future generations. Sometimes, individuals inherit new characteristics that give them a survival and reproductive advantage in their local environments; these characteristics tend to increase in frequency in the population, while those that are disadvantageous decrease in frequency. This process of differential survival and reproduction is known as natural selection. Non-genetic changes that occur during an organism's life span, such as increases in muscle mass due to exercise and diet, cannot be passed on to the next generation and are not examples of evolution." Accessible at: http://www.pbs.org/wgbh/evolution/library/faq/cat01.html#Q01 (as of 4/2/09)
61   Darwin, 1859. p. 158.
62   Behe, 1996.

"Can any of you think of biological systems that might be irreducibly complex, that would have needed many parts to evolve at the same time?"

A timid girl in the back, who wanted to major in zoology, raised her hand. "What about birds? They have hollow bones, big chest muscles, feathers, a fast metabolism, a flow-through respiratory system, and only one ovary."

"That's a good example," I encouraged her, "All of those things are part of an integrated system in a bird. None of them, on their own, would be a great advantage and some would be a definite liability. Imagine how dangerous it would be to have thin, lightweight bones if you couldn't fly. It would be like having osteoporosis...not an advantage. Or would it be helpful to have a fast metabolism if you didn't need all that energy? It would just make you hungry all the time...like teenagers. What use would wings be if the chest muscles to operate them were absent? Or consider the flow-through respiratory system; how would that be an advantage to a land-bound organism and how well would a bird cope without it? But all these things together allow a bird to fly."

Ramy then volunteered a suggestion, "When we were studying proteins, you talked about the blood complement system and how one protein cleaves another and there is a cascade that ends with an infected cell having a tube inserted in it to blow it up. If you took away one of those proteins or if one did not work, then the system would be useless." Ramy was hoping to become a doctor.

"Yes, and there are many genetic diseases known to be a result of a problem with one of the proteins in the complement system," I added.

"So," challenged Nathan, who had been sitting in the back with his arms crossed over his chest, "Are you saying that God must exist because evolution can't explain the complexity in life? A kind of God of the gaps theory?"

"No," I answered, "ID is science and so it can't tell us about God, only about whether intelligence is suggested. It cannot tell us what the nature of that intelligence is...it might be an alien. I'm just giving you the arguments that have been put forward to suggest that macroevolution is insufficient as a theory to explain the origin of a species. In fact, some evolutionists arbitrarily assert that any design we see in nature is only apparent.[63, 64] This in itself looks like a religious, not a scientific, statement. It might also be that there is another so far undiscovered theory of origins out there and you might be the one to come up with it."

"But, do *you* think that it's God?" he persisted.

---

63 Crick, 1988.
64 Dawkins, 1996, p. 4.

"Nathan, I cannot talk about that here because this is a biology not a philosophy class.[65] But, if you want to talk further, we can meet in my office."

Manaar, a feisty covered Muslim woman, spoke up, "Well, I think it's obvious. Allah is the Creator."

Nathan turned on her. "No intelligent scientific person believes that. It's just religious crap."

Here Nathan was using the popular, not legal, definition of religion, since the U.S. Supreme Court defines *any* belief about origins as religion.[66] This includes the belief that only natural causes are possible. But, I wanted to avoid the religious implications of this subject matter as much as possible.

I also clearly needed to regain control of my classroom before the arguing escalated, "Okay, let's finish the lecture. You can talk after class."

I then reminded my students of the various levels of scientific certainty that they'd learned about in the first lecture. "Although there is some controversy about these definitions, I am going to give you what your textbook says. Laws are the most certain, having been tested extensively and never disproven. Theories can and have been tested, but not as extensively as laws. They are an evidence-based explanation for an observed phenomenon.[67] A hypothesis is the least certain; it is a proposed explanation for a set of facts that can be tested, but has not undergone testing yet. Microevolution is a theory, but actually macroevolution does not fit neatly into any of these categories since it is a historical science and is more difficult to test. Regardless, we do know one thing. Any new hypothesis or theory must be in accord with known laws. Otherwise it is not scientific."

I then explained the law of biogenesis that says life always comes from prior life and the laws of statistics that show that there has not been enough time for the positive mutations needed for present day life to have evolved from bacteria.[68] Therefore, I concluded the lecture with a challenge. "Since macroevolution, if you include the origin of life, appears to contradict known laws, is it a viable theory? Think about the evidence: do you think that complex life came about through macroevolution, Intelligent Design, or another as yet undiscovered process?"

"Dr. Crocker, if we can think of another process, will you give us an "A" for the course?"

---

65   I made this clear on more than one occasion, but it is documented in letters from two students, December 22, 2004 and May 4, 2005. Student identities have been withheld at their request. Letters may be found in Appendix II.

66   *Lee v. Weisman*, 1992. 505 U.S. 577.

67   Raven and Johnson, 2005.

68   Johnson, 2009.

I laughed, "Yes, I will. But, remember, it must account for all the evidence and not go against any known laws. If you can manage that, you might even get a Nobel prize!"

This topic covered, we were coming up to the end of the course. Because of in-class discussions and exam results, I was very aware that many of my students had not yet grasped the basic concepts of the course, so I determined to have one last try at helping them do so, while also making it possible for them to raise their grade.

"So, I want to talk about the final exam." The class became quiet. "I've decided to make it an essay test," I announced to groans from my students. I pressed on, "There will be ten questions posted on the board tomorrow. Of those, five will be on the exam and you'll be expected to answer three."

Hands flew up around the room, "Hey Doc, d'you mean that you'll show us the actual questions that'll be on the test ...the exact same ones?"

"Yes, the questions cover the course content and so, if you learn the answers, we both benefit. You'll get a good grade and I'll be happy you learned the course material."

"Can we check our answers with you beforehand?"

"Yes, I'll tell you where you need to improve, so there's no reason why you shouldn't get 100% on this exam." As it was, only about ten of my students sent me answers to check so, as a last ditch attempt to prepare them for the next course, I held an optional review session where I covered the answer to each of the questions. Only fifteen students turned up and I realized that poor grades are not necessarily the fault of the teacher.

Final exam time came around and the nervousness in the air was palpable. One particular student, Evan, seemed even more nervous than the others. He had not tried particularly hard during the semester, only turning up for class about 50% of the time and rarely turning in homework. But now, he was hopping from one foot to the other, "Dr. Crocker, Dr. Crocker, I need a "C." Please, I'll do ANYTHING!"

I tried to be gentle, "Evan, I don't think that it's possible now. Earlier in the semester I suggested studying, but now the best you can do is a "D." I'm sorry. You'll have to try again next semester."

"But I *neeeed* this class to graduate. How about giving me an extra credit project?"

"Evan, I told you what you needed to do earlier in the semester, but now, your past grades have been too bad. There's nothing I can do."

I got up and went to my office, gathered my things and then proceeded to my car, with Evan following me all the way. He continued to beg and became more and more adamant and agitated. I once again explained about consistent study habits, but he seemed not to hear. Eventually, I got in the car and drove away as he was still talking.

The next day Evan appeared in my office. Again he was agitated and this time I noticed he was trembling and sweating. "Dr. Crocker, you have to let me turn in an extra paper or something. I can't repeat the class. Or I could do some work on your house...or, or, or fix your car. Please, *anything*. I have to get a "C.""

I had to be tough, "No, Evan, it's no use. I cannot give you any advantage that other students don't have. You should have worked during the semester. I warned you repeatedly then. Our conversation is over, so you should leave."

At this, Evan did not leave, but drew in closer, so much that I could smell his sweat. I became nervous and edged towards the door of the faculty office as he spoke. He was a big person and his voice grew progressively louder. At this point I was relieved when a fellow teacher entered the office and, seeing my predicament, told Evan to leave in no uncertain terms.

The next day, Evan turned up as I was doing some photocopying just before class. However, I was prepared and because he was frightening me, I had warned security. When he followed me to the class, they escorted him away. It was not something I enjoyed having to do, but it did have a good effect. I met Evan several years later, still at NVCC, but now working hard and succeeding. Surprisingly, he remembered me with affection as the one who finally convinced him that there was no way to do well in school except through hard work. He later took a different and more advanced class from me and earned a B.

And so, the final exam and the end of the semester arrived. I had mixed feelings: I would miss my students, but not the grading. I was buzzing with ideas about how to improve next semester, but nervous about having to prepare an entirely new course, the second semester of general biology, Bio 102.

Arriving for the final, I was pleasantly surprised to find a couple of thank you cards and a box of chocolates on my desk. I said thank you to my students, but made a mental note not to open them until after I'd finished the grading.

"Okay, its time to put away your books and notes. Now, please take out your Scantron sheet and your exam notebook and turn them in. Then I will redistribute them. If you get a notebook that already has an answer in it, be sure to turn it in immediately so you don't get penalized for cheating." Because I had intellectual honesty as a core value, I was also fairly tough on cheating.

A murmur of dismay went around the classroom. They hadn't expected this. "I already wrote my name on my booklet," objected one student.

"That's okay. The person who gets it will just cross it out," I answered.

After the exchange, I was handed two exam books with notes already in them. My heart sank. I'd been warned about possible cheating, but had not wanted to believe it. I gave those people new booklets, but didn't pursue the ones who had attempted to cheat since I knew they wouldn't know the material anyway.

The results of the final were pretty much as I expected with a few pleasant surprises. Most of those who did very well had also worked hard during the course. Many who did poorly had also not studied enough during the semester, so the final did not affect their grade. However, there were a few who had worked like crazy and got over 90% on the final when their course grade was much lower. In that case, I did as I had promised and raised their grade by a full grade, even though a strict average would not usually have this effect. I figured better late than never for learning the material. The grades were entered into the NVCC computer system and the semester was over. I had learned so much: something of how to teach undergraduates, at what level to pitch a course, that students today are very different from what they were 20 years ago, and most of all…that teaching is awesome. I realized again that I could happily do this for the rest of my life.

REFERENCES

Anonymous. "Biography of Prof. Derek Burke." *The Faraday Institute for Science and Religion*. http://www.st-edmunds.cam.ac.uk/faraday/Biography.php?ID=94 (as of 3/31/09).

Anonymous. 2003. "My DNA." *Dolan DNA Learning Center; Cold Spring Harbor Laboratories*. http://www.dnai.org/text/mediashowcase/index2.html?id=585 (as of 3/31/09).

Anonymous. 2004. Letter from GMU pre-med student to Caroline Crocker. December 22. The author's identity has been withheld by request.

Anonymous. 2005. Letter from lawyer and GMU student to "Karen Anderson." May 4. The author's identity has been withheld by request.

Anonymous. 2008. "mRNA Processing." *ndsuvirtual Cell Animations Project Animation*. March 3. http://www.youtube.com/watch?v=YjWuVrzvZYA (as of 3/31/09).

Anonymous. 2008. "Protein Synthesis: Translation Process." May 7. www.youtube.com/watch?v=B606uRbID388NR=1 (as of 3/31/09).

Anonymous. 2008. "The Inner Life of the Cell." BioVisions. October 6. http://www/youtube.com/watch?v=BVvvx5HGpLg (as of 3/31/09).

Anonymous. 2009. *Coalition for the Public Understanding of Science*. February 2. http://www.copusproject.org (as of 3/31/09).

Behe, Michael J. 1996. *Darwin's Black Box: The Biochemical Challenge to Evolution*. New York, NY: The Free Press.

Burke, Derek C. (editor). 1985. *Creation and Evolution (When Christians Disagree)*. Leicester, UK: Inter-Varsity Press.

Crichton, Michael. 2008. "'Aliens Cause Global Warming'," reprinted in *Wall Street Journal*, November 7.

Crick, Francis. 1973. "Directed Panspermia." *Icarus* 19: 341-346.

Crick, Francis. 1988. *What Mad Pursuit: A Personal View of Scientific Discovery*. New York, NY: Basic Books.

Darwin, Charles. 1859. *On the Origin of Species by Means of Natural Selection*. London, UK: John Murray.

Dawkins, Richard. 1996. *Climbing Mount Improbable*. London, UK: Viking. p. 4.

Dembski, William A. 1999. *Intelligent Design: The Bridge Between Science and Theology*. Madison, WI: Inter-Varsity Press.

Dembski, William. 2002. *No Free Lunch: Why Specified Complexity Cannot Be Purchased Without Intelligence.* Lanham, MD: Rowman & Littlefield.

Dembski, William A. 2004. *The Design Revolution: Answering the Toughest Question about Intelligent Design.* Madison, WI: Inter-Varsity Press.

Einstein, Albert. 1936. Letter from Albert Einstein to Phyllis Wright, dated January 24, AEA 52-337. In Einstein. His Life and Universe, edited by Walter Isaacson. 2007. New York, NY: Simon and Schuster. Forssmann, Werner. 1931. "Münchener Medizinische Wochenschrift/20 March 1931 Contrast representation of the cavities of the living right half of the heart, Eberswalde." In MMW, *Münchener medizinische Wochenschrift* 120 (14): 489. April 1978. PMID 347275

Einstein, Albert. 1999. *The World as I See It,* Secaucus, New Jersey: The Citadel Press, pp. 24-29. http://www.stephenjaygould.org/ctrl/einstein_religion. html (as of 4/29/09).

Gates, Bill. 1995. *The Road Ahead.* New York, NY: Penguin, p. 188.

Gould, Steven J. 1982. "Darwinism and the Expansion of Evolutionary Theory." *Science* 23(216):380-387.

Humphries, Donald. 1975. Sermon series given by Reverend D. Humphries at Warwick University Chaplaincy, Coventry, UK, October.

Johnson, Donald E. 2009. Probability's *Nature and Nature's Probability: A Call for Scientific Integrity.* Riverside, CA: Big Mac Publishers.

Kettlewell, H.B.D. 1955. "Selection Experiments on Industrial Melanism in the Lepidoptera." *Heredity* 9:323-342.

Kurtz, Paul. 2003. *Science and Religion: Are They Compatible?* Amherst, NY: Prometheus Books, p. 13.

Lenski, R.E. 2004. "Phenotypic and genomic evolution during a 20,000-generation experiment with the bacterium, E. coli." *Plant Breeding Reviews* 24:225-65.

Linton, Henry Alan H. 2001. "Scant Search for the Maker." *Times Higher Education Supplement,* Book Section, p. 29.

Marshall, B.J. and J.R. Warren. 1984. "The Bacterium *Helicobacter pylori* and its Role in Gastritis and Peptic Ulcer Disease." Lancet 1, pp. 1311–1315.

Mayr, Ernst W. 2000. "Darwin's Influence on Modern Thought." *Scientific American* 283(1):67-71. July.

Meyer, Stephen C. 2009. *Signature in the Cell. DNA and the Evidence for Intelligent Design.* New York, NY: HarperCollins.

Raven, P.H., G.B. Johnson, J.B. Losos, S.R. Singer. 2005. *Biology* 7th Edition, Dubuque, IA: McGraw- Hill.

Russell, Jeffrey Burton. 1997. "The Myth of the Flat Earth," presented during the American Scientific Affiliation Conference at Westmont College, August 4. http://www.veritas-ucsb.org/library/russell/FlatEarth.html (as of 3/2/09).

Wells, Jonathan. 2000. *Icons of Evolution: Science or Myth?* Washington, D.C.: Regnery Publishing Inc.

White, Elwyn B. 1952. *Charlotte's Web.* New York, NY: Harper Collins.

Chapter 3: Learning through Experience

This was my second semester at NVCC and I was actually starting as a semi-experienced college teacher. Full of enthusiasm, I wanted to be the best I could be. So, I decided to make more changes in order to increase the pass rate without using the huge curve employed by so many teachers. I pored over the old exams, studying which questions were missed most and why. I looked through old lab reports, seeking the most common errors. I chatted with those students who were still in contact with me to get their ideas on how their learning experience could have been improved. I talked with Dr. Buckley to find out the level at which courses should be pitched. I have always been a perfectionist and my teaching career was going to reflect this.

Then, I was given a copy of the course objectives for Bio 102 and a list of the chapters to be covered. "Oh my goodness, now what do I do?" I whispered. The course was to cover animals and their organ-systems, plants and their function, and ecology. My last exposure to botany had been in high school and I didn't remember ever studying ecology. Skimming through the chapters did not help my panic. The depth of coverage was such that I would need three semesters to deal with the set subjects. So, I turned to my fellow adjunct teachers for advice.

The first colleague I found was an elderly man with a yellowed beard wearing a rumpled suit and tie. He leaned back in his chair, "Well, I've been an adjunct professor here ever since I retired from teaching high school and I've found that, as long as you touch on all the objectives, no one seems to care whether one is covered more thoroughly than another. Me, I really like plants, so I cover two animal organ-systems per lecture and only spend two lectures on ecology. The rest of the time I teach botany."

I figured I could make use of his expertise, "I really know very little about botany. Would you mind if I sit in on some of your lectures and labs at the beginning of the semester, just to get an idea of what to teach and how? I might even like to sit at a lab table and pretend to be a student."

"No problem. My lectures are on Mondays and Wednesdays at 8:00 am and the lab is after that at 10:00." I took advantage of his offer and found it very helpful, especially in labs where we were just supplied with a bunch of plants on a cart with no sign of what species each plant was.

Here another teacher chimed in, "I don't teach 102 that way. I think ecology is the most important subject to teach in these days of global warming and the destruction of our environment." She stood up, her voluminous skirt swirling around her ankles, and began sorting through her overflowing bookcase, "I'm sure I have a copy of my syllabus somewhere." After a time she gave up. Flipping her rather wild-looking hair out of her eyes, she said, "Anyway, I skip most of the animal systems and the plants. Instead, I spend over half the semester on ecology…we take field trips and the kids really seem to like it… Of course, I also have treats for when we get back."

I repressed a smile at the idea of this eccentric teacher with her rather distinctive mode of dress traipsing across a meadow, pointing out its various features with a class of 25 college students in tow, returning to feed them milk and cookies.

Just then a clean-cut man in his fifties with a military bearing entered the room, "Good morning all. Ready for the new semester?"

"Actually," I replied, "We were just talking about that. This is my second semester here and I'm teaching Bio 102 for the first time. Do you have any advice on how to tackle it?"

Here Dr. Walsh drew himself up importantly and adjusted his tie, "Don't take any nonsense from 'em. Most students want to be spoon-fed and be given a grade without having worked for it. I don't stand for any crap and just fail 'em. The way I see it, there are two types of people—us and them. We're the ones who work and study hard and we made it. Most of the students here are "them." They're lazy and dishonest; they'll cheat and even try to make you lie for them. Take one student I had last semester—he came in after the last day to drop and asked me to sign the paperwork necessary because he was failing. In order for him to be allowed to withdraw, I needed to sign that he had extreme circumstances, like a death in the family. I asked him how he dared to ask me to lie for him. He denied it, but that's what he was doing and I didn't let him get away with it…" And Dr. Walsh went on, getting progressively louder.

Since the other teachers had quietly become scarce by this time and we were alone, I began to feel uncomfortable and moved towards the door, finally pleading that I had another appointment to get to. I later found that this man was not at all dangerous to fellow teachers and had a wonderful sense of humor, but he did have a reputation for making students cry. I often heard him yelling at an unfortunate victim through the closed door of a classroom and was glad that he considered me "one of us"!

With all this advice under my belt, I began to prepare the course. I decided to do as the other teachers do and concentrate on what I know, skimming over the other subjects. Therefore, I determined to spend most of the time on animal organ-systems, about three weeks on botany,[69] and one week on ecology.

---

69 Definitions can be found in Appendix I.

Now that I had decided on the course content, what changes should I make to ensure the students would learn it? The first problem to be tackled was the tendency of students either to not take notes or to be furiously copying what was on the slides and not listen to what I said. Since the university provided teachers with web space, I designed a website that would include copies of all the PowerPoint slides used in the course, the syllabus and schedule, lab assignments, contact information, a FAQ section, a scrolling announcement line, and sample exams. The problem, of course, was that if students could obtain all the slides online, why come to class? Instituting a rule that more than four missed classes would result in being withdrawn or failed solved this. My experience from the previous semester was that students who skipped class failed anyway, so it wasn't as harsh a rule as it seems. Because taking roll was mandatory at NVCC, it was also easy to accomplish.

Memories of the questions I was asked during exams brought me to another change in the course structure. I had noticed that students were often tripped up by questions that included scientific terminology. Since a large part of science is simply learning vocabulary, it was important to devise a scheme that would force the students to memorize words. Here I realized that it was possible to kill several birds with one stone. If I opened each lecture with a quiz on ten vocabulary words that had been introduced in the previous lecture, I would solve the persistent problems with tardiness, help ensure students learned the science words, and force them to read their lecture notes at least once before studying for the exam. These words with their definitions would be posted on the website, allowing students ample time to do the memory work.

My perusal of the old exams also showed me that it was the questions with complex sentence structure that were often missed. "Of course," I thought, "Most of the students are not native English speakers." Going through the exams and simplifying the sentence structure would easily solve this. I decided against using the supplied test bank since that seemed more like an English than a biology test. In the future, I would have my exams reviewed by honor students from various countries, so they could give me input about which questions were confusing because of the language barriers. Finally, I gave a copy of my first exam to Dr. Buckley, who kindly went through it and marked all the questions he felt were too difficult. Amazingly, those were the ones I got from the testbank.

Finally, I tackled the problem of missed labs. Because university technicians set up the labs, if someone missed a lab, for any reason, they couldn't make it up. Therefore, I decided to visit the Natural History Museum in Washington, D.C., making up a worksheet as I went. If a student missed a lab, or just wanted to skip one, they could make it up by going to the museum and turning in the worksheet. It proved to be a popular option and last time I checked NVCC professors were still using my worksheet.

Finally the syllabus was written, the website was up and running and the first day of the new semester began. The first thing I noticed upon walking into the tiered lecture hall was the heat. Although the room had been fairly comfortable previously, it was now at least 85° F and this was in January. The warmly dressed students were red-faced and sweating. Many were fanning themselves. I quickly slipped out and went to the office to speak to the friendly redheaded administrator for the department.

"Susan, it's way too hot in the lecture hall. Is it possible to get someone from maintenance to turn the heat down?"

Susan shook her head. She'd worked at NVCC for years. "No, it's always this way. Hot in the winter and way too cold in the summer. You just learn to dress in layers."

Dr Buckley overheard us, "If you think it is hot there, just wait until you get into lab."

As I made my way back to the lecture hall, I again noticed the sagging, discolored ceiling tiles and the peeling paint. I passed by a lab with its antiquated equipment. Some of the slides were so old that I had joked with the students that they contained dinosaur blood. I knew that community colleges are run on a shoestring to keep prices low for students. Except for the price of books, this was accomplished admirably. Just that semester, the faculty had been informed that state funding was being cut further, so student costs would go up, but not by much. The education received in the small classes of a community college is often better than that obtained in the huge lectures of a state-run four year institution, so it was certainly worth the cost. But, I was frustrated because the condition of the facility was an impediment to student learning. How can one stay alert enough to take in information when the room is 85° F? And my hope was they would also think about and use the information.

I re-entered the lecture theater and introduced myself to my waiting class, apologized for the heat and advised them to dress in layers, as was suggested by Dr. Buckley. I then passed out the syllabus and turned to starting up the computer so that my students could see the syllabus and PowerPoint slides. At NVCC the computers are kept in cabinets with padlocks to prevent theft, but I found that this did not provide enough security. The computer booted up without a problem, but to my frustration, the mouse wouldn't work. I soon discovered the reason. Someone had stolen the ball from inside of it. Rather pointless, but it was done. Getting out the chalk, I explained the syllabus and website and did the lecture on the board, as I had the previous semester. I made a mental note to bring my own mouse in the future. But the next time I had a problem, someone had actually stolen the entire guts of the computer, so the extra mouse didn't help.

"Please get out your syllabus. Note that you are in Bio 102 and that my contact information and website address are on the front of the syllabus. This means you can and should contact me and that you should mark the website as a favorite."

"What if I don't have a computer?" asked Paco, a sleepy-eyed young man who had comfortably situated himself with his head pillowed on his sweater, which was conveniently placed up against the wall.

"There are lots of computers in the library and in the study halls. Use one of those."

"But I work full time. I don't have time to go messing with computers and libraries," he said, adjusting his makeshift pillow into a more comfortable shape.

I had learned the previous semester that full time work and success in school do not mix and decided to be cruel to be kind, "If you don't have time to fulfill the requirements of the course, then you shouldn't take it. This course is difficult and will require two hours of your time for every hour spent in class. If you're going to do well, you'll need to make it a priority."

I then continued, "If you turn to page two of the syllabus, you'll see how the course is graded. There will be four exams and a final, daily quizzes, and lab work. Please note that the quizzes are given during the first five minutes of class and, if you miss one, you cannot make it up."

There was an instant buzz in the room.

"What if we're late or absent?" worried Anna, a chubby blonde lady dressed in a business suit.

"That's the point. I've noticed that those who come, and come on time, do best in school, so I'm using these quizzes to encourage you in these habits."

"But, what if we're sick or have a flat tire?"

"If you notice, the total points allocated to the quizzes add up to 10 points more than they should. This will allow you to miss two quizzes without receiving a grade penalty. On the other hand, if you make it to all of them, you'll have 10 points extra credit."

Anna thought about this for a minute, "That's not fair. I have work right before this class and if my boss keeps me late I'll lose points."

"I'm sorry you don't like it, but that's why we go through the syllabus on the first day of class. It's like a contract between us. You do have the option to take another class where you like the syllabus." I was growing hard-nosed with experience. After all, in order to succeed, it was vital that the students saw that the course would require a significant time commitment. Otherwise, it was a waste of their time and money.

Ignoring the murmurs about what a hard teacher I was, I pressed on and began the first lecture of the term. I didn't mind being perceived as hard if my goal of helping students learn was accomplished.

After class two young men approached me. Claus was chunky with an arrogant tilt to his chin; Andrew was dark-haired, diffident and shy— but they had the same story.

"Dr Crocker, I have a learning disability. See, the disability office told me to give this to you so you can make accommodations for me."

I read the forms through. Basically, both Claus and Andrew had problems with writing and needed to have help from another student in taking notes. They would also require assistance with doing the research paper that I'd assigned. I assured them of my assistance and signed their forms. I was to discover, however, that there can be a world of difference in how students having similar disabilities cope with them.

The next time the class met, I asked for volunteers to take notes for students with learning disabilities. Helen, who had taken Bio 101 from me previously, immediately raised her hand. Since I knew that she was extremely meticulous, I accepted her offer. Another girl, Elhaim, sitting right in front of me, also offered. I was pleased because this meant if one of them was absent the other could cover. It was now up to the students requiring help to make arrangements with those who could offer it.

Immediately after class I could see that there were going to be problems. Claus was talking to Helen and I heard him say, "The way it works is this. You take notes on the class, photocopy them and give me the photocopies, hole-punched and in a folder."

Stunned, I listened for Helen's response. It seemed to me he was asking for a lot more than was necessary.

Helen looked distressed, "I don't have money to do the copying. Will someone reimburse me for it? And where do I get the folder?"

"How would I know? Go to the office and ask."

Here I stepped in, "Claus, since it's you who knows where the disability office is, how about you go and get these questions answered. After all, Helen is doing you a favor."

Claus sniffed, raised his chin higher and turned to me, "Dr. Crocker, I'll also not be able to do the research paper, so you'll need to waive that requirement."

Remembering my new toughness, I was unperturbed as I replied, "I'm afraid that won't be possible. Accommodation means that I will help you fulfill the course requirements, not that I will change them." I was glad that NVCC had provided information on what "accommodation" means at the pre-semester orientation.

For the first time, Claus appeared flustered, "I'll have the office call you… you'll see." He then stalked out of the classroom, leaving behind a worried Helen.

"Don't be upset, Helen. You're volunteering and no one can force you to do something you don't want to do. Remember you always have the option to say 'no'." I then turned to Andrew, who had been waiting quietly.

"Can you explain more fully what it is you need in the way of accommodations?"

"Yes," he said, fumbling in his bag, "Look, I brought carbon paper. That way Helen or Elhaim can just put it under the page as they take notes and then give me the copy after class."

"That's a great idea. Where do you get the carbon paper?"

"Oh, the disability office provides it. I can get more any time," he answered, blushing furiously at my praise.

"How about the research paper? How can I help with that?"

Andrew thought for a moment. "Well, I've done papers before, but I have real problems with writing anything down. If you think it is okay, in the past I've had someone just write what I dictate…unless that's cheating," he finished anxiously.

"No, it sounds like a great idea. Executives do it all the time. They don't think it's cheating. And if you need further help, just let me know."

It was not much of a surprise for me to find that Claus dropped the class before the first exam and that Andrew finished with an "A," even earning a high mark on the research paper.

The next class was also the first quiz. I made sure that I arrived early and that all the computer parts were present and accounted for. Watching the clock, I posted the quiz on the screen exactly as the second hand reached the 12. I wanted the students to get the idea that I meant what I said about being on time. It would be good practice for the working world. Exactly five minutes later I removed the projection of the quiz and asked that the papers be handed in.

A breathless young lady came running in just as I collected the last paper.

"Did I miss it?" she asked as she plopped into her seat.

"Yeah," answered the student next to her.

"@$#*&" she replied.

I pretended not to hear and started the lecture. As the semester went on I would become more lenient with students who had real reasons for being late (difficult bosses, late babysitters, traffic), but wanted to establish discipline from the start.

After class, I got the quizzes out and began marking. Since the words and their definitions had been listed on the website, and all they needed to do was match them by writing a, b, c, etc. I thought they probably would have done well. I was right. I was gratified to see that 80% of the class achieved 10/10. However, there were things that disturbed me. I noticed that those who made mistakes often got the exact same things wrong as their neighbor. In addition, I noticed that two quizzes had different first names on them, but were written in the same handwriting. Looking at my class roster, I saw that Kameela and Khalida had the same last name, but I doubted it was possible to have identical handwriting.

The next quiz I had the students write down definitions instead of letters, thinking it would be easier to discern cheating in this way. At the end of lecture, I called Kameela and Khalida to the front of class and dismissed the others.

Pulling out their quizzes, marked clearly with a "0" each, I asked which of them had done both quizzes.

"Dr. Crocker, I promise we each did our own," protested Kameela.

"But, the handwriting is the same."

"We're sisters; our handwriting is very similar."

"Really? Show me the notes you took today." A quick look showed me that Kameela had done both quizzes. "Kameela, these quizzes are both in your handwriting. Was Khalida absent?"

Kameela looked aghast. "No, Dr. Crocker, honestly, we would never do such a thing. Please don't give us '0's,' you're being unfair!"

"Okay, I'll check with the head of department. If he agrees that these are the result of cheating, the mark stays. If not, I'll restore the points you lost."

It was interesting to me that Khalida had not said a word throughout the entire exchange. Was it possible she'd not been aware of what her sister had done?

The girls left, muttering under their breath, but I hoped they were also resolving not to try cheating again. They never did admit to the offense, despite the fact that the department head agreed with my assessment of the situation, and they both dropped the class soon afterwards. In fact, in all my years of teaching, I only once had a student who was caught red-handed cheating admit to and apologize for the offense. Teaching intellectual honesty was to prove difficult in more ways than one.

The lab part of the Bio 102 course was challenging, for both the students and the teacher. On the first day, students were instructed to go to the bookstore and purchase a fetal pig for dissection beginning the following week. Unfortunately, the lab was extremely hot and lacked any windows or ventilation, so the smell and the effect of the preservative on the eyes was extremely unpleasant. Pinning the animal onto ancient, cracked and dirty dissection trays, groups of four students peered at the pigs. One of them cut it open with an old and rusty scalpel and began to probe around looking for the various organs and structures.

"Dr. Crocker, do you have any newer scalpels? These won't cut."

"Just a minute. I'll check in the back."

I slipped into the prep room and asked the technicians for new blades.

"They're here if you want them, but we give the students the old ones so that they won't cut themselves."

Since I could not see the logic of this, I made no reply but simply thanked them, picked up some new blades, and made my way back to the lab.

The students were soon busy cutting open their pigs, rinsing out the excess latex paint that had been used to dye the blood vessels, and locating the assigned structures. When I came by, they would look at me blearily with red-rimmed eyes, hoping I would not ask them to show me the location of a particular part of the pig.

Eventually, after having studied the digestive, circulatory, and nervous systems, we came to the lab on the excretory system. Here, after locating the pig's kidneys, bladder and other parts of the system, the students would have a chance to experiment on themselves.

"Okay, please put away your pigs and wash your hands. Then take your seats to wait until the rest of the class is ready." I waited for the commotion to die down.

"For this part of the lab you're going to obtain a specimen of your own urine and do experiments on it, so please come forward and pick up a disposable cup."

"Dr. Crocker, do we have to? Can't just one of us provide the pee?" wailed a girl in the front.

"No, for safety reasons, everyone must work on their own urine and not someone else's. If there are reasons why you cannot participate, come and see me privately." I had resolved that, in the case of a girl menstruating or someone having another good excuse, I would provide that person with artificial urine. Although adequate for the purposes of the lab, using artificial urine did reduce the interest level, so I wanted to keep it to a minimum.

I passed out the cups and the students trooped off to the various bathrooms.

"Dr. Crocker, look!" beamed a muscular young man, Carson, as he reentered the room, "My pee is frothy. And, I nearly filled the beaker."

"Very good, Carson. Now, put it down before it spills." I was used to Carson bragging about most everything -- his face, his body, his dress-sense, but this was amazing.

Carson sneered at his lab partner, a shy Japanese boy called Senichi. "Hey man, Sen, is that *all* you could do?"

Senichi was quiet, but had a good sense of humor, "I go for quality, not quantity."

Smiling, I turned to Carson, "Okay now, settle down. What's the first thing you need to write about your urine?"

He looked confused. "Uh, how much?"

"No, look at your lab book. You need to observe the color and whether it's cloudy," I pointed at the spot on the page, "Write it down here."

I then moved on to the next table to watch a studious group of young men writing down their observations. This particular lab group consisted of mostly "A" and "B" students. Leaning over to see what they were writing in their lab notebooks, I was startled to see that one of them had reported his urine as being green.

"Luis, which urine is yours?"

He pointed at a container of yellow-orange fluid.

"Oh, you haven't had much to drink today, have you?"

Sheepishly, Luis hung his head, "I only just got up in time to come here. I didn't have time for breakfast."

"Okay, that doesn't matter, but why did you write that your urine is green?"

Luis looked at me in astonishment, "Because it is...look at it."

"Dude," drawled his lab partner, "It's orange."

A suspicion formed in my mind, but it would be the next lab, on the senses, before it was confirmed that Luis was, in fact, color blind.

I continued round the lab, checking on student progress, when I was stopped by a whisper from Una, a lovely-looking European girl. "Dr. Crocker, could you look in my microscope?"

I stopped and had a look. Students were often surprised to find that urine can contain crystals and epithelial cells. However, her urine sample was full of sperm. "Umm yes, that's very interesting," I said, not really knowing how to respond, moving towards the front of the room.

Una looked worried and followed me. Reaching my desk, she asked, "Do I have some awful infection?"

I glanced at her bare ring finger, "No, I think maybe you have a boyfriend."

After a moment the penny dropped and Una, blushing, made her way back to her bench.

Later I found out that she was dating Carson. Wouldn't he have been proud.

Only a week later I had to tackle the chapter on the reproductive system. The textbook started with external anatomy, but I suspected the students would know this. I elected to skip it and avoid the guffaws that would accompany the labeling of a penis on the screen. Instead, I started with the internal anatomy and an explanation of how the reproductive systems in males and females work. We then covered a bit of embryology and finished with a discussion of how things can go wrong with the reproductive system. Since over 50% of the sexually active population will have Human Papilloma Virus (HPV) at some time in their lives,[70] 20% have Herpes,[71] nearly 4% have Chlamydia and more have Trichomoniasis,[72] not to mention a variety of other diseases, I felt it important to lay out the facts. In these days of political correctness, many students had been instructed in "safe sex", but had not been told condoms do not entirely prevent many of the incurable sexually transmitted diseases (STDs). They certainly did not know about the seriousness of the situation.

Halfway through the lecture there was an audible groan, "Oh, no!"

Several students tittered. I stopped for a moment, waiting to see if there was a question. Finally one came, but from the other side of the room.

"Dr. Crocker, are you sure about those numbers?" challenged a young man sitting towards the back.

"Yes, many of the statistics came from the Center for Disease Control (CDC) publications. The other facts are known, but not well publicized. For example, did you know some scientists claim that wearing a condom only reduces your chance of contracting HIV by 70%?[73] The National Institutes of Health (NIH) has reported that the number is 85%.[74] Either way, it is better than not wearing one, but not good enough in my opinion."

He looked worried, "But these days most STD's, except of course AIDS, are curable, right?"

I did not like to add to his anxiety, but knew that honesty was what was needed. "If you know you have one, and 80% of the time people don't, and it is bacterial, then it is usually curable. Unfortunately, many of these diseases cause infertility before they are detected." I had more bad news, "But, there is no cure for a virus. If you get Herpes or HIV, it's for life. Some people manage to fight off HPV, which is caused by a "wart virus", but others don't. HPV is known to be cause of almost all cases of cervical cancer in the United States."

---

70   Koutsky, 1997.
71   http://www.cdc.gov/std/Herpes/STDFact-Herpes.htm
72   http://www.cdc.gov/std/default.htm
73   Weller, 1993.
74   http://www3.niaid.nih.gov/about/organization/dmid/PDF/condomReport.pdf

The student groaned, "What a bummer!" This brought outright laughter from the rest of the students, but I suspect summed up what most of them were feeling.

After class, a rather diffident, slender and delicate girl, Chuntao, approached me. Up until today she'd never spoken to me, but sat curled up in her seat, her arms wrapped around her knees. I did wonder, at times, how she could balance on the lab stool in that position without falling off.

"Dr. Crocker, could I talk to you in private?"

"Of course, let's go to the adjunct office and see if anyone is there."

I was glad to see the room was empty and we went in.

"Um, could you close the door?" Chuntao asked, blushing.

Since the office was lined with windows I figured this would be okay, so did as she asked, sat down and waited.

For a while she just sat in front of me, fiddling with her bag, never meeting my eyes. Finally, she spoke. "I haven't told anyone, but I can't take it any longer. I'm so scared. And now…well now I guess I probably have a disease."

From previous conversations, I knew that Chuntao's religion strongly prohibits pre-marital sex, so I probed gently, "Why, do you have a symptom?"

"No, no, I don't think so. But…well, last month I was on my way home from work…I work as a teller at Safeway…and someone jumped out of the bushes…"

Here she covered her face and began to sob. I passed her a Kleenex and waited for her to continue.

"I did fight, but he was too strong…the bruises are gone now…but I did fight," she trailed off.

I figured I probably knew the answer to my question, but asked anyway, for the sake of clarity, "Did he rape you?"

Chuntao nodded miserably, and moved to sit in her usual position with her knees under her chin.

"Did you report it?"

"No, then my family would find out and my dad would be dishonored. I don't know what they would do to me."

"Okay, but you do need to see a doctor," I persisted.

Chuntao looked worried, "But, what if the doctor tells my parents?"

Here I could provide reassurance, "That would be illegal. Since you're an adult, all of your medical information is private to you. But, you do need to go…to set your mind at rest about diseases and also because you might possibly be pregnant."

Her shoulders slumped, "My period is late and I did wonder…"

Although teacher – student contact is forbidden, I did at this point take her hand, "Chuntao, go to a doctor. If you're scared, I'll come with you."

She did not pull away, but held on tightly, "Okay, I…I think I'll be alright on my own, but can I come and tell you what happens?"

My heart went out to her, "Of course, call me any time. This is my home number; don't be shy about using it."

Chuntao did come see me the next week with the news that she had not contracted an STD, but she was pregnant. Inevitably, she had to tell her parents, who forced her to have an abortion, which she told me felt like more of a violation than the rape. I was extremely grateful that her parents, whose religion specified that she should be severely punished for pre-marital sex even if it was not her fault, did not kick her out of the home. Chuntao called me regularly for the next few years when she needed advice, reassurance, or just a listening ear. Even though she ended up dropping the course, she regularly gave me updates on how and what she was doing. Eventually, Chuntao did recover, got married, and even had a baby boy, but her parents never knew the role her professor had played. It was a privilege to be trusted like this, but it made me more aware than ever about the responsibility to be as honest and accurate as possible in what I taught.

Of course, because the Bio 102 course was meant to cover the structure and function of animal and plants, the book also spent quite a lot of time on evolution, giving this as the explanation for the increasing complexity of organ-systems in the higher animals. I had covered evolution the previous semester, when some of the students had me as their teacher. Therefore, in a part of one lecture, I decided just to cover the part of the evidence for evolution most relevant to this course: the fossil record. I started with a question.

"Today we are going to talk about the fossil record and evolution. Has anyone read the chapter?"

A few hands were raised.

"How does the fossil record support the theory of evolution?"

Immediately, many students raised their hands. "The lowest layers of the earth have the simplest organisms, like bacteria, and the more complex organisms, like us, are closer to the surface," answered Andrew.

"Right, and that does seem to suggest evolution from a common ancestor. Fossils of the unicellular organisms have been dated to about 3.5 billion years ago. After that, fossils of algae were found that are dated at about 1.2 billion years ago. Then, fossils of most of the different types of animals from the Cambrian era begin showing up at about half a billion years ago. People only appeared about 200,000 years ago. But, the fossil record does pose a significant problem for evolutionary theory. Does anyone know what that is?"

Luis said, "The Natural History Museum in Washington, D.C. says that the fossil record shows layers with the sudden appearance of highly varied and complex forms of life. I guess that means there were no intermediate forms between the layers, but surely evolutionary theory requires that there are loads of intermediates before we get to where we are. Still, the Natural History museum does say that life evolved." Here was a student who really paid attention during his extra credit visit to the museum.

"Okay, now, let's think about this." I put the postulated evolutionary tree of life up on the screen. "This is how modern evolutionary theory says the variety in life occurred. An organism experienced a change in its genome because of a mutation. This made it better able to survive and thus, more fit. It made more offspring and out-competed others or filled a different niche. Then there was another mutation and on and on. One would then expect there to be a fossil record of all these transitions. But, Darwin said that the fossil record did not show this,[75] as indeed it still doesn't."

Andrew responded immediately, "But he lived over a hundred years ago."

"That's right, and you would think that we would have found those transitional forms by now, especially considering how hard we are looking. But, there are so few transitional forms that every time a 'presumed' intermediate is found it is trumpeted in the press. It should be the norm, not the exception. Instead, as said by evolutionist Niles Eldredge, 'Most families, orders, classes, and phyla appear rather suddenly in the fossil record, often without anatomically intermediate forms smoothly interlinking evolutionarily derived descendant taxa with their presumed ancestors.'[76] This is very similar to the claim put forward by evolutionist E.C. Olson about bats, '…there is absolutely no sign of intermediate stages…the first evidence of flight in mammals is in the fully-developed bats of the Eocene epoch.'"[77]

Senichi leaned forward, "I have never heard this before."

"Yes, in fact, a map of the fossil record looks more like a meadow than a tree, with many organisms suddenly appearing at the same time and then some of them becoming extinct. This suggests that there may be problems with the theory of evolution as it now stands. A proposal called Punctuated Equilibrium has been put forward, which suggests animals evolved quickly, leaving hardly

75   Darwin reprint, 1979. p. 292.
76   Eldredge, 1989, p. 22.
77   Olson, 1966, p. 180.

any fossils.[78] Not all scientists accept this idea, but it is growing in popularity, possibly because it attempts to explain why so few intermediate fossils are being found."

I was pleased to see that Andrew was thinking hard about this. It was my aim to encourage students to be intellectually honest and critically consider the facts. He then asked, "Okay, but what about all the evidence that man came from apes or that horses evolved?" Now, I knew that this was not an accurate description of evolutionary claims, but did not feel that a public correction would be the best way to encourage this student to continue in the thinking process.

"Good, I'm glad you asked that. It shows you don't just believe everything I say. To answer your question, evidence from geologic events can be very confusing and there is a lot of disagreement about how to interpret what has been discovered. Many scientists believe that the order, age, and similarities between some fossils points to common ancestry. However, from what I understand, those who are questioning evolution from the viewpoint of paleontology would say that finding one fossil under another does not mean that one was the ancestor of the other. Kind of like finding two skeletons in a graveyard does not prove they were related. In fact, Henry Gee, a senior editor of *Nature* magazine, published a statement that said, 'To take a line of fossils and claim they represent a lineage is not a scientific hypothesis that can be tested, but an assertion that carries the same validity as a bedtime story— amusing, perhaps even instructive, but not scientific.'[79] On the other hand, some of the genetic evidence does suggest common descent, even though it appears that random mutation could not have been the mechanism.[80] There is obviously still a lot of work that needs to be done."

It was time for class to be dismissed, although I could see several students did not want to leave. Surely, that was a good sign. They would be discussing this topic on their own, at home, and maybe even doing independent research. This was my goal since the purpose of education is to enable and encourage students to become informed and independent thinkers.

* * * *

We were nearly at the end of another semester. The familiar panic of students who were hoping to make last minute restitution for failed efforts ensued. Others began to challenge grades earned early in the semester in hope of extracting another point. All the chaos made me begin longing for a quiet summer. I had enjoyed my year of part time teaching and felt that I'd learned a lot. During

---

78 Eldridge and Gould, 1972.
79 Gee, 1999, p. 116-117.
80 Behe, 2007.

moments of quiet reflection, I realized that I would like to make a career of teaching, so I turned in applications for fulltime positions to both NVCC and the local four-year university, George Mason University (GMU).

I soon heard from GMU. It seemed they needed help with teaching microbiology labs, but there would not be an opening for full time work until the following January. NVCC responded after a couple of months with a rejection of my application. Rumor had it that applications from those with teaching experience or a Ph.D. were discarded immediately because the funding to pay them was not available. So, I agreed to teach part time at both places, as well as teaching Bio 101 at the local military base. I would be busier than a full time teacher, but would be paid far less. Such is the life of an adjunct professor.

On the first day of the fall cell biology class at NVCC, my attention was drawn to a bright-eyed attractive Persian girl, Neshat. Seated in the front of the class, she nodded comprehension when a concept registered, smiled at my jokes, and was always the first to raise her hand to answer a question. Next to her was a plump, older, serious-looking lady, Maureen. Maureen also paid rapt attention, writing everything down furiously. Just behind them was a bespectacled young man, Adam, who appeared to have come straight from work, wearing a shirt and tie. When class started, he pulled out his laptop and proceeded to take notes by typing. A highly organized single mother of three, Shanice, who had a dream of becoming a doctor, rivaled him. She always came with a wheeled suitcase containing her books, folder, and of course a laptop. At the back of the class, pacing up and down to stay awake, was the night watchman, Mwenye. These students were to become the hard-working core of a very successful class.

Immediately after the introductory lecture, Neshat came forward and stood by my desk diffidently, waiting until I had finished putting away my things, "Dr. Crocker, I just wanted to tell you thank you for teaching us. I'm looking forward to learning all about biology from you. Please, could you tell me how I can do well in your class?" She flashed me a shy smile.

"Just do the work suggested in the syllabus. Be sure you're prepared for the vocabulary quizzes, read the chapters, study for the tests, and come to the study groups."

Neshat looked apprehensive, "But will that be enough? I really want to go to medical school and I need good grades."

"Don't worry. I've had very few students who work hard and don't do well. It's those who come late, sleep during class, and rarely study who fail." I tried to reassure her.

"Oh, I will work hard. I like biology…it is so interesting."

Next in line was Mwenye. In heavily accented English, he said, "Dr. Crocker, I work nights and go to school in day. It is hard to wake. But, I want better job one day."

Because I saw where he was going, I interrupted, "It's quite alright with me if you need to walk around at the back of class to stay awake. But, I have to tell you that you can't hope to do your best work if you're so tired. Is it possible to cut down on your hours?"

He shook his head, "I have wife and two children to support. But, I want do more than a security job. It is difficult…"

"I admire you for trying. Do what you have to; I'll not object."

As I predicted, that semester Mwenye's performance in the course was not consistent with the level of ability that he displayed in his interactions with his classmates and me. However, he did pass and eventually got a degree.

I didn't have a chance to speak with Shanice until I saw her in the hallway before the first lab, "I love that book bag on wheels. It's such a good idea. I think I'll get one."

Shanice smiled wearily, "I use all my energy just to manage school, work and three little ones. This may be unfashionable, but it helps, and that's all I care about."

How easy I had it going to university while being supported by my parents! We entered the lab. "What do you do with your kids while you're at school?"

"Oh, my mom helps. I couldn't do it without her. She believes in me and thinks I can make it to medical school. I sure am going to try not to disappoint her."

I stopped to take in Shanice's air of quiet determination and the intelligence that was evident in her face. "You know, from what I see so far, I don't think you will." Shanice did not disappoint anyone. She was so determined that she even brought her children to class when she couldn't get a babysitter. Shanice achieved the highest grade in the class and I had the privilege of writing a recommendation for her admittance into medical school.

Maureen was the student who showed me the power of grueling determination and extreme effort. Older than the average student, she was returning to school after raising her family. As such, she found the course extraordinarily difficult. Her last science course had been over 20 years ago. At first, I was rather disconcerted to see tears running down her face as I explained a complex concept to the class, but I was to become accustomed to it. She told me that it seemed as if she had no sooner learned one subject than I introduced another. But, Maureen did not give up. Her dream was to be a nurse and sheer hard work got her there.

In fact, this class inspired me so much that I began implementing other measures to assist students in completing their schooling as successfully and inexpensively as possible. I frequently helped international students in editing their English papers, gave advice on which courses were necessary and which were not, and even helped them in their dealings with governmental red tape. I also collected textbooks for the use of students who could not afford bookstore prices. Although I continued this uncontrolled loaning of textbooks for the entire time I taught, I never had a problem with them not being returned. I even took the step of inviting entire classes to my home for Thanksgiving and Christmas. Fortunately, only those who were genuinely alone responded to this offer and I never had to feed more than 20 people at a time.

"Class, give me your attention. For this part of the lab, you will be studying osmosis by observing water uptake by raisins. First weigh a raisin while dry, then allow it to soak in distilled water for two hours. Weigh it again and write down how much weight was gained. At the end of the period, turn in your calculation of how many molecules of water were absorbed per gram of raisin per minute."

Hearing this as I walked by a class being taught by Dr. Walsh, the teacher who scared his students, I couldn't believe my ears. He expected freshman to be able to do this? Unable to resist the temptation to tease him, I stepped into the classroom, "Dr. Walsh, what kind of an assignment is that? You're a sadist."

The students laughed, but I could detect that they were a little anxious about his reaction. Would he hit me or just shout?

However, they need not have worried. With a glint in his eye he told me, "Maybe your students can't do this, but mine can. Just shows who's the better teacher."

Walking away chuckling under my breath, I began to think, "Maybe my students would be able to do it. Certainly the more able ones might enjoy the challenge." I resolved to present this as an extra credit assignment. After all, one important goal of teaching is to help the students become independent learners. All the information needed for the calculation was in their books, but I had not gone through it.

The very next day, I wrote this assignment on the board and waited for the class to arrive. Reactions were predictable. Shanice and Neshat, who sat together, immediately got out their books and began to discuss how the problem could be solved. Maureen turned red and tears began to flow. Many of the students pronounced me unfair, despite the fact that it was extra credit, and didn't even bother to try. Adam surprised me by losing his official look and becoming positively enthusiastic. Was it possible that what I'd interpreted as self-importance was actually boredom? After working furiously for a time he came forward to my desk.

"Dr. Crocker, I think I have it. Look!"

Here he proceeded to lead me through his thinking and calculations.

"Well, you're very nearly right. But you forgot an important step. Think about it some more."

Frowning with perplexity, Adam returned to his bench. When his lab partners attempted to speak to him, he moved to another table. He was determined to beat this.

"OOHH!" he suddenly exclaimed, making everyone jump, "I got it! I know I'm right this time!" He came forward to show me his answer (Figure 8).

$$\frac{\text{Grams of H}_2\text{O absorbed}}{2 \text{ Hours}} \times \frac{2 \text{ Hours}}{120 \text{ Minutes}} \times \frac{1 \text{ Mole H}_2\text{O}}{18\text{g H}_2\text{O}} \times \frac{6 \times 10^{23} \text{ Molecules}}{1 \text{ Mole}} = \frac{\text{Molecules}}{\text{Minute}}$$

Figure 8 *This equation shows how Adam solved the extra credit problem. He weighed the raisin before and after two hours of soaking it in water. The difference between these two weights would be due to water absorbed. After performing the above calculation, Adam could tell me how many molecules of water the raisin absorbed in a minute.*

"You got it," I congratulated him.

Just then Dr. Walsh walked by my class and saw the assignment on the board. Walking in, he pointed to it, "What's that I see? After giving me a hard time."

I laughed, "Really, I thought it was a good idea…and Adam here did it! How many of your students got it?"

"Four," he answered glumly.

I turned to the class, "Okay guys. We need to beat Dr. Walsh's record and prove who has the better class. I'm counting on you."

In the end, half of my class did it, but it wasn't really a fair test. Adam was far too excited about his answer to keep it to himself. But, Dr. Walsh didn't need to know that!

REFERENCES

Anonymous. "Genital Herpes CDC fact sheet. *Department of Health and Human Services Centers for Disease Control and Prevention.* http://www.cdc.gov/std/Herpes/STDFact-Herpes.htm (as of 4/1/09).

Anonymous. "Sexually transmitted diseases." *Department of Health and Human Services Centers for Disease Control and Prevention.* http://www.cdc.gov/std/default.htm (as of 4/1/09).

Behe, Michael J. 2007. *The Edge of Evolution: The Search for the Limits of Darwinism.* New York, NY: The Free Press.

Darwin, Charles. 1979. *The Origin of Species.* Crown, New York, NY, Reprint, p. 292.

Eldredge, Niles and Stephen J. Gould. 1972. "Punctuated Equilibria: An Alternative to Phyletic Gradualism." In *Models in Paleobiology*, edited by T.J.M. Schopf, pp. 82-115. San Francisco, CA: Freeman, Cooper & Co.

Eldredge, Niles. 1989. *Macroevolutionary Dynamics: Species, Niches, and Adaptive Peaks.* New York, NY: McGraw Hill, p. 22.

Gee, Henry. 1999. *In Search of Deep Time: Beyond the Fossil Record to a New History of Life.* New York, NY: Free Press, pp. 116-117.

Koutsky L. "Epidemiology of Genital Human Papillomavirus Infection." *American Journal of Medicine*, 1997, 102(5A), pp. 3-8.

National Institute of Allergy and Infectious Disease (NIAID), National Institutes of Health (NIH). 2000. "Scientific Evidence on Condom Effectiveness for Sexually Transmitted Disease (STD) Prevention," http://www3.niaid.nih.gov/about/organization/dmid/PDF/condomReport.pdf (as of 4/1/09).

Olson, E.C. 1965. *The Evolution of Life.* New York, NY: The New American Library, p. 180.

Weller, S.C. 1993. "A Meta-analysis of Condom Effectiveness in Reducing Sexually Transmitted HIV." *Social Science and Medicine* 36(12):1635-44.

Woodruff, David S. 1980. "Evolution: The Paleobiological View," *Science* 208:716.

Chapter 4: Teaching Excellence

"Dr. Crocker, I just don't get it. Why'd you take a point off for my answer? I'm sure that all my calculations are right." Samantha, a nursing student, was red-faced with frustration. She was certain I was wrong this time.

"Well, let's forget the calculations for a minute and just think about your answer logically. You say there were 10^{-5} bacteria present on the Petri dish. Does that make sense?"

"Yes, we did the dilutions right and everything and those are the results we got."

"Tell me, what does 10^{-5} mean?"

"Ummm....oh, I remember! You said that you put a "1." and move the decimal point back five times."

Smiling encouragement, I replied, "Okay, but what does that *mean?*"

Looking even more confused, Samantha muttered, "I don't know what you're asking."

"Well, how does 10^{-5} translate into a fraction?"

Here Samantha's lab partner joined in, "I know! It's 1/100,000."

"That's right. Now, is it possible to have 1/100,000 bacteria on a plate?"

"I think so." pondered Samantha, "They're very small."

Now, I had to think. How could I help these students to visualize what numbers mean in reality? "Let's go over to the blackboard." I drew a circle on the board. "Okay, show me the circle cut in half (1/2)."

Samantha drew a line down the center of the circle.

"Good. Now make it in quarters (1/4)."

Samantha did this, as well.

"Now make it in 100,000 pieces (1/100,000)."

Samantha laughed. "I can't. They would be too small and it would take too long."

"So, how about if we were to cut a person into 100,000 pieces. Would that be possible? They're bigger than the circle."

Samantha's partner chimed in, "No, it would kill them."

Suddenly understanding dawned on their faces. "Ooohhh, so that's why you can't have 10^{-5} bacteria on a plate."

"Yes, if you were to do that, you would have way less than one. The only way to do it would be to explode a bacterium and then it would no longer be a bacterium."

The girls nodded their understanding, so I decided to go a step further. "So, would it be possible to have 10^{-5} bacteria/ml?"

Samantha's brow furrowed in thought and she scribbled numbers on a piece of paper. Then she smiled, "Yes, but unless you had more than 100 liters of media, the bacterium would be very lonely."

Working at George Mason University (GMU), even as an adjunct microbiology lab teacher, was to prove very different from NVCC. The course content was strictly regulated, there were weekly prep sessions, the methods of evaluation were standardized, and oddly enough the vast majority of the students were female. I found myself giving lab quizzes for the first time. These were a real eye-opener when I saw how little of the lab students really understood.

I'd found that it was best to keep on the move during lab so I would be accessible to my students and the students would be able to ask me any questions as they came up. My eye was caught by a young lady, Deepti, who was doing almost everything possible wrong. In attempting to transfer a colony of bacteria from one plate to another, she heated the wire loop used for picking up bacteria to red hot and put the loop onto the colony. She hadn't waited for it to cool, so there was a sizzling sound and the agar[81] growth medium spattered. Deepti blushed as she noticed me watching. She then reheated the loop, but remembering that it should be allowed to cool, she blew on it before applying it to the new agar, closing the plate and placing it in the incubator.

"Deepti, do you think anything will grow on that plate?"

She looked offended, "Of course, but it'll take 48 hours."

"Okay, lead me through what you did just now."

"Well, I heated up the loop so it would be sterile."

"Good," I encouraged her, "and then what?"

"I picked up a colony from the plate."

"Did you make a mistake?"

She hesitated, but remembered that I'd been watching. "Well, yes, I forgot to let the loop cool, so the agar spattered."

"Right, and what do you think that might have done to your bacteria?"

Deepti thought for a while, "I guess it might have killed them."

I smiled, "I think you're right. Now, what did you do next?"

"I heated up the loop in case it had become contaminated."

"Yes, and if there were any live bacteria on it, what happened to them?"

"They died?" she said, looking a bit worried now.

"Yes, so now you have a sterile loop. Then what did you do?"

"Well, I learned from my mistake and blew on the loop to cool it before putting it onto the new plate."

---

81 Definitions can be found in Appendix I.

"So, do you think it was still sterile after you blew on it?"

Color slowly seeped up Deepti's face, "No, I hadn't thought of that."

"Okay, so if you get growth on that plate, will it be what you wanted?"

Ruefully, Deepti shook her head, "No, I killed the bacteria I want and inoculated the plate with contaminants from my breath. It's good you noticed." Deepti did the procedure again, this time without mistakes.

I learned to watch carefully as the students worked in the microbiology lab. I also learned to ask them questions as I did, in order to make sure they understood what they were doing. I wanted them to not just understand, but also be able to assess and apply what they were learning.

Just before Christmas I was approached by Dr. Sullivan, the interim head of my department. "We're looking for a full time teacher in the new year. This person will primarily be responsible for teaching the Cell Biology course and I wondered if you'd like to apply."

"I sure would. I'll have my application in to you by the end of the week."

"Great," she smiled, "I'll look forward to getting it."

I sent in my application and heard from Dr. Sullivan almost immediately. After an interview where I gave a demonstration lecture and was quizzed by several members of the faculty, Dr. Sullivan told me that term positions were usually for one year in the first instance. Then, depending on the departmental need and the faculty member's performance, the contract would be extended by one, three or five years. However, since I was beginning in January, Dr. Sullivan told me that she would advocate for me to start with a longer contract. Normal practice, then, would be for the renewal to be for three or five years. Therefore, I was pleased to begin my full time teaching faculty position with an 18-month contract. I would be teaching one cell biology lecture (150 students) and four labs per week.

Just before the beginning of semester I received an e-mail from the Information Technology department offering a class on the use of the audiovisual equipment in the lecture hall. "What's this?" I thought, "Will there be more than just a computer and projector?" I registered for the class and attended.

I hadn't seen a lecture hall at GMU up until then and was amazed. The only similarity to NVCC was the tiered seating. In marked contrast to my previous experience, the room was well ventilated and comfortable. It was also three times as big. At the front there was a stage with a huge podium covered by a myriad of buttons and controls. A screen with the ability to show two separate displays covered the entire front of the classroom. The lecturer could project PowerPoint slides on one half and anything he or she wrote while at the podium on the other. Help from the IT staff was instantly available any time. No more struggling with stolen mouse balls, recalcitrant computers, missing parts, and projectors that would not work because of the heat in the room. Paper, markers, and supplies were also at hand. It made me feel quite important.

Moving into my office was just as exciting. Instead of sharing a desk, a computer that usually did not work and space with numerous other adjunct faculty, I had a room with a desk and my own computer. I was to share with another teacher, Dr. Faulkner, but he also had his own desk and computer. When I arrived, the secretary handed me all kinds of treasures, including a stapler, notepads, pens and pencils, paperclips, and even my own hole punch. In the office itself, I had a bookcase *and* a filing cabinet to myself. When Dr. Faulkner told me that it would be okay to move the furniture around and decorate as I liked, I thought I was in heaven. That semester and in the following ones I had students illustrate and summarize chapters on posters to earn extra credit and help them learn the material. The winner for the class would get a prize and those posters became the wallpaper for the office. When I finally cleared out my office at the end of my time at GMU, it was extremely distressing to find these posters torn down and crumpled in a corner.

Of course, now I had to settle down to prepare yet another set of lectures and PowerPoints, because the text used by GMU for cell biology was different from that used by NVCC. Again I was unsure of what to include and how hard it should be. Dr. Alekseev, a colleague who had been teaching the course for years, kindly allowed me to have a copy of his lecture notes. So, armed with textbook, notes and a computer, I began. The course was called "Structure and Function of Cells," but the description in the course catalog said it would cover the chemistry, metabolism, genetics and *evolution* of cells.[82] I noticed that the notes I had been loaned by Dr. Alekseev included referrals to evolution in almost every lecture. As I had done before, I decided to teach most of the course as scientific facts only (there were plenty of those) and leave the theory of evolution to just one out of the approximately 25 lectures to be given. Otherwise, I prepared the lectures with his notes on one side, the book on the other and my computer in the middle. I also prepared the new course web pages for GMU, making sure to take into account the huge class size which necessitated just having ten vocabulary quizzes per semester, offering four study group sessions per week, and not giving out my home phone number.

I then spent some time chatting with the other teachers in the biology department to learn about the rules and regulations in force at the four-year college. The first rather surprising one was that professors were neither allowed to take at-

---

82   http://www.gmu.edu/catalog/0405/courses/biol.html Course description can be found in Appendix VI.

tendance nor allow any part of the student grade be based on attendance. In other words, it was up to the individual student to decide if they felt like going to class.

I was shocked, "Surely that sets the students up for failure, doesn't it?" I was well aware that for many of the young people this opportunity to skip class without apparent penalty would be a huge temptation. However, my experience at NVCC had shown me that virtually all students who missed more than four lectures also failed the course.

Dr. Abramson sympathized with my view, "I'm afraid so, but those are the rules."

"Well, can we do things to encourage them to come, like give pop quizzes that can't be made up?" I wanted to make sure my students would have every chance to do well in the course and form good study habits for the future.

"Oh yes, but you need to be prepared to grade all of them."

"I don't see that I have much choice if I want the students to succeed. I'm going to try it. It might also encourage them to come on time."

Dr. Abramson smiled, "I just lock the door when class starts. Those who are late can't come in."

I guess everyone finds their own ways of dealing with students.

The first day of class arrived and I walked into the lecture theater early to be sure that I would be able to set up with the rather complex equipment. I slipped the CD containing the PowerPoint lectures into the computer and watched as the first slide appeared on the huge screen. I then turned on the paper projector to see the syllabus appear on the other half of the screen. I couldn't repress a grin. This was going to be great.

The students began arriving. Looking at them as they filed in, some nervous, others happily chatting with friends, and still others bored already, I again noticed the huge mix of nationalities. I was glad that I didn't have to take roll because pronouncing names correctly might be a challenge. Soon a line of students began to form, waiting to speak to me.

"Dr. Crocker, I tried to sign up for this class online, but it was full. Can you force add me? I really need this to graduate."

"Teacher, I missed my lab class and now I've been dropped from the course. What do I do?"

"Miss, is this the right book?"

"Hey Doc, can I record the lectures? My other teachers let me."

Clearly, I could not answer all the questions on an individual basis. The class was just too large and it was time to start, "Please take your seats. I'll answer most of your questions during the lecture time and, if I don't, you can see me afterwards."

The university policy stipulating that students who do not attend the first lab be immediately dropped from the course would prove to be a big problem every semester. Since this course was mandatory for all biology majors, it was always over-subscribed and every seat in it was treated like gold. Therefore, for a student to find they'd been dropped was upsetting, to say the least. In order to get back into the course, the student would have to find a lab teacher willing to add them to a lab. By the beginning of semester these were the teachers who had been assigned the 7 am or 7 pm labs, not always a popular choice among students. Only after the lab was assigned, could the student apply to the lecture teacher and be added to the lecture. Unfortunately, it was not always possible to explain this to a nervous student who was convinced that I was just being mean.

After class I was again deluged with students, many of whom had not been listening during the lecture and needed to have policies explained on an individual basis. It was not really worth getting frustrated, so I just patiently repeated myself again and again. Looking up, I caught the eye of an intelligent-looking young man, Don Willcox, who seemed to have the ability to see past my face into my mind. He was obviously amused at how I had to keep saying the same thing time after time. I quickly looked away before he could make me laugh. Don was to be one of my best students, so much so that if he got something wrong on an exam, I would assume I had made a mistake on the answer key.

"Dr. Crocker, I want to introduce you to my friend, Melinda," said a middle-aged lady, "She is deaf and I'm her helper."

Melinda was an attractive brunette who was busily signing as her helper spoke to me. Rochelle signed back and then turned to me again.

Rochelle went on, "The way it works is that Melinda signs to me and I tell you what she's saying. While I speak, you must look at her and, when you answer, speak to her. Pretend that I'm only her voice."

I found this much easier said than done, but made a valiant effort, "Okay, what can I do for you?"

Rochelle translated, "I need you to sign this disability form, saying that you'll make reasonable compensations for my disability."

"What are those?"

"I need a note-taker, I need extra time on exams, and Rochelle needs to sit on the stage next to you while you lecture, so I can see what you are saying."

"Well, the PowerPoints are on line, so I'm not sure you need a note-taker, but I don't mind if you have one. I also don't care if Rochelle is next to me, but she can't be there during quizzes or tests. But, why would you need extra time on exams? They are written."

"Because this is a hard course and English isn't my first language."

I shook my head, "The course is hard for everyone and most of the students are not American. I'm afraid that being unable to hear does not give you the right to have more time on exams."

I crossed out that compensation on the form, signed the paper and they left, busily discussing with their hands.

I made my way to the lab. As I approached, I noticed that the halls were lined with students, many sitting on the floor, obviously waiting for me. "Of course," I thought, "The lab is locked when no one is there." I quickly checked for the password and opened the door. The first lab was always short, involving going through the lab syllabus and the safety rules. Then, after taking role, the students were dismissed. To my surprise, given the difficulty of getting into the class, three of the students did not attend. According to the rules, I had no choice but drop them immediately. Still, it was difficult because one of the absentee students was Melinda. I knew she wanted to take the course, but she had not come to lab, even though the rules had been explained during the lecture. As I left lab, I spotted her in the hallway, but without her helper.

"Melinda, why didn't you come to lab?"

She indicated that she did not understand and offered me a piece of paper and a pen. I wrote my question down.

She answered on the paper, "Nothing happens in the first lab."

I then wrote, "You *have* to come so you aren't dropped from the class."

"PLEASE don't do that."

"I have to keep the rules, but if you attend another lab session and get that teacher's signature, I won't drop you."

"Okay, thanks," she wrote and went on her way.

I made my way back to my office and sat down to plan the study groups that would be necessary for every student to be able to have access to help. Because past experience had shown me that participation in this kind of an opportunity is only about 20%, I decided to offer four groups per week, on different days and at different times, so that most students would have one time when they could attend. The first group was to be the very next week. I announced the groups in class, explained how they help with understanding of the material, reserved the room, and bought snacks (always important for students). Three people came: Don and two shy girls, Hamideh and Termeh. I decided to proceed as if the room had been full.

"Welcome, I'm so glad you came. Help yourselves to something to eat," I waited for them to sit down and get out their books. "Do you have any questions about the first chapter's material?"

"Can you give us the answers to the vocabulary words?" asked Hamideh.

I thought for a while and then answered, "I think you'll learn them better if you review your lecture notes looking for the words. Remember that the definitions are on the website; they're just in a different order from the words, so you can match them yourself. This will encourage you to read ahead."

Termeh joined in, "Can you check if I got them right?"

"Of course," I answered her and reviewed them for her. Naturally, as soon as I was done, Termeh showed the answers to Hamideh and she copied them all.

Next Don had a question, "What's going to happen during these groups? What's the point?"

"Well, the purpose is to let you have a chance to ask questions in a small group setting and get individual help on difficult concepts. Also, if you don't ask questions, I will. That'll help you know how well you understand the material. Finally, in some cases, the material is better understood through hands-on activities. In that case, those will be done here."

"I have another question," Don grinned, "Where's everyone else?"

"I don't know…maybe they'll come nearer to the exam or maybe they just didn't remember the group. I'll advertise again."

Termeh volunteered, "I passed some people in the hall talking about the group. They said it was at the wrong time for them."

"Okay, I'll ask the class what time is best and we'll do them at the most popular times."

During the next class I talked about the groups and had the students sign up for their favorite time. I then made sure that either my teacher's aide or I would be available during those times. However, much to our disappointment, even when I came in on weekends, few if any students showed up. I usually only filled the room during the week before exams.

But then, I never knew what to expect because students are amazingly unpredictable. Just how much so I learned in one lab session that I'll always remember. During this lab the students were instructed to extract DNA from an onion and detect it using a reagent made with a strong acid. Since lab coats were not mandatory, I spent quite some time at the beginning of lab explaining the procedure and especially the safety precautions to be taken when using strong acids.

"Turn around and look at the back of the lab," I instructed, "See the hood on your right? That's where you'll find the acid. Be sure you pipette it in the hood. Bring the container for the acid to the hood; do not fill the pipette and then carry it, dripping, around the lab." I began to demonstrate to be sure they got the point.

Just then, I was distracted by a young man in the front row who stood up and removed his shirt, shaking it furiously as he stood there bare-chested.

"Marcus, what are you doing?" I asked, losing my train of thought. The students stared as they realized what I was talking about.

"Uh, well, I was sitting on the grass before class and I think a bug got in my shirt." he answered, appearing not to be embarrassed in the least.

The class giggled.

I took a breath, "Okay, well, did you get it out?"

"Yeah, I don't see it."

"Then please put your shirt on again," I began to laugh, "I must admit. I've had students do all kinds of things in class, but none has ever done that. I don't actually remember where I was in the lecture."

A student in the back helpfully shouted out, "You were telling us how to use acid."

"Thanks," I answered and continued my explanation of safety procedures.

When I was done, the students began to chop and grind onions, hoping to produce DNA. The lab smelled like a kitchen. I made sure everyone knew what they were doing and sat down to grade the quizzes they had just completed when I was interrupted by a chubby young man by the name of Nick.

"Dr. Crocker, my stomach itches," he complained.

I looked up to find the offending party in my immediate line of sight. "Nick, there's a hole in your shirt."

"Is there? I don't think it was there this morning." He looked down with a frown.

I noticed a sour smell and a wisp of smoke coming from the edge of the hole. "You got acid on your shirt. Take it off and rinse your stomach with lots of water." I looked up at the class and caught Marcus' eye. "Marcus, go with Nick to the men's room and make sure he gets himself clean."

Marcus' lab partner became interested, "Can I go too? I'm wearing an extra shirt that Nick can use."

The young men exited the room and I called the class to attention, warning them again of the hazards of working with acids.

After class Marcus approached me with a worried look. I thought he was probably going to apologize for stripping off during class. Instead he shared a problem.

"Dr. Crocker, I'm most likely not going to be in class for the next couple of weeks."

I frowned, "Why not? You're a good student and that will for sure mess up your grades."

He hung his head, "I won't have a choice. You see, I was driving a bit too fast and got a reckless driving ticket." Here Marcus hesitated, "Actually, I was going a lot too fast and it wasn't the first time. I'm probably going to jail."

"Marcus, that's terrible! How fast were you going?"

"They clocked me at 126."

"Are you going to do it again?"

Here his eyes flew up to meet mine, "Oh no, no way! My family is shattered. They have to drive me everywhere because my license was suspended and now I'm going to jail. I learned my lesson."

I thought for a minute, "When's the court date? Would it help if I came and told the judge that missing two weeks would mess up your grades and maybe even prevent you from getting into medical school?"

"It's Monday at 9 am. Would you do that?"

"Sure, I'm free then. Ask your lawyer if it would help. If it might, I'll be there."

The next day Marcus e-mailed to tell me that it would help. I went, and it did. Marcus did have to do jail time, but because of my intervention he was allowed to serve six weekends, instead of two solid weeks, meaning his schooling was not affected. He assured me that he would never speed again.

The lecture I gave on evolution at GMU was much the same as the one I had been delivering at NVCC, but was shaped to be more intellectually challenging and relevant to cell biology. It was also shortened to take up only one lecture period, instead of two, as it had in Bio 101 at NVCC. I started with a definition of evolution and natural selection, as described by the textbook. Since many students were now becoming aware of the media attention to the tension between Darwinists and Darwin-doubters, I drew their attention to the fact that, in marked contrast to the textbook's claims,[83] it was obviously not true that all scientists agree about neo-Darwinian evolution. Even evolutionists argue among themselves.[84] To show this, seven of the ten quotes used in the lecture were taken from evolutionists and only one from an intelligent design proponent. The other two were from non-scientists. I then attempted to give them the scientific facts related to this controversy, leaving out the contributions of philosophical differences as much as possible. We briefly went through the problems with the fossil record and other evidences listed in their book, but then went on to more cell-based science.

---

83 Campbell and Reece, 2002.
84 For example, there are advocates of gradualism versus people who support punctuated equilibrium, those who believe in common descent and those who believe life started in multiple places, and more.

First, I pointed out that, in most disciplines, the existence of code is accepted as a sign of the action of an intelligent being. After all, we never claim that hieroglyphics just happened over time[85] and in the movie, *Close Encounters of the Third Kind*, the repetitive tune was assumed to be communication by aliens, not just radio static. I decided to give a close-to-home example.

"So, say you go into the living room and find the Scrabble pieces on the floor. What could've happened?"

"Probably my brother dropped the game box and was too lazy to clean it up," answered Alison, a young lady who looked disgusted at the idea.

"Okay, but what if the letters said, 'My sister is a jerk.'?"

She involuntarily made a fist. "He'd be dead meat!"

The class laughed.

"Okay, but would you believe him if he said it happened by accident?"

"No way, I'm not stupid."

"I'm sure you're not," I said soothingly. "But, let's think about why you would assume your brother did it."

Alison knew the answer, "Because I know whether something is an accident or deliberate."

I persisted, "But, how?"

The class was silent.

"We all almost instinctively figure out whether the events we see around us are caused by natural laws, accidents, or intelligent intervention. In fact, forensic science, the Search for Extraterrestrial Intelligence (SETI), and archeology are all based on the idea that it is possible to discern whether an event or phenomenon is an accident, the result of a natural law, or the deliberate act of an intelligent being. ID is simply applying those rules to other types of scientific evidence."

Because the students had by then been exposed to DNA and molecular biology, we went on to discuss the specified complexity of the DNA code. In fact, this is an example of what has been called "designoid" by evolutionists.[86] Something that is designoid looks designed, but many Darwinists say it actually isn't.[87] This is not an assertion based on the evidence, but rather based on the presuppositions by which they understand science. However, there is no good scientific reason why something in the natural world cannot be designed. In addition, there is no rule that says science cannot measure the action of an intelligence, be it natural, artificial, or supernatural. In fact, science seeks to measure and detect intelligence in many different ways, IQ tests being just one example.

---

85   Bullock, 2006.
86   Williams, 2004.
87   Dawkins, 1986, p. 196.

I then went on to remind my students of things they had already learned about in the course. Since evolution is said to be a result of random positive DNA mutations resulting in "fitter" organisms that are then chosen by natural selection, I touched on the fact that the vast majority of DNA mutations actually range from near neutral and just a bit negative all the way to deadly, while positive mutations are difficult to document at all.[88] Those mutations that lead to positive changes do so by breaking a previously functioning system. For example, if a cell experiences a random mutation that damages the "door" where a virus enters, that will be beneficial in situations where that cell is exposed to the virus. But, random mutations do not lead to new information, new protein-protein interactions, or novel molecular machines. As Michael Behe would say, that would be beyond the "edge of evolution."[89]

"Remember the various ways DNA can be point-mutated or changed." Here I wrote sentences consisting of three letter words, just like that contained by DNA, on the board as follows:

The cat sat and ate the rat.	
The ats ata nda tet her at.	(deletion mutation)
The eca tsa tan dat eth era t.	(insertion mutation)
The rat sat and ate the rat.	(substitution mutation)

"You can see that none of these mutations actually cause the sentence to make more sense. Of course, we can also have transpositions, where a long piece of DNA gets moved from one place to another, sometimes resulting in a serious genetic disease, if not death. Duplications of entire portions of DNA also occur (some do not appear to have much effect), as do other more major mutations, but our present-day experience with those is that they do not usually produce good changes. One exception is in the anti-freeze protein, but even this does not

---

88   "As the controversial evolutionist Lynn Margulis said, "We agree that very few potential offspring ever survive to reproduce and that populations do change through time, and that therefore natural selection is of critical importance to the evolutionary process. But this Darwinian claim to explain all of evolution is a popular half-truth whose lack of explicative power is compensated for only by the religious ferocity of its rhetoric. Although random mutations influenced the course of evolution, their influence was mainly by loss, alteration, and refinement. One mutation confers resistance to malaria but also makes happy blood cells into the deficient oxygen carriers of sickle cell anemic [sic]. Another converts a gorgeous newborn into a cystic fibrosis patient or a victim of early onset diabetes. One mutation causes a flighty red-eyed fruit fly to fail to take wing. Never, however, did that one mutation make a wing, a fruit, a woody stem, or a claw appear. Mutations, in summary, tend to induce sickness, death, or deficiencies. No evidence in the vast literature of heredity changes shows unambiguous evidence that random mutation itself, even with geographical isolation of populations, leads to speciation." Margulis, 2003, p. 29.
89   Behe, 2007.

make a new protein machine, but unfolded, nonspecific 'junk in the gutter,'[90] preventing ice crystal formation. Remember how a simple mutation like having three, instead of two, copies of the smallest somatic chromosome (21) results in Down's syndrome?"

Alexi joined in, "Yes, and having three copies of any other chromosome, except the sex chromosomes, almost always results in a miscarriage."

The students nodded as they remembered. In an attempt to make the course interesting to the majority of the students, who were aspiring physicians, we'd studied some of the deleterious effects of mutations that affect cell function, resulting in cystic fibrosis, sickle cell anemia, fragile X syndrome, and hemophilia.

Now, I went on to give them information about recent research. I wanted their knowledge base to be as up-to-date as possible. "This principle, that mutations are neutral or negative, is used extensively in research into how cells work. A protein is deliberately mutated and observations are made about what changes this makes to the function of the cell, system and organism. No one ever expects things to improve, but it does give an idea about what parts of a protein and, indeed, which proteins are important for certain processes."

The students looked confused, so I explained further, "Think back to the lecture on cell communication. We talked about how cells have receptors, like doorbells, on their surfaces that recognize signals from their surroundings. The cell passes the message from chemical to chemical, kind of like a game of Telephone, until it reaches the nucleus so the cell knows how to react. The message isn't whispered, but is passed by events like a protein changing shape, a phosphate being passed, calcium being released, or cAMP being elevated. This is similar to sending a message through a room full of people by one person whispering, another text messaging, another using hand signals, and another writing notes. The message is the same; the means of transmission is different. In order to find out how a particular message is passed in a cell and which of the tens of thousands of proteins in the cell are involved, scientists systematically knock out the activity of one of the proteins they think might be involved at a time. If the message doesn't get through, then the protein is probably involved in transmitting the message (Figure 9)."

---

90   Behe, 2007.

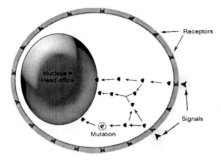

Figure 9 *The figure shows how a chemical signal (or message) stimulates a receptor (intercom) so that the message is passed through a series of intermediate steps until it reaches the nucleus. A mutation in the DNA coding for one of the intermediate proteins may prevent that protein from being able to pass on the message. Alternatively, it may prevent interaction with the transduction of another message. It might even cause a message to be transmitted continuously so that the stimulus cannot be "turned off." All of these events will cause the cell to malfunction. In life, cancer is a common consequence of problems with signal transduction.[91]*

"Oh, I get it," responded an older lady in the front row who'd worked in the government, "kind of like finding the glitch in a computer program."

Not knowing much about computer programming, I just nodded and went on. "Another issue is that for macroevolution to occur, you often need to have a change in the morphology or shape of an organism. That is, new information is required."

Nathan had spent some time looking into these things on his own, "Yeah, and I was reading on the Internet that no one has ever been able to produce a change in morphology by mutating a gene."

I added, "Well, scientists have produced some weird creatures using mutations, like a four-winged fruit fly, but it's a cripple and not really an example of macroevolution. However, you're right, according to according to Professor Margulis, 'new mutations don't create new species; they create offspring that are impaired.'"[92]

Next, I reminded the students of the scientific laws they had learned about during the course: the Second Law of Thermodynamics, the Law of Biogenesis and Cell Theory. A simplified view of the first says that the disorder of the universe always increases. Some scientists have argued that this makes spontaneous increasing complexity, as is claimed by macroevolution, unlikely. However, physicists correctly state that this is an oversimplification of thermodynamics and is not strictly applicable to the evolution argument. I made sure to stress this, since I wanted the students to honestly consider the evidence for themselves. The latter two laws state that life comes from prior life and that cells (the

---

91 Signal reception and transduction are more complex than what is depicted here. For example, not all receptors are on the surface of the cell; some are intracellular. Also, responses to signals vary from being direct and immediate to requiring a change in gene transcription. In my opinion, the permutations of cell communication may be even more complex that that of human language.
92 Margulis, 2006.

fundamental unit of life) come from prior cells. The discrepancy between these tried and proven scientific laws and the primordial soup or spontaneous generation ideas for the origin of life is obvious. The Campbell Biology test bank makes the astonishing claim that life could have evolved from nonlife 3.8 billion years ago simply because conditions were different then.[93]

After mentioning and briefly explaining irreducible complexity as I had at NVCC, I showed how evolutionary mechanisms could only result in cumulative complexity and summed up with a slide inviting the students to think about the scientific evidence for themselves.

"There is some evidence for microevolution, but there is also evidence that strict Darwinism is out-dated in view of the discoveries made since the time of Darwin. This evidence includes: 1) the fact that DNA is the genetic material carrying incredibly complex information and 2) the inner complexity and specificity[94] of cells and their protein machines."

I hoped to enable the students to use their critical thinking faculties and left them with a challenge to come up with a better theory or just to be able to defend their beliefs about the subject with scientific facts. My goal was to impartially give the facts. I knew I had achieved this when months later several students told me that, at the end of the lecture, they had no idea what I personally believed about the subject. In fact, one student later wrote,

> On the subject of evolution, you taught what was necessary for cell biology students to learn... During the first lecture, you said outright that this biology course could not answer the 'who' or 'why' questions pertaining to the operation of physical life, that these questions were for philosophy or theology courses. When you did mention evolution in your lectures, you did not assert your opinion above any other. In actuality, I found it difficult to ascertain your opinion in most cases. Even when some students asked if you were suggesting the existence of God, you did not declare your opinion as fact. You only taught what you should have, that there are different theories. For each theory, you even gave the scientific facts to support or refute each claim. You provided your students with critical thinking skills and the knowledge, the known facts, to make up their own mind on the subject of evolution versus intelligent design.[95]

---

93 Campbell Biology Test Bank v. 6.0
94 Complexity has been defined as having many parts in intricate arrangement (low probability). Specificity is an arrangement that is easy to describe because it fits an independently identifiable pattern. Something that has a purpose could be said to be specific.
95 Letter to Caroline Crocker, dated December 22, 2004. The author's identity has been withheld by request.

The semester continued and I became aware of a problem with teaching a large, crowded class that had not seemed nearly as significant when dealing with a smaller one -- cheating. Possibly because the students thought I would not notice or care, some would try at every opportunity. Early in the semester I'd devised a system for ensuring the students would get to class on time, even when there was no quiz. They would get a point of credit simply for signing their name on a sheet of paper. But, I often found that at least one pair of names would be written in identical handwriting, once in the same color crayon. Someone had signed their friend in, as well as themselves. Upon being confronted, the students inevitably denied any wrongdoing.

Another favorite was to sit outside class and copy the worksheets and lab assignments from someone else. It was impossible to prevent this, although I tried by insisting that all work be handed in before the beginning of class. This prevented students from being late and succeeded in making some very angry, but I soon found it wasn't necessary. Those who cheated would happily and mindlessly copy wrong answers too, and usually did. The better students had worked for their grade and were reluctant to share, especially after I instituted a rule that giving someone your answers would result in the same penalty as was given to those receiving the answers. The result was that the students who cheated usually failed, but were pretty angry with me as well.

Next, I had to face copying during exams. Since I used Scantrons, it was easy for one student to look at another's answers and copy them. How to prevent this? Here I hit on using three versions of the same exam. Even so, there were some who would copy their neighbor's answers and then write their neighbor's exam version number on their answer sheet as well. So, I began to have the students write their name on their exam sheet and on their answer sheet, checking if they matched before grading. It was a lot of trouble, but very necessary. One young lady, Hiroko, turned in a Scantron sheet identical to that of Elise, the student sitting next to her. She also had Elise's exam version written on her Scantron; it did not match her exam sheet.

"Hiroko, you have the wrong version written on your Scantron, look."

"Oh," she answered airily, "I just got confused about it." She changed the version.

"Now look, Hiroko, your answers are identical to Elise's answers," I challenged her. "You know cheating isn't allowed."

Hiroko looked indignant, "I wasn't cheating. I just happened to choose the same answers."

"But, you had a different version of the exam." I was amazed at her denial.

"So, are you calling me a liar? How can you accuse me of cheating!" Hiroko flounced out of the room.

Because we had been told at faculty orientation that it was mandatory to report cheating, I sent the evidence to the honor committee. Hiroko was found guilty. We then found that she had been cheating in the lab, as well. Hiroko, who seemed a little slow at realizing when she should stop, had notes penciled on the back of her Scantron during the very next exam. Another student, Maya, informed me, I saw it, and sent the evidence to the honor committee. Their decision was that Hiroko should leave the university. It amazed me that Hiroko still persisted in misbehavior and then followed Maya around, threatening her, until Maya phoned me at my home in tears. It did not take long for me to contact the Dean of Students, a lovely man, who soon made a phone call and put a stop to the nonsense.

Final exam time came quickly. I had noticed that grades were poor overall, with about 3% of the students consistently producing "A's" and 30% failing. Since I'd taught the same course with the same exams at the community college and had the opposite student results, I knew this was a problem related to class size. I decided, once again, to make the final exam available online prior to the exam. I also held a study session where the answers to the essays on the final were discussed. I hoped this would help, but it didn't. Some students came, but many found it too much trouble to learn the content of the ten answer slides displayed.

As I was dismally entering the grades into the computer, I heard a knock on my door. Glad of the distraction, I got up to open it.

"Hey, Dr Crocker, I thought I would stop by and say thanks for being a great teacher. I really enjoyed your class," Don Willcox offered his hand to be shaken.

I smiled, "Don, come in and have a seat. It's good to see you. Thanks. What're you planning on doing next?"

"Oh, I have another year and then I hope to go to graduate school."

"I'm sure you will do well. If you need a reference, let me know."

"Actually, Dr. Crocker, maybe you can help me with something *now*. I need some extra cash next semester and I wondered if you need a TA."

"Well, those are usually provided by the department, if we get one, but I noticed that the Center for Teaching Excellence (CTE) is offering a stipend for a Teacher's Aide who does a project. I was thinking about recruiting someone and you might just fit the bill."

Don leaned forward, "What did you need?"

"Okay, I'm entering the grades for the course and I have to say I'm disappointed. The students at NVCC did much better in the same course. It looks like the huge classes really impede student performance. I'd love to do a project on improving student learning in large class settings."

"That sounds interesting. I'd like to help with that."

And so, a very fruitful partnership was born. Don and I applied for a grant from the Center for Teaching Excellence.[96] It was funded and we began working together, brainstorming for ways to help students learn cell biology.

We decided to move the vocabulary quizzes to before the relevant lecture, rather than after. This way, we hoped to encourage students to have read those chapters before coming to the lecture. Even if they didn't, at least they would understand the words I was using. Then, because so few took advantage of the study groups, we decided to implement a worksheet over each chapter. These would be due before the lecture after that chapter was finished, so that students would have to review the course material continuously. These worksheets would also be the subject of the weekly study sessions. Then, the correct answers to the worksheets would be posted on the website, allowing students to self-correct before taking the exam.

Next, we came up with activities that could be done during class, allowing students to further comprehend material. For example, we made props so that student volunteers could "do protein synthesis" in the form of a play during class. Finally, we decided to have a large review session before each exam, where questions could be asked and the concepts that the coming exam would cover would be explained once again. Don would help with writing the worksheets and would do some of the extra grading. He would also be available to help individuals with the worksheets and proctor exams. At the end of the semester, Don analyzed student grades, found that we had been successful in raising them significantly, and presented the results as a poster.[97] The CTE liked our work so much that they asked me to do another project, but by then I had a new boss, "Dr. Carter," who was not happy about my work with the CTE, so I declined. I was never certain why he was so opposed to their help; I did not ask.

Dr. Carter was an interesting man. About 60 years old, he was tall, suave and definitely liked to be in charge. In fact, one of the first things he said when we were introduced was "Hi, I'm Dr. Carter and I'm the one in charge here." It was a rather surprising statement, but I assumed it was a joke and responded, "I'll be sure to remember that."

---

96   A copy of the first page of the Center for Teaching Excellence grant application can be found in Appendix V.

97   Willcox, 2004, Powerpoint can be found in Appendix V.

Shortly after meeting Dr. Carter, I made an appointment to see him.

"Dr. Carter, I'm so glad that you are going to be taking over coordinating the cell biology course. There are significant problems with it that I'd love to help you to address." Here I outlined the changes I was making with Don, but also pointed out the issues with the labs: the TA's were untrained, the labs were elementary, and there were numerous mistakes in the lab book. His answer astonished me.

"Those who complain do not get their contracts renewed," he intoned ominously.

I looked at him in surprise, "I'm not really complaining, just pointing out things that need work. I'm willing to help." I protested.

"Okay," he said, settling back in his chair and steepling his hands, "What do you suggest?"

Encouraged, I went on enthusiastically, "Well, it would be great if we had a prep session for the labs. That way, all the TA's would know what they should do. Last semester we were not even told what lab was next. Also, I have three lab exercises that I wrote while working at NVCC that you might find helpful. They illustrate lecture material much more adequately than the present book. Finally, maybe the lab book should be revised. It contains numerous mistakes. I can help with that, if you like."

Dr. Carter appeared to warm up towards me, "I'm in the process of doing the revision, but I'd like to see the labs you wrote. Can you e-mail them? Also, I was already planning on having prep sessions on Fridays."

I summoned up a smile, "That would be good. I'll look forward to it. See you then."

I returned to my office and, just in case, made a mental note to be careful to always defer to Dr. Carter, to laugh at his remarks about the intelligence level of students, and to never let down my guard. Unfortunately, in time his cultured manners won me over; I forgot this last resolution and paid dearly for it.

Dr. Carter and I became quite friendly. He often discussed problems related to the course with me and asked for my opinion in lab meetings; he appeared to really care about teaching. The labs I wrote were included in the new version of the lab manual[98] and Dr. Carter asked me to produce the artwork needed for implementation of one of the labs. Since excellence in teaching was also close to my heart, I spent many hours at home, trying to do the best job possible. Towards the end of the spring semester, when my original contract was running out, I was overjoyed to receive a new contract, this time for three years.

---

98   Fox and Christensen, 2005.

Despite the fact that Dr. John Evans, a former dean who had worked on a departmental committee developing a policy for renewal of term faculty contracts had informed me that it was normal practice to either offer a contract for the same length of time (my original was for 18 months) or increase the time,[99] I was so happy that I showed it to the secretary to make sure I was reading correctly. She assured me that I was. I then phoned my husband, Richard.

"Guess what? My contract was renewed…this time for three years! That's enough to finish putting James through college." I was almost too excited to speak. Our son's overseas education bill had been a worry to me and now it looked like we would be okay until he was finished. As I walked back to my office to pack up my things, I ran into Don. He was delighted to hear the news since he maintained that I was a gifted cell biology teacher.[100, 101] After inviting him and his family to a celebration dinner at my home that night, I took the contract home with me and showed Richard and an international student who was staying with us at the time. "Look, I have a job until May, 2007… just enough!" Finally, I phoned my parents to share the news. Soon afterwards I received a communication from Human Resources asking if I would prefer to be paid only during the months I was working or have that payment spread over 12 months for the next three years. I responded that I would prefer the latter option. (The spreading of payments never happened, but I assumed it was just an oversight and did not follow up.)

It seemed that Dr. Carter had forgiven me the original infraction of suggesting the course could be improved and had accepted me as a capable colleague. This was confirmed in my mind that next week after the lab meeting when I was walking back to my office with Dr. Carter. He was depressed because he couldn't find anyone to teach the other section of cell biology next semester. "It's just that I have so much to do with running the department and teaching the grad students. Now I have to do lectures, too."

I volunteered to help him. "Why don't you let me do it? I love teaching and doing two instead of one lecture really would not be a problem," I said.

"That's an idea. Let me think about it. I'll get back to you."

The next week Dr. Carter brought up my suggestion as we walked back to our offices after the weekly lab meeting, "You know, I think that it would work for you to teach both sections. I could give you only one lab and then you could do both lectures."

"Would I have a TA? The grading would be the only problem."

99 Telephone interview of Dr. J.C. Evans by Caroline Crocker, March 2009.
100 Letter from Donald Willcox to "Karen Anderson", April 2005. Letter can be found in Appendix II.
101 E-mail from Donald Willcox to Caroline Crocker, February 2009, E-mail can be found in Appendix II.

"I'm sure I could do that. In fact, I would rather get you one than have you involve the CTE. I really don't like their interference," he answered. As an afterthought, he added, "Of course, we'll need to change your contract to reflect your new responsibilities. Can you bring your copy of the old contract to my office?"

I did not see a problem with this, but got busy and forgot. A couple of weeks later, Dr. Carter burst in on me while I was teaching a study group. "Mary Lou told me that the contracts are overdue in the head office. Could you just sign this now…it's changed to reflect your new teaching duties…and back date it to reflect what is here?" Dr. Carter pointed at the relevant part on the second page, which had been printed onto the back of the first page. He then turned it over for me to sign the third page.[102]

I obediently signed.

Dr. Carter then said, "Okay, I'll have this one photocopied and leave a copy in your box—I also need you to give me your copy of the old contract."

"Umm, the old one is in my office," I answered, "I'll just throw it away."

Dr. Carter studied my face for a couple of minutes, "Be sure you do. It's not good to have two around."

Not thinking about this any more, I threw the old contract away as soon as I got back to the office. I believe in keeping my word. I did not receive a copy of the new one in my box, but was not worried since I knew it would be in my file.

Soon it was the end of the semester. The students were doing better under the new regimen. In fact, my TA presented a poster showing that there had been a 22% decrease in students dropping the class and an 11% increase in grades.[103] The labs had improved under Dr. Carter's watchful eye, and I began looking for a new challenge. I noticed that "Technology Across the Curriculum" (TAC) grants were available and decided to apply. As a first stop, I consulted with Dr. Carter.

"These are the kinds of things my tenure track faculty should be doing," he pointed out with a frown.

I wasn't sure what this had to do with me, "I understand, but what do you think about my ideas?"

"Write them up and I'll sign off on them. They sound good. By the way, what are your career goals? Would you like to have a tenure track position?" He leaned back and crossed his legs.

---

102   A copy of this contract can be found in Appendix V. Note that, because the first and second page had been printed on the front and back of the same sheet of paper, when the second and third page are displayed, the first page, where the length of the contract is specified, is hidden.

103   Willcox, 2004. "Cell Biology Comprehension and Communication: Optimizing Large Class Instruction." Poster presented at George Mason University Center for Teaching Excellence Conference, February 9.

I was surprised by this question, but answered honestly, "Yes, eventually I would. But, I think that would first require completing postdoctoral research and I have yet to do that."

Dr. Carter did not seem to think this was a problem, "You could probably find someone here who would allow you to work in their lab. Think about it."

I said I would and stood up to take my leave of his office.

I wrote two grants, one for implementing the use of a reference managing program, Endnote, in the biology course and the other for teaching the students PowerPoint in the course of a lab presentation.[104] I was pleased to hear that they were to be funded consecutively. At the first lab meeting in the fall of 2004, Dr. Carter introduced me to his wife who had just been hired to teach biochemistry in his department. I was pleased to hear that she would be helping me on the TAC project, not realizing that working with the boss's wife can be tricky.

Soon after the beginning of the next semester, Dr. Carter e-mailed me a faculty evaluation, requesting that I sign it and return it to him. I was shocked at what I read. Despite my receiving grants from the CTE and TAC, having created new lab exercises and having been given responsibility for teaching all the cell biology that semester, Dr. Carter had written that my teaching performance was just average. It was true that my average from the student evaluations was slightly less than that received by the teacher who was lecturing the other section of Cell Biology, but the difference was not significant (within one standard deviation). Also the other teachers, perhaps knowing that faculty were being evaluated on the basis of student reports only, did not report cheating. As I pointed out to Dr. Carter, being a good teacher, not accepting tardiness or cheating does make some students angry and as a result many of them will then give a teacher low marks. The Dean of Students told me that I was the only teacher from our department to report on cheating in many years. I knew not doing so was against the official rules, but it seemed as if it would have been better for my reputation to do the same. In addition, although the faculty handbook stipulated that teachers also be evaluated on the basis of someone observing their teaching and improvements they make to the course, this was not done in my case, despite my continued requests that it should be.

Finally, I decided to put aside my hurt feelings and calmly asked, "Dr. Carter, how would you like me to change or improve my teaching?"

His answer surprised me, "Just carry on doing what you are doing. The student grades are up and that's enough."

---

104   Copies of the first pages of the two Technology Across the Curriculum grant applications can be found in Appendix V.

I persisted, "What about insisting on attendance and reporting cheating? Doing that lowers the student evaluation scores."

Dr. Carter repeated, "Keep doing what you are doing. It's good."

Just the same, I wrote up the results of that meeting and had it added to my departmental file. I was beginning to distrust the suave smooth-talk of this man.

On my way back to my office, I met a former student, Darren. This man was older and had earned an A+ in my class. He was trained and had practiced as a lawyer, but now wanted to also go to medical school.

"Dr. Crocker, I'm glad I caught you. I just wanted to let you know I got my MCAT[105] results. They're great and I owe it all to you."

"What do you mean? You took the exam, not me," I reminded him with a smile.

"I know, but while I was taking your class, I hated the way you made us do vocabulary quizzes all the time. It was so boring!" he answered, "But, when I was doing the MCAT, I saw the point. Knowing those words got me through most of that exam."

"I'm so happy for you. So, have you applied for any schools?"

"I'm in the process now. Would you write me a recommendation?"

"With pleasure. I know you'll be a great physician."

I thanked God for students like Darren. Whenever life would knock me down, it seemed that one of them was always there to build me up again. I was to find this continued to be true, even through the exceedingly difficult days that lay ahead. I wrote the supportive letter of recommendation that Darren had earned as an excellent student and he was to return the favor later by writing a strong letter in my support[106] when I was falsely accused of professional misconduct.

---

105 Medical College Admission Test
106 Letter from lawyer and GMU student to Caroline Crocker, May 4, 2005. The author's identity has been withheld by request. The entire letter can be found in Appendix II.

REFERENCES

Anonymous. 2004. Letter from pre-med student to Caroline Crocker. December 22.

Anonymous. 2005. Letter from lawyer student to Caroline Crocker, May 4.

Behe, Michael J. 2007. *The Edge of Evolution: The Search for the Limits of Darwinism.* New York, NY: The Free Press.

Bullock, Roddy. 2006. *The Cave Painting. A Parable of Science.* Colorado Springs, CO: Access Research Network.

Campbell, Neil A. *Biology* Testbank version 6.0, San Francisco, CA: Benjamin Cummings

Campbell, Neil A., and Jane B. Reece. 2002. *Biology* 6th Edition. San Francisco, CA: Benjamin Cummings.

Center for Teaching Excellence Grant Application. 2003.

Dawkins, Richard. 1986. *The Blind Watchmaker: Why the Evidence of Evolution Reveals a Universe Without Design.* New York, NY; W. W. Norton and Company.

Evans, J.C. 2009. Phone interview of J.C. Evans by Caroline Crocker, March.

Fox, Donna H., and Alan H. Christensen. 2005. *Cell Structure and Function Lab Manual* 2nd Edition. Dubuque, IA: Kendall Hunt.

Margulis, Lynn and Dorion Sagan. 2003. *Acquiring Genomes: A Theory of the Origins of the Species.* New York, NY: Basic Books.

Margulis, Lynn. 2006. Quoted in Darry Madden, "*UMass Scientist to Lead Debate on Evolutionary Theory,*" Brattleboro (Vt.) Reformer, February 3.

Plantinga, Alvin. 2007. "Religion and Science." *Stanford Encyclopedia of Philosophy.* http://plato.stanford.edu/entries/religion-science/ (as of 2/03/09).

Schwartz, Jeffrey H. 1999. *Sudden Origins: Fossils, Genes, and the Emergence of Species,* New York, NY: John Wiley & Sons.

Technology Across the Curriculum Grant Applications. 2004.

University Catalog George Mason University, Biology. 2004. http://www.gmu.edu/catalog/0405/courses/biol.html (as of 4/1/09).

Willcox, Donald. 2004. "Cell Biology Comprehension and Communication: Optimizing Large Class Instruction." Poster presented at *George Mason University Center for Teaching Excellence Conference*, February 9.

Willcox, Donald. 2005. Letter from Don Willcox to "Karen Anderson", April.

Willcox, Donald. 2009. E-mail from Don Willcox to Caroline Crocker, February.

Williams, Peter S. "Is Life Designed or Designoid? Dawkins, Science, and the Purpose of Life." Access Research Network, Colorado Springs, CO. http://www.arn.org/docs/williams/pw_purposeoflife.com (as of 2/22/09).

Chapter 5: The Unforgivable Sin

The fall of 2004, my 4th semester of full time teaching at GMU had been the busiest one so far, with 300 students and the responsibilities of the research paper assignment resulting from the TAC grant. I was exhausted. I calculated that I had been putting in over 60 hours per week for a salary equivalent to what is normally earned by a secretary.[107] It's good that money was not my motivation. Before collapsing during the Christmas vacation, I made an appointment with Dr. Carter. Because he had not attended the meeting with the TAC people, I needed to inform him of the outcome of our project. I also wanted to discuss some ideas about the upcoming semester. In particular, I had decided to write a course manual, including the PowerPoint slides, quizzes, worksheets, sample exams and more for use in the Cell Biology course. Since I'd made contact with a company willing to publish it, Kendall Hunt, I thought it time to let Dr. Carter know about my intentions.

The meeting went quite amicably at first, talking about the past semester and the TAC project, but then it turned in an unexpected direction. I was already standing, ready to leave, when without preamble, Dr. Carter announced, "I've been told by several students and faculty that you're teaching 'creationism.' I am going to have to discipline you. You won't be allowed to teach lectures this coming semester, but will fulfill your hours by teaching labs." He stood up as he spoke.

I was flabbergasted. Feeling the heat flood my face and then drain, leaving me dizzy, I grasped the arm of a chair for support, "Dr. Carter, are you serious? I haven't been teaching anything of the sort! You've always had access to my lecture notes—they're online and you have the password, so you know what I teach. I do usually teach a lecture on the evidence for and against evolution, but it is not creationism, and I *didn't even do* that lecture this semester. There was no time because of the time I spent teaching the students how to write a research paper."

Dr. Carter was adamant, "I warned you before about this," (which was not true), "and now you've done it again. Many people, both faculty and students (also not true), have complained and I have no choice but to take action."

Again I tried to defend myself, "Please, ask the students. I presented a balanced and objective look at the facts about evolution in the past, but I *didn't do that lecture* this semester. When I did the lecture in the past, I don't think I even mentioned the word, "creation." If you like, I won't ever give the lecture where I question evolution again!" Because I enjoyed teaching so much, I was desperate enough to promise anything. In retrospect, I may have responded too hastily on that point.

---

107   http://swz.salary.com/salarywizard/layouthtmls/swzl_compresult_national_OF13000055.html

Here Dr. Carter changed the instructions for the course, "You shouldn't teach evolution at all in this course. That's reserved for Animal Biology."

This was also confusing, "But, the course description in the 2004-2005 GMU catalog says cell biology covers the chemistry, metabolism, genetics, and *evolution* of cells.[108] The book also covers evolution and even the cell biology lecture notes that Dr. Alekseev gave me discuss evolution extensively."

Dr. Carter's height made him appear menacing as he came out from behind his desk. "Our discussion is finished. You've been teaching creationism (this was his mischaracterization of what I had taught) and I've made the decision that you must be disciplined. Go straight to Mary Lou's office and have her sign you up for four labs. You will not be allowed to teach lectures."[109]

On my way out of the door I paused, "What about the fall semester?" This was when I planned to implement use of my Course Workbook.

"I'll decide about that at some time in the future," he answered haughtily.

I left the office and, in a subdued voice, asked Mary Lou to sign me up for the labs. Looking at my face, she did not dare to ask what had happened. I then made my way back to my office, trembling and nearly in tears. When I got there, there were two students, Jameerah and Tushar, waiting outside my door. During the last class I had announced that I was going to apply for another grant from the CTE to work on improving the efficacy of study groups. Any student who wanted to be a recipient should let me know. They were there to apply.

I invited them into my office and tried to compose myself, but to no avail. I sank into my chair as another wave of dizziness hit.

"Dr. Crocker, are you okay? You look terrible!" asked Jameerah, wrinkling her face in concern.

Her friend, Tushar, joined in, "You're shaking! What happened?"

Summoning up my strength, I answered, "I'm okay. I just had a bit of a shock. What did you guys need?"

Tushar volunteered, "We want to apply for the CTE grant that you talked about in class. How do we do it?"

I hadn't wanted to tell students about what just happened, but now saw that I would have no choice in the matter. "Oh, I'm so sorry," I sighed, "It won't be possible to do that project now, unless you do it with someone else. I've just been told that I won't be allowed to teach lecture next semester."

The students looked aghast, "What? Why not?"

---

108 http://www.gmu.edu/catalog/0405/courses/biol.html Copy can be found in Appendix VI.

109 According to lawyer, John H. Calvert, this was a violation of the Establishment Clause—promoting a particular religious belief—materialism, and a violation of title VII. The course catalog took me into a religious sphere (origins) and Dr. Carter was punishing me for fulfilling my duty to act neutrally in that sphere.

I had not yet had sufficient time to come up with an answer that would protect my supervisor's reputation, so I just told them the truth, "Well, my boss seems to think that I've been teaching creationism, even though that is not true. He's disciplining me by removing me from teaching lectures."

Jameerah, a hot-tempered young lady, jumped to her feet. "Who is he? Dr. Carter? I'll tell him that someone was lying to him! You never taught creation! You taught biology, and you're the best teacher I've ever had!"[110]

I smiled gratefully, "Thanks, but it won't help, and it might hurt you. Just keep this to yourselves; I want to let things settle in my mind before anything is done. If I need your help in the future, I'll let you know."

"Well, if you're sure. That just makes me so mad. You try so hard for us and now…" Tushar and Jameerah left, angrily discussing how silly these charges were and I wearily packed my things to go home. I still had some grading to do, but couldn't face it just then.

As I was leaving the office, another person appeared at the door. It was Steve, a graduate student who was doing some teaching for the department. He also noticed that I was looking rather ill. I decided that there was no harm in telling him what had happened, especially since he had the same boss. I figured he might find a warning useful.

"You mean he's disciplining you, even though there's no written documentation of the offense?"

I shook my head, "Well, if there is, I've not seen it."

Steve looked incredulous, "Has there been a hearing at least, to find out if you did what you are accused of?" The 2004 GMU Faculty Handbook, Section 2.10.3, mandated this procedure.[111]

"No, I was told today and the discipline happened immediately."

"#*%&#, that means that if a student does not like her grade and falsely accuses me of sexual misconduct I can be disciplined without due process?" Steve scratched his head.

"Pretty much. Makes you feel kind of insecure, huh?"

"Wow, I'll be glad when I get out of this crazy place." he answered, bending over to retrieve some papers from his briefcase. Steve shook a stack of marked papers in my direction. "Over half of these are getting a C or less— makes my job really tough and kind of depressing. This makes it even harder."

I nodded sympathetically, but had no encouraging words to give him.

---

110   Within days Jameerah wrote a furious letter in my support, the contents of which can be found in Appendix II (December 19, 2004).
111   Contents can be found in Appendix VI.

That evening, after discussing things with my husband Richard, I phoned Dr. John C. Evans, a close friend and former graduate dean at GMU, to ask for his advice. He listened to my story in stunned silence.

"Wow, I don't know what to tell you," he paused, "What happened isn't right, but I'm not sure you can fight it."

"What should I do?"

"Well, let's see. I think your options are to move to a different university, or file a grievance, or just let things cool off and talk to Dr. Carter again."

"Do you think that'll help?"

"Probably not. But, we can pray. Still, just in case things go even more sour, you should write him an e-mail confirming your perspective of what transpired in the meeting so that you both have a record of it."

"Okay, thanks for your help. I'll let you know what happens."

I decided to sleep on it and write the e-mail, let myself cool down for a couple of days, and then send it.[112] As I opened my computer mailbox to do this, I noticed that I'd received an e-mail from Tushar. He said that he and Jameerah were very unhappy about what happened to me and that they and some other students wanted to put together a protest of sorts. This I answered immediately, thanking him for his concern, but warning them that doing this might put their academic futures in jeopardy. Instead I requested that they just write letters saying what I do teach, in case I should need them in the future. Over the next few months I received many letters from various former students, all stating that I was an excellent teacher and had not taught creationism. Jameerah wrote the following:

> I am very disturbed to hear that Dr. Crocker may not be a lecture professor any longer… I took Dr. Crocker's Biology 213 class this fall 2004 semester, and would like to address the idea of her teaching creationism in her lectures. I am unbiased about the subject of creationism, and am shocked to hear that she is being falsely accused. I have attended all of her lectures and I have followed along the lecture notes that she provided. She does not cover any other material in her lectures than what is outlined in her lecture notes. In addition, not only has she not taught creationism in particular, she even skipped the section on evolution…[113]

---

112   E-mail from Caroline Crocker to "Peter Carter", December, 2004. Contents can be found in Appendix IV.
113   Letter to Caroline Crocker, December 19, 2004. The author's identity has been withheld by request. The entire letter can be found in Appendix II.

Darren, the lawyer student who took the class a semester before so that he could also go to medical school, wrote a wonderfully articulate and furiously passionate letter.

> In regards to the above-mentioned allegations against Dr. Crocker, any and all claims of Dr. Crocker teaching creationism in class or Dr. Crocker being a poor teacher are absolutely false. In fact, any negative or derogatory claim against Dr. Crocker cannot have any merit whatsoever. Obviously, my comments are based on my experiences from the 2004 spring semester and while I cannot directly comment about anything that may or may not have happened in the 2004 fall semester, I believe my comments would still generally apply.

> As to the spurious claims of Dr. Crocker teaching creationism in class, this must be summarily dismissed. At no time did Dr. Crocker ever teach creationism or any "theory that humankind was created by a divine being" as defined by the United States Supreme Court. At no time did Dr. Crocker utter the word "God" or any other word referring to any "divine being." From my recollection (as I never missed a class) and my review of my Biology 213 notes, Dr. Crocker did give one lecture regarding evolution and discussed the theories of microevolution (natural selection), macroevolution, and intelligent design; moreover, Dr. Crocker presented "only scientific explanations for life on earth" and, if any, only "scientific critiques of evolution" as outlined by the United States Supreme Court. I find it incredible how any reasonable and prudent student could honestly believe or state that creationism was being directly or even obliquely taught by Dr. Crocker. This claim is absurd. Furthermore, even after that lecture on evolution and having sat through every lecture, I have absolutely no idea what Dr. Crocker believes religiously or scientifically or realistically as to the origins of life.[114]

Christmas that year was subdued. I tried not to let the unfairness of it all affect me, but it was always at the back of my mind. When the next semester started, I realized that I would be wise to place various documents in my departmental file in case of future trouble. Therefore, I went to see Mary Lou and gave her a copy of the e-mail I had sent to Dr. Carter, which had not been answered, and two of the student letters. I then said, "Mary Lou, can I ask you a question?"

"Sure," she answered amicably, sitting down at her desk.

"Have you heard anything about what's happening to me?"

---

114   Letter from lawyer and GMU student to Caroline Crocker, May 4, 2005. The author's identity has been withheld by request. The entire letter can be found in Appendix II.

"Well, yes, I know that you are not being allowed to teach the lecture part of cell biology," she tucked her hair behind her ear.

I persisted, "Do you know why?"

"Yes, I heard that you're being disciplined for teaching 'creationism'," Mary Lou answered honestly.

"It seems so strange to me to be disciplined for something I didn't do...and without due process," I mused, "Do you know of anything else I did to upset Dr. Carter?"

Mary Lou shook her head, "As far as I know, Dr. Carter doesn't have any problem with you except that you taught creationism. I think a student complained. Maybe you should try talking to him again."

My shoulders slumped as I fought tears, "I can't, Mary Lou. I am so upset about it all that I would just get emotional. Also, I think he's pretty angry. He didn't answer the e-mail I sent before Christmas."

Mary Lou grimaced, "I can imagine how you feel. But, I also know he had a pretty hard holiday season. Maybe he just didn't have time."

A couple of days later I decided to go see the person who hired me at GMU, my former boss Dr. Sullivan. She greeted me and invited me into her office.

After the usual pleasantries, I plunged right in, "Dr. Sullivan, have you heard about what happened to me?"

She nodded, "If you mean that you've been banned from lecturing, yes. But, tell me what happened." Dr. Sullivan had always impressed me as a no-nonsense and fair-minded person.

I related the events of the meeting where I was told that I would need to be disciplined. I also asked her if she had heard of any other reason that Dr. Carter should be upset with me. I still could not believe that such an "offense" would result in being removed from teaching.

Dr. Sullivan thought for a moment. "No, I don't think so. As far as I know, the evolution issue is the only problem he has with you."

"What should I do? You've known him longer than I have."

Dr. Sullivan frowned, "I do know him quite well and I found out the hard way that he isn't one to tangle with." Here she shared her own story, which I am not at liberty to divulge. "You could file a grievance, but that probably wouldn't bring the results you want. It would be better to wait until the middle of this semester, then abjectly apologize, promise not to do it again, and hope for the best for the fall semester. By the way, how is the course workbook coming? Did the Kendall Hunt Acquisitions Editor contact you?"

"Oh, it's nearly done except for the artwork. That takes a lot of time. Thanks for putting me in contact with Curtis Ross. We signed a contract and I'm looking forward to using my own workbook when I teach in the fall."

I stood as the conversation ended. It was a small comfort to me to realize that I was not the only one who had been treated badly by Dr. Carter, but I was not happy about submitting to injustice. I knew that Dr. Carter was probably just acting to save his own skin, but it was me who was being sacrificed! I thanked her for her time and candor and went to my office to mull things over. I didn't want to promise never to speak doubts concerning the scientific validity of neo-Darwinian evolution again, and in retrospect, I was aware that my rash promise to do just that didn't help my situation. But, one nagging question kept coming back to me: didn't the university stand for academic freedom? I knew I'd seen this in the faculty handbook, "the right to unrestricted expositions of subjects (including controversial questions) within one's field...in a professionally responsible manner...without fear of censorship or penalty."[115] The same handbook also said that faculty have "the right not to be excluded from the classroom until sufficient grounds for exclusion have been found and a committee of five have approved such discipline (to be done within three days after such exclusion)." I hadn't even received a complaint in writing, much less been given a warning or a hearing.

George Mason was the father of the Bill of Rights and yet the university that is named after him trampled on the very rights that he sought to institutionalize. I hoped that Dr. Carter would take the time to consider his actions and change his mind about disciplining me. But then, I also knew he was probably just protecting himself from a perceived threat to his own job or reputation.

Meanwhile, since teaching four labs left me with a lot of free time, I decided to go back to NVCC and see if there were classes available for me to teach. The Head of Biology there was now a lovely Christian lady, Dr. Brinkerhoff. She was amazed at what had happened to me and wanted to help by giving me adjunct teaching. However, the only class that still had no teacher was Anatomy and Physiology for students hoping to be medical assistants. I hadn't taught this before, but figured it would keep me busy enough, so I accepted. I also decided to give more time to the Cell Biology workbook I'd been working on.

Three weeks had now passed and Dr. Carter still had not replied to my e-mail. Just in case it never arrived (or he might claim it didn't), I decided to give him a hard copy of the e-mail, a letter explaining why I was giving it to him, printouts from the GMU website about academic freedom and a description

---

115   George Mason University Faculty Handbook 2004, Section 2. Contents can be found in Appendix VI.

of the course content, and one of the student letters. I gave this package into his hand on January 24, 2005 in the presence of one of the lab teachers. I then checked my departmental mailbox and found a letter from Dr. Peter Stearns, the GMU Provost (the second I had received) congratulating me on my "unusually high student rankings" the previous semester.[116] The irony of it all amazed me.

> Dear Professor I. Caroline Crocker:
>
> We write to congratulate you and thank you for an outstanding performance in the general education course you taught last spring term, as evidenced by unusually high student rankings. This kind of teaching quality is essential for this vital educational program, and we're very grateful for your successful efforts.
>
> Our review of student rankings represents a first level analysis given the fact that the data are ordinal (ranked) data. As you know, it is our goal to review the general education curriculum and recommend possible adjustments after the first few years of implementation. As a part of our review, we have identified outstanding student rankings of courses (equal to or >4.75, Question 6 "The Overall Rating of this Course"), and your course was included in this noteworthy group.

What was Dr. Carter so frightened of? I had not been teaching religion, but objective science; all I did in previous semesters was to point out problems with certain scientific data said to support Darwinism and offer my students some of the new ideas emerging out of the scientific community. If evolutionary theory was to qualify as science and not religion, surely challenging it should be allowed. Something that cannot even be questioned is dogma.[117] This reaction by Dr. Carter suggested he viewed evolutionary concepts as unassailable. I knew that several evolutionists lament the fact that some people adopt evolution with an almost religious fervor. Michael Ruse, a prominent philosopher and evolutionist, complained "Evolution is promulgated as an ideology, a secular religion."[118] Perhaps that's why people say, "I believe in evolution," but never, "I believe in gravity." It appeared to me that people at GMU were using their positions of power to advance their religiously held faith in Darwinism.

* * * *

---

116   Letters from Peter Stearns to Caroline Crocker, December 23 and March 22, 2004. A copy of these letters can be found in Appendix III.
117   "A specific tenet or doctrine authoritatively laid down, a settled or established opinion, belief or principle." http://www.dictionary.com
118   Ruse, 2000.

Classes were starting for the Spring 2005 semester, and students assailed me even before my first lab began.

"Dr. Crocker, why aren't you teaching? The course catalog said you are, and I signed up for you, but it's not you. It's some woman who doesn't seem like she knows what she's doing at all."

I remembered my own struggles to learn how to teach cell biology well and empathized with the new instructor. Maybe she had not taught the course previously; I suspected that she had been forced to take it on at short notice.

"Dr. Crocker, remember me? I had you last semester…remember? You flunked me, but it was my fault. I wanted to take you again. I signed up especially for your class, but it's not you teaching it."

"Dr. Crocker, I heard you're suspended from teaching. Is that right?"

I also got e-mails like the following:

I was wondering if you might ever teach a class other than 213, like micro or genetics?? I know I'm not the only one wondering this, several of my classmates this semester, as we study for our current class were wondering if you might teach other classes. We feel like [we] benefited and learned a lot from your class and are worried about having an unorganized, unclear teacher for a really challenging class such as micro. This is probably a very odd-sounding e-mail, I don't think any of the other kids I know who are wondering this actually have e-mailed you, but I am very curious.[119]

It was difficult to know what to say. I wanted to be professional and knew it would be wrong to say anything disloyal about my boss, so skirted the issue. I did wonder where the students had heard that I was suspended. Was Dr. Carter talking? I knew he frequently spoke about students with teachers, but had not heard him extend the practice to speaking to students, faculty, and staff about faculty. However, the fact that both Mary Lou and Dr. Sullivan knew all about the problem suggested he had, at least, discussed me with faculty and staff members.

"Oh, I'm taking time off this semester to write a workbook for use in teaching cell biology," was my standard response to students. At least this was partly true.

"Okay, so should I drop the class and wait for you next semester?"

I was not sure how to react. This was such a huge compliment. "Umm, well, I'm not sure what I'll be doing then. Probably you should just take the class now. I'll be available if you need help." I did not know whether I would be relegated to teaching labs only for an indefinite period.

---

119   E-mail to Caroline Crocker, May 17, 2005. The author's identity has been withheld by request. A copy of the e-mail can be found in Appendix II.

It was nice to hear the good things from the students, but upsetting to know that my integrity and reputation were being sullied in retribution for an offense that I hadn't committed. Feeling alone, I decided to go to the Fellowship of Christian Faculty for the first time since I began teaching at GMU. Afterwards, I shared the problem with the Campus Crusade representative, Randy Newman, and a faculty member. They both advised that this was a direct violation of my right to academic freedom and due process and urged me to take action. I still was not sure where to turn for help.

Finally a friend suggested that I go to the Office of Equity and Diversity Services. I did this and met a friendly lady, Lakisha, who kindly made enquiries with Dr. Carter. But, when I phoned her a week later, I was told that Dr. Carter had told her that students had complained (he had previously said to me students and faculty complained) and that he is in the process of writing me a letter (this letter never appeared). He also told her that term faculty do not have any rights, so she should not pursue helping me further.

I shook my head in amazement. How could he say this? I pleaded with Lakisha on the phone, "But, that's not true. Chapter 11 of the faculty manual says nothing about the right to academic freedom and due process being denied to term faculty.[120] It just says that their service cannot be applied to consideration for tenure!"

Lakisha was sympathetic, but definitely did not want to get involved, "I'm sorry. I can't help you. Maybe you should try the dean of your department."

Because it appeared that nothing else would work, I requested a meeting with Dean Struppa. After getting past the necessary red tape with his administrative assistant, the meeting was duly scheduled. When the day was near, I received an email from Daniele Struppa saying that, because this was a dispute between Dr. Carter and me, he would like Dr. Carter to attend as well. This should not have surprised me because I'd heard that the two were good friends. Since my confidence that I would obtain justice had already been shaken, and I knew that two males could easily shout down a lone female, I agreed, but asked that Dr. Murray Black, a full professor and respected member of the university, also attend. Dean Struppa immediately responded to this by saying he had decided that meeting with me would be inappropriate. He advised me to file a grievance.[121] I felt completely unsupported and alone and wondered if justice was only a dream.

Just then, there was a knock on my office door. I stood and opened the door, "Oh hi, Rashida, come on in. Have a seat."

---

120   George Mason University Faculty Handbook, 2004, Chapter 11.
121   E-mails between Daniele Struppa and Caroline Crocker, February 7-9, 2005. Contents can be found in Appendix IV.

Rashida was one of my better students from a previous semester, but she had to work hard to achieve good grades, "Hey Dr. Crocker, I heard what's going on with you. Are you okay?"

My heart warmed to her, "I'm fine, Rashida. It's annoying, but not life-threatening."

"What're you going to do?" she asked me, obviously still worried.

"Well, I'm not sure right now. But, I've been advised to talk to the dean. It's just he doesn't think it would be good to talk to me."

Rashida pondered this for a couple of minutes and then volunteered, "How about if I take a bunch of us students to see him? He might listen to us."

"No, but thanks. I'm beginning to see that this thing is bigger than I imagined and I'm worried that doing something like that might hurt your academic future."

"Well, okay. But let me know if you change your mind. You're a great teacher and it's so unfair that this happened."

I decided to change the subject. Rashida had been to see me during the previous semester because she was struggling with depression and had even become suicidal. At that time I'd sent her to the school counselor and given her some of the motherly attention she'd been missing while at school. "So, how are you doing now? You look well."

"Oh, I am. I feel so much better. In fact, I'm going to get married next month. Would you come?" She showed me her ring.

"Rashida, I'd be happy to. Thanks for asking. Who's the guy?"

And so our conversation went on. It was so good, once again, to hear the happy chattering of a young person.

Another source of light during this rather dark time was my Anatomy and Physiology class at NVCC. Many of these students had a goal to become medical assistants and I knew that, unfortunately, some of them would not make it. Although I simplified the course material and structured the course in the way I knew worked for Cell Biology, it did not help with this course. The first quiz consisted of learning short definitions of ten words, but most of the students failed abysmally. Still, they were a pleasure to teach simply because they were so friendly and fascinated by the subject matter, especially when I related the material to diseases and conditions with which they were familiar.

After finishing the lecture on the main chemicals found in the body, I decided to try for some practical application of the knowledge.

"How many of you have seen medicines that lower cholesterol advertized on the TV?"

Hands raised all over the classroom.

"What do they do?"

A few hands dropped but Bessie, a lady in the front of the class, answered, "They lower cholesterol levels. My mom is on Lipitor."

"Good, now has anyone heard the list of side effects for these medicines that they read on the TV?"

A number of students giggled and one said, "Those lists make you wonder why anyone would take anything, really."

Bessie answered again, "Muscle pain seems to be the big one and, if you ignore it, kidney and liver problems. But, my mom is getting forgetful. I looked it up on the Internet and that seems to be a problem more people have. Then again, maybe it's just menopause. She's started having a lot of hot flashes."

The class chuckled at her candor.

Chung Ye joined in, "My dad's allergies have gotten a lot worse since he started on Crestor. That's another drug that fights cholesterol. But, I don't think that's related."

"Okay, now let's think about this. What does cholesterol do?" I asked, hoping that the students would be able to apply what they learned in class.

Chung Ye answered, "It causes heart attacks."

"Well, actually, that is still being debated.[122] But, what I wanted was for you to think about why our bodies make cholesterol in the first place. It must do good things or we wouldn't make it."

A young man dressed in scrubs, Robert, answered me in the exact words they had been given to learn for a quiz, "It is a precursor for some hormones."

I nodded encouragingly, "Good, can you give me examples of steroid hormones?"

Answers rang out, "Estrogen," "Testosterone," "Cortisol."

"Right, now, is there anything else you know that cholesterol does?"

Students began shuffling through their notes. Chung Ye answered, "Oh, I know! You find it in cell membranes where it stops them from being too rigid."

I wrote the side effects the students were coming up with on one side of the board and the good effects of cholesterol on the other, "Can anyone relate this side of the board to the other? How do you think these drugs might cause these side effects?"

Bessie looked thoughtful, "If they reduce cholesterol, they might also reduce estrogen. Maybe that could even bring on menopausal symptoms."

I encouraged her, "Good thinking. I don't know if they do, but it seems possible, based on what we see here. What else?"

122   Rosedale, undated.

Chung Ye pondered the board, "If a person has less cholesterol in their blood, wouldn't the amount of cholesterol in their cell membranes also be less? Then the membranes would be more rigid. I wonder if tearing of the cell membranes when muscle cells change shape causes the pain."

"Excellent thinking," I smiled at him, "and how might the drugs be related to allergies?"

The students looked confused. This was too hard, so I told them, "Cortisol reduces inflammation in the body. That's why inflammation is often treated with cortisone. If a person has less cholesterol, they might have less cortisol, making their allergies worse. This is something the drug company would need to investigate and test before releasing the medication."

Robert frowned, "Well then, why are those drugs even legal? Seems to me nobody should take them."

The other students were nodding their agreement.

I was pleased because one of my major goals in teaching was to enable students to use what they learn and apply it to life, but knew they still needed more information.

"Actually, that brings us to an important point about drug use. There's something called a cost/benefit ratio. All medications have bad and good effects. The decision on whether to take it should be based on an assessment of whether the benefit exceeds the cost."

Then Yolanda, who always sat at the back, raised her hand. I knew she worked as a medical assistant already, but was just doing courses to qualify for a higher pay rate. "Dr. Crocker, those drugs do lower cholesterol, but not below normal levels. I don't see how that would cause side effects."

This was great. Now they were not only applying their knowledge, but also questioning what the teacher says. This was always my goal in teaching: not only to give students information, but also to encourage thinking through issues independently, hopefully generating intellectually honest scholars. I still lived by what I had been told in my first year of university, "Think about it. If it is true, you can think about it and it will still be true. If it isn't, it wasn't worth believing in the first place."

* * * *

Despite a high degree of student participation, the results of the first exam were terrible. When I asked Dr. Brinkerhoff about this, she informed me that the students always do extremely poorly in this class. I decided to take this as a personal challenge.

For the next exam, I went through the questions word-for-word in the pre-exam review session. I knew that all these students had jobs and that they did not have much time to study, so I figured they could use some assistance. They took notes, but it did not help. What else could I try? I was determined that my students should succeed. So, for the third exam I not only told the students what I would expect them to know, but also allowed them to bring in a sheet of notes. I was sure that now they would do well. I was wrong. Finally, I gave each of them a copy of the fourth exam during the pre-exam review session, instructing them to look up the answers and learn them. (All the exams were multiple choice.) The students elected not to do this and instead furiously copied down the questions. I was sure that, armed with the questions for two days before the exam, most would achieve scores of 100%. But, to my amazement, on the day of the exam many of them failed. I was not looking forward to seeing their evaluations of my teaching.

I decided that some extra credit was in order. Therefore, I made a trip to the National Museum of Health and Medicine in D.C., taking along a pen and paper so I could make up a worksheet asking questions that were a little out of the ordinary so I would know they had actually gone. For example, "How old was the man who died of mega-constipation?" I then posted the worksheet on my website and invited the students to go to the museum, fill out the worksheet, and turn it in for extra credit. Since the museum was full of medical exhibits, I thought this would be a useful exercise for students wanting to have careers in healthcare. The idea was well-received and those who participated enjoyed it.

For the final, I once again gave students the questions prior to the day of the exam. The class still did poorly, but I was to find that you can never predict what students will do. After the exam, several students shyly approached my desk with cards and little gifts. They thanked me for being a great teacher. How could that be? Half the class had received a D or an F. The teacher evaluations were just as kind. In fact, one student wrote, "Dr. Crocker is a great teacher. We were just an amazingly dumb class." I had to smile. After all, there are human qualities that are much more important than academic prowess—like honesty and kindness. I had a feeling this class contained some great future medical assistants.

Meanwhile, I was thinking about whether a grievance procedure over my dispute with Dr. Carter would be wise. I was told that filing a grievance would not affect my future chances of employment and assured that I would receive a fair hearing.[123] After this encouragement, I e-mailed Dean Struppa and as a first tentative step requested that he assign a committee to my case, which he did. To my surprise, Dr. Carter, who claimed that term faculty did not have the right to a grievance procedure, challenged this. The question was put to the committee, they determined that term faculty have the same rights as anyone else, so the way was open for me to file a grievance.

---

123   George Mason University Faculty Handbook, Section 2, 2004.

Just after this, I was e-mailed by three very different people. One was Curtis Ross from Kendall Hunt, the publisher for the Cell Biology Workbook I was writing, the other a student, Cheryl, whom I was to come to know quite well, and the last a reporter for *Nature* magazine, Geoff Brumfeil. All were hoping to meet with me.

The meeting with Curtis was mostly business, talking about cover design, whether I would want to use figures from other books, and when I anticipated finishing. Here I explained that I would be creating all my own artwork, since I wanted to retain themes throughout the manuscript for the sake of visual learners. I also talked about how the title page of each chapter would be a pictorial summary of all the information in that chapter. I was excited to see how this would help students learn the material.

We also talked about deadlines and when I would want to start using the book. Although I originally had intended to use it for the first time in the fall, now I was hoping to use a draft copy at NVCC for a summer course. This, I hoped, would allow me to catch the inevitable mistakes. The publisher assured me that using photocopies for a small class in this way would not be a problem. So, I worked on the book during every spare minute that I had.

The one topic I did not broach in our discussions was the disciplinary action meted out to me at GMU. There were several reasons for this. First, I genuinely expected that the issue would be resolved come fall and that it would not affect publication of my workbook. Second, I had put hours upon hours of labor into this book and could not face the prospect of it never being published because the few pages that showed the evidence for and against neo-Darwinian evolution might be perceived as politically incorrect. Finally, even though I did not believe that I had done anything wrong, the persistent questions from students, the ominous silence from Dr. Carter, and the knowledge that the biology faculty and staff had been told about the discipline made me feel the shame of an outcast. No amount of reason could quite dispel that feeling.

The next e-mail was a joy to answer. Cheryl and her friends wanted to set up a group where questions about evolution and intelligent design could be discussed in an informed and free manner. The e-mail had been sent to all science faculty, but I was the only one who responded. How strange! One would think that faculty would be only too happy to help open-minded students to thoughtfully consider questions that interest them. It was incomprehensible that they would not even want to discuss some issues. In response to my e-mailed answer, Cheryl came to my office to talk about how I could help.

"Dr. Crocker, the point of the IDEA (Intelligent Design and Evolution Awareness) club is to invite people with different views about this subject to come and talk to us about why they believe what they do.[124] We hope that will spark informed debate. The purpose is not to convert anyone to another viewpoint, but just to help us think about the issues. Personally, I haven't made up my mind. I want to be very careful to invite the same number of evolutionists as others, but I haven't had much luck with anyone answering." Cheryl was at pains to be clear about how the IDEA club was designed to educate people about both sides of the issue and not to try and change their minds.

Here I told Cheryl what had just happened to me. "I suspect that other faculty, knowing what is being done to me, would be frightened to get involved with something like this." I gave her a brief synopsis of what had occurred.

Her jaw dropped in amazement, "You're kidding! I had no idea, but I'm so sorry. But, do you think you could help anyway?"

I smiled at her fresh features, bright eyes, and earnest manner. "Sure, I'll do what I can. I do know some faculty on both sides who might be willing to speak and can give you an introduction to them."

"Would you speak to us, as well?"

"Okay, just let me know when and what about."

"Thank you so much. Oh, I just remembered. Can I give your contact information to the other person who is leading this group? I know he would want to meet you."

"No problem. I look forward to hearing from you both."

Cheryl left to continue her organizing efforts.

The request for an interview from *Nature* magazine was quite a different prospect. I did not yet know whether I wanted speak about my experience. As a first stop I e-mailed Dean Struppa and Dr. Carter to ask whether speaking to a reporter would be permissible. Dr. Carter did not respond, but Struppa replied quickly saying that it would be okay. He stressed that I was to make it clear that I was not speaking as an official representative of GMU. So, I replied to the reporter that I would be willing to speak to him, having no idea that this would kill my chances for future tenure-track positions at most secular universities. I was still under the illusion that all of this trouble was just a minor glitch in life that could be overcome with some persistence on my part.

Little did I know what I was to discover about that in the coming months.

---

124   http://www.ideacenter.org

REFERENCES

Anonymous. 2005. E-mail from former student to Caroline Crocker, May 17.

Anonymous. 2005. Letter from student who is a lawyer ("Darren") to Caroline Crocker, May 4.

Anonymous. 2004. Letter from student to Caroline Crocker, December 19.

Anonymous. Undated. Salary.com. http://swz.salary.com/salarywizard/layouthtmls/swzl_compresult_national_OF13000055.html (as of 4/1/09).

George Mason University Course Catalog for Biology, 2004 – 2005. 03/01/09, http://www.gmu.edu/catalog/0405/courses/biol.html (as of 4/2/09).

Crocker, Caroline. 2004. E-mail from Caroline Crocker to "Peter Carter", December 17.

George Mason University Faculty Handbook. 2004. No longer available on the Internet.

Luskin, Casey. Undated. Intelligent Design and Evolution Awareness Center website. www.ideacenter.org (as of 4/1/09).

Rosedale, Ron. Undated. "Cholesterol is NOT the Cause of Heart Disease." http://articles.mercola.com/sites/articles/archive/2005/05/28/cholesterol-heart.aspx (as of 6/2/09).

Ruse, M. 2000. "How evolution became a religion: creationists correct?" *National Post*, May 13, p. B1,B3,B7.

Stearns, Peter. 2004. Letters from Peter Stearns to Caroline Crocker, December 23 and March 22.

Struppa, Daniele. 2005. E-mails between Caroline Crocker and Daniele Struppa, February 7-9.

Chapter 6: What Academic Freedom?

On March 1, 2005 the *Nature* magazine interview rolled around. Having never given an interview before I was extremely nervous, but bearded reporter Geoff Brumfiel quickly put me at ease. He *seemed* nice enough. Since my office was shared with two others, we found an empty lab and sat down to talk. Geoff asked some general questions about my scientific credentials, and then we came to the issue at hand.

I was careful to explain myself clearly, "My goal in teaching the evidence for and against evolution was to help the students to think about issues in an informed manner. I'm passionate about stimulating curiosity and creating lifelong learners. I'm also extremely interested in teaching critical thinking skills and advocating intellectual integrity. After all, deliberate distortion of experimental results is not good science and not informing students about inaccuracies or omissions in their textbooks is not good teaching."

"But, wasn't this all based on your religious views?"

"No, it definitely wasn't. I freely admit that I am a Christian and attend a mainline denomination church, but I made that decision when I was 18. I only began to question neo-Darwinian evolution about 20 years later. In addition, ID is not religion but an application of the methodology developed in some branches of science to detect the operation of intelligence. It says nothing about what that intelligence is."

"Did you teach creationism?"

"No, I didn't. Creationism is not synonymous with ID and I didn't teach anything about creationism. During the semesters when I gave the single lecture on evolution, I did spend a few slides on ID, but I mostly just gave the students facts about evolution; the vast majority of the quotes came from evolutionists. And, as I said, I didn't even give that lecture during the semester before I was disciplined."

I feared that he might not have heard what I said, but could only hope for the best.

Geoff then asked me if I was planning on filing a grievance against Dr. Carter.

I thought for a moment. "I don't know yet, but I'm thinking about it. I guess I'm trying to decide if it will help. The faculty handbook says that filing a grievance cannot hurt your future employment, but I would be surprised if that were true."

After the interview I e-mailed Dean Struppa, just to keep him informed and to express my concerns that the reporter from *Nature* may not have completely understood what I had said. He answered immediately with a message of encouragement, which was surprising in the light of what I read that he said in the published article in *Nature*.[125] Apparently, when asked about my situation, Daniele Struppa told them that he is a Hindu, but does not teach Hinduism in science classes. This made it clear to me that Struppa either had no idea about what had happened in my case (that I had not taught creationism or religion and had not even given that lecture during the Fall 2004 semester) or that he was being deliberately obtuse. It was also a great concern to me that the *Nature* article reported that many of the biology department faculty had said I had simply gone too far, *but none of them had ever been to a lecture*. No one had ever approached me about the situation nor asked about what I was teaching. So, I wondered what their basis was for making these comments? Why would anyone betray a colleague by making such a remark to the press? Were they fearful for their own jobs or was something else going on? It did confirm my suspicion that Dr. Carter had been discussing my case with other members of the faculty.

Meanwhile, Dr. Carter had not answered any of my e-mails and did not speak to me in the hall. Perhaps he was just uncomfortable with confrontation. Regardless, it was a very unpleasant situation and I realized that waiting and hoping for it to get better was ill-advised. The head of the grievance committee, "Dr. Anderson", contacted me and said that if I still wanted to file I would need to do it by April so that there would be time to respond. She sent me the web address for the necessary forms and evidence, as well as the procedures. At the same time I received a circular e-mail from Mary Lou, the departmental administrator, asking me about the fall cell biology teaching schedule she had attached to the e-mail.[126] Since I was not on the schedule, I could not answer her, but decided that filing a grievance was in order.

The report was to have four sections: the name of the alleged offender, a statement about which sections of the faculty handbook had been violated, pieces of evidence showing the violation had occurred, and a request for remedies sought. When doing the necessary research, what I suspected was confirmed: Not only had two sections of the handbook been violated (2.12.1 on academic freedom and 2.10.3 on not being excluded from the classroom without due process),[127] but also the 1st, 6th, and 14th amendments to the constitution. Since this seemed unbelievable, I checked these facts with my friend Tim, who is a lawyer. He concurred with my conclusions.[128] I then turned to amassing the evidence: a copy of the e-mail confirming the proceedings in the fateful meeting, three letters from students and one from a teaching assistant stating that, at no time, did I teach creationism and that I did not

---

125   Brumfiel, 2005.
126   E-mail from "Mary Lou Oakley" to Caroline Crocker, 2005. Contents can be found in Appendix III.
127   George Mason University Faculty Handbook, 2004. Contents can be found in Appendix VI.
128   Since then lawyer John Calvert has informed me, "yes to the first and 14th, but no as to the sixth."

even do that lecture during the semester preceding the discipline, and copies of the relevant pages from the faculty handbook. Finally, I added an excerpt from the university course catalog showing that teaching of evolution in the context of the *Cell Structure and Function* course was entirely appropriate, since it said that the course would cover "the chemistry, metabolism, genetics, and evolution of cells."[129]

For the "remedies sought" portion of the grievance, I requested that I be reinstated to teaching the lecture starting in the fall, negative documentation would be removed from my file, and Dr. Carter would not be the sole person in charge of evaluating my teaching performance and renewing my contract in 2007. Almost exactly a week after the e-mail from Dr. Anderson, the grievance was in the mailboxes of each member of the committee.[130] I also put a copy in Dr. Carter's mailbox.

And so I continued teaching labs with a cloud of uncertainty about my future hanging over my head. Even more difficult was the fact that the students grumbled about the lecture teachers, Dr. Carter and an apparently inexperienced lady who taught the other lecture section. I felt for the lecturers. After all, I was sure that students had also complained about me—I do not know of any teacher who escapes this kind of treatment.

"Dr. Crocker, we're way behind in the syllabus. We won't get to enzymes for at least a week. So, how are we supposed to understand this lab?" asked a student seated in the front row, Abdul.

I stopped my explanation of the procedure. "You were supposed to have covered enzymes last week," I stated in surprise.

"Well, we didn't. In fact, at this rate, we won't have covered even two thirds of the set material by the end of semester," answered another student, Karim, looking disgusted.

"Oh…well, if I have to take time to explain enzymes to you, there won't be time to finish the lab. It's a long one." I thought about it for a minute. "I know, we'll just team up the class to do the exercise. Each table will do one part of the experiment and you can share the data." I then went on to give a lecture on enzymes during lab time.

The other lab teachers also complained about this problem. Many of them were not qualified to do the required teaching, but had no choice because the lecturers were so far behind that the students had not yet come across the material covered in the labs.

So, even though I had been banned from doing the lecture part of the course, I found that I was lecturing anyway. It became common practice for me to preface

---

129   http://www.gmu.edu/catalog/0405/courses/biol.html Contents can be found in Appendix VI.
130   Letter from Caroline Crocker to College of Arts and Science Grievance Committee, March 11, 2005. A copy can be found in Appendix IV.

every lab with a lecture on the material simply because the lecturers were running so far behind. Here I found the course workbook I was writing to be very helpful, since I'd been working on presenting the same concepts pictorially. A diagram could easily be posted on the blackboard and the students told me that the shortened lectures I gave in lab were clearer than what they were getting in class.

During lab one day, several students approached me. "Dr. Crocker, why aren't you giving the lectures? You were listed as a teacher in the printed schedule of classes," asked Karim.

"I know. There were some last minute adjustments, so I'm doing labs this semester." I tried to continue walking around the classroom so I wouldn't have to answer any more questions.

Karim was persistent, "But, why? I took you last semester (and failed because I didn't study) and now I have Dr. Carter. He's using the exact same techniques for teaching of the lecture part of the course as you did: pop quizzes, worksheets, and pre-exam study sessions."

I pretended I had not heard. However, if imitation is the sincerest form of flattery, Dr. Carter obviously thought I was an excellent teacher, despite his silence about these things on the teacher evaluation.

"Yeah," Abdul, who was also retaking the course, joined in, "but with a big difference. He's lazy. He uses the book's PowerPoints and just reads from them. His exams are a joke. They come straight from the book's website and even have the little clickable boxes still on them."

Rachael, a gentle blond, stuck up for Dr. Carter, "I like him. The exams are easy since you know the questions ahead of time. Also, I think his explanations are very helpful, even if he is behind in the syllabus."

Her friend, Katie, replied, "Yeah, but he's obviously bored stiff by the whole topic."

Ling, the last person in that lab group, was finally stirred up enough to participate in the discussion. "Well, you guys are lucky. I have Ms. Novelle as my teacher and she isn't even a cell bio teacher. She's got no idea what she's doing."

It was amazing what you could overhear in lab class. I felt bad for the other teachers—I knew how student criticism, justified and unjustified, felt. However, I pretended I did not hear and just continued my rounds, making sure the students were doing the experiment correctly. But, I did wonder why Dr. Carter still refused to communicate with me, even though he obviously did not enjoy the teaching. In particular, I continued to wonder about my "discipline" for an unsubstantiated allegation. Surely there was more to this than a difference in opinion about whether both sides of a scientific issue should be taught!

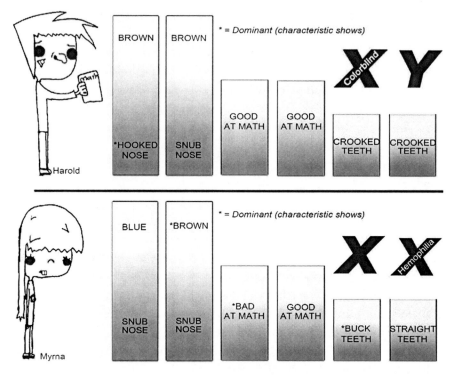

Figure 10 *Here we have Harold and Myrna with their four pairs of chromosomes next to them. Each rectangle depicts one chromosome containing one or more specified "genes" coding for specific characteristics. The characteristic with an asterisk is dominant. Thus, since having a hooked nose is dominant to having a snub nose (in our example), Harold has a hooked nose. Poor Myrna, on the other hand, failed math and has buck teeth. Note that Harold also has an X and a Y sex chromosome and carries color blindness on his X. His clothes never match. Myrna carries hemophilia on one of her X's, but since she also has an unmutated X, she is healthy. Her sons, however, have a 50% chance of being hemophiliacs.[131]*

Putting these questions aside, I prepared to teach one of the labs I'd written for helping students understand cell division and genetics. Because I'd noticed that the vocabulary of genetics[132] was confusing to students, I spent time brainstorming on a way to demonstrate some of the concepts in an interactively. While still part-time at NVCC, I hit on the idea of making chromosomes out of cardboard that had various heritable traits or "genes" written on them (blue or brown eyes, hooked or snub nose, bow legs or pigeon toes, good at math or bad at school, crooked teeth or buck teeth). These were put into a Ziploc bag with a drawing of the mythological person

---

131   In reality, these characteristics are encoded by combinations of genes (sometimes hundreds) and people have more than four pairs of chromosomes (23). However, this exercise was created for the purpose of teaching students about cell division and inheritance in a hands-on fashion and additional complexity would have been counter-productive.

132   Definitions can be found in Appendix I.

(Edna, Gertrude, Myrna, Harold, Albert, and Edwin) illustrating the characteristics encoded in their genes (Figure 10). After seeing them during the previous semester, Dr. Carter requested that I produce enough of these for all the cell biology labs and have them laminated. I did and as far as I know, they are still in use.

I would then take the students through the story of their "person," starting with childhood and ending with their offspring.

"Now, on the bench in front of each group there are the chromosomes of a mythical girl or boy. You know they're mythical because they only have four pairs of chromosomes and they are made of cardboard."

"Dr. Crocker, our person is really ugly. Can we trade?"

"No. Now, your person has reached five years old and while running, fell down and skinned their knee. They need to make new skin cells to cover the scrape. How does this happen?"

Rachael, one of the brighter students, answered, "By mitosis."

"Good! Now, we are all going to put our chromosomes through mitosis or cell division to see how an identical cell is made." And so, the groups of students were led through the necessary cell replication events by executing them using the laminated chromosomes on their lab bench. Although I had previously walked through mitosis on the board for my students, it was always instructive to see how much (or little) of the information penetrated their thinking. Most groups would require help in translating their head knowledge into "doing it" on the lab bench. Physically manipulating the chromosomes through the processes involved in cell division seemed to cement a better understanding in their heads.

"Okay, now your person has reached puberty. So, pretend that the bench in front of you is an ovary or a testicle, depending on the sex of your person."

"Dr. Crocker, those girls are looking at our testicles!"

"We are not!"

Laughter ensued.

I was glad that the students were enjoying the lab. This would actually help the learning process.

"Now, how are sperm and egg cells made?"

Again Rachael answered, "Meiosis."

"Right, so what has to happen first in meiosis or cell division to make gametes?"

My students remembered what I told them about mitosis and applied their knowledge, "The DNA has to be replicated."

We then went through the steps of meiosis, showing how the cell division to make eggs and sperm (meiosis) differed from that to make new skin cells (mitosis).

"Alright, now you have either sperm or eggs in front of you. The generic term for these is gametes. Your subject has grown up and needs a partner. Find a lab group with a "person" the opposite sex of your subject, get married, and then make a baby."

Abdul looked confused. "How?" he asked, scratching his head.

The room exploded with laughter and he turned red, realizing what he had asked. His buddies were not shy about explaining the process!

I waited for the uproar to settle and then explained, "Give your partner one of your gametes. They will join it to one of theirs. Then get one of their gametes and join it to one of yours. These will grow and be born as babies."

The students roamed around the class looking for a suitable partner and finally settled down with their "babies." Unfortunately, the giggling started again when I had to remind one group that two females cannot make a baby together, even though the cardboard chromosomes on the lab bench do not make this obvious.

As a final part of the exercise, I had the students look at the genes found on the chromosomes and decide what characteristics their "baby" would display. This was a good exercise in learning about dominant and recessive genes, co-dominance, and sex-linked traits. At the end, I was gratified when one student told me that she had learned more about genetics in that one lab than in an entire course taken the previous semester.

* * * *

After waiting for a month to hear from the grievance committee, I e-mailed Dr. Anderson and asked if Dr. Carter had responded to the grievance and, if so, when I would get a copy of it. She answered on April 7, 2005, saying that he had written to the committee, but did not answer as to whether I would get a copy.

Concerned by the inequity of the treatment, where the hurt party was required to disclose all immediately, but it seemed as if the perpetrator of the offense could keep his response secret, I spoke with a personal friend, the Reverend Canon George I. Kovoor, who also happened to be the president of a college in the UK and chaplain to the Queen of England. He strongly advised I bring in legal counsel. Since I did not have money for this kind of thing, I talked about the details of the case with my friend Tim, showing him the relevant documents

Tim, being a lawyer, sat quietly reading for a time and then responded. "This is a very strong case, even in a civil court. But, what measures will you be allowed to take to be sure that the hearing is fair?"

"What do you suggest?"

"Well, if possible, I suggest taping the meeting. That way no one can dispute what was said or not said." Tim frowned as he thought further. "If they won't allow this, you should at least be allowed to have a friendly faculty member present as a witness."

This seemed reasonable to me so I e-mailed Dr. Anderson with a list of questions, receiving a reply with the time of the hearing, but nothing else. Feeling the need for some support, I then e-mailed the supportive faculty at the university and asked for a meeting. It felt as if the biology faculty were avoiding me and now it seemed that I would not be granted equal access to information before the grievance procedure. I still had not received Dr. Carter's answer and now Dr. Anderson was not answering my questions about the nature of the hearing and whether taping would be allowed. The supportive non-biology faculty members agreed to meet and were sympathetic, but expressed their doubts that much could be done for me. However, two of them wrote letters of support for me to Dr. Anderson and Dr. Black volunteered to accompany me to the hearing. I was grateful for their friendship.

Just five days before the hearing, on April 27, 2005, I finally received a response to my questions from Dr. Anderson where she told the truth: Dr. Carter had not yet sent in his response to them, but had been ordered to do this by the Friday before the Monday of the hearing.[133] At the hearing I would be allowed fifteen minutes to speak and answer questions, then Dr. Carter would get fifteen minutes, and then the committee would deliberate and make their decision. In addition, I would not be allowed to tape the hearing. The inequity of the treatment bothered me, but I was now committed and had no choice but to proceed. I knew that the committee was supposed to be impartial and I had a forlorn hope that the hearing would be fair, but that belief was growing increasingly shaky.

On Friday, April 29, 2005, I finally received Dr. Carter's response to my complaint. It astounded me with the number of points that I felt to be inaccurate.[134] He first claimed that, as the associate chair, he had the right to decide who should teach the lecture and who should teach the lab (true) and removing me from the lecture was just him exercising his right to do that. But, this completely begged the issue of him withdrawing me from teaching the lecture at the last minute, after the catalog had been published, and then *telling me and others* that the reason for it was to *discipline* me for teaching creationism. It was also strangely inconsistent with his demand that my contract be changed to reflect my lecturing responsibilities. Next, he went back to his old claim that rights in the Faculty Handbook only apply to tenure-track faculty, an assertion

---

133   E-mail from "Karen Anderson" to Caroline Crocker, April 27, 2005. Contents can be found in Appendix IV.
134   "Peter Carter's" response to the Grievance document, April 29, 2005. Contents can be found in Appendix IV.

that the committee had already found to be false. He also claimed that I was not excluded from the classroom, merely reassigned to classes I was better at teaching, again seeming to forget that I was *told* I was being disciplined and that both Mary Lou, the departmental administrator, and Dr. Sullivan had confirmed this, not to mention all the faculty members who spoke with the *Nature* reporter.

In the next breathtaking paragraph Dr. Carter claimed that I had been removed from teaching because I was a "below-average" teacher and that I had been warned about this repeatedly. This assertion blind-sided me since I had received two commendations from the provost[135] and been offered three grants in the last two years.[136] Also, Dr. Carter had no real way of knowing what kind of teacher I was. He had never been to one of my lectures, despite my continued pleas that he come and visit my class. He had not even attended the poster presentation given by my TA, Don, showing the improvement in student grades after implementation of the strategies the TA and I developed.[137] In fact, he had assessed me solely based on student evaluations and, evidently, his personal issues with anyone who suggests any scientific problems with the theory of evolution. As I had told Dr. Carter at the meeting with him that we had right before he assigned me to teach *two* lecture sections, student evaluations alone are not a good measure for teachers who are strict about tardiness and cheating. At that time, Dr. Carter agreed and had instructed me to carry on as I had been. Documentation to this effect had been placed in my file. This fact that he had assigned me to teach two lectures right after the supposedly low student evaluations was not mentioned in his response.[138] He also did not mention that, even as the grievance procedure was in progress, he was using the labs I had written and the very teaching methods for his lectures that I had developed while working on the CTE grant. Not exactly what you would think he would do with the teaching approach developed by a "bad" teacher like myself.

In addition, Dr. Carter went on to claim that I was on a 9 month, not a three-year contract. This flabbergasted me because it seemed that it would be so easy to prove him wrong. I had e-mails asking about the fall semester from the departmental administrator,[139] a workbook contract with Kendall-Hunt,[140] and of course the contract—or so I thought. Then, I remembered that when Dr. Carter had me sign the new contract to allow me to teach two lectures in the fall

135   Letters from Peter Stearns, George Mason University Provost, to Caroline Crocker, May, 2004 and December, 2004. Copies can be found in Appendix III.
136   Copies of the first pages of the TAC and CTE grant applications can be found in Appendix VI.
137   Willcox, Poster presented February 9, 2004. Copy can be found in Appendix V.
138   Contract of Caroline Crocker with George Mason University, 2004. Copy can be found in Appendix VI.
139   E-mails between "Mary Lou Oakley" and Caroline Crocker, February and May, 2005. Contents can be found in Appendix III.
140   E-mails between Curtis Ross and Caroline Crocker, 2005. Contents can be found in Appendix V.

and one in the spring, I had been unable to make a copy, being in the middle of a class and had not received the copy he promised. Therefore, I immediately requested a copy of my contract from Human Resources, but knew it would not arrive until after the grievance hearing.

Finally, Dr. Carter alledged that the complaints from students had come in the spring of 2003, not December 2004 when he implemented my discipline, and that they had refused to put them in writing. He then claimed he requested that I remove evolution from the syllabus and that I had done so. The fact that my syllabi did not and had never shown this did not seem to faze him. He claimed that so much time was spent on evolution that I had not been able to cover the other course material, which was again easily falsified.[141] I always covered all the assigned material unlike those who taught the course during the time I was being "disciplined." Finally, Dr. Carter wrote that the cell biology course should not include evolution, backing it up with syllabi from other teachers who had taught it in the past. The facts that the course description included evolution of cells as a topic, the assigned text talks about evolution in almost every chapter,[142] and that Dr. Alekseev mentioned evolution in almost every lecture were not mentioned.

Although it was not easy to produce a response in the three days he left me, I e-mailed a rebuttal responding to all the erroneous and misleading points by the next day to the members of the committee.[143] I also sent several letters from students and faculty supporting my claims.

I wish to lend my professional support for Dr. I. Caroline Crocker and her 'Reinstatement of Dr. Crocker's Current Term Teaching Position in the Department of Molecular and Microbiology.' In a professional capacity at GMU I have known Caroline for several years. I am also knowledgeable of the general facts surrounding this particular case. I also have been both an administrator and a professor at GMU for twenty years and in that capacity I have both defended and cherished the vision of our wonderful university as a community of scholars dedicated to preserving and 'evolving' the emergent concept of a great and highly diversified place of learning and sharing ideas and lives. I am both aware and a defender of our Provost's and President's stands on both diversity and academic freedom for faculty and students. Moreover I am highly respectful of the important responsibility your [grievance] committee maintains, and I am a supporter of due processes for GMU faculty as defined in the GMU Faculty Handbook. Thank you for allowing me to submit this letter of support for the current case.

---

141 Letter from student to Caroline Crocker, December 19, 2004. Contents can be found in Appendix II.
142 Campbell and Reece, 2002.
143 E-mail from Caroline Crocker to College of Arts and Science Grievance Committee, 4/29/05.

I have first hand knowledge of Dr Crocker's academic speaking and lecturing characteristics. I have attended lectures by her and have witnessed the following characteristics of her presentation style:

1. Excellent audience eye personal contact.
2. Friendly and supportive audience manners.
3. Enthusiasm in the entertaining of audience questions.
   Excellent preparation of lecture materials.
4. Openness to alternative ideas and opinions from the audience.
5. Excellent pre-preparation of visual aids.
6. Focus and reinforcement of the topic of the presentations.
7. Deep knowledge of the material.[144]

Finally the day of the hearing arrived. I walked across the campus on May 2 of 2005 towards the designated building, trying to enjoy the sunshine, blossoms on the trees, the smell of freshly-cut grass and the breeze on my face. But, in spite of my whispered prayers, my hands were moist and my stomach was churning. As I entered the building, I noticed Dr. Murray Black, the full professor and former Dean in Engineering who had volunteered to accompany me.

A tall, handsome man in his 60's, he bent towards me and asked compassionately, "Hi. How are you coping?"

I tried to quell the tremor in my voice, "Oh, I'm okay. Just a little nervous. I'll be glad when it's over."

Dr. Black led me towards the waiting room. "I've been here for a while. This is where I was told we have to wait. Let's have a seat."

We sat down and I began to show him the papers I had prepared, rebutting Dr. Carter's assertions. Among them were several supportive student and faculty letters.[145, 146, 147] The door opened and Dr. Anderson poked her head around. "We'll be ready for you in five minutes."

"Okay, and I wanted to ask….can Dr. Black come in with me? He won't say anything."

"I'll ask the committee," she answered with a discouraging frown.

Dr. Anderson soon returned, "No, you have to come in alone." She then left, closing the door behind her. Since I was also not allowed to tape the pro-

---

144 Letter from Dr. David Rine to College of Arts and Science Grievance Committee, May 2005. Copy can be found in Appendix III.
145 Letter from Donald Willcox to "Karen Anderson", April 26, 2005. The entire letter can be found in Appendix II.
146 Letter from Chemistry student to faculty, January 31, 2005. The author's identity has been withheld at their request. The entire letter can be found in Appendix II.
147 Letter from pre-dental student to "Karen Anderson", April 2005.

ceedings, this effectively meant there would be no record of what went on. After reading Dr. Carter's document, I was pretty insecure about being treated fairly.

Dr. Black sighed, "That's disappointing. Well, let's pray before you go in."[148]

We bowed our heads, committed the time to the Lord, and all too soon it was time for me to enter the lion's den. Tim had been willing to come, but I did not want to inflame matters by bringing legal counsel. Now as I went in alone I was re-thinking that decision.

The first thing I noticed as I entered the room was how stuffy and dark it was. Four people were seated at a long table that nearly filled the room, three opposite me, and Dr. Anderson beside me. First they asked me for my statement. In response I briefly outlined the essence of my grievance and then summarized my rebuttal of Dr. Carter's answer to it.[149] I looked at their faces and wondered if they had been told to sit in stony silence. None of them showed even a flicker of interest and I certainly received no encouraging smiles. I wondered if they'd been listening at all. Perhaps this was what they perceived as "being impartial"? When I finished, a little nonplussed by the total lack of human reaction, the committee members had several questions for me.

"Dr. Crocker, academic freedom provides for the discussion of subjects that have some recognition within the scholarly community. Has intelligent design ever been published in the scientific literature?"

I was distressed because they obviously had not heard me say that I *had not done that lecture in the semester preceding the discipline*.[150] In addition, most of my lecture on evolution in previous semesters had merely given the scientific evidence for and against evolution, which was well documented; I'd taught very little about ID.[151] However, I decided to just answer the question, "Well, I know that lots of books written by heavily credentialed people have been published and I have been told that there are papers out there, not the least of which is the paper that was published causing Rick Sternberg to be penalized by the Smithsonian."

---

148 Even several years later, Dr. Black remembered this incident in an e-mail sent 2/27/09. "I do remember the rejection that I received when I asked if I could either testify or at least attend your appeal hearing before the College of Arts and Sciences Appeals Committee. I may have that title incorrect. Otherwise, I recall meeting with you, John, and Dave and on your behalf, I recall being rather frustrated about the situation. I also met with my old friend Don Kelso, and he was very nice, and in a rather "non-committal" way, I sensed that he was sympathetic to a point. He did mention in passing that the department had ruling regarding evolution-creation, but frankly, I have forgotten the details of what he said."

149 E-mail from Caroline Crocker to College of Arts and Science Grievance Committee, April 29, 2005. A copy can be found in Appendix IV.

150 Letter from a student to Faculty, December 19, 2004. The author's identity has been withheld by request. A copy can be found in Appendix II.

151 Letters from students to Caroline Crocker and College of Arts and Science Grievance Committee, December 22, 2004 and May 4, 2005. The author's identities have been withheld by request. Copies may be found in Appendix II.

"Can you give us references for any of these papers?"

I shook my head, "No, I'm too nervous for much of anything to come out of my memory, but I will e-mail each of you a list as soon as I get to a computer."[152] I then promised, "That will be today."[153]

They changed their approach. "Do you believe that a course coordinator has the right to choose what should be taught in his course?"

It sounded like they had read what Dr. Carter had written, but not my response to it. I tried to be clear. "Yes, he or she should decide which book and chapters are covered, basically deciding on the course objectives. But, I believe that the professionalism of the teachers should be recognized and they have the freedom to decide in what order and manner they feel the assigned subjects are best taught."

"By teaching creationism, which is outside the scope of the cell biology course, you used time that should have been used for teaching the set subjects," one man said in an accusatory tone.

Again, although unsuccessfully, I tried to set the record straight, "I did not teach creationism. You have several letters in front of you from students testifying to that." I put additional letters on the table. "Here are some more." They did not pick them up, so I continued my defense. "In addition, I covered all the assigned subjects and chapters, not leaving any out."

"But, evolution is not a set subject for cell biology."

I shook my head, "That isn't true. Evolution is mentioned in every chapter of the text and is specifically listed in the course description."

One of the men leafed through his papers until he found the course description, "What is listed is evolution of cells, not of organisms. You talked about experiments involving organisms."

I found it hard to believe the hair-splitting. "Yes, in that one lecture out of the total of about twenty-five 75 minute lectures, I did briefly mention evolution of species for the sake of completeness, but I spent much more time on DNA and proteins. Actually, Darwin did not know much about cells, so he did not cover evolution of cells either. I also spent much less time on it than I would have had I talked about evolution in every lecture like Dr. Alekseev, whose notes I referenced before I began teaching here."

I did not understand their concern when I *had* actually covered the *entire* set of assigned subjects every semester. This was not easy because there was a *lot* of set material. I knew that Dr. Carter had not accomplished this in the current semester because the students told me they were worried about how they

152   E-mail from Caroline Crocker to College of Arts and Science Grievance Committee, May 2, 2005. Contents can be found in Appendix IV.
153   http://www.discovery.org/scripts/viewDB/index.php?command=view&id=2640

would cope with future courses, having been inadequately prepared. However, the committee had clearly been kept ignorant of this fact.

"Looking at the slides from that lecture, I see you also have cartoons," a committee member pointed out reproachfully.

I was astonished. Surely they were not suggesting that lectures must be humorless. "I find that students learn better when they are engaged. I put a couple of cartoons in all my lectures and often use funny pictures. I think it helps them to remember. I know that when I was at university I found the jokes helpful for remembering material." I looked around the room to find some indication of understanding. I was disappointed. The faces looked as if they were made of rock.

Finally, Dr. Anderson looked at her watch. "Okay, our time's up. We'll meet with Dr. Carter, spend some time deliberating and let Dean Struppa know what we decide. He will then let you know the verdict."

I left the room and found Dr. Black waiting for me. "How was it?"

"Well, the best thing I can say is that it's over. But, I don't think they have any intention of helping me or giving me justice."

I went home, looked up and found references for many scientific papers questioning tenants of Darwinism published in reputable journals such as *The Journal of Molecular Biology*,[154] *Annual Review of Genetics*,[155] and *The Proceedings of the Biological Society of Washington*[156] and immediately e-mailed them to the committee. I also found an article on irreducible complexity published in the journal *Philosophy of Science*,[157] and many books published by mainstream publishers sympathetic to intelligent design. Even though several of the faculty wrote supportive comments about me to the committee, I didn't have much hope that it would make a difference. An excerpt from Dr. Black's letter follows:

> My concern in this case is the manner in which the change was handled. I believe that the rights of Dr. Crocker were violated and due process was not followed. At the very minimum, the process was not handled in a professional manner that I would expect of any chair at our university. Apparently, Dr. Crocker was told of "students and faculty" complaining that she was "teaching creationism" (nothing about her technical competence in teaching). The issue of the appropriateness of creationism is one I shall not deal with at this point. Rather, I am concerned that apparently none of the faculty ever heard her teach at all and none ever approached her about what

---

154   Axe, 2000.
155   Lönnig and Saedler, 2002.
156   Meyer, 2004.
157   Behe, 2000.

or how she was teaching her class. In fact from what I observe, Dr. Crocker is a very thorough teacher…[158]

I still did not understand the lengths to which people will go to silence someone who exercises their right to teach objectively, but I was going to find out.

The *Nature* article had been published just a few days before my hearing. Reading it, I felt it was slanted towards presenting Darwin doubters as religiously motivated, but the article overall wasn't as bad as I had feared. What I was not prepared for was the reaction of the public. Although I did get a nice e-mail from a self-identified creationist who was happy thinking that I was teaching creationism, I also received several very nasty e-mails and one misspelled and extremely unpleasant letter. The basic message of all of these was that, in their opinion, "You are a *&&%$# idiot and deserve to be fired," for even questioning neo-Darwinian evolution. I tried to reply to the most reasonable of the negative e-mails, thinking that maybe the person would value a mature conversation, but his response showed me that he really did not want to do more than vent his anger and call me names. I deleted the e-mails, seeing no advantage in keeping them.

It was with great relief when, a few days later, I boarded the airplane with my husband Richard and one of our sons, bound for a short vacation in Florida. We spent several lazy days at the beach, visited Cape Canaveral, and enjoyed fresh seafood. The only work I took was the semi-final copy of the cell biology workbook, which I finished while the men played pool. It was a very necessary break, especially in view of what was yet to come.

* * * *

The first thing Richard always does when coming home is to check the mail and this day was no different. On the top of the pile was a slim letter from GMU, containing my contract. Now, at last, I would be able to disprove Dr. Carter's persistent claim that my contract was over, so giving me teaching in the fall was impossible. I unfolded the paper, began reading how I was to teach two lecture sections in the fall and one in the spring (I had not been allowed to do this, but guessed this breach of contract did not matter) and then came to the length of my term. A wave of dizziness hit me as I read that my contract was for nine months and was now over.[159] "Richard, look at this. It says my contract expires now, not in two years time!"

---

158   Letter from Dr. Murray Black to College of Arts and Science Grievance Committee, May 3, 2005, A copy of this letter can be found in Appendix III.
159   Contract between Caroline Crocker and George Mason University, April 20, 2004. Contents can be found in Appendix VI.

Richard looked over my shoulder. "I'm sure that isn't the contract I saw last year. That one was for three years; I remember we kept looking at it because we were so happy. I'm pretty sure that one was also a more generic contract and did not specify the amount of lecture teaching you would do."

Then, I remembered. After asking me to do two lectures, Dr. Carter had said that my contract would need to be changed. I'd agreed to sign another one and he had presented me with the new one while I was with students. I'd signed without reading it, especially since he was hurrying me saying that the contract was already overdue in the Dean's office, even instructing me to backdate it. I remembered throwing away the old contract in obedience to his request, having seen no good reason to keep it. Because the new contract had been signed so late, I'd not been provided with a copy in the hurry to get it sent to the Dean's office.

All the peace I had gained during the vacation fled. I was frantic. It seemed to me that Dr. Carter had set me up for this over a year ago. After all, he wrote he received the oral complaint about my teaching well before this "discipline" was instigated. And, in retrospect, it was strange that he asked me to teach *two* lecture sections *after* receiving a complaint. But, how could I prove it? I immediately went to the GMU Human Resources department. Of course, Dr. Carter had already had plenty of time to do something about old records, but I didn't believe that he would stoop to that level or that the corruption would be that widespread. I asked to see my files. The lady behind the counter looked worried. "Just a minute, I need to see if that's allowed."

I waited for 45 minutes and then asked again. This time, I was taken to a little room and given a slender file. In it was a copy of the new contract, but nothing else. There were no copies of degree certificates, no documentation of yearly reviews, no letters from references, no copy of my document requesting to be paid monthly, not even my letter of application. I could not prove anything, but it looked like the file in the Human Resources office had been cleansed, perhaps as a result of a phone call made during the 45 minutes that I was made to wait. Then again, I surmised that if Dr. Carter had been planning this for some time, there would have been plenty of time to cover his tracks prior to that day. I could see that it was unlikely I would ever find a copy of the original contract or that I would find anyone willing to admit that they typed it. In fact, since the end of semester, I'd found that no one in the GMU biology department answered my phone calls or e-mails. In March of 2009 I tried to get in contact with Mary Lou, the administrative assistant who had dealt with the contract, through a mutual friend. Her response was to request that the friend not divulge Mary Lou's phone number to me and to tell me to talk to the GMU lawyers. Since I had not yet made public the fact that there were issues with my contract, this was suspicious in the extreme. I wondered if both then and now the GMU staff and faculty were following orders.

However, I did know some faculty members who would put honor above orders. One of those was Dr. John Evans, an astrophysicist and former Graduate Dean who had chaired the Physics and Astronomy Department. It was he who first told me of the GMU Physics and Astronomy Department policy of reinstating term faculty on contracts for either the same length of time or for a longer period, if they were to be renewed. He had rejoiced with me when I received the three year contract and was amazed when I told him of the switch.

Later during a meeting of the Physics and Astronomy Department termfaculty committee, Dr. Evans discussed my particular case in the Biology Department. The committee's policy recommendation for the Physics and Astronomy Department was that as standard procedure all changes in an amended contract should be explicitly made known to the term faculty member before the document was signed. Unfortunately, Dr. Evans' workload as a graduate program advisor and active researcher meant that he could not follow up my case.[160] Dr. David Rine also remembered the three-year contract and was astonished by its replacement,[161] but how could the one-year contract be challenged when I had indeed signed it?

The next day I went to GMU to pick up the ruling on the grievance. It was brief, stating that Dr. Carter had not done anything wrong in removing me from teaching and that I would not be reinstated because my contract was over. It also said that no negative documentation had been added to my record.[162, 163] Of course, I knew by then that *all* documentation, negative and positive, was missing.

The final blow of the semester came with an e-mail from the acquisitions editor at Kendall Hunt Publishers. Wanting to be honest, I had told Curtis Ross that I might not be teaching in the fall. He was astounded at the reason, but regretfully told me that Kendall Hunt would not be able to publish the workbook because I could not guarantee producing the students to buy it.[164] This was entirely reasonable, but at that point, it felt like rejection. I'd spent almost every evening that semester writing the book and creating the illustrations that would make cell biology, a difficult course, accessible to the average student. The methods used had been proven to improve grades and student retention of material. Could this really be the result of spending a few minutes explaining to students why some aspects of evolutionary theory remain controversial?

---

160   Telephone interview of J.C. Evans by Caroline Crocker, March 2009.
161   E-mail from David Rine to Caroline Crocker, March 4, 2009. Contents can be found in Appendix III.
162   Letter from College of Arts and Science Grievance Committee to Daniele Struppa, May 9, 2005. Contents can be found in Appendix IV.
163   Letter from Daniele Struppa to Caroline Crocker, May 17, 2005. A copy can be found in Appendix IV.
164   E-mails between Curtis Ross and Caroline Crocker, 2005. Contents can be found in Appendix V.

REFERENCES

"Anderson, Karen." 2005. E-mail from "Karen Anderson" to Caroline Crocker. April 27.

Anonymous. 2002. Letter from chemistry student to faculty, January 31. The author's identity has been withheld by request.

Anonymous. 2004. Letter from pre-dental student to "Karen Anderson", April. The author's identity has been withheld by request.

Anonymous. 2004. Letter from pre-med student to Caroline Crocker, December 22. The author's identity has been withheld by request.

Anonymous. 2004. Letter from student to faculty, December 19. The author's identity has been withheld by request.

Anonymous. 2005. Letter from student and GMU lawyer to "Karen Anderson", May 4. The author's identity has been withheld by request.

Axe, Douglas A. 2000. "Extreme Functional Sensitivity to Conservative Amino Acid Changes on Enzyme Exteriors," *Journal of Molecular Biology*, 301:585-595.

Behe, Michael J. 2000. *Self-Organization and Irreducibly Complex Systems: A Reply to Shanks and Joplin*, Philosophy of Science 67:155-162.

Black, Murray. 2005. Letter from Murray Black to College of Arts and Science Grievance Committee, May 3.

Brumfiel, Geoff. 2005. "Intelligent Design. Who has Designs on your Students' Minds?" *Nature* 434:1062-1065. April 28. http://www.nature.com/nature/journal/v434/n7037/box/4341062a.html

Calvert, John. 2009. E-mail from John Calvert to Caroline Crocker. April.

Campbell, Neil A. and Jane B. Reece. 2002. *Biology*. 6th Edition. San Francisco, CA: Benjamin Cummings.

Center for Teaching Excellence Grant Application, 2003.

"Carter, Peter." 2005. Response to Grievance filed with the College of Arts and Science Grievance Committee, April 29, 2005.

College of Arts and Science Grievance Committee Recommendation. 2005, May 9.

Contract between Caroline Crocker and George Mason University. April 20 2004.

Crocker, Caroline. 2005. Grievance filed with the College of Arts and Science Grievance Committee, March 11.

Crocker, Caroline. 2005. Letter from Caroline Crocker to College of Arts and Science Grievance Committee, May 2.

Crocker, Caroline. 2005. Response to "Peter Carter's" Response, April 29, 2005.

Evans, J.C. 2009. Telephone Interview of J.C. Evans by Caroline Crocker, March.

George Mason University Course Catalog for Biology, 2004 - 2005 http://www.gmu.edu/catalog/0405/courses/biol.html (as of 4/2/09).

GMU Faculty Handbook. 2004. No longer available on the Internet.

http://www.nature.com/nature/journal/v434/n7037/full/4341062a.html

Lönnig, W.-E. and H. Saedler. 2002. "Chromosome Rearrangements and Transposable Elements," *Annual Review of Genetics*, 36:389-410.

Meyer, Stephen C. 2004. "The Origin of Biological Information and the Higher Taxonomic Categories," *Proceedings of the Biological Society of Washington*, 117(2): 213-239.

"Oakley, Mary Lou." 2005. E-mails from "Mary Lou Oakley" to Caroline Crocker, February 28 and May 12.

Rine, David. 2005. Letter from David Rine to College of Arts and Science Grievance Committee, May.

Rine, David. 2009. Letter from David Rine to Caroline Crocker, March 4.

Ross, Curtis. 2005. E-mails between Kendall/Hunt Publishing Representatives and Caroline Crocker, May 20-25.

Stearns, Peter. 2004. Letter from Peter Stearns to Caroline Crocker, December 23 and March 22

Struppa, Daniele. 2005. Ruling from Dean Daniele Struppa for Caroline Crocker, May 17.

Technology Across the Curriculum Grant Applications. 2004.

Willcox, Donald. 2004. "Cell Biology Comprehension and Communication: Optimizing Large Class Instruction." Poster presented at *George Mason University Center for Teaching Excellence Conference*, February 9.

Willcox, Donald. 2005. E-mail from Donald Willcox to "Karen Anderson", April 29.

Chapter 7: Legal Help?

It was hard work to avoid sliding into depression, but the summer 2005 semester at NVCC was starting and I had work to do. I was going to pioneer a summer class in cell biology. My heart wouldn't let me give up entirely on the workbook I'd written, so I decided to make the chapters available online. That way it could be tested in a real class situation. This required a complete overhaul of the website, which kept me very busy. I was also excited because Dr. Brinkerhoff had given me a free hand as far as the labs were concerned; she gave me great opportunities that I'd not had at GMU. I tailored the labs so that they would coordinate with the course material and made use of a neighboring university's generosity in providing high-tech labs to community colleges. So, I was happily submerged in preparation for the course.

While teaching at GMU, I'd noticed that students frequently struggle with both cell and microbiology because they had forgotten math skills learned many years before. Therefore, I started the lab part of the course with a math worksheet that I'd written while at GMU. It was meant to serve as an indication for students about where a review of specific math concepts might be helpful. Even though exponents and fractions are taught in junior high school, the university students frequently found them challenging. Despite my no longer being welcome at GMU, this worksheet was still in use there and may be to this day for all I know.

Then, in addition to the usual spectrophotometry, microscope, and DNA extraction lab exercises, I added two labs designed to help familiarize students with techniques used extensively in research today: ELISA and DNA gel electrophoresis.[165] The first, otherwise known as Enzyme Linked Immunosorbent Assay, is a simple but powerful technique that is regularly used for determining concentrations of various substances in professional laboratories.

The principles behind it form the basis of many other commonly used procedures in modern research laboratories. The students were thrilled to have an opportunity to learn the technique and better prepare themselves for the science job market.

The second new lab was modeled after CSI, making it of great interest to my TV-saturated community college classes. Students were asked to ascertain the identity of a criminal based on the DNA found at the crime scene and that obtained from suspects. To do this, it was necessary to extract the DNA (we practiced this using an onion.), cut the DNA up with enzymes (the helping uni-

---

165   Definitions can be found in Appendix I.

versity did this part for us), and separate the pieces on a gel. The pattern seen for DNA from the various people is distinctive for that person, so the DNA from the crime scene could be matched to the guilty suspect (Figure 11).

Since these techniques are not just used in forensics, but also in genetic engineering work, I felt that exposure to them would be a valuable experience for the students. It was not difficult to put this together because GMU had offered a similar lab and I had written the scenario for them. Since they were now using my work, without giving credit to me, I figured I could use it, too. Basically, the students were told that the lab was the scene of a crime. An empty soda bottle had been found on the lab bench, suggesting that someone had been drinking while in the lab (against safety rules). We'd obtained saliva from the mouth of the bottle, as well as DNA samples from the teacher and the students. Their job was to ascertain who committed the crime. This made the lab a bit more interesting and it was always fun to see their faces when they discovered that the teacher was the culprit.

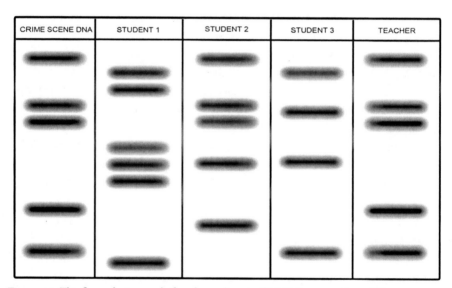

Figure 11 *This figure depicts a gel after electrophoresis of DNA fragments from different suspects. The DNA obtained from the crime scene is on the left. Since that obtained from the teacher matches the pattern from the crime scene, the teacher is guilty of breaking the lab safety rules.*[166]

Soon the semester started and I was again faced with an amazingly diverse group of students. In a class of only 22, there were people from England, Iran, Mexico, China, Korea, Iraq, Pakistan, Germany, Bulgaria, Switzerland, Uganda and of course the USA. There was no majority race or nationality and seem-

---

166   The DNA ladder has been omitted for the sake of clarity.

ingly little, if any, prejudice. In fact, the students enjoyed the mix and a lot of good-natured ribbing went on. This was diversity as it was meant to be, where everyone was accepted.

"Hey Seen," said my irrepressible Bulgarian student, Angel, while in lab class, "Meet my good friend, Sanchez." He referred to everyone as a good friend.

Sean repressed a smile. "My name is Sean, not Seen."

Carlos nodded, "And my name isn't Sanchez. It's Carlos."

Angel, who was a young man with sparkling eyes and an infectious smile, shrugged. "*Buenos dias*, Well, you know what I mean."

Although Angel was good at languages, he seemed to have problems with names. I had also heard him call Wilhelm "Sven" or "Manfred" at different times. Amazingly, Wilhelm always answered. Although the name was incorrect, at least the nationality was close and Angel was so contagiously friendly.

Thinking about the importance of names, I was reminded that thanks to the *Nature* article[167] and resultant blogs, my name was also becoming known. Early in the list of people who contacted me were two representatives, Logan Gage and Mark Ryland, from an organization called the Discovery Institute.[168] They congratulated me on my courage and asked if we could meet for lunch. Since I hadn't heard of Discovery before, I was a little suspicious. I didn't want to be associated with some of the groups I'd read about where the "experts" seemed to have little scientific credibility. But when I looked up Discovery Institute I found it to be a nonpartisan think tank for public policy with a division for research in science and culture. I read some of what they had to say and admired the scientific and philosophical solidity of their publications. In addition, I was impressed that many of the authors on the subject of evolution and intelligent design whose work I had come to admire were, in some way, associated with the institute.

Early in the summer, Richard and I met with Mark Ryland and Logan Gage at my favorite restaurant. After the usual introductions and pleasantries, these two men began to tell Richard and me about the work of the Discovery Institute in the area of evolution and intelligent design. To my surprise, they again congratulated me on my courage for publicly questioning Darwinism. I had never considered it to be particularly brave to teach students all the scientific facts about evolution or encourage them to think for themselves in an intellectually honest manner.

---

167   Brumfiel, 2005.
168   http://www.discovery.org

I smiled wryly, "I didn't mean to cause such a stir…I only wanted to give students both sides of the story presented with scientific accuracy."

Mark responded, "Didn't you realize it would be risky?"

"No, I thought universities stand for academic freedom and are a place where students are encouraged to think and form their own opinions. I guess I was pretty naïve." I felt embarrassed to have been so politically obtuse.

"Well, at least you're not alone in the struggle," Logan said encouragingly.

I was amazed. "You mean that there are others who've lost their jobs because they taught both sides of the controversy?"

"Oh yes, and more. Rick Sternberg was an editor for *The Proceedings of the Biological Society of Washington* and was persecuted terribly for allowing a paper that favored ID to be published, even though it had been peer-reviewed by others.[169] He's only one. But, lots of scientists have been denied tenure, pushed out of jobs, harassed, and have been restricted in their work. In fact, I talk to many scientists who doubt Darwinism, but it's better for their careers if they keep these ideas to themselves. There's a list of the names of those who are public about their opinions on the Discovery site."[170]

I shook my head, "I wish I'd realized how serious this was before I allowed *Nature* to publish it. Now, I guess, I'm going to have trouble finding another job."

Logan nodded sympathetically, "Unfortunately, that's probably true."

Smiling sadly, I said, "You know, I got an e-mail a couple of days ago. It was from a Russian professor. He said, 'You in America say you have freedom, but I can question evolution!' What has happened to our freedom to think or speak?"

Here Richard joined in, "I guess if we don't keep fighting for it, we'll lose it."

Since I'm not a naturally political person, this was all rather overwhelming for me. "So, what do you guys suggest I do now?"

Mark began counting off ideas. "Well, you could just look for jobs and hope that your possible employers have not heard about you. But, employers do "Google" prospective employees. Alternatively, you could write a book or file a lawsuit and make what happened known to everyone, maybe working as a speaker. This might provide impetus for things to begin to change. Obviously,

---

169   http://www.rsternberg.net/smithsonian.php
170   This list currently numbers over 800 PhD's and MD's. It is no longer on the Discovery Institute website, but can be found at http://www.dissentfromdarwin.org. The list includes "people who hold doctorates in biological sciences, physics, chemistry, mathematics, medicine, computer science, and related disciplines from such institutions as Oxford, Cambridge, Harvard, Dartmouth, Rutgers, University of Chicago, Stanford and University of California at Berkeley. Many are also professors or researchers at major universities and research institutions such as Cambridge, Princeton, MIT, UCLA, University of Pennsylvania, University of Georgia, Tulane, Moscow State University, Chitose Institute of Science & Technology in Japan, and Ben-Gurion University in Israel."

it advances our cause if injustices like this are brought to light. But, you need to do what works best for you."

I pondered this for awhile. "You know, my fighting spirit says to go ahead and make a big noise, but I have kids in college who need me to earn money. I'm also kind of thin-skinned and really don't like people being nasty to me. I love to teach, but prefer to teach those who want to learn. I usually avoid arguments. I'll need to think about it."

Mark handed me his business card. "When you've thought it over, if you want to talk to a lawyer, let me know. I have someone I can suggest."

"Thanks. I'll be in touch," I replied. Richard and I stood up. "And, thanks for the lunch."

As Richard and I drove home, we discussed what had been proposed. Should I try to go back to teaching or should I go for a job where people were less likely to be prejudiced against Darwin-doubters? Should I try to forget the pain inflicted by the unfair treatment at GMU or should I sue them? If I decided not to sue, would this just encourage GMU and other state-funded institutions to deprive others of their academic freedom and suppress the objective teaching of accurate science? But, what about the cost to my family? How would the children handle the stress? Also, would we win a lawsuit? We certainly could not pay for a lawyer. Around and around we went.

Our decision was made a few days later when I received a phone call from Barbara Bradley Hagerty with National Public Radio (NPR). She requested an interview about what had happened at GMU to include as part of her story on Intelligent Design and Academic Freedom. I'd heard many good things about her. My husband and his boss knew her and thought this would be a good chance to have my position fairly stated. Another advantage was that she would be going out of the country for awhile, giving me a hiatus time to look for jobs and think about what to say.

Fame (or infamy) was strange to me. I'd never before had the press interested and now a *Washington Post* editorial writer was writing to me, someone from CBS "Eye on America" kept leaving phone messages, and a German newspaper reporter asked me for an interview. When I went to the controversial preview of the *Privileged Planet* at the Smithsonian,[171] I was amazed to be led around afterwards by the director of the Discovery Institute, Bruce Chapman, and introduced to David Berlinski, some of whose publications I'd read. What was more astonishing was that he said to me, "I've heard about you." When I embarked on trying to give students a balanced view of evolution and encouraging them to

---

171   Nguyen, 2005.

think through the facts in an intellectually honest manner, I never thought this would be the result. Why would the presentation of the evidence for and against a scientific theory lead to all this fuss?

But then, big advances in science have always led to controversy. The suggestions that continents move, the universe began with a Big Bang, or DNA is the genetic material were all opposed and made fun of. Even gravity was questioned when Newton first proposed it.[172] Perhaps the violent opposition to consideration of Intelligent Design is simply because ID is a relatively new concept. Regardless, neo-Darwinian evolution is a theory suffering from a number of problematic pieces of key evidence and unresolved questions and does require objective re-evaluation.

Since many scientists proposing any change in the *status quo* have been persecuted in the past, why would I expect to be treated differently? Science may be a quest after truth, but many scientists, being human, would prefer to just remain comfortable in their well-worn and well-funded, if inaccurate, theories. According to an eerily accurate "news report" in Michael Crichton's novel, *Next*,

> The ultimate lesson is that science isn't special—at least not anymore. Maybe back when Einstein talked to Neils Bohr, and there were only a few dozen imported workers in every field. But there are now three million researchers in America. It's no longer a calling, it's a career. Science is as corruptible a human activity as any other. Its practitioners aren't saints, they're human beings, and they do what human beings do—lie, cheat, steal from one another, sue, hide data, fake data, overstate their own importance, and denigrate opposing views unfairly. That's human nature. It isn't going to change.[173]

This notion was strengthened in my mind when I was invited to the GMU IDEA club to speak about the evidence on both sides of this debate. Cheryl, the coordinator, met me at the door and showed me where I should set up. I began to get my things out and she began to talk.

"Dr. Crocker, why do people get so mad about ID?"

"What do you mean?" I questioned, only half-listening, turning on the computer, getting out my notes, and attaching the microphone to my pocket.

"Well, I sent an e-mail to the profs you suggested and one of them, an evolutionist, sent back a really nasty answer." Cheryl's eyes filled with tears.

I stopped my setting up. It could wait. "Really? What did he or she say?"

---

172   Cohen and Smith, 2002, p. 12.
173   Crichton, 2006, p. 62.

Cheryl looked embarrassed at the memory, "He said that anyone who doubts Darwin is just too dumb to be bothered with and that all reputable scientists agree with him. He sounded really angry."

"Wow! That's quite a claim. I don't think all reputable scientists agree about anything. Could you forward me the e-mail?"

"Yeah, but what should I do about him? I don't want him mad at me. I tried to be very even-handed, but he really hurt me," she hesitated, "To be honest, I don't even know what I believe about evolution—I just wanted to explore the options."

The irony of the fact that this open-minded searching after truth was prohibited in academia struck me again. "Well, you could try going to talk to him and explaining the idea of the club once more, but I can't guarantee he would listen. Probably you shouldn't go alone."

Actually, Cheryl, at just 18-years-old, proved herself a woman of character and did go see this man who was three times her age. She bravely explained the purpose of the club. The result was that she won a friend and he also agreed to come and speak to the IDEA club. I was glad that it turned out this way. On a later date this professor, a professing humanist, heard me speaking about my experiences while giving a talk at another IDEA gathering. Afterwards, he came up to apologize for the conduct of his colleagues. It wasn't as good as getting a job offer, but it was nice to hear. I guess sometimes, in our passion about disagreeing with someone else's viewpoint, we forget they are also a person with feelings. How great it would be if our academic institutions really were places where people would listen to each other and consider new perspectives instead of being places of rigidly enforced indoctrination into one-sided religious dogma.

When students began to arrive, I soon heard that things at GMU had not become easier after I was banned from lecturing. Two of my former students told me, independently of one another, that the first thing they were told in their animal biology class was that they were not allowed to discuss intelligent design or creation, even though evolution would be covered extensively. Another helper at the IDEA club told me of how any announcements advertising the IDEA club in the biology building were pulled down within an hour of being posted. Therefore, when a lovely pre-med student, who had earned an A⁺ in my cell biology class, told me that she was going to do research in the evolution/ID

debate for a seminar class and that this project had been approved, alarm bells
went off in my head.

"Oh Evelyn, can't you do something else?"

"Why?" she asked in surprise.

"I just don't trust it. The department is violently opposed to even breathing
doubts about Darwin. And you want to go to medical school. I don't think getting known as a Darwin-doubter would be a good move for you. They need to
provide recommendations in order for you to get into medical school."[174]

Evelyn frowned, "The teacher didn't seem to mind. She just wants me to
be sure to give evidence for both sides of the debate."

I did not want to be paranoid, but I also wanted to protect this brilliant
young lady from those who might not hesitate to ruin her future. "Okay, just be
sure that you're careful about what you say."

"Would it also be okay for us to meet, to talk about any questions I have
about the project?"

I smiled, writing my phone number on a scrap of paper. "Sure, why don't
we get together at Starbucks. We can talk then."

As it turned out, Evelyn did stay in contact with me by e-mail up until the
time she gave her presentation, although we didn't have a chance to go for coffee.
She shared her own journey towards doubting neo-Darwinian evolution. However, after her presentation, I did not hear from her again. Cheryl, a friend of
hers, told me that this was because a group of faculty members had confronted
Evelyn about her views on evolution, leaving her shaking and in tears. It was
so painful and frightening that Evelyn had decided that in order to secure her
future she should never again mention her doubts about neo-Darwinian evolution. In addition, she resolved that she should also never again speak to me.
Unfortunately, her decision came too late; I later learned that she was denied
entrance into medical school. I found it hard to believe that this was happening
in America, where we pride ourselves on our freedoms.

After hearing about cases like this, my concerns deepened, and I decided
that investigating the possibility of a lawsuit would be in order. If nothing else,
maybe I could help others like Evelyn. I phoned Mark Ryland and requested a
meeting with him and the lawyer that he was recommending. We agreed to meet
at the Discovery Institute office in Washington D.C. and I jotted the date down.

---

174   I recently communicated with a California graduate student reporting that his/her school requires
all pre-med students to sign a document certifying that they will not challenge evolutionary theory. He/she
refused and was forced to change majors. Student's identity is withheld at their request. The case is currently
(as of 11/2009) under investigation.

I knew this might mean finding a full time job would be even more difficult, but felt it important that someone stand up for what is right.

Meanwhile, my class at NVCC was well underway. We had reached the chapter on proteins, one that was challenging to teach clearly, but fascinating to me. I always liked to start with a quotation from the former president of the National Academy of Science (NAS) in 1998, Bruce Alberts. "The entire cell can be viewed as a factory that contains an elaborate network of interlocking assembly lines, each composed of large protein machines (enzymes)...Why do we call (them) machines? Precisely because, like the machines invented by humans..., these protein assemblies contain highly coordinated moving parts."[175]

I then went on to explain that the blueprint for these protein machines (enzymes) was the DNA, which sits in a separate compartment of the cell. When enzymes need to be made, the blueprint is copied into another molecule called RNA and the RNA goes to ribosome "factories" to be used as instructions for making the enzymes. But, in order for this to occur, enzymes and proteins need to control every step of the process from making DNA to copying it into RNA, to processing the RNA, to attaching the RNA to a part of a ribosome, to putting together the entire ribosome, to attaching the parts of the enzyme protein together, to folding it when made and making sure it gets to the right place (Figure 7, Chapter 2).

A hand waved in the air. "But, Dr. Crocker, you just said that this is how enzymes are made. How can you need enzymes to make enzymes? And don't you need enzymes to copy DNA? Which came first?"

"Well, if you are asking which was there in the primordial soup, I would have to say neither. Proteins and DNA are both information-containing molecules that do not just happen. Some people say that some of the parts of RNA might have been there at the beginning,[176] but there is no suggested explanation of how information became a part of these molecules. The challenge is not only how the molecules would be made, but even more importantly, how they came to contain information."

I paused and then continued, "But, if you're asking about the cell itself, since our current understanding of cell theory is that every cell comes from a pre-existing cell, I would say the enzymes are there first." I thought for a minute. "But, if you don't have the DNA code, which you need enzymes to make, then

---

175   Alberts, 1998.
176   Francis Collins, former Director of the Human Genome Project, does not agree, "Despite substantial effort by multiple investigators, however, formation of the basic building blocks of RNA has not been achievable in a Miller-Urey type of experiment, nor has a fully self-replicating RNA been possible to design." Collins, 2006, p. 91.

you don't have a living cell. So, maybe the DNA came first…but, that got made by the previous cell."[177]

The class started to laugh. Sean piped up, "Looks like we stumped the teacher."

I smiled, "Actually, there are a lot of processes in cells where it is very hard to speculate how they could have started. And you'll be glad to know that we're going to learn about a lot of these complicated processes in great detail."

Now the class groaned. I continued the lecture.

* * * *

The time to meet with Mark Ryland and the lawyer had arrived. I took the metro into D.C. and walked to the building that houses the D.C. branch of the Discovery Institute. The office was on an upper level, so I took an elevator, stood for awhile looking for the place, and then smelled—coffee! I hoped that would be the right office and it was. The receptionist told Mark I was there and he and another debonair man emerged from a conference room. Mark shook my hand and introduced me to Edward Sisson, a partner at Arnold and Porter since January 1, 2000, a large D.C. law firm, then led us back to the conference room. The receptionist brought us coffee and I tried to relax, sipping the fragrant brew.

Edward started by telling me about his work in the 2005 Kansas evolution hearings, where many Ph.D.'s testified to the scientific gaps in the theory of evolution and many evolutionists had refused to testify. He also impressed me with his knowledge of the scientific arguments, gained by his personal reading of books by authors on both sides of the debate, as well as complex science textbooks. He had earned a bachelor of science from MIT in architecture, and had actually read, understood and retained most of the highly-detailed Bruce Alberts cell biology textbook I used in many of the classes I taught at GMU.[178] He was obviously a highly intelligent individual.

Mark then joined in, telling me that introducing me to Edward did not mean that this would be an official Discovery Institute case and that my communications with him would be confidential. The usual lawyer-client relationship would be observed. Discovery would not make a financial or indeed any contribution to my case.

---

177 "The calculations presented in this paper show that the origin of a rather accurate genetic code, not necessarily the modern one, is a *pons asinorum* which must be crossed to pass over the abyss which separates crystallography, high polymer chemistry and physics from biology. The information content of amino acids sequences cannot increase until a genetic code with an adaptor function has appeared. Nothing which even vaguely resembles a code exists in the physiochemical world. One must conclude that no valid scientific explanation of the origin of life exists at present." Yockey, 1981, p. 26.
178 Alberts, 2004.

I felt a bit overwhelmed, "Thanks, but I need to make it clear that I have no money. I'm out of a job and don't know how long it will take for me to get another. My son's college education and some of our living expenses were being paid from my salary, so really now we're just going further into debt every month. We cannot afford legal counsel."

Here Edward answered, "After I get the facts, I'll take this back to my firm and they'll decide if I can represent you *pro bono*."[179]

Then, Mark added, "If not, there are people we can contact who might be willing to sponsor a lawsuit so important for the cause."

"Okay, but just as long as you know we can't pay anything."

They assured me that if I had to pay, the case would not proceed.

Edward led the meeting with a number of questions, taking notes in true lawyer style. "When did you start working for GMU and how long did you work there?"

"I started as an adjunct microbiology lab teacher in 2001 and was hired by Dr. Sullivan as a full-time term faculty member to teach cell biology in December of 2002. She negotiated with her superiors and got me an 18 month contract. This contract was renewed by her successor, Dr. Carter, in the spring of 2004 to end in 2007. My job ended a couple of months ago."

"May, 2005?" he questioned, wanting to make sure the timeline was accurate.

"Yes, that is, I've heard nothing about going back in the fall except for two circular e-mails from the departmental administrator: one asking what kind of a classroom I require and the other asking if the teaching schedule was okay with me.[180] She has not answered my e-mail to her, in fact no one from the department, except Dr. Sullivan, has spoken to me or answered e-mails since the end of the semester." I was later to learn that this kind of silent treatment is a common experience for scientists who commit the crime of questioning Darwin.

"Okay, so let's get back to the incident that started all this. Describe what happened."

And so, Edward expertly led me through the entire ordeal, frequently asking questions on points that required clarification. I gave him copies of the original grievance, Dr. Carter's response, my response to that, the record I had kept of the proceedings during the semester, letters from students and faculty in my support, the verdict from the dean, and several other documents.[181] I also made it clear that I had not taught the offending lecture during the semester before I was disciplined. He promised to review the documents and get back to me with

---

179   For free
180   E-mails from "Mary Lou Oakley" to Caroline Crocker, 2005. Contents can be found in Appendix III.
181   Many of these documents can be found in Appendices II-IV.

an answer on whether there was a hope of winning a lawsuit and whether his firm would be willing for him to do the work *pro bono*.

Our business done, we then went on to discuss the current state of the suppression of academic freedom related to the subject of Darwinism. They asked if I knew various people, all of whom had suffered in their careers for questioning neo-Darwinian evolution. I did not, but their names were soon to become very familiar to me.

* * * *

The first summer semester at NVCC was drawing to a close and I still had not heard back from Edward. I sent him an e-mail asking if he had any news for me. Apparently, his firm was still having discussions; I would have to be patient. This was frustrating because the consequences of the dispute were having an effect on my future job prospects. I applied to a firm that specialized in placing teachers in private schools, but because I could not get a reference from GMU, I would not be listed. I applied for a position teaching general and cell biology at another local community college, but did not hear back. I did, however, meet the person who got the job while in the faculty lounge one day at NVCC. She told me, "I don't know why I got the job. I'm not at all qualified."

"What do you mean?" I questioned.

"Well, I've never taught cell biology before. I only teach anatomy and physiology."

"That's interesting. I applied for that job and didn't even get an interview. What was the interview like?"

Here she pulled a face, "It was all about evolution. I had to give a sample lecture on it and most of the questions were about my views on it."

"What are your views?" I asked her, curiously.

She hesitated, "Hmm, I guess I can tell you, I have big doubts. The science just doesn't add up. But, I needed the job, so I went with the party line."

I gathered my things, ready to leave for the day, "Well, congratulations on getting that job. It looked like a good one."

I felt rather depressed, realizing that I might not get a job teaching in academia again. My conscience would not allow me to lie to students and teach them that the information in the textbook was complete and reliable in this area. I had been interviewed at a local Christian school, but they wanted someone part-time and were specifically interested in hiring a young-earth creationist. That was not me. It seemed that few were comfortable with just teaching the science facts and letting students think for themselves. Was it really true that, in a country where freedom is highly prized, the freedom to think was not an option?

Because the law firm seemed to be dragging their feet, I decided to try and gain some justice for myself. First, I contacted J. Chapman Petersen, a friend who at the time was a State Delegate in Virginia. He is now a Democratic State Senator for Virginia. Chap was astonished at what had happened and wrote to Alan Merton, the president of GMU, on my behalf.[182] He received a letter in response stating that my contract was not renewed and that this was a neutral action on the part of the university.[183] This seemed unlikely given that the number of students at GMU increased and that they had found it necessary to hire Dr. Carter's *wife* as biology faculty to help.[184] The president did not comment on the fact that I had been *told* that I would be *disciplined* for teaching creationism (even though I didn't). Chap wrote again,[185] but it did not help.

Early in August 2005 I received a letter from Edward's firm agreeing to represent me *pro bono*. I signed and returned the contract. An appointment was made for me to meet with Edward at his Law Office. I had read on his firm's website how they have certain values, like treating each customer's case as if their reputation rests on that, building a tradition of *pro bono* service, and embracing diversity. This seemed hopeful. On the day of the appointment, I dressed up and took the metro to the city. The mammoth firm employs over 700 lawyers and the building was impressive, to say the least. I mounted stairs, announced my presence to the receptionist, and was shown to a sumptuous waiting area. After about ten minutes, Edward arrived and gave me a tour of the building, which featured an awe-inspiring open courtyard with glass running from top to bottom for several stories. He then showed me to his office. Here we discussed the past history of lawsuits regarding the freedom to teach all the scientific evidence pertaining to evolution and brainstormed about tactics we thought might work to secure some justice for me.

Edward's advice was to try the low-key route first and we settled on a letter written to the president of GMU, basically requiring that they reinstate me. There were several reasons given: 1) My original contract was for three years, 2) Being removed from teaching for disciplinary reasons without the benefit of a hearing was a violation of my constitutional rights (and a breach of the new contract), and 3) The faculty handbook provides that faculty should be allowed,

---

182   Letter from J. Chapman Petersen to Alan Merton, June 28, 2005.
183   Letter from Alan Merton to J. Chapman Petersen, July 22, 2005.
184   http://mason.gmu.edu/~dpolayes/
185   Letter from J. Chapman Petersen to Alan Merton, August 3, 2005. A copy of this series of letters can be found in Appendix VI.

"unrestricted expositions on subjects within one's field…without fear of censorship or penalty."[186] Clearly, evolution was covered in the course textbook, was listed as a topic in the course catalog,[187] and was included in the lecture notes I received from a colleague, so it was an "allowable" topic, provided the rest of the course content was covered, as it always was. However, the letter went on, I was removed from teaching because Dr. Carter believed that the scientific content of that one lecture might influence the religious beliefs of some students. Therefore, it was an act of religious discrimination, even though I did not teach religion.[188] Edward sent the letter and we anxiously waited for a response.[189]

Two weeks later a lawyer from GMU sent a letter to Edward.[190] The reply was disappointing, but not surprising. The question of academic freedom and religious discrimination was completely avoided and they merely asserted that my contract was for one year. Since my personnel file was virtually empty, without even degree certificates and reference letters, it was not surprising that the original contract would also be missing. They also claimed that Dr. Carter had removed me from teaching the lecture because of my student evaluations. This was clearly false for many reasons as explained before. The most obvious was that the evaluations are done in the spring and Dr. Carter had the results *before* assigning me to *two* instead of the usual one lecture section in the fall. Second, at the time of the evaluation I had told him about how my policy of reporting cheating and not allowing late work affected student evaluations and asked his advice. He told me to carry on in the same way. This was documented in my file. Third, I had presented numerous letters from students extolling my virtues as a teacher.[191, 192] Fourth, I had two letters from the provost congratulating me on my excellent teaching. Finally, there remained the simple fact that I was called into the office and TOLD I was going to be disciplined for teaching creationism (Dr. Carter's mischaracterization of what I had taught) and that this was why I was being removed from the lecture. No mention was made of this, even though the departmental administrator and the former interim head of the department had told me that they were aware of it.

Edward informed me that he would need to think about what the next step should be. Would it be wise to sue or would this simply ensure that I would become even more unemployable? I'd already experienced the effects of being

---

186   George Mason University Faculty Handbook
187   http://www.gmu.edu/catalog/0405/courses/biol.html
188   Calvert, 2009.
189   Letter from Edward Sisson to Alan Merton, August 15, 2005. Copy can be found in Appendix VI.
190   Letter from Alan Merton to Edward Sisson, September, 2005.
191   Various notes and e-mails from students can be found in Appendix II.
192   Recommendation for Outstanding Teacher Award, 2004. A copy can be found in Appendix V.

blacklisted and was growing anxious about my mounting bills. Because Richard had a steady job in the area, moving was not an option, even though I had job offers from two scientist friends in other states.

* * * *

Meanwhile, we had nearly reached the end of the summer semester at NVCC and I gave the lecture on the eukaryotic genome, which is the DNA contained in all cells that contain a nucleus. I started by describing the structure and talking about the difficulty of having what, in humans, amounts to 46 long strings of information.

"The average human cell is about 30 micrometers in size. That is, you could fit 10,000 of them on the head of a pin. The amount of DNA contained in each of these cells would measure 2 to 3 meters in length if it were stretched out."

Some of the students looked confused, so I tried to make it more under-standable. "So, if we were to blow up a cell to 1 cm in size, about the size of a small marble, the length of DNA packed into its nucleus would be 1000 km or over 600 miles long."

Now I could see the penny dropping.

Carlos looked amazed, "Dr. Crocker, you mean I've got six feet of DNA in me?"

"Not only that, you have six feet in each of your cells. Now, the cell has two problems. First, you can imagine how these long strings might get tangled when put in such a small space." Here, I paused. "Does anyone here have a sewing or a fishing box?" A few hands went up. "How many of you have a hopeless tangle of thread at the bottom of it?" Again, some of the students nodded. "Well, my mother-in-law loves to embroider and she has a system for not getting the threads tangled. She winds each thread around its own bobbin and puts them in order of color. That works to keep them untangled. But the cell has another problem, too. It needs to be able to find the right piece of information at the right time, so it needs to "know" where every part of the genome "thread" is kept."

A hand went up, "Can't it just read the string until it reaches the relevant part?"

"Not really," I answered, "You see, we're talking hundreds of encyclope-dias-worth of information. The cell would be in big trouble if it had to take even as long as we do to find the right encyclopedia, let alone the right page."

Angel, a student gifted in visualization of processes, began to think out loud. "Is that why people with non-familial Down's syndrome, who have an extra chromosome, but none missing, have so many symptoms? Their cells can't find the right genes?"

I nodded, "It might be. In the same way, translocation mutations, where genes trade places in the genome, also cause huge problems, possibly because the information is 'lost' to the cell. You know how, if you lose a tool, you might as well not have bought it. You can't use it either way."

Here I went on to explain the exquisite organization of the DNA. "It is first wound around proteins called histones, then gathered up with other proteins, and next, those loops are looped into a thicker thread." (Figure 12)

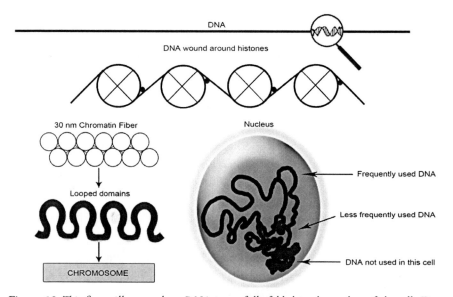

Figure 12 *This figure illustrates how DNA is carefully folded in the nucleus of the cell. First, it is wound around histone proteins, then this is condensed into a fiber that is 0.00000003 m wide. This fiber is gathered into loops and the final folding into chromosomes occurs when the cell divides. In non-dividing cells DNA that is used frequently is much less tightly folded than DNA that is used infrequently or DNA that is not used at all. This is comparable to the way we organize our homes. Those items we use a lot are out on the counter, those we use less are in a cupboard, and those that we use infrequently are packed away in the attic.*

In each cell of the body, those genes that aren't needed are packed away and those that are used frequently are available for use. Of course, which genes these are vary with the cell type. A skin cell does not need access to genes that code for liver enzymes." Since many of the students were interested in medicine, I then pointed out that this is why cancer cells are called "deranged." Not that they are crazy, but that the control of their DNA expression is messed up so they make things that they shouldn't. Of course, their growth is also out of control.

I then reviewed the way that the cell recognizes which gene to read and use by piling on lots of proteins called transcription factors, how the cell regulates how many times the gene is read, and more (Figure 13). But, transcription factors are proteins that are coded for by DNA and making these is also regulated by transcription factors. By the end of this session, most students were overwhelmed, but also in awe of the processes they had glimpsed. I had only touched the surface of the complexity, but it was enough for sophomores.

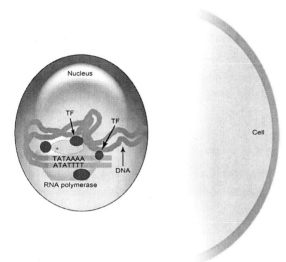

Figure 13 *This figure shows a few of the ways that the cell tells the nucleus which machine is needed on the factory floor and, thus, which gene should be copied into mRNA (mRNA is not shown in the figure). Proteins called transcription factors (TF) bind to the beginning of the required sequence, allowing the enzyme that does the copying (RNA polymerase) to begin its work. Other transcription factors bind to control sequences on the DNA as well as the promoter region of the DNA sequence to be copied; this is one way that the speed and frequency of the copying can be controlled.*[193]

Around this time I was invited to a lecture at the D.C. office of the Discovery Institute. Dr. Jonathan Wells would be speaking on his newly released book, *The Politically Incorrect Guide to Darwinism and Intelligent Design*. Since I was featured in the book, and was always interested by what this gracious and highly intelligent man had to say, I went. But, this time I came away more disturbed than enlightened, since he informed me that being known as someone who questions Darwinism would very likely result in my never securing another teaching position at a secular university. After hearing this, it was difficult to concentrate on his talk, even though I was sitting by his very sweet mother! My entire future was up in the air, and it was not a good feeling.

---

193 Control of gene expression is actually much more complex than depicted, but the above is sufficient for the purposes of this book.

REFERENCES

Alberts, Bruce, Alexander Johnson, Julian Lewis, Martin Raff, Keith Roberts, Peter Walter. 2004. *Molecular Biology of the Cell, Fourth Edition.* New York, NY: Garland Science.

Alberts, Bruce. 1998. "The Cell as a Collection of Protein Machines: Preparing the Next Generation of Molecular Biologists." Cell 92:291-294. February 8.

Anonymous. Undated. "A Scientific Dissent from Darwinism." http://www.dissentfromdarwin.org (as of 4/1/09).

Brumfiel, Geoff. 2005. "Intelligent Design. Who has Designs on your Students' Minds?" *Nature* 434:1062-1065. April 28. http://www.nature.com/nature/journal/v434/n7037/box/4341062a.html (as of 3/2/09).

Calvert, John. 2009. "Kitzmiller's error. Use of an Exclusive Rather than an Inclusive Definition of Religion." Address given at Liberty University School of Law, February 6.

Cohen, I. Bernard, G.E. Smith. 2002. *The Cambridge Companion to Newton.* Cambridge, UK: Cambridge University Press.

Collins, Francis. 2006. *The Language of God.* New York, NY: Free Press, p. 91.

Crichton, Michael. 2006. *Next.* New York, NY: Harper Collins.

Discovery Institute. http://www.discovery.org (as of 4/1/09).

George Mason University Faculty Handbook 2004. No longer available on the Internet.

Merton, Alan. 2005. Letter from Alan Merton to Edward Sisson, September.

Merton, Alan. 2005. Letter from Alan Merton to J. Chapman Petersen, July 22.

Nguyen, Tommy. 2005. "Smithsonian Distances Itself from Controversial Film." *Washington Post,* CO1, June 2. http://www.washingtonpost.com/wp-dy/content/article/2005/06/01/AR2005060101986.html (as of 4/1/09).

"Oakley, Mary Lou." 2005. E-mails from "Mary Lou Oakley" to Caroline Crocker, February 28 and May 12.

Outstanding Teacher Award Recommendation. 2004. June 17.

Petersen, J. Chapman. 2005. Letter from Chap Petersen to Alan Merton, June 28.

Petersen, J. Chapman. 2005. Letter from Chap Peterson to Alan Merton, August 3.

Sisson, Edward. 2005. Letter from Edward Sisson to Alan Merton, August 15.

Sternberg, Richard. 2008. "Smithsonian Controversy." *Richardsternberg.org.* http://www.rsternberg.net/smithsonian.php (as of 4/1/09).

University Catalog George Mason University, Biology. 2004. http://www.gmu. edu/catalog/0405/courses/biol.html (as of 4/1/09).

Various Notes and E-mails from students, 2004-5.

Yockey, Hubert P. 1981. "Self-Organization Origin of Life Scenarios and Information Theory." *Journal of Theoretical Biology,* 91(13), p. 26.

Chapter 8: We are Expelled!

So, I applied and applied and applied for jobs. I tried for teaching positions in universities, at high schools, for research positions with the government and in industry, for jobs as a science writer, and even considered getting out of science completely. Some applications required four lengthy essays and receipt was not even acknowledged. Although in our increasingly callous culture, this has become standard practice, I became a bit suspicious that many of the employers "Googled" me and decided to not even respond. After all, I was certainly well qualified, even over-qualified, for the positions to which I responded. Finally, I was offered a job teaching high school biology to aspiring ballerinas. Although an intriguing possibility, the pay was so low that it would barely have covered the cost of the commute and I decided to keep looking.

Finally, having not received any other job offers, in August I agreed to teach cell biology and general biology as an adjunct professor for NVCC. I decided to have my cell biology workbook photocopied by the college and sold to students at cost, instead of being made available on the website. I asked Dr. Brinkerhoff if this would be possible and she said she would check with the authorities. A week later the answer came back in the negative. I knew this would pose a hardship for the students, since the printing costs in the library would be considerable. When I went directly to her boss, the Dean of Math, Science and Engineering, I found that, as is so often the case, he had chosen the easy option, instead of what would be best for the students. After some discussion, where I pointed out other teachers who were doing exactly what I was proposing, the man understood that what I was requesting was not strange or unusual and he finally agreed. The books were printed and put in the bookstore at cost. It did make me wonder if the issues with academic integrity were possibly more to do with laziness than principle. After all, the teachers and administrators might have to seek further education in order to really understand scientific issues instead of just regurgitating what is in the textbooks.

Just before the beginning of term I was again contacted by Barbara Bradley Hagerty of NPR. She was back from her assignment in England.

"Thank you for agreeing to meet with me. Now, what is the best place and time for you?" Barbara asked politely.

"Well, I don't have a private office at NVCC, but we could probably find a place before or after a lecture or lab."

"That sounds good. Also, I'll want to use some background classroom noise and maybe a sound bite of your lecturing. Can I come to a lecture, maybe the one on evolution?"

"In Bio 101, that lecture does not come until the end of the semester," I answered. "It would be hard to do it earlier just because the students would not have the knowledge base to understand it."

"Alright, I can just come to another lecture. Do you mention evolution at all any other time?"

"Yes, in the first chapter of the assigned text, the book mentions the diversity of life. It also points out that life is unified; all known life forms use DNA. The book ascribes both of these observations to evolution.[194] I just say that this is one theory, but not everyone agrees on it."

"Would it be okay for me to come to that lecture?"

"Hmm, I don't know college policy for reporters coming to class, but I'm sure we could find out."

"Oh, don't worry about that. We'll get the appropriate permissions. And then we can talk further after the lecture."

Thus, it was arranged that Barbara Bradley-Hagerty would attend my first lecture that semester.

We agreed to meet outside the classroom 15 minutes before class, hopefully before too many students turned up. When I arrived, teaching materials in hand, Barbara was there already. I was a little surprised to see the huge black furry microphone; it was almost bigger than the trim, dark-haired reporter. I was clearly suffering from a lack of experience with the media. It was even more nerve-racking when I started the lecture and discovered that Barbara would follow me around as I wrote on the whiteboard, crawling on the floor in front of me, despite her elegant business suit. Naturally, it was also a bit distracting for the students, but I explained who she was and they soon became engrossed in the lecture. At the end, after answering the inevitable student questions about the coming course, I led Barbara to a relatively quiet room for the actual interview. We covered the natural questions about what I taught (and did not teach) at GMU, why I did it, and what happened as a result. I felt that the radio report generated was a fair and accurate reflection of the state of affairs, but I heard that the fall-out on Barbara was ridiculous, even including death threats. Perhaps the untenured professor who told her that voicing his doubts about evolution would be a "kiss of death" to his career had a point.[195] I feared that Barbara would not be allowed to speak on this issue again.

---

194 Campbell and Reece, 2002, Chapter 1.
195 All Things Considered with Barbara Bradley-Hagerty, November 10, 2005 on NPR, Washington DC.

* * * *

Soon afterwards I had a phone call from a teacher at a local junior high school, Mrs. Black. She wanted me to come to her class and speak about intelligent design.

"How did you get my name?" I wondered out loud.

"Oh, I'm teaching a debate class and wanted the students to learn about the evolution/Intelligent Design issue that's on the news so much. I asked my principal and was told that both sides of the debate must be presented. So, I called the (NAS) and asked them to provide both speakers, but they only had one for the Darwinism side. They suggested you for the other."

Now, I was well-aware that prominent Darwin-doubter, Dr. Phil Skell, is a member of the NAS, but they obviously preferred to keep this quiet because of his unpopular views on neo-Darwinian evolution.[196] So my surprised response was, "What? They know me?"

"I guess so."

"Wow! I had no idea I was so famous. Well, could you tell me about where your students stand with regard to their knowledge of biology? That'll help me make my presentation age-appropriate."

So, Mrs. Black gave me a run-down on their education so far. We got along very well, since teaching clearly was close to both our hearts.

"Oh yes, one more thing," she said as we prepared to hang up the phone, "Would it be acceptable for a reporter from the *Washington Post*, Shankar Vedantam, to attend?"

I did not yet have a full time job, so had to answer in the negative. The last thing I needed was more press and I didn't know this person.

Mrs. Black answered, "I think he just wants to get background on a story he's doing. I'm sure he wouldn't use your name if you didn't want him to. He seems very pleasant."

I was not happy with the situation, but decided to agree, "If that's the case, that everything is off the record, then okay. Does he seem trustworthy to you?"

"Oh yes," she repeated, "He seems like a very nice man."

And so I prepared the presentation, complete with a worksheet, and tried to explain intelligent design in terms that junior high students could grasp. Their questions revealed that some did and some did not understand the presentation, but Mrs. Black assured me that it was much more student-accessible than the presentation given the previous week by the NAS representative.

---

196 Skell, 2005.

After the talk, Shankar asked if I would be willing to tell him about what had happened to me, just off the record. He suggested we go to a nearby restaurant; the only place in the vicinity was McDonalds. So, we walked across the street and it came to be that the *Washington Post* treated me to a cheeseburger.

Shankar proved to be a very good listener (an important quality in his line of work) and drew the entire story out of me, including my hurt at the abusive e-mails and letters and my frustration at not being able to find another job. He explained that his main interest was not in the rights and wrongs of neo-Darwinian evolution versus intelligent design, but the reason why the debate seems to elicit such strong feelings. His goal was to write an article that suggested people discuss the topic as rational human beings, not resorting to name-calling and threats. It sounded like a good if underutilized idea to me, but I suspected that any further press coverage would guarantee my future as an unemployed scientist, so was reluctant to be involved. I did, however, mention to him that our church was doing a seminar series of lectures on controversial subjects and that there he could gain access to scientists with a variety of opinions ranging from subscribing to theistic evolution, intelligent design, young or old-earth creationism, or combinations of them. All of these scientists would probably be Bible-believing Christians and many were very highly regarded in their fields, heading labs at National Institute of Standards and Technology and NIH, for example. A couple of the expected participants were professors at GMU. Shankar was very interested in attending this event and we exchanged e-mail addresses.

* * * *

One thing I definitely wanted to do before putting together and printing the Cell Biology Workbook for use at NVCC was to update all the information and make it current with the most recent peer-reviewed scientific publications. Textbooks usually run two or three years behind. I also decided that it would be best not to tackle the part on evolution as one lecture, the way I had in the past, but to integrate it into the entire course, as was done by my colleagues at GMU and in many biology textbooks. Therefore, in the introductory chapter where the assigned text[197] stated that the unity and variety in life is attributed to evolution, I also introduced the reality that there is an ongoing debate about whether neo-Darwinian evolution is the best explanation of all the scientific facts. After all, one would only need to read the newspaper to be aware of the issue.

Since this textbook chapter also covered the scientific method, in my workbook I mentioned how science progresses and how some theories thought to be

---

197   Campbell and Reece, 2005, p. 15.

fact by one generation are found to be the result of incomplete understanding by the next. I felt it important to stress that scientific understanding evolves.

I challenged my students to think of some examples of how scientific understanding has been modified in the past.

"How about the way people once thought the earth was the center of the universe, and now know it's not?" asked one student.

"Yes, that's one. Any others?"

A hand waved desperately, "Oh, oh, Dr. Crocker! I know! In my microbiology course we learned that people used to think that bugs were spontaneously generated from rotten stuff, but some scientist showed that this wasn't true by sterilizing the stuff and then using a curvy neck flask."

I suppressed a smile at the lack of scientific precision in Febron's description, "Right, I think Pasteur had something to do with that. This is now called the Law of Biogenesis."

A young lady I knew to be interested in physics, Fulmala, then contributed, "Professor, in my physics course we learned that Newton's laws of motion are very good approximations, but that Einstein's theories of relativity are more accurate, especially at high speeds."

"That's right. And people are still working to refine Einstein's ideas even now." I then changed the subject slightly. "Has anyone noticed another scientific theory that is a source of debate right now?"

Many students nodded and one spoke up, "Evolution. People sure seem to get mad about that one."

"You're right. They do. So, in this course, I'm going to mention the evidence for evolution and some of the problems with that evidence. Some of you probably learned about evolution in high school. But, much of the information in this course you will never have heard before. But, at least knowing both sides of the story, you'll be able to understand the reason for the debate."

Many students looked happy about this idea, although Alex, a chubby young man seated in the front row, scowled and slumped down in his seat. I heard him mutter, "People who doubt evolution are #&%* idiots." I chose to pretend I had not noticed. Name-calling and profanity are not the best way to engage a teacher in conversation.

In my workbook, I included parts of the debate about neo-Darwinian evolution in seven of the 20 chapters, giving each point less than one slide (average of 25 slides per lecture) to evolutionary issues (about 1% of the course). For example, in the workbook chapter introducing cells and the one on cell division, it was necessary to start with Cell Theory, which is closely related to Pasteur's Law of Biogenesis. These theories/laws are not really debated among scientists, but I thought it would be interesting to invite the students just to think about whether the spontaneous generation theory of the origin of life is consistent with the accepted scientific fact that all cells come from pre-existing cells. I wanted them to think about and apply what they were learning, not just memorize and regurgitate what the professor says.

Paiva, an older woman who I grew to know quite well, piped up, "But, Dr. Crocker, the textbook says that the origin of biological molecules from the conditions present on early earth can be duplicated in the lab. In fact, a couple of guys did it."

"I know what you're referring to. The experiments of Miller and Urey, right?"

"Yeah, that's them."

"Well, what the textbook does not tell you is that some scientists think that Miller and Urey started with the wrong gases. They also did not allow for the escape of hydrogen. There is debate about whether the conditions they postulated even approximated those found on the early Earth."[198, 199, 200, 201]

Fumala answered, "The book says that amino acids were made."

I agreed, "True, and other organic compounds as well. But, not all the amino acids were made, and those that were made were made in a racemic mixture.[202] This means both right- and left-handed molecules were formed."

Many of the students looked confused, so I explained, "Remember that carbon, which is the basis of organic chemicals, can make four bonds. When it does this, the elements it bonds with are arranged in a tetrahedral fashion, kind of like the three legs of a tripod with another leg sticking up, around the central carbon. If all the elements bonded to the carbon are different, mirror image compounds or enantiomers can be formed. These rotate light in different directions and are called left-handed and right-handed even though they don't really have hands (Figure 14). The chemical behavior of these compounds is the same, but the biological activity is different because life distinguishes between them. Living organisms only use left-handed amino acids and right-handed sugars."

198   Rosing and Frei, 2004.
199   Lahav, 1999, p. 138-139.
200   Fitzpatrick, 2005.
201   Miller, 1994.
202   Miller, 1953.

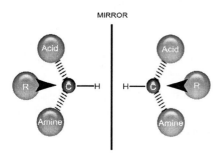

MIRROR

Figure 14 *All amino acids have the same general structure having a central carbon atom bound to a hydrogen atom, an acid group (COOH), an amine group (NH2) and an R group that has twenty variants and determines which specific amino acid it is. The four connections are in a tetrahedral shape, making mirror images possible. No matter how the molecules are rotated, they cannot be superimposed on each other. Only the "left-handed" versions of amino acids are used in living organisms.*

Paiva frowned, "How's that possible as a result of random forces?"

"I don't know, but some suggest it has to do with polarized light in space, others suggest issues with solubility,[203] but these do not really seem to address the issue. Additionally, the book does not tell you that when the amino acids were forced to react with each other in the Miller-Urey experiments they did not always form peptide bonds (Figure 15).

$$
\begin{array}{c}
\text{C} \downarrow \quad \text{R} \quad \downarrow \quad \text{R} \quad \downarrow \quad \text{R} \\
\| \quad \quad | \quad \quad \quad | \quad \quad \quad | \\
\text{O—N—C—C—N—C—C—N—C} \\
\quad | \quad | \quad \| \quad | \quad \| \quad | \\
\quad \text{H} \quad \text{O} \quad \text{H} \quad \text{O} \quad \text{H}
\end{array}
$$

Figure 15 *This figure shows the peptide bond that occurs between amino acids in proteins. The R groups also contain parts that can and would bind together in an uncontrolled environment. In fact, these attractions are what help proteins to assume their shape as functioning machines. However, in life the proteins are carefully constructed so that the first bonds that form are those between the amino group (NH$_2$) of one amino acid and the acid group (COOH) of the next. The peptide bonds are those between the O of the C=O and the H of the N-H.*

That is, it was not always the NH_2 and COOH groups that reacted. Those bonds are what is needed to form proteins. In a watery environment such as a primordial soup, formation of any bonds is highly unlikely. In fact, Stanley Miller (of Miller-Urey fame) is on record as having said that any amount of material from the primordial soup would be too small to "contribute to the origin of life."[204] Furthermore, even if only the left-handed molecules had reacted and they had only reacted at the amino and carboxy termini, the main mystery is not how the protein molecules were made, but how they came to form exquisitely functioning machines. Finally, we all know that a protein is not alive. As has been noted previously, "…Urey and Miller did not realize the essence of life to

203   Anonymous, 2006.
204   Miller, 1994.

be its structure, not its building blocks. It is the precision arrangements of different amino acids in long chains that is the big issue."[205]

Alex, who had been pulling faces and rolling his eyes while I was speaking, jumped in, "Just because there are questions, it doesn't mean 'Gawd' did it!" He deliberately exaggerated the word to show how unutterably stupid he considers anyone who thinks about these issues.

"That's right, and that is not what we're discussing. We're merely evaluating the Miller-Urey experiment scientifically and objectively deciding exactly what it does show us. In fact, it is now generally agreed that it explains very little about the origin of life. Because Miller and Urey believed that early Earth was a strongly reducing atmosphere, this is what they used in their experiments. But, some modern geologists tell us that the atmosphere at that time was oxidizing.[206, 207] Doing the experiments in the presence of oxygen would not result in amino acids, but an explosion. In fact, scientists really have no idea how life originated. According to H.P. Yockey, "You must conclude that no valid scientific explanation of life exists at present... Since science has not the vaguest idea how life originated on earth, ... it would be honest to admit this to students, the agencies funding research and the public."[208]

An older lady, Nora, with genteel manners, raised her hand, "Why do they include it in the text?"

"That's a good question. I suspect it might be because updated texts are just slightly adjusted from older ones without a thorough review of the facts. Teachers do not always have time or inclination to assess whether the assigned textbooks are accurate. Some have suggested it is a deliberate attempt to deceive. Personally, I reserve judgment but, in the interests of scientific integrity, do think it important to give you the full story."

Later in the workbook-based course, I talked about the cytoskeleton (muscles and bones of cells). Here it was necessary to introduce the students to cilia and flagella, which are hair-like projections on the surface of cells that respectively allow them to move liquids over their surfaces or allow them to move through a liquid. These molecular machines are amazingly complex, much like the other equipment found inside the cell, so I used this opportunity to introduce the controversial idea of irreducible complexity. After all, these were college students and exposure to alternative viewpoints should be part of any course. I

---

205   Hoyle and Wickramasinghe, 1993, p. 29.
206   Simpson, 1999, p. 26.
207   Scherer, 1985, p. 92.
208   Yockey, 1981.

had not gone into anything close to this type of detail at GMU, but now knew I had nothing to lose by being less cautious.

Febron raised his hand, "I don't get it."

I pondered to come up with a simple example. "Okay, let's think about your laptop. Say that the screen stopped working. Would the computer be useful to you?"

"Not very!"

"What about the hard drive, or the battery, or the keyboard?"

Febron thought about this, "Well, I might be able to use it a bit, but it would not work good."

"That's right. A scientist named Michael Behe showed how a mousetrap is irreducibly complex. That is, it doesn't work as a mousetrap unless all its parts are functional. Now, if we were to suggest that a mousetrap evolved over millions of years, we would have to be able to prove that you could go back a step or remove a part and still have a working machine. You can't claim something evolved by small steps if you can't go back a step and still have something that is functional so that natural selection can work on it."

Nora joined in, "I see. Every step along the evolutionary path of an organism or a cell or even a molecular machine needs to be the result of natural selection of the entire organism. But, natural selection can't select things that don't work."

"Yes, now in the case of the bacterial flagella, if one of the proteins involved in one of these machines is dysfunctional, then the machine does not work, or works less efficiently than it otherwise would. For example, a defect in axonemal proteins, important in eukaryotic flagella and cilia, is known to cause male infertility because the sperm cannot swim as efficiently.[209] Because cilia are important in keeping bacteria out of our lungs, this genetic defect is also connected with respiratory system problems."

In fact, these irreducibly complex structures are complexes of many proteins, all of which fit together with extreme specificity. But, even HIV, which has a mutation rate so great that Behe speculates it may have "mutated as much as all the cells that have ever existed on earth,"[210] has never made a new molecular machine.

At the beginning of the next lecture, I was pleased to find that the students had been stimulated to do some independent research. Fumula waived her hand.

---

209   Escudier, 1990.
210   Behe, 2007.

"Dr. Crocker, I looked irreducible complexity up on the Internet and found a really cool quote from Darwin where he said that the existence of even one irreducibly complex organ would wreck his theory."[211]

I smiled, "He did say something like that, but I suspect it was meant as a challenge, not a concession. Still, it is true that Darwin lived over 100 years ago and had no idea about the amazing complex and functioning machines that exist in a cell."

Alex had also been busy, "Look, it's been proven that co-option explains things that seem irreducibly complex."

Since a number of students looked confused, I asked Alex to explain further.

"Co-option is when several genes or proteins that are needed for one process develop independently and then are co-opted to be used in a new structure or trait," he said.

I thought for a moment. How could I make this understandable to the class? "So, co-option is a bit like a person building a soapbox car from odd pieces of lumber, wheels from a baby buggy, and left-over house paint. The idea is that the already-functioning and independently-developed proteins in the cell come together to make a new machine with a new function and the organism with that new function would be 'fitter'."

Fumula looked skeptical, "Yeah but, a person makes a go-cart. The parts don't just come together by themselves, even if they are functioning. I was reading how cells add each part to their complicated machines in order and may even carry new parts on kind-of railway tracks. Co-option doesn't come close to explaining that."

I agreed, "That's true. There are many questions left unanswered. But, that's the point of college -- to make you think! Maybe some of you will even be inspired to go on and do research to find the answers to some of these questions." Several students nodded in agreement.

The next mention of evolution came in the lectures on mitochondria, an organelle that allows animals and plants to generate cell-accessible energy from sugar and oxygen, and chloroplasts, which allow plants to make sugar from carbon dioxide and water. Both mitochondria and chloroplasts are small semi-independent bacteria-like structures contained within some cells. Although mitochondria and chloroplasts contain some of their own DNA and have the machinery needed to read the DNA and make proteins, they are missing the DNA for most of the proteins they need and are unable to survive on their own. The theory of endosymbiosis suggests mitochondria and chloroplasts were originally

---

211   Darwin, 1859.

bacteria that got stuck inside a larger cell. Since evolution is supposed to proceed by competition, not cooperation, the scientist (Lynn Margulis) who suggested this theory was ostracized and denied grants.[212] In fact, there are several biological factors that may support her ideas and a number of scientific inconsistencies that are unexplained, none of which I will mention here. However, in class I was careful to impartially provide as much information as possible.

Since we were then into the DNA and protein synthesis part of the course, it was natural to introduce my students to the idea of the information contained within DNA molecules and to bring up the question of how an information-rich molecule could evolve. It was also interesting to consider how the information content of a molecule could be improved by spontaneous errors in copying, as is claimed by Darwinism. After all, typos have never been known to improve the quality of a book. I gave the history of scientific thinking about this issue and mentioned the current theory of intelligent design, but only on the final line of the slide.

Meanwhile interest from the press continued. I was contacted by a reporter for a Romanian newspaper, another from *Legal Times*, and another from *Mannheimer Morgen*. Since I doubted future employers would read any of these publications, I agreed to interviews. The last interview, with reporter Marcus Günter from the German newspaper was the most interesting. He was embarrassed to be taking me out to what was basically an upscale hamburger joint, Fudruckers, but felt much better when I told him that the *Washington Post* reporter had taken me to McDonald's. The interview itself was rather disappointing since it was very difficult to get past his preconceived notions of me as a frothing-at-the-mouth religious fanatic who was totally uninformed about science. When I finally convinced him that I am, in fact, an informed individual with a PhD, publications, and an ability to think rationally, he again got the wrong end of the stick. For him, it was just not possible for a Christian to also be a scientist. So, soon after the article was published in Germany,[213] I received a concerned e-mail from a young German lady who wanted to know why I don't believe in God. I wrote back to her, set the record straight, and we began a pleasant friendship by correspondence.

Soon after this interview, I met with my next general biology class of 52 students. It was like déjà-vu: again the room was hot and sticky, the new freshman seemed to come from all corners of the world, and they looked at me apprehensively as if I might sprout horns and eat them at any time. I tried to smile reassuringly and passed out the syllabus. By now, I had this down to a fine art.

212   DiProperzio, 2004.
213   Günther, 2006.

I pulled my website up on the computer and led my students through the syllabus, my expectations, and the use of the website.

"Umm, what was your name again?" asked an Asian student, Seung, seated in the front row.

I pointed to where I had written it on the board, "I'm Dr. Crocker. You can find all my contact information in the syllabus and on the website. However, it's better to contact me by e-mail because I don't have my own office and messages there can get lost. I check e-mail several times a day."

Another student, Masani, timidly raised her hand and asked in a heavy accent, "The website, you mean all PowerPoint lectures are available now?"

"Yes, the purpose of this is so that you have time to listen to the lecture and not just be furiously writing what is on the screen. I encourage you to print out the slides and bring them to class so you can annotate them during the lecture."

"That is good," she nodded. This was to be one of my better students, despite her obvious difficulties with the language.

Next, a good-looking young man, Shunnar, sitting with his legs straight in front of him and his arms across his chest, asked laconically, "So, if everything's online, why come?"

I was glad he'd asked the question on everyone's mind, "Because you'll understand the material much better if you hear it explained. To encourage you to attend, there are almost daily quizzes that can't be made up."

Seung looked panic-stricken, "Quizzes! What about?"

Patiently, I again showed them the syllabus where it said that the quizzes were on vocabulary that could be found on the website. I also showed them where the answers to the quizzes were located, also on the website.

With all syllabus-related issues resolved, I began the introductory lecture on what biology is, giving a general overview of the entire course.

Finally, a month after the fall semester at NVCC started, I received a phone call about a possible job. It was from a Dr. Weidman, asking me to come for an interview for a Department of Defense position as a post-doctoral fellow working on signal transduction in T-cells. Two days later, another scientist contacted me from Yale, asking me to come and work for him, also in T-cell research. This offer was made on the strength of my qualifications and recommendations, even without an interview. I wondered if they had heard about me and didn't care or if it was only in academia that intellectual freedom was suppressed. Regardless, I was happy to hear from them.

On the day of the interview with Dr. Weidman, I left two hours early to be sure that I would find the place. After the 40 minute commute to the military base in Bethesda, I spent half an hour looking for the building. I was glad I'd left so early. When I finally found the room, I met a slender man in his forties with a disturbing tendency to gaze at a person without saying a word. I found myself rather unnerved and chattering to cover the silence. Soon Dr. Weidman offered to show me around the labs and introduce me to the lab personnel. I was astonished to note that every machine, flask, and test tube was labeled "Weidman lab" and wondered if they had a problem with stealing. We then walked up and down countless sets of stairs and around even more hallways as he showed me the way to more equipment scattered around the buildings. I wondered if the biggest challenge in this job would be finding my way. Eventually, after some brief discussion, Dr. Weidman offered me the position.

Since Richard had an interview scheduled in New Haven and I had a job offer at Yale, I couldn't give him an immediate answer. However, when later Dr. Weidman assured me that he had (NIH) grant money for three years, Richard decided that the New Haven job was not attractive enough to pull me away from something about which I was so enthusiastic. I turned Yale down and accepted the position with the Department of Defense. So as not to jeopardize my new job, I decided to postpone further pursuit of a lawsuit until after it had started and I let my attorney Edward know about that decision.

The day after accepting the position, I went to see Dr. Brinkerhoff at NVCC to tell her that I would not be doing any adjunct teaching the following semester. I knew she was already planning on my teaching cell biology in the spring. Her assistant told me that she was with someone, so I took a seat outside her office to wait. To my amazement, I overheard Dr. Brinkerhoff and a couple of people from the NVCC administration talking about me.

"She's been in the newspapers and on the radio. You have to get rid of her."

Dr. Brinkerhoff loyally protected me, "Dr. Crocker is a good teacher. She gets excellent student ratings and the young people clamor to get into her classes."

"Is she going to be here next semester?"

"I don't know. She's looking for a job, but hasn't heard anything yet."

"Well, we're not happy about her teaching here. It gives us a bad name."

I felt sorry that Dr. Brinkerhoff, who had been so supportive through all my difficulties, was getting grief on my account. The people from the administration left her office, walking past but not recognizing me. After all, they had never bothered to meet or talk to the "troublesome" teacher.

I entered Dr. Brinkerhoff's office, pleased to be able to tell her of my job offer and thereby take pressure off her.

She was genuinely happy for me, "Congratulations! Tell me all about it!" Then she paused, "Does this mean you won't be able to finish the fall semester?"

"No, I'll finish. The job is very interesting and I could start right away, but it wouldn't be fair on you or the students to leave. I told my new boss that I'll be available in January." I knew this would mean a financial loss of about $10,000 because adjunct faculty are paid so little, but I wanted to do what was right.

"Thanks," she said with a smile, "And maybe you can teach an evening cell biology class for us in the spring."

"Oh, I don't think so. It's a long commute and I'll have a lot of new techniques to learn. I think I'll be pretty absorbed in this job."

"Okay, well, keep in touch." She smiled at me, "I hope you change your mind."

Meanwhile, the semester was progressing nicely. My general biology class was very enjoyable, with pleasant students and all kinds of personalities. However, the cell biology class was a challenge. Although most of the students were cooperative and hard-working, Alex continued to be resistant to my attempts to engage him. He would mutter through the lectures, shake his head at imagined mistakes, be late for lab, and write nasty notes to me on his worksheets. I tried to break through by inviting him to show the class how calculations should be done (he was temporarily happy about this), showing interest in his personal life (he frequently spoke of having been recently married), and even over-looking the nasty notes, but to no avail. I found that I had to stand behind the computer so that I would not be distracted by his grimaces while lecturing. His grades, which started as A's, dropped steadily; it looked as if he was not studying at all. He began turning his homework in late and I started to suspect there was more to this than simple dislike of the teacher. When he didn't even bother taking the third exam, ensuring that he would fail the course, I was convinced.

Finally, at the end of the semester, I found out what was happening because of a conversation I was having with Paiva, another student in the class. Paiva, who had struggled through as an adult immigrant, told me that she'd spent years on anti-depressants, simply due to the fact that she was homesick. But, she hated how they made her feel.

I agreed with her, "I know what you mean. A few years ago I experienced a significant personal tragedy. I went to the doctor, was prescribed anti-depressants, tried them for a week, and decided I would rather struggle through the grief. Actually, I found the pain made me grow as a person, even if it wasn't fun at the time—and I did recover." I gave her a wry smile.

"Yeah, I also stopped taking them. I feel much better just by exercising regularly. Then I don't need to take drugs."

Alex, who had been listening to us with interest (this was fairly typical of his behavior: sometimes pleasant and friendly and other times downright nasty), joined in, "I know what you guys mean. Several years ago I got a diagnosis of bipolar, but I think I can deal with it. So, even though my wife hates it, I don't take medication."

My opinion is that far too many Americans are taking anti-depressants. Some of them have been banned in the U.K., and for good reason.[214] In some cases, life-style changes would be just as beneficial, if not more so. For others, it might be that temporary pain would cause the person to grow stronger, as it did me. But there are cases where medication is needed. I suspect that Alex was one of those. I was not surprised to look at the comments about me on ratemyprofessor.com and see some particularly nasty ones some of which have since been removed.[215] I knew their source; many I had already seen on his worksheets.[216]

Soon afterwards, in the fall of 2005, Shankar Vedantam from the *Washington Post* got in touch with me again. The date for the seminar at my church was approaching and he wanted to meet me outside the church building and then go somewhere to talk. But next came a twist in the storyline that caused me to be sorely tempted to stand him up.

The next day I received a phone call from a lady at Arnold and Porter, the law firm where Edward Sisson was a partner. She wanted to know whether I would object if they took GMU on as a client, since doing so could present a potential conflict of interest. I was surprised that it was not Edward who phoned, but said I did not mind. After all, I reasoned, the law firm was doing me a favor and I was not going to deny them possible income. She then asked if Edward and I were actively doing anything on my case. I explained that I had asked him to hold off on further action until I started my new job in January. We would resume proceedings then. She repeated, "But, right now, there is no action on the case, is that correct?" I agreed.

Less than a week later I received a phone call from Edward informing me that his law firm was going to fire me as a client because they had accepted GMU's offer to represent them and GMU had objected to me as a client. Although Edward had no specific knowledge about this, his experience as a partner made him think that this contract for an unrelated paying commercial matter between Arnold and Porter and GMU could net the firm tens of thousands of dollars in billings. In comparison, since I had no job and no way to pay for legal representation, they had been handling my case pro bono. Edward also told me that he would be leaving the firm by January 9th, less than three months away.

---

214   http://www.guardian.co.uk/science/2003/dec/10/drugs.sciencenews
215   Bergman, 2008, p. 234.
216   Compare comments at http://www.ratemyprofessors.com/ShowRatings.jsp?tid=649890&page=2 to those in Appendix II, which preceded my "discipline."

"You mean to tell me that GMU bought your law firm and they even agreed to throw you out to sweeten the deal?" I questioned in astonishment. This seemed more like a John Grisham novel than reality. I felt dizzy with the shock.

Edward, of course, could not answer this type of suggested accusation. "No, my job is over for unrelated reasons. GMU has engaged Arnold and Porter on a paying commercial matter. Even though the firm has hundreds of lawyers and the two cases are entirely unrelated, GMU objected to Arnold and Porter representing you. This is not a customary course of action, but it is within their rights as a client. I was not consulted about this pronouncement, but it has been decided that we fire you."

A few days later I received an e-mail from Edward confirming that his law firm would no longer be representing me.[217] In addition, he gave me his new e-mail address since his current one would soon be discontinued. I wondered if lawyers involved with GMU would also monitor his office e-mail. I did not trust anyone at that moment. It felt terrible to think that my questioning neo-Darwinian evolution had not only caused me to lose my job but might also make it difficult for Edward to find another job. In fact, just recently Edward told me that his willingness to associate himself publicly with the "Darwin-challenger" position has brought a substantial amount of Internet invective and denigration. He feels this has been a substantial deterrent to his ability to get new work since leaving Arnold & Porter four years ago, but anticipated it might occur when he first decided to take-on the Kansas evolution hearings.[218]

For this reason, when I met Shankar at the church seminar, I told him that I'd changed my mind about speaking with him, even off the record. He could see that I was pale, trembling, and nearly in tears, so asked me what was wrong.

"I don't really want to talk about it," I said as firmly as I could.

But, being a very experienced reporter, he was not put off so easily, "I can see you're very upset. Let's just go listen to the seminar and we can talk later."

After the seminar, I introduced Shankar to the government physicist from the NIST, who is a believer in God and in theistic evolution. He also met a GMU Dean who questions evolution but does so from a non-biological perspective, a politician who worked for Rick Santorum, and a reporter for a prestigious science magazine who is a firm, but necessarily undercover, believer in intelligent design despite the fact that his employers ardently espouse the "fact" of neo-Darwinian evolution. Shankar was amazed as these people consistently told him the same thing; it is important to follow scientific facts where they lead but that

---

217   E-mail from Edward Sisson to Caroline Crocker, November, 2005. A copy can be found in Appendix VI.
218   E-mail from Edward Sisson to Caroline Crocker, March, 2009.

faith is not based on science and a belief in intelligent design is a poor substitute for right theology. Christianity is based on the historical facts of the life, death and resurrection of Jesus Christ and on the experience of His continued presence here on Earth, not on science. Intrigued by the opinions and obvious intelligence of these believers, Shankar asked me if he could attend a church service.

"Of course, when would you like to do it?"

"How about next week? But…I'm a Hindu. Would that be okay?" Shankar looked uncertain.

I was happy to reassure him, "Yes, we don't keep anyone out. I'll meet you outside at 11 am. And then, why not come for lunch with me and my family?"

"Thanks. That would be great. I'll see you then."

Of course, the next week Shankar had not forgotten how upset I'd been the previous week. "So, what exactly was so troubling for you?" he asked during a hymn.

I did not want to answer and put him off until after the service, which he found fascinating, but then I had nowhere to hide. I decided that because Shankar had shown himself trustworthy in the past I would tell him the truth.

Trembling, I confessed, "Listen, you can't print this. I'm scared of what people might do to my family and me. But I'll tell you off the record, okay?"

Shankar assured me that he would not print anything that I did not give him permission to print. I examined his face and decided to trust. My faith was not misplaced.

So I continued, "I just found out that GMU offered my law firm a contract worth thousands with the condition that they drop me as a client. They did, and then Arnold and Porter also told my lawyer they no longer needed him, despite the fact that he was a partner with the firm."

Shankar's jaw dropped, "This is amazing!" He shook his head, "What does GMU and the law firm think they're doing? Don't they know that reporters are going to start wondering why you are no longer being represented?"

I had not thought of that, "Do you think anyone will notice that my lawyer no longer has a job or that I lost my pro bono representation when Arnold and Porter started to represent GMU?"[219]

"It'll only take one. But about you, I don't think that an article would put you or your family in danger. In fact, it might make people sympathetic to you if they knew how you're being persecuted for your belief in academic freedom."

I shook my head, "That hasn't been my experience. People only hear what they want to hear. I do get e-mails from those who are supportive of my stance,

---

219   The Coral Ridge Hour (television), August, 2006.

but have not yet heard those who disagree with my perspective say that I should be allowed to discuss my views without fearing the backlash. I do get nasty e-mails from lots of folks."

"Do you have copies of any of the nasty letters or e-mails?"

"No, I delete them because they are too negative. Folks seem to think that if they can't see your face its okay to take a swing at it. But, I'm told that there are all kinds of unkind remarks on the Internet about my intelligence, inability to teach, and even quotes on theology that I never said. My father reads this stuff, but I don't. My daughter told me that reading what people say about me made her cry. I just figure that it's not really worth reading the comments from people who talk *about* me, but not *to* me."

"Okay, well, I still think that an article in the *Washington Post* magazine, not discussing the pros and cons of evolution, but just questioning why the issue makes people abuse each other wouldn't hurt you and might help. People usually rally to help the underdog."

I understood his wish to write about this, but also realized that it probably wouldn't help me at all. I had seen bullying behavior before and knew that some people are just as likely to kick as help someone who is under attack.[220] However, Shankar had been pleasant to my family and me while we ate together. Surely, since someone was bound to write about it, it would be best to have him do it. He seemed fair and even sympathetic. So, I agreed, with the proviso that publication be delayed until a couple of months after my new job started. Shankar convinced his boss and the date for a formal interview was set. But, first, he wanted to attend the general biology lecture on evolution. I assumed he would get the necessary permissions and gave him the date of the lecture.

Since I knew that this would probably be my last teaching position and I had nothing to lose, I decided that in this last lecture on evolution I would be honest with the students about my views. After all, these were university students, not little children. Up until now I had made sure that my students would have no idea what I believed, so as to allow them maximum opportunity to draw their own conclusions on the basis of the scientific evidence.

I met Shankar outside the class and introduced him, as well as his photographer, to my goggle-eyed students. Shankar then requested permission to address the students.[221]

"I'm doing an article for the *Washington Post* magazine about the reaction of the public to people who question evolution. After the lecture, I would love

---

220   For a nice example of "kickers," see P.Z. Myer's blog at http://scienceblogs.com/pharyngula/2006/02/heck_yeahcaroline_crocker_shou.php

221   Sometime in November, 2005

to interview any of you, either by name or not. Also, we'll want a photograph of Dr. Crocker, and you're welcome to stay in the background for that."

So, I began my last lecture as a professor on the evidence for and against evolution. But, this time I did go much further than I ever had before in my discussion of the evidence for evolution, the problems with that evidence, and the new theory of Intelligent Design. The students had heard about the controversy over evolution in the papers and on TV, so it was not news to them, but I wanted to make clear to them the extent to which academic freedom was being suppressed. It appeared that many in academia are very opposed to "teaching the controversy."[222]

"So, in these two lectures you've heard the evidence that the book presents for evolution, the scientific problems with those experiments, and the outline of a new theory that is being proposed by some scientists."

One of my more confrontational students, Hector, waved his hand, "This intelligent design…isn't it just a front for religion?"

"No, it isn't. We have already developed methods for detecting whether an accident, a natural law, or an intelligent being has caused a phenomenon.[223] We apply that methodology in forensics, archeology and even the Search for Extraterrestrial Intelligence (SETI). The ID approach just applies those same accepted methods to biological systems and observes the results. Detecting an intelligence behind the DNA code does not support a particular religion."

Hector stuck out his chin, "Yeah but, 'intelligence' is just another word for God."[224]

I tried to make myself clear, "That is a decision you will have to make and I cannot address here. Science does sometimes have philosophical implications, but those must be independently assessed."

Hector tried one last time, "So, according to intelligent design, the DNA code could have been written by the purple-headed spaghetti monster?"

To his surprise I answered in the affirmative, "Yes, science sometimes cannot determine what the source of intelligence is. I personally would be surprised to meet such a being, but you are free to believe in him, her, or it." The class giggled at the thought.

I returned to the lecture. "Now, about whether the variety in the world came about through evolution, intelligent design, a combination of the two, or

---

222 Scott and Branch, 2003.
223 Dembski, 2002.
224 Note that, similarly, lack of intelligence is a "front" for "no god." ID and neo-Darwinism are not religion, but both have religious implications.

by another process entirely,[225] you will have to decide," and here I went further than I ever had before, "but I want to warn you that this decision is not without consequences."

The students leaned forward in their chairs. One asked, "What do you mean? Will you give us a bad grade if we don't agree with you?"

I laughed, "No, not that kind of consequence. That's really pretty minor. I don't care what you think, provided you back it up with facts. But, having politically incorrect opinions can lead to being persecuted."

Masani then changed the subject, "Dr. Crocker, will you be here next semester? I want to take you for Bio 102."

"No Masani, I won't be teaching second semester general biology or any other class. In fact, I won't be teaching at all."

"Why not?" asked several of my class, expressing surprise.

"Well, I've taken another job doing research. I love teaching, but I lost my job at GMU for presenting a lecture similar to this one and the administration here isn't happy with me either. They want me to leave."

Shunnar, a dapper young man whose father was in the medical profession, asked for clarification. "You mean you're not going to be allowed to teach at GMU or NVCC because you taught us about the science on both sides of the evolution debate?"

"Yes, pretty much. And I need to tell you that, if you have doubts about neo-Darwinian evolution, you need to keep them to yourself until you're in a secure job."

Seung found this hard to believe and asserted, "This is America, where we have freedom of speech. It's okay to say anything."

I shook my head sadly, "No, it's not. A scientist at the Smithsonian was severely harrassed for allowing a paper supporting ID to be published,[226, 227] graduate students are denied their Ph.D.,[228] faculty are denied tenure,[229] and my former lawyer cannot find a job,[230] possibly for supporting those who question neo-Darwinian evolution. It is serious business. If you want to get into medical or graduate school, my suggestion is that you don't let anyone know if you have any questions about neo-Darwinian evolution. I've seen too many people get hurt."

---

225   It is important to note that there are only two options when it comes to design: something either is or is not designed.
226   Klinghoffer, 2005.
227   Cashill, 2007.
228   http://www.insidehighered.com/news/2005/06/10/osu
229   http://www.freegonzalez.com/tenure.html
230   http://www.youtube.com/watch?v=6lCe5ICSKI0

The classroom was silent. Then Masani, a committed Christian, spoke up. "I will not be silent. I will speak to the reporter. In my country, persecution is an honor."

Another girl timidly ventured that she would also talk, but only anonymously. She did not want to jeopardize her future career prospects.

A couple of young men also volunteered to be interviewed anonymously.

So, I dismissed the class, posed for a photo with those who remained, and left Shankar in charge of the interviewing of students.

* * * *

All too soon the semester was over. I marked the exams, tallied the grades, posted them, and cleared my desk. I quickly discovered that NVCC was only too glad to be rid of me, which was underscored by the fact that they removed my website and e-mail address from their system less than a month (instead of the normal semester or longer) after the end of the class. Students are supposed to be able to contact their teachers and challenge their grades for up to a semester, so I did not see the sense in this. I assumed that their association with me embarrassed them and this inconvenience to potentially disgruntled students was the result.

REFERENCES

Anonymous. 2005. "Not so Intelligently-Designed Ph.D. Panel." *Inside Higher Ed.* June 10. http://www.insidehighered.com/news/2005/06/10/osu (as of 3/20/09).

Anonymous. 2006. "The Intelligent Design Controversy in Higher Education." *The Coral Ridge Hour* (TV), August 13.

Anonymous. 2006. "Right-handed Amino Acids were Left Behind," *New Scientist* (Reed Business Information Ltd) (2554):18, June 2.

Behe, Michael J. 2007. *The Edge of Evolution: The Search for the Limits of Darwinism.* New York, NY: The Free Press.

Bergman, Jerry. 2008. *Slaughter of the Dissidents.* Port Orchard, WA: Leafcutter Press, p. 234.

Boseley, Sarah. 2003. "Drugs for Depressed Children Banned." *The Guardian.* December 10. http://www.guardian.co.uk/science/2003/dec/10/drugs. sciencenews (as of 3/2/09).

Bradley-Hagerty, Barbara. 2005. "Intelligent Design and Academic Freedom." All Things Considered. *National Public Radio.* November 10, http://www.discovery.org/a/3083 (as of 3/15/09).

Campbell, Neil A., Jane B. Reece. 2002. *Biology* 6th Edition. San Francisco, CA: Benjamin Cummings.

Campbell, Neil A., Jane B. Reece. 2005. *Biology* 7th Edition. San Francisco, CA: Benjamin Cummings.

Cashill, Jack. 2007. "Peer-harassed Scientist Rocks Evolutionary Boat. Not So Intelligently Designed Ph.D. Panel." *Worldnet Daily,* February 15. http://www.worldnetdaily.com/news/article.asp?ARTICLE_ID=54257 (as of 4/1/09).

Darwin, Charles. 1859. *On the Origin of Species by Means of Natural Selection.* London, UK: John Murray.

Dembski, William. 2002. *No Free Lunch: Why Specified Complexity Cannot be Purchased Without Intelligence.* Lanham, MD: Rowman and Littlefield.

Di Properzio, James. 2004. "Lyn Margulis: Full Speed Ahead." *University of Chicago Magazine.* http://www.mindfully.org/Heritage/2004/Lynn-Margulis-Gaia1feb04.htm (as of 3/1/09).

Escudier, E., D. Escalier, M.C. Pinchon, M. Boucherat, J.F. Bernaudin, J. Fleury-Feith. 1990. "Dissimilar Expression of Axonemal Anomalies in Respiratory Cilia and Sperm Flagella in Infertile Men." *Am Rev Respir Dis.* 142(3):674-9.

Fitzpatrick, Tony (2005)."Calculations Favor Reducing Atmosphere for Early Earth – Was Miller–Urey Experiment Correct?" *Washington University in St. Louis*, September 7. http://news-info.wustl.edu/news/page/normal/5513.html (as of 4/1/09).

Günther, Marcus. 2006. "Stammt der Mensch vom Affen ab?" *Mannheimer Morgen*, May 10.

Hoyle, Fred and C. Wickramasinghe. 1993. *Our Place in the Cosmos: The Unfinished Revolution*. Phoenix: London.

Iowa State Alumni. Undated. "Tenure Criteria and Denial." *Freegonzalez.com*. http://www.freegonzalez.com/tenure.html (as of 4/1/09).

Klinghoffer, David. 2005. "The Branding of a Heretic," *The Wall Street Journal*, January 28.

Lahav, Noam. 1999. *Biogenesis: Theories of Life's Origins*. New York, Oxford, NY: Oxford University Press.

Miller, Stanley L. 1953. "Production of Amino Acids Under Possible Primitive Earth Conditions." *Science* 117:528, May.

Miller, Stanley L. 1994. "From Primordial Soup to the Prebiotic Beach." Interview of Dr. Stanley Miller by Sean Henahan. http://www.accessexcellence.org/WN/NM/miller.php (as of 6/2/09).

Myers, P.Z. 2005. "Heck yeah—Caroline Crocker Should Have Been Fired." *Pharyngula*, February 5. http://scienceblogs.com/pharyngula/2006/02/heck_yeahcaroline_crocker_shou.php (as of 7/4/09).

Ratemyprofessor Comments, 2005.

Rosing, M.T. & R. Frei. 2004. "U-rich Archaean Sea-floor Sediments from Greenland—Indications of >3700 Ma Oxygenic Photosynthesis." *Earth and Planetary Science Letters* 217:237–244.

Scherer, S. 1985. "Could Life have Arisen in the Primitive Atmosphere?" *J. Molecular Evolution* 22(1):91–94, p. 92.

Scott, Eugenie C., Glenn Branch. 2003. "Evolution: What's Wrong with Teaching the Controversy." *Trends in Ecology & Evolution* 18(10):499-502, October 1.

Simpson, S. 1999. "Life's First Scalding Steps." *Science News* 155(2):24–26, p. 26.

Sisson, Edward. 2005. E-mail from Edward Sisson to Caroline Crocker, November 11.

Sisson, Edward. 2006. Podcast, May: http://www.youtube.com/watch?v=6lCe5ICSKI0

Sisson, Edward. 2009. E-mail from Edward Sisson to Caroline Crocker, March.

Skell, Philip S. 2005. "Why do we Invoke Darwin? Evolutionary Theory Contributes Little to Experimental Biology." *The Scientist* 19(16):10, August 29.

Yockey, H.P. 1981. "Self-organization Origin of Life Scenarios and Information Theory." *Journal of Theoretical Biology* 91:13-31.

Chapter 9: Strange Doings

It had now been a year since I was told I would be disciplined for teaching both sides of the evolution controversy and I had moved on with my life. I wanted give my best to my new job as a post-doctoral fellow engaging in cancer research for the Department of Defense. I began working with Dr. Weidman in January of 2006. Since he had to be away for the first few weeks after I started, it was up to me to figure out what to do. I was pleased to make contact with Elizabeth, a veterinarian and member of the lab who was finishing up her Ph.D. She ushered me to my desk and lab bench, showed me where to get supplies, gave me a tour of the building, and got me hooked up with a computer. She was also instrumental in helping me get started in the research I needed to do. Because of my past research and teaching experience, I had varying degrees of familiarity with many of the techniques the research group used, but there was also a lot to learn. I'd taught genetic engineering to undergraduates in lecture and lab classes, but I now found myself in an environment where I and others were actually *doing* it. It was tremendously exciting.

"Elizabeth, would you mind explaining as you work on this procedure?" I asked with some hesitation, knowing that having me look over her shoulder might slow her down.

She was a gracious and superb teacher, "Not at all. In fact, I have to do this twice, so I'll do it the first time and you can do it the second." I learned the all-important molecular biology techniques of restriction digests, ligation, electrophoresis, and transformation from Elizabeth.[231]

"Galina, where do you keep the equipment for the Westerns? I'm writing it all down, so that I'll be able to find stuff in the future." Dr. Weidman's group worked in several labs; reagents, equipment, and supplies could be found all over the building complex.

Galina showed me, "But, do you know the procedure?"

"Oh, I've been watching and writing down what you and Elizabeth do. Still, I wouldn't mind if you check to be sure I got it right." There was no Standard Operating Procedures manual in this lab, so I figured writing one would be a good use of my time, allowing me to simultaneously learn the procedures and perform a service.

A couple of days later another member of the lab by the name of Joshua approached me. "Dr. Weidman e-mailed me and said that he wants me to show

---

231   Definitions can be found in Appendix I.

you how to prepare slides with activated T cells and then how to use the confocal microscope."

"Okay, when will you be doing it?"

"I'll be showing someone from NIH[232] tomorrow. How about if you join us?"

So, I did—I watched and took notes, over ten pages of them. To say the confocal was a complex instrument would be a great understatement. I later found out that weeklong training seminars are considered standard for initial instruction in the use of this microscope. The next day I decided to try what I'd learned for myself. I entered the darkened microscope room, but felt pretty nervous. So, I gave myself a pep talk, "Now Caroline, Joshua said you can't hurt the machine. You have the notes; just do what they say. First it's this switch…"

Just then I noticed a face pop out from behind a computer in the back of the room. It was Joshua. I hoped he was not the type to go back to the lab and tell everyone that the new post-doc talks to herself. It turned out he was very discreet and also very patient, helping me every time I got stuck. He taught me so well that I soon found others, even from other research groups, asking *me* for help!

Finally, after nearly a month, Dr. Weidman returned to work. I expected he would now give me instructions about what to do, but he didn't. So, I continued my work making the DNA constructs and transfected[233] cell lines that Joshua had suggested I try. I also asked Dr. Weidman for a copy of his current grants. Maybe I could figure out my project from them. I discussed the issue of not having been assigned a project with Elizabeth. She nodded understandingly, "Dr. Weidman won't talk to you unless you talk first. You always need to ask him, and push him for an answer if you want one." So, I decided to just come out and ask Dr. Weidman if he had a particular project he wanted me to tackle.

"Actually, there are three," he began. "Eventually, I hope you'll be able to work on them all at once, but start out with this one." He then outlined the goals of the projects, giving little, if any, detail. Not having done a post-doc before, I assumed figuring it out was my job and started making a plan.

February was a mixture of joy, worry, challenge, and just plain stress. I was happy with the new position, but the long commute and the demands of my job were tiring. Then, Shankar contacted me, wanting a formal interview for the *Post* article. I had been expecting this, but it reminded me that Dr. Weidman did not know of my history. When the article came out, would I lose another job? Finally, I was finding that the molecular biology techniques were not foolproof and took some practice to get right. In despair, I apologized to Dr. Weidman. He was very encouraging, "You're doing great. Most people take a year to get these

---

232   National Institutes of Health
233   Definitions can be found in Appendix 1.

things down. You're well ahead of schedule." But, I'd been hoping to impress him so much that he wouldn't want to let me go, even if he did find out about GMU. Frankly, I was scared.

Eventually, Shankar phoned and told me that the article was going to come out in the *Washington Post* magazine that next week.[234] I realized that it would be worse for Dr. Weidman to find out by reading the paper than for me to tell him, so I took my courage in both hands and knocked on his office door.

"Dr. Weidman? Do you have a minute?"

"Sure, come in. Sit down." He sat back with his hands comfortably behind his head.

"Okay well, I have something to tell you that you might not like. Well, actually, I haven't done anything wrong in the lab or broken anything, but there is something I didn't tell you at my interview." I was falling over my words in my anxiety.

Dr Weidman was very good at sitting still and that's just what he did.

The words tumbled out, "So, you see, while in my position at GMU, I was accused of teaching creationism. The complaint was never put in writing and is, in fact, not true. I did teach a lecture on scientific evidence regarding neo-Darwinian evolution, but tried to impartially cover both sides of the debate. I figured that this would be what scientific integrity requires. Anyway, the result was my boss told me he was going to have to discipline me, even though he had no evidence, and he removed me from lecturing. He also made sure my contract was over at the end of the semester—that's a long story. I did have a lawyer because it was a clear infringement of my right to academic freedom, but GMU offered the law firm a contract and the law firm fired me as a client. So, now I don't have a lawyer and, actually, my former lawyer doesn't have a job."

"Wow! That's almost unbelievable. But, why are you telling me now?"

"The *Washington Post* magazine is going to publish an article about me this weekend. I thought you would rather hear from me than read it and be surprised."

"Well, thanks for letting me know. But, I really don't care about what the personal views of my staff are, provided it doesn't affect their work."

I shrugged, "How would thinking that evolution has problems as a theory stop me from doing good research?"

Dr. Weidman answered enigmatically, "Well, it might."

---

234 Vedantam, 2006.

This did not make a lot of sense to me, but I decided not to argue and just reassured him, "It won't affect my work, but the attitudes of those who oppose me might affect you."

"How do you mean?"

"Well, in my past job, people phoned my boss and were nasty to her for letting me work there. They wanted me fired. I've tried to keep it secret that I work here, but if it leaks or someone finds out, they may bother you."

Here Dr. Weidman came through like a hero, "If I get any phone calls like that, they'll be very short!"

I was immensely grateful for his support and again made a private vow to do my very best at my work. I also realized that since Dr. Weidman knew about my "secret," I would be at liberty to accept the speaking and other engagements I was being offered. It was strange that in a free country I was so concerned about being exposed as someone who believes in academic freedom and scientific objectivity, but there was good reason for my caution.

A rather exciting opportunity that came along that spring was a request from Coral Ridge Television to do a story on me. The reporter was a member of our church, so it was a natural contact. But, what fun! The flowers were blooming, so the camera crew sat me on a chair in front of an azalea bush in my backyard. I was nervous as we went through the interview, but it was nice to be able to stop and do a re-take whenever I got tongue-tied. Then, we moved to the kitchen. They were going to film me making a cup of tea. Of course, it was all acting. I made the tea with cold water, and then walked to the front porch to sit and pretended to drink, gazing soulfully into the distance, as if contemplating the unfairness of it all. Since I'm a scientist and not an actress, I found it very challenging not to laugh. The best fun was when I was told to change into work clothes. Then Richard and I were instructed to leave the house through the front door, with him walking me to my car, giving me a kiss, and seeing me off to work. This was not even close to reality because in order to avoid traffic I would always leave while it was dark and long before Richard was awake. It seemed very silly to me that we would play-act like this, but I was assured it would make for good television.

The television crew's next stop was to interview my ex-lawyer Edward Sisson, who backed up my entire story. He also admitted that he still did not have a job, which was distressing to me, since it felt like it was my fault.[235] The Coral Ridge program was well done and sympathetic but because it was on Christian

---

235   Interview of Caroline Crocker and Edward Sisson by Coral Ridge Television, August 13, 2006. Go to http://www.coralridge.org/medialibrary/default.aspx, click on "date," then on "2006," then on "August." Scroll to the bottom of the page and click on page "4," then on "more."

TV it had a very limited audience. There was none of the resulting uproar that I'd expected. In fact, the only result was some congratulations from people at church, a couple of invitations to speak at a local mega-church and a smaller one, and a nice e-mail from a friend.

The talks that I gave at the churches were always different from those I gave at universities, even when addressing a private group like the IDEA club. It is vital that people do not base their faith on science, so I felt it highly necessary to explain the difference between science and philosophy or theology, making sure that my audience understood what each can tell us about our world. I would start with the definitions of science (study of the natural world obtained empirically), philosophy (exploration of reality, knowledge, or principles obtained by logical reasoning), and dogma (a statement of ideas considered to be absolutely true).

Science, because of its empirical basis, can only tell us about the natural world. I have found Dr. Norman Geisler's distinction helpful here concerning two different approaches to science: what he calls "operations science" and "origins science." Operations or empirical science is what most experimental scientists use; it seeks to find describable regularities by repeated testing and observation.[236] It cannot, as is claimed by some Darwinists, prove that only the natural world exists. It also cannot tell us much about the supernatural (even though, by empirical means, it may detect the influence or operation of an intelligent being that could be supernatural). Origins science is more like forensics; it seeks to find an explanation for a historical event or unrepeatable singularity, such as the origin of the universe. According to Geisler, both ID and macroevolution fall into the category of origins science; neither are empirical since an origin is a one-time (not repeatable) event.

Philosophy investigates another type of knowledge, but is a discipline no less valid than science and like science employs the use of logic. This is a discipline that could possibly yield some limited information about God.

Dogma is a word often applied to faith in a god, but is also applicable to faith that there is no god. Both are religion, as it has been defined legally. There is no room for discussion when it comes to neo-Darwinian evolution, and that's a clear indicator of dogmatism or religion. One only needs to watch the Discovery Channel or read *National Geographic* to observe neo-Darwinian evolution being presented as irrefutable dogma.

It is my understanding that to study the supernatural world we need philosophy, theology, history, experience, and revelation. No person can be known

---

236   Geisler & Anderson, 1987.

intimately unless they are willing to reveal themselves or open up to us. We could test a person's blood, run experiments on their physiological responses, and even study their home. This might assure us that they exist (or existed), but we would not really know them as a friend. Even more so, God, because He is God, cannot be really known on a personal level by our scientific experiments, but only through His revelation of Himself. That is, we might be able to use science and information theory to detect that an intelligence probably was involved in the origin and design of life and can even reasonably surmise some characteristics of that being (organized, powerful, etc.), but we cannot do much more than that. Faith that is based strictly on science without any consideration of revelation is theologically problematic and subject to revision every time a new scientific discovery is made. Therefore, it can lead to fear of new scientific discoveries that might challenge old beliefs. Science that is based on faith is also in danger of closing its eyes to anything that appears to be a threat to that faith. But, if God is real, we should be able to study as much as we like without losing sight of the fact that He is. There is no fear when we are free to base our science on scientific evidence discovered in the natural world and our faith on truth discovered in history, experience, and of course revelation. What I was told so long ago, "Think about it. If it is true, you can think about it and it will still be true," seemed to be a message worth repeating.

In addition, when speaking to lay audiences, it was often necessary to refresh their memories on science. After all, some of the evidence for biological intelligent design is only understood by those with a good understanding of the inner workings of the cell. However, contrary to the popular opinion expressed among some scientists, I found that lay people are generally more than able to understand the science once it is explained and are therefore perfectly capable of making up their own minds about the issue. They did not need protection from having their minds polluted and were happy to be challenged to think. This was directly contrary to the beliefs of many Darwinists, who think informing students about the evidence challenging current scientific dogma (or even that there is a debate) is irresponsible.[237]

* * * *

Immediately after I finished my talk at the mega-church, several people approached me. One showed me a recently published book that had a page all

---

237 "Although there are scientific controversies about the patterns and processes of evolution that are appropriate topics for the science classroom, and there is a continuing social controversy in certain circles about the validity of evolution, it is scientifically inappropriate and pedagogically irresponsible to teach that scientists seriously debate the validity of evolution." Scott and Branch, 2003.

about me. I'd never met the author and the incident they described was clearly either made-up or greatly exaggerated. But, it wasn't particularly offensive. In fact, I laughed when I read the description of myself as a soft-spoken redhead who mesmerizes her audience just by entering a room. The author certainly had not asked my family about the quietly spoken part and I'm sure my students would disagree about the mesmerizing part. Even the hair color was wrong, although I do have the fiery temper one would expect from a redhead!

Another person asked me, "Are you suing GMU?"

I smiled, "No, I don't have a lawyer now because my last one lost his job at the same time as his firm dropped me as a client. I would feel bad if I caused someone else to end up unemployed. I even reported Arnold and Porter to the D.C. Bar Association, but got nowhere. They just did what law firms do. It was GMU that was acting strangely by refusing to allow the huge law firm to represent both of us, thereby depriving me of my pro bono representation. It seems as if money, not justice, rules."

"But what about the Christian Legal Society or the American Center for Law and Justice?"

I shrugged, "I don't know. My past experience shows there is little hope that it'd help. I have a job now, one that I enjoy and find challenging. It's on the cutting edge of biology. I don't want to jeopardize that or waste time on something that wouldn't help anyway."

"What exactly are you doing in your job?"

"Well, it's kind of hard to explain in lay terms. Basically, I do a kind of cancer research. There are receptors on the surface of cells— kind of like doorbells on a house. Imagine a person speaking through an intercom system outside a building. The receptionist answers and relays the message to her boss. If it's important, he relays the message to the big boss. If *he* considers it important, action is taken.

Cell communication is kind of like that. When a receptor is stimulated, a cascade of communication to the cell's control center takes place, like knocking down a series of dominos. Proteins bind to the next protein, or pass a phosphate group to it, or cut the next protein up. But, one difference from doorbells or intercoms is that each cell has thousands of receptors and usually each of the receptors is specific for only one signal." (See Figure 9, Chapter 2)

I hesitated, looking for signs that I had not lost my listeners along the way. Heads nodded encouragement. I was aware that I was over-simplifying, but wanted to help them understand. "There's a different cascade for each receptor, although some cascades interact or have common elements. It would be like a company responding to thousands of messages given through intercoms and having a logical coordinated response. In a cell, proteins in the nucleus may eventually turn on certain genes. That means the information in those genes is used to make new proteins, causing the cell to change its behavior in some way." I stopped and thought for a minute. "Well, actually, that's not the only way that signals from receptors are acted on, but to explain that would just get too involved."

I continued, "Each cell has to constantly analyze all the signals it gets and determine an appropriate response. Our group is looking at how messages travel from one type of receptor on one type of cell to one of the proteins that causes the DNA to respond. We're looking at the cascade of proteins involved because a mutation in one of them causes a type of cancer."

"So, if you're successful, will you cure cancer?"

I shook my head, "No, cancer is like a symptom. It has many different causes. We're investigating just one cause of one type of lymphoma. For us to discover anything of real significance we'll need to collaborate with lots of others who are studying other aspects of this cascade. Imagine lots of fleas working together to make a road map of an elephant. Eventually, they will be able to put the picture together, but it will require lots of cooperative effort."

A high school biology teacher leaned forward, "How do you study the action of a protein while it's still inside a cell?"

Since most of the others looked confused, I declined to answer fully. "You know, that just gets even more complex, but we basically make the proteins fluoresce in different colors by genetic engineering of the DNA that codes for them. I'd love to tell you more because it's really cool, but I'm afraid I have another appointment this afternoon and don't have time."

Most of them nodded in relief. A lawyer in the group leaned forward and changed the subject, "Did you ever get your legal file back from the firm?"

"I didn't. Isn't it their property?"

"No, it's yours. Why don't you request it and then send it to the American Center for Law and Justice (ACLJ)? They may be able to help."

I thought this was a pretty good idea, so I wrote a letter to Arnold and Porter, obtained my file, and contacted the ACLJ. They gave me the name of a lawyer who would be willing to review the file, Brett Lucas. Without opening the file, I slipped it into a FedEx box and shipped it to him. I then proceeded to forget all about it because my post-doctoral work was so totally engrossing.

* * * *

Within a few months, I'd mastered all the techniques needed to do my work for Dr. Weidman and had even been assigned a summer student to supervise and train. Using the manual I'd written, she was able to learn the laboratory techniques in a very short time. This seemed to be an ideal job. My boss trusted my scientific judgment, I liked teaching, I was enjoying being back in the lab. It was especially enthralling to be able to view proteins that I had modified to fluoresce in the cell interacting with each other (Figure 16). And to think that, until so recently, scientists had believed the cell was just a bag of undefined protoplasm.

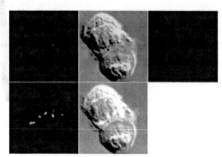

Figure 16 *This is a photograph obtained with the confocal microscope. It shows several views of a T cell (top) attacking a cell it perceives as foreign. The top middle view is a 3-D image of the cells; the two left views are of different proteins that have been rendered fluorescent. The top right shows where the fluorescent proteins may be communicating with each other and at the middle right is a combination of all the views.*

A couple of months later, I was contacted by a film company wanting to make a documentary about intelligent design with Ben Stein as the interviewer. It sounded exciting, and having what I thought was secure employment, I agreed to be interviewed. Mark Mathis, Associate Producer of the film, phoned to discuss my case.

"Do you have copies of any of the documents pertaining to your discipline?"

I hesitated, "Well, yes, but I'm not sure what's legal to release. After all, can I give you a letter written to me by someone who doesn't know I gave it to you?"

Mark answered, "In this lawsuit happy country you can sue a hamster if you wish. But, we have legal experts who will be looking over all of the material we include in the film. They will do this to protect you and to protect the company. People may get angry with us, but if what we say is true, bringing legal action will be an expensive gamble with poor odds."

He told me that the film would probably be released in 2008 and promised to be in touch about the interview with Ben Stein in the near future.

But in the summer of 2006 I experienced yet another setback. First, Dr. Weidman told me that he was concerned about his funding situation. Apparently, the Uniformed Services University had cut his funding for one post-doctoral fellow. It made for a nervous summer. Dr. Weidman told me that he had applied for grants and was getting answers in July and September, so I planned not to begin to look for a new job until September, just to maintain my sanity (my daughter's wedding would be in August). Meanwhile, I continued my work with a renewed determination, even starting a new project directing the writing of a computer program that would cut confocal microscope data processing time from a week to seconds. Within a couple of weeks, Dr. Weidman called me into his office to tell me not to worry about losing my job. He would find the money to keep me. Still a little concerned, I requested that, if he decided to let me go, he give me at least three months notice. Dr. Weidman laughed and assured me that I would have six. So, I did not look for a job, but poured my heart and time into doing the best possible work I could.

It did not make any difference. Near the end of October, 2006 Dr. Weidman called me into his office, "Caroline, I have some bad news for you."

This was too reminiscent of the past and I became quite tense.

Dr. Weidman continued, "My grant isn't being renewed. I'm running out of funds and so your job will be over by December 30."

I felt my face turn red and blurted out, "But, you promised! You said that you'd let me have at least six months notice. This is less than three!"

It was to no avail. I was frustrated because I had turned down a post-doctoral position at Yale on the strength of Dr. Weidman's word that this job would be for a minimum of three years.

Although my mind understood that this was nothing personal, my heart did not. I was hurt. I had worked so hard and was now on the edge of completing all the initial studies needed. I was confident that I could put a publication together given four months, but I only had two. So I spent them working at a near frantic pace, trying to get enough data to publish. But, cells take time to grow, most of the experiments took a week to complete, and even with doing them in an overlapping fashion, I could only complete the confocal data by December 30. It laid a good framework for a compelling paper or two, but I didn't have time to do the confirming experiments. Since I knew I needed to be spending all my time job-hunting, I decided not to fight for a publication. This was just as well since I was later told that Dr. Weidman would have found publishing a paper with my name on it detrimental to his academic future. Since I knew that he had a three-year NIH grant when he hired me, I wondered if his discovery of this fact had led to my being let go so much sooner than expected, but at that time it was only a fleeting thought.

* * * *

By March, 2007 I'd received four other government post-doctoral fellowship offers, two at NIH, but all fell through. I was told that it was due to lack of funding, but did wonder why the unfunded jobs had been advertised. I was later advised that the NIH, which are closely allied with the Smithsonian institutions, do not hire anyone who is known to have questioned neo-Darwinian evolution.

This notion was strengthened by the fact that I was called in for numerous interviews, which went very well, for positions for which I was eminently qualified and experienced, but was not offered those positions. Whereas before I became "known" as a Darwin doubter I was always offered every job for which I applied, now I was being turned down every time. My suspicions were later confirmed in a government report that stated, "*NMNH[238] officials have made clear their intent to prevent any scientist publicly skeptical of Darwinian Theory from ever being appointed as a Research Associate, no matter how sterling his or her professional credentials or research. This is discrimination.*"[239]

So, I decided to try other avenues. I applied for jobs in industry as a scientist, as a medical writer, and even in teaching. I noticed that the job I had at GMU was being advertised, but decided against applying there. But this clearly showed that their claim that they let me go because they had no more need or money for a Cell Biology teacher was false. As Shankar had said in the *Washington Post* article, "If…scientific rebels were once punished by the dogma and authority of the church, these (ID) advocates now believe they are being punished by the dogma and authority of science."[240] Actually, if the truth be told, science is not dogmatic. Rather, it was the dogma and authority of the non-theistic religious beliefs that have been imported by some enterprises that hold themselves out to be scientific that were causing the problem.

Having spare time, I also turned my thoughts back to the lawsuit and wondered what Brett had determined about my file. Because I'd not heard from him for months, I e-mailed him and got a rather strange reply. Apparently, he did not feel there was enough evidence to press for a lawsuit. I asked him to send the file back, so I could use the documents as references in writing this book. What a surprise. All the important documents were missing. I'd kept a daily record of proceedings since the day Dr. Carter had told me he would discipline me. It was missing. I had given Edward a copy of my grievance and the evidence in support of that grievance. They were missing. I had given Edward the letters from students and teachers in my support, the reply to my grievance from Dr. Carter, and my reply to him. They were also missing. What could have happened? Did Brett just misplace them?

---

238   This is the National Museum of Natural History at the Smithsonian Institution.
239   United States House of Representatives Committee on Government Reform Report, December 2006.
240   Vedantam, 2006.

I e-mailed him to ask and he answered immediately.[241] Although he said it was not impossible for him to have lost the papers, if he had, it would have been the first time ever. He'd never before misplaced a client's documents and did not find mine in a search of his office. He also said that he didn't remember seeing them, but admitted he had reviewed my file a long time before and may have forgotten. This seemed mysterious to me.

I knew Edward wouldn't have mislaid the documents because I'd been in his office and it was very tidy. I also knew he would not have had reason to launder my file. But, Edward was not the one who had returned my file to me. The whole thing made me feel uncomfortable and a little angry. Was it possible that the firm had done a Watergate in response to a request from GMU? After all, my file in the personnel office at GMU was also strangely empty. I didn't know and knew it likely wouldn't be possible to ever find out. However, the fact that those documents were missing would explain why Brett said there was insufficient evidence. Since the missing documents were key to supporting my claim that there was substance to my case, I decided to replace them (I had copies, having learned my lesson at GMU) and sent the file to yet another lawyer. This man responded within one working day. It was not good news. "Why did you take so long before seeking legal help? The statute of limitations has run out. You would have had a good case, even on the basis of religious discrimination, but now it's too late. I'm so sorry."

I was frustrated. If only I had checked the file before sending it to Brett Lucas, the ACLJ lawyer, if only I'd bothered him so he would not have sat on it for so long, if only... I realized that those who sought to suppress academic freedom and scientific objectivity had won this round. I'd lost my job because I advocated for open and honest discussion of the scientific facts about evolution, but it appeared to me that GMU had covered their tracks by exchanging my contract and pretending that I was a bad teacher. They had then refused to allow Arnold and Porter to represent me, resulting in my case being dropped. Finally, because my file was incomplete, the ACLJ lawyer didn't feel I had a case. I realized that it was useless to hope for justice through legal action. But then I thought, that's not the best way to raise awareness of the threat to our intellectual freedoms. It was becoming increasingly obvious to me that an alarm must be sounded and that I should be on the leading edge of those who made the most noise.

---

241 E-mail from Brett Lucas to Caroline Crocker, 2007.

REFERENCES

Anonymous. 2006. "The Intelligent Design Controversy in Higher Education." *The Coral Ridge Hour* (TV). August 13. http://www.coralridge.org/medialibrary/default.aspx (as of 4/1/09).

Geisler, Norman, Kirby Anderson. 1987. *Origin Science*. Grand Rapids, MI: Baker Book House.

Lucas, Brett. 2007. E-mail from Brett Lucas to Caroline Crocker, September.

Scott, Eugenie C., Glenn Branch. 2003. "Evolution: What's Wrong with Teaching the Controversy." *Trends in Ecology & Evolution*. 18(10):499-502. October 1.

United States House of Representatives Committee on Government Reform Report. 2006. "Intolerance and the Politicization of Science at the Smithsonian." December 11. http://www.kolbecenter.org/Intolerance.pdf (as of 4/1/09).

Vedantam, Shankar. 2006. "Eden and Evolution." *The Washington Post Magazine*. p. W08. February 5.

Chapter 10: What Now?

There is companionship in troubles, and the more public my case became the more others experiencing the same type of persecution contacted me and shared their own stories. Over 800 intellectually honest colleagues admit to seeing flaws in the theory of evolution[242] and as a result many have suffered attacks on their careers and reputations.[243] I was told of Nancy Bryson, a chemistry professor at Mississippi State University, who nearly lost her job for teaching the evidence for and against neo-Darwinian evolution to honors students, despite the fact that universities are supposed to be places for open inquiry and academic freedom. The university decided against demoting her only after her story was made public.[244] In comparison, the case of the immunologist who lost his job after 30 years of stellar research has not been made public, simply because he still hopes to secure another position.[245]

Since I was still writing graduate school recommendations for former students I was also alerted to the case of Bryan Leonard, a graduate student denied the right to defend his doctoral dissertation simply because he committed the "crime" of teaching high school students scientific criticisms of evolutionary theory.[246] Considering that archaeology students routinely employ ID techniques, I wryly wondered if they should also be "disciplined" in some way. Through other friends I met Richard M. von Sternberg who, as the editor of a scientific journal, had allowed a peer-reviewed ID friendly paper to be published. He consequently was pressured to resign and had his name/reputation smeared.[247] Sternberg was also featured in the movie *Expelled*, as was Guillermo Gonzalez, a highly published and brilliant astronomer.

This kind and gentle man with a shy smile committed the "crime" of co-authoring a book suggesting a universe demonstrating evidence of design.[248] Gonzalez was then denied tenure and lost his job at Iowa State University,[249] despite the fact that he discovered a couple of extra-solar planets! E-mails from his colleagues show that they clearly do not support intelligent design (or, apparently, academic freedom and objectivity in science). One atheist religion professor

---

242   http://www.dissentfromdarwin.org/
243   Bergman, 2008, Ch. 3.
244   Bhattacharjee, 2003, p.247.
245   Interview of immunologist by Caroline Crocker, January, 2006. His identity has been withheld at his request.
246   Bergin, 2005, p. 23.
247   http://www.rsternberg.net/smithsonian.php
248   Gonzalez and Richards, 2004.
249   Hauptman, 2007.

opposed Gonzalez by circulating a petition that read, "Intelligent Design ... has now established a presence, even if minimal, at Iowa State University. Accordingly, if you are concerned about the negative impact of intelligent design on the integrity of science and on our university, please consider signing."[250] Obviously, being a religion professor, Avalos was probably not so much worried about the science as about a challenge to his religion. Even my lawyer Edward did not find another job, having made the "mistake" of standing up for those who question the reigning orthodoxy.[251] His character is evident in that he is still representing the persecuted and the underprivileged, albeit *pro bono*.

What about the all-important freedom to think in an unrestricted fashion in research institutes and university classrooms? In the United States, our inventiveness and ability to think outside the box is a large part of what makes us competitive in the global marketplace. Unfortunately, it appears that our freedom to espouse and consider different points of view is fast disappearing. Many evolutionists insist that evolution is a fact and must not be questioned. Take Michael Ruse who said, "Evolution is fact, FACT, **FACT!**,"[252] or Richard Dawkins who said, "It is absolutely safe to say that if you meet someone who claims not to believe in evolution, that person is ignorant, stupid or insane (or wicked, but I'd rather not consider that)."[253] It appears that the consensus among many is that our vulnerable university students, who are old enough to smoke, drink, and go to war, must be protected from dangerous ideas like questioning neo-Darwinism. Certain thoughts are banned; objective teachers are gagged.

Is this good for us as a nation? I would suggest that it is not. We are being stifled into a politically correct ideology and scientists are being motivated more by fear about their reputations and hunt for money than by curiosity. Freedom of inquiry is allowed only within the context of accepting the "fact" of neo-Darwinian evolution. This will have a huge negative impact not only on science, but also on our well-being and economy. One only needs to remember the consequences of Lysenkoism to understand.[254] Here, too, scientific dissent was outlawed and those who opposed the prevailing dogma lost their jobs (and sometimes their lives). Since the enforced scientific view was incorrect, people

---

250 E-mail from Hector Avalos to colleagues, sent 8/2/2005.
251 http://www.youtube.com/watch?v=6lCe5ICSKI0&feature=related
252 Ruse, 1983, p. 58.
253 Dawkins, 1989, p. 3.
254 Wells, 2006.

starved to death, science stagnated, and Russia suffered both economically and scientifically.[255]

GMU provides many excellent examples of the suppression of scientific objectivity and the erosion of our first amendment freedoms. My tutoring brings me into contact with many students, so I hear much about what occurs in their classrooms. I have seen first hand that GMU is a good school and certainly offers a science education superior to what can be obtained at many private institutions. However, the mandatory indoctrination (which is by no means unique to GMU) is troubling. At GMU, all biology majors are required to take Animal Biology; a class that Dr. Carter told me explicitly was given for the purpose of educating students about evolution. These students are subjected to an entire semester of "proofs" for neo-Darwinian evolution with Campbell's *Biology* textbook as the authoritative source.[256] Problems that are brought up by students are quickly dismissed. An ecology major at a university on the East Coast told me that if ID is mentioned, it is only in a derogatory fashion with no attempt to accurately explain the thinking of ID theorists.[257] This is obvious in the Campbell *Biology* test bank,[258] which contains questions such as,

The theory of evolution is most accurately described as
a. An educated guess about how species originate
b. An opinion that some scientists hold about how living things change over time
c. **An overarching explanation, supported by much evidence, for how populations change over time**
d. An idea about how acquired characteristics are passed on to subsequent generations

Obviously, the above is not only about science, but rather makes sure that the student answers according to the prevailing consensus (see footnote). This particular question (and answer) would be more accurate if it only asked about

---

255 According to author (and MD) Michael Crichton, this is a great threat in America today. "I regard consensus science as an extremely pernicious development that ought to be stopped cold in its tracks. Historically, **the claim of consensus has been the first refuge of scoundrels; it is a way to avoid debate by claiming that the matter is already settled**. … Let's be clear: the work of science has nothing whatever to do with consensus. Consensus is the business of politics. Science, on the contrary, requires only one investigator who happens to be right, which means that he or she has results that are verifiable by reference to the real world. **In science consensus is irrelevant**. What is relevant is reproducible results. The greatest scientists in history are great precisely because they broke with the consensus. There is no such thing as consensus science. If it's consensus, it isn't science. If it's science, it isn't consensus. Period." (Emphasis added)
256 Campbell and Reece, 2002.
257 Interview of GMU ecology student by Caroline Crocker, March, 2009.
258 Campbell Biology Testbank v. 6.0

microevolution and left out the over-the-top "overarching" part! Other questions from this test bank ensure that the student understands that 1) macroevolution is merely speciation (no mention of the need for entirely new morphologies and information), 2) that ID as an explanation for irreducible complexity is as ridiculous as suggesting that the absence of a murder weapon and a suspect means there could not have been a murder, and 3) that aliens may well have seeded life on Earth.

Just recently a student, "Steve," who is agnostic about evolution contacted me after he was completely disgusted by the way his professor was teaching the students in his class. Steve reported to me that the students who brought up scientific evidence challenging neo-Darwinism were verbally crushed in class. It appeared that the teacher had been specifically prepared to put down challengers. Steve was horrified to see some classmates literally shake after a confrontational encounter with the imposing professor who arbitrarily dismissed their very legitimate concerns. The importance of this indoctrination to the authorities at GMU is demonstrated by the fact that, after the time spent on evolution, only the last third of the Animal Biology course is left to teach about the organ systems.[259]

It looks much as if GMU is extremely uneasy about even the possibility of having open-minded teachers on their faculty. I was informed that while the Animal Biology teacher was lecturing on evolution (Fall, 2008), a high-level professor was present in the room all the while taking notes.[260] Making sure Darwinian orthodoxy was being maintained? Another student, "Tasha," told me that when privately having coffee with one of her professors, this man admitted to doubts about the ability of neo-Darwinian evolution to explain his observations in physics. However he became very frightened when Tasha suggested the possibility of intelligent design, hastily informing her that, "We don't talk about such things." Taken aback, Tasha began to question him, but the nervous professor quickly changed the subject.[261]

Both teachers and students are only too aware of the risks associated with being known as someone who thinks outside the box. I suspect that this is the reason for the pro-evolution and anti-creationism signs that decorate many faculty office doors; ID is also slammed at every opportunity.[262] Only months after

259 Interview of GMU pre-med student by Caroline Crocker, December, 2008. The student's identity has been withheld at their request.
260 Interview of GMU student by Caroline Crocker, November, 2008. The student's identity has been withheld at their request.
261 Interview of GMU student by Caroline Crocker, July, 2008. The student intends to pursue graduate work, so her identity was withheld at her request.
262 http://www.youngcosmos.com/blog/archives/362

I lost my job, the Mason Gazette ran an article on what their "experts" say about ID[263] (nothing good). In case that was not enough to counteract the "damage" resulting from my balanced presentation of the scientific facts, less than a year after my "discipline" the National Center for Science Education's Eugenie Scott was invited to GMU to lecture against ID.[264] One must be a loyal party member, or a "good comrade" as Ben Stein puts it in the movie *Expelled*.[265] GMU does not seem as worried about accurate science as it is about the promotion of a particular kind of religion by suppressing any scientific evidence that supports another.

The suppression of academic freedom and scientific objectivity is not just found at GMU. During the Louisiana House Educational Committee hearings on SB 773 in Baton Rouge in May of 2008, Bryan Carstens, a Louisiana State professor spoke proudly of how he and 59 other biology professors at LSU have signed a document confirming their public agreement with evolution.[266] Since I was present at the hearing, I recall a revealing exchange when a house member wryly asked him what would happen to someone who refused to sign. The silence was deafening. The paranoia engendered by the active persecution of all who dare to question any aspect of neo-Darwinism was exemplified in the testimony of Barbara Forrest, who breathlessly and repeatedly informed us, "Discovery Institute is watching your every move!"[267]

At a recent conference in Hawaii I was approached by a group of about eight students lamenting about how only one side of the evolution issue is taught in their classrooms and that anyone who suggests that there may be scientific evidence on the other side is ridiculed. In fact, at universities throughout the country, faculty and administrators harass students who attend Intelligent Design and Evolution Awareness (IDEA) club meetings, where they just want to openly and freely investigate the evidence supporting evolution versus intelligent design. The IDEA club organizers at some universities complain that their activities are severely discouraged by those in authority, presumably so no student even has a chance of being "infected" with such subversive ideas. One leader at a university in California told me,

> Within a year, the climate became very hostile against ID. The trouble started when a professor complained to administrators about our IDEA meetings. At the time the resistance from administration started, I was ar-

---

263 http://gazette.gmu.edu/articles/7155/
264 http://gazette.gmu.edu/articles/7537/
265 Stein in *Expelled: No Intelligence Allowed*, Documentary released in April, 2008.
266 http://www.2theadvocate.com/news/19165269.html
267 http://www.evolutionnews.org/2008/06/how_to_rebut_barbara_forrest_e.html

ranging for pro-ID scholars to present at our campus. After monies were already allocated for speakers and travel costs, our IDEA Club was told by administrators that we were not allowed to publicize our events where pro-ID speakers would be presenting. Pressure from administrators suffocated the IDEA Club within the same academic year... Any given professor that ignorantly speaks against ID may be the one who will give me a shot at an internship or research project. Starting an IDEA Club on my campus would be academic and professional suicide.[268]

Another student wrote that when he tried to start a club, "I received support from the philosophy department, but harsh antagonism from the biology department,"[269] and a graduate student told me that participation in an IDEA club would seriously jeopardize her chances of completing a graduate degree.[270] A postdoctoral scientist at the NIH informed me that he needs to stay *in cognito* about his Darwin-doubting ways,[271] as did a biologist in the University of California system.[272] Both were hoping to protect their research futures. Still another scientist privately told National Public Radio's Barbara Bradley-Hagerty that to admit to doubts about evolution would mean an end to his advancement in academia.[273] In fact, many of the scientists who question neo-Darwinian evolution advise their students to remain silent about such questions until after receiving tenure. It very much appears that, at every level of academia, it is necessary to "sign on the dotted line" and fully subscribe to Darwinism in order to succeed.

For me, student-relayed news of so many of my former colleagues decrying me in their classes, continued rejection letters from prospective employers, and nasty comments about me on the Internet made me realize that I would have to earn a living in some other way. I chose a possible career path where I hoped I would be able to avoid the blacklisting and to bring in some very necessary income and decided to start a tutoring company under my maiden name. After all, I had enjoyed most aspects of teaching and those parts I did not like (dealing with cheating and politics) would not be a part of tutoring. I also hoped to be able to spend some time helping promote objectivity in science.

---

268 E-mail from former IDEA club leader to Caroline Crocker, May 2008. The author's identity has been withheld at their request.
269 E-mail from former IDEA club leader to Caroline Crocker, June 2008. The author's identity has been withheld at their request.
270 E-mail from student to Caroline Crocker, June 2008. The author's identity has been withheld at their request.
271 Interview of NIH postdoctoral scientist by Caroline Crocker, October, 2007. Identity has been withheld at their request.
272 Interview of tenure-track University of California biologist by Caroline Crocker, March 2009. Identity and specific campus have been withheld at the scientist's request.
273 Bradley-Hagerty, 2005.

My first student was a young lady, Maria, who was having difficulties with biology. I was amazed to find that a 7th grader was studying at the same level as introductory biology students at GMU, but we gamely worked through the structure of cells and the systems of the body. Her mother, Felicita, and I were both gratified when Maria's grades showed immediate improvement.

The first challenge came when Maria's teacher started the unit on evolution. During our tutoring session I noticed that her textbook claimed that embryology recapitulates phylogeny (pre-birth development parallels evolutionary history) and included a reproduction of Haeckel's embryos, which allege to show striking similarities between different animal embryos during the early stages of their development. These illustrations have been known to be a hoax for about 100 years and most embryologists are now well aware that the drawings by Haeckel are inaccurate.[274] Nonetheless many biology textbooks continue to offer them as evidence for neo-Darwinian evolution.[275] The text also asserted that "Darwin's" finches are proof of evolution, even though Darwin did very little with finches. Perhaps not a significant point, but I believe this is symptomatic of the idolization of the man that exists among followers of this ideology. More importantly, Maria's textbook said that recent research on finch beaks conducted by the Grants demonstrated a change of beak size in response to a drought, but did not mention the return to typically sized beaks the following year.[276] It also did not specify that this is hardly a demonstration of how dinosaurs supposedly evolved into birds or a single cell eventually gave rise to human beings. I was willing to say, "This is what your text says," but wondered what Felicita, a staunch Catholic, would think. Despite the risk, my conscience would not let me take the easy route and, as we stood in the doorway chatting after a tutoring session, I asked her, "About evolution, do you want me to teach the real science or what the textbook says?"

"What do you mean? Is the textbook wrong?" Felicita looked confused.

"Well, yes. In previous chapters the book was just out-of-date or in other instances it over-simplified to the point of inaccuracy; I pointed those out to Maria. But in this chapter it's downright erroneous in places and misleading in others. This is probably because of the current social climate, so I wanted to check what you would like me to do." I knew that being honest about my independent stance with regard to neo-Darwinian evolution might lose me a pupil, but was convinced that I should be true to what I stand for: scientific integrity.

---

274 Cushmann, 2001, p. 18
275 Wells, 2000.
276 Grant and Grant, 2002.

"I want her to learn the truth!" Felicita exclaimed, revealing that she is a member of the 70-80% of Americans who would like to see science taught in an objective and intellectually honest manner.[277, 278]

Here I hesitated, "Listen, being vocal about this issue probably lost me three jobs and resulted in my being blacklisted from getting many others. Students are also being intimidated into following the party line. If I teach Maria both sides of the issue, I strongly advise that you instruct her not to challenge her teacher."

"But, the teacher should also know the truth. After all, it's a Catholic school and committed to excellence in teaching."

"What you tell Maria to do is your decision, obviously, but please consider carefully. The thought police are hot on this issue. I know she's only in seventh grade, but you definitely need to carefully consider if it's worth the risk. Is she up to the possible consequences of being outspoken on this issue?"

After due consideration and more conversation, Felicita asked me to teach Maria the truth, but to instruct her to keep it to herself. The result was that Maria found the chapters on evolution fascinating (kids love a controversy) and she got an "A" on the test, just by "telling the teacher what she wants to hear." She had been educated without being indoctrinated.

I ran into the same issue but with a different result with a high school student taking AP Biology. Gerome's ambition was to either become a physician or a sports star, whichever came easier. His attitude towards school reflected these goals; I had a suspicion that hiring a tutor was his parents' last-ditch effort to help Gerome succeed academically. When we reached the evolution chapters, I asked him if he wanted to learn what the chapters said or more than that. Hardly surprisingly, unlike Felicita, he chose the first option. This was fine with me; it just had to be his choice. Unfortunately, academia does not agree with me and students are not given the choice of learning one or both sides. Only one side is allowed and only one side is presented.

Over next couple of years I tutored college level chemistry (inorganic and organic), physics, botany, genetics, ecology, English, and even some mathematics. As I had not taken many of these courses since I was 16 or 17 in community college, it meant reading the book before the students arrived and then explaining it. Nonetheless, many of them told me that they wished their teachers would explain things the same way I do. Maybe it was because much of the material was now new to me; I knew what would confuse them because it had just confused me. It was a joy to receive letters of thanks when the students did well in

---

277 Zogby Poll, 2009.
278 Steinberg Poll, 2004.

their classes.[279] It was great to guide a research student through writing her first ever abstract for her summer research project and amazing to hear that her professor had decided to use the student's abstract instead of his own in his grant application! Even better was the fact that he was funded. I smiled at the thought of the professor's shock should he discover he was using material that I'd guided and edited. Even being "exposed" by *Skeptic* magazine as an alleged fraud who, after being blacklisted from employment, had the gall to try and earn money under her maiden name,[280] did not take away from that satisfaction. It amazes me how many presume to speak authoritatively about my case when they have never made an attempt to contact me.

Soon after starting the tutoring company I received a surprising phone call from the Discovery Institute inviting me to give a short presentation on my GMU experiences at a conference in Seattle. Since I was eager for the opportunity to meet others with experiences similar to mine, I accepted. Arriving in Seattle in August of 2007, I took a taxi to the hotel, unpacked and wandered across the street to the restaurant hosting the Discovery Institute reception. I was seated next to an elderly gentleman who informed me that he is one of the few members of the National Academy of Science who doubts evolution. His name was Phil Skell. After the usual small talk, Dr. Skell and I had a fascinating conversation about the actual contribution of evolutionary theory to practical science. That is, we discussed how much the theory influences what experiments are done and the direction new research takes. In my experience, I informed him, evolutionary theory did not influence my choice of experiments or interpretation of results at all. That is, the investigation of how a glucocorticoid regulates the release or secretion of immunomodulatory chemicals or how stimulation of the T cell receptor results in a virtual ballet of protein movement does not require any pre-existing dogma, only controlled experiments and careful observation. Dr. Skell nodded eagerly, "Yes, that's what almost every practicing scientist with whom I have spoken says; evolution makes no difference to their research!"[281] Interestingly enough, Dr. Skell's opinions are discounted on many neoDarwinist websites because he is an organic chemist and not a biologist. I wonder how that prevents him from being able to accurately poll practicing scientists from other disciplines.

During dessert, I and others with similar experiences were asked to speak on what happened to us as a result of our suggesting that neo-Darwinian evo-

---

279   For example, "Because of your tutoring, I got an A in inorganic chemistry even though over half of my class had to drop the course," or "Thank you for your help with cell biology. It made all the difference. I got an A!"
280   Sager and Bottaro, 2008.
281   Skell, 2005.

lution may be out-dated or ill-supported scientifically. Our stories were even shocking to those who were familiar with the persecution of Darwin-doubters. After the negative and harrowing experience of finding myself banned from the career I had worked so long and hard to attain (ten years of university, not to mention time spent teaching and conducting research), it was wonderful to be affirmed and even admired. When I thought about it, it does take certain amount of courage to stand up against people who apparently would do almost anything to silence you. I was glad to be, at least for a short time, in the company of those who clapped for me instead of those who ignorantly sneered out of prejudice against anyone who would challenge the prevailing dogma.

The next evening we had a special treat. The producers of the movie for which I had interviewed months before were going to show us a preview. Since, for personal reasons, I was out-of-town when Ben Stein was there, Mark Mathis had conducted my interview and I'd made incorrect assumptions about this movie. Basically, I'd assumed it was to be similar to the other informational ID-related DVDs. I was not expecting much. We were ushered into a theater with about 100 others and seated before a large screen. Without further preamble the "bad boy" music began and I saw the title of the movie, *Expelled: No Intelligence Allowed.* I was astonished to see myself in the trailer on the screen and impressed by the quality of what little we saw. We were then told that this was slated to be a major blockbuster, opening in over 1000 theaters nationwide. Looking at the trailer, I could see why. It was not a low-budget production, but would be a professionally done, innovative, entertaining and fascinating documentary starring Ben Stein. Walking out of the theater with all the other stunned people, I wryly observed that it was just as well I had not found a job because I would almost certainly have lost it as soon as the movie was released. My decision was confirmed. Since I had nothing left to lose, I decided to go as public as possible about the suppression of academic freedom and scientific objectivity within American academia. Who could be better prepared than me to understand the loss of our hard-won freedoms, the need to preserve what is left and to fight to win back the freedoms that have driven success in the United States and everywhere else they are enjoyed?

Not long afterwards, Casey Luskin contacted me about working for a non-profit organization called the Intelligent Design and Evolution Awareness (IDEA) Center.[282] I'd been a speaker at IDEA club events, so knew something about the Center, but was intrigued to know more. The IDEA Center was conceived by a group of students at the University of California at San Diego. This same group

---

282 www.ideacenter.org

started the first IDEA Club in 1999 out of frustration at the one-sided nature of the teaching their professors offered, organizing a gathering where students from all points of view were welcome. The purpose was to discuss origins issues, the scientific evidence, and its philosophical or theological implications in a friendly and open atmosphere.

After a major IDEA Center conference, students from other universities became interested, so the founding members of the club organized into a non-profit organization. IDEA clubs started up all over the country and even overseas. Now the board felt it was necessary to hire an executive director. It sounded like a great opportunity. I was honored when they invited me to consider the position and, after some consideration, accepted in January of 2008. Finally my passion for intellectual integrity in considering all the scientific evidence had *gained* instead of lost me a job.

More encouragement soon followed when I received a letter from Biola University. I was informed that the 2008 Phillip E. Johnson Award was to be conferred on Ben Stein for his work in *Expelled* and secondarily on three of the scientists who are featured in the movie, Richard Sternberg, Guillermo Gonzalez, and me.[283]

We were all invited to an award banquet and ceremony where we would each give a short presentation on how we stood up for "the causes of liberty and truth in science and academia." A particular highlight for me was when Ben Stein arrived at the banquet and called across the room, "Caroline, it's so great to finally meet you!" To this day I am still flabbergasted when folks recognize me. As for Ben, I was utterly amazed when I observed that he either knew or quickly learned everyone's names in the room. In fact, this is what he did in every place I saw him from then on; learning up to 100 names when introduced to each person only once did not seem to faze him. That ability to make everyone feel like his personal friend was truly impressive; I wished it were contagious.

After the dinner, we were escorted to our seats under the protection of security, having been told that there would be over 1000 people in attendance. Fortunately, there was no problem. In fact, this was probably the most supportive large audience I'd spoken to thus far. We had been instructed to keep our talks to ten minutes, but part way through I began to worry if this was including or excluding audience cheering and clapping time. I was high on the adrenaline for hours afterwards.

As we left the building, Ben asked me, "So, what do you think about being a movie star?"

---

283   http://www.uncommondescent.com/expelled/expelled-at-biola-ben-stein-receives-the-phillip-johnson-award/

I answered truthfully, "I'm not sure what to think."

In response, he encouraged me, "There's nothing about it *not* to like!"

For someone who certainly receives a lot of media venom, this was an incredible statement. Later, when I began to see unflattering reports about him and about myself on the Internet, I remembered his words and how such criticism did not faze him.

* * * *

The media requests began to pour in once again and I started to feel less like an expelled scientist and more like a "movie star." I received an invitation from Matt Barber of "Concerned Women for America" to interview on their radio program,[284] again about the unfair treatment I had received at the hands of GMU and my involvement in the movie, *Expelled*. I figured I might as well accept and took the Metro to their office in Washington, D.C. Upon entering the suite of rooms, I was recognized and warmly greeted by the receptionist and introduced to many of the CWA staff. They were so friendly and normal that I quickly regained control of my nerves and settled into an enjoyable interview. However, I did chuckle at the erroneous initial (and edited out) statement that I was one of the producers of *Expelled*!

This was followed by more speaking requests from schools and churches and I embarked on a whirlwind of these engagements. It was extremely gratifying to find that many events were standing room only. Obviously, people wanted to hear about this issue. A team of people volunteered to help me; they were all much needed and appreciated. I was amazed by how many people it takes to put together a successful talk: people to man the book table, run the electronics, solve the inevitable hiccups, and even rescue me after an hour of questions. Although there was always some antagonism to the message, most of the questions I was asked were eminently answerable.

"Dr. Crocker, thank you for a most informative and frightening talk. What I would like to know is how can parents prepare their children for what they'll encounter at university?"

This was a heartfelt and common question at many of these engagements. After all, state schools and universities have a definite agenda regarding the necessity of promoting neo-Darwinism and eradicating any belief in a god. Consider, for example, this statement from one of the primary magazines used in educating biology teachers, "When young children are indoctrinated into believing that for which there is no evidence (God, Heaven, Hell, etc.), a habit of mind is being developed that is inconsistent with the open, enquiring mind

---

284   Barber, 2008.

needed for scientific study…the habits of mind are inconsistent between science and religion."[285] Of course, this is an incorrect use of the word religion, since any belief about origins is religion, including belief in natural causes. Basically since the magazine is advocating for eradication of theism, another religion is being promoted (atheism or humanism).

Do not be misled. Atheism is not the absence of religion, but is itself a religion, as are humanism and even agnosticism.[286] This means that, when origins science is not taught objectively and evolution is linked to secular humanism, there is no separation of church and state. Some say that this is why over half of the students who start university as Christians change their faith to atheism or agnosticism before leaving.[287]

The atheist author of *The God Delusion*, Richard Dawkins converted to this faith after being indoctrinated into neo-Darwinian evolution at school.[288] So did Cornell University Professor Will Provine, seen in *Expelled*, who emphatically spouts on about the absence of purpose in life and his own intention to commit suicide.[289] The story of how Joseph Campbell, a famous author, mythologist, and atheist, exchanged his Roman Catholic faith for atheism after being taught neo-Darwinian evolution can be seen on Youtube.[290] These are just a few examples of the many people who were influenced by the incomplete or philosophically biased teaching of the science relating to evolution, and who then adopted atheism as their personal faith. For Dawkins, his faith in atheism is even evangelistic, "…I think a case can be made that faith is one of the world's great evils, comparable to the smallpox but harder to eradicate."[291]

Therefore, I would always carefully answer parental questions about preparing their children to face the mandatory neo-Darwinian evolution indoctrination they would face at state schools: "I think it's important to educate your children. Don't leave it to the schools, and don't shy away from presenting all sides of this issue. After all, it's better if they hear all the facts from you rather than some of the facts from their neo-Darwinist teachers and professors. Then, make sure your sources are very accurate and have scientific merit. Some professors will not hesitate to crush rather than correct a student who they believe gets something wrong. Others might be sympathetic, but not allowed to admit it. Personally, I would recommend checking out the information available at Probe

285 Good, 2003.
286 7th Court of Appeals, August, 2005; *Lee v. Weisman*; *United States v. Seeger*.
287 Nowicki, 2008.
288 Dawkins, 2006.
289 Provine, 1998.
290 http://www.youtube.com/watch?v=vJmNBxbExuA
291 Dawkins, 1997.

Ministries,[292] the IDEA Center website,[293] and in the book, *Explore Evolution.*[294] Finally, teach your kids to think logically and give them some grounding in philosophy. After all, it's simply illogical to say that evidence for microevolution (changes within a type of organism) proves macroevolution (development of entirely new structures). It's also incorrect to say that, because empirical science can't measure the supernatural, it doesn't exist."

I do realize that to accomplish all of this requires a lot of work on the part of parents. In these days of public education, the responsibility to learn and pass on information has largely been abdicated to the state. However, the state is now behaving irresponsibly and I suggest that parents need to reclaim the right and responsibility to educate their children.

* * * *

Voicing another common response to my presentations, an older gentleman in Hawaii (Nov, 2008) stepped up to the audience microphone and spoke in a worried tone. "We've always taught our children to stand up for what they believe, but after hearing your talk, I wonder if I should advise my daughter to stay quiet about her beliefs until after she graduates from college."

I nodded sympathetically, "If she wants to go into science, I would advise her to keep doubts about neo-Darwinism to herself for much longer than that. After all, according to a US House subcommittee report about the Smithsonian, NMNH [National Museum of Natural History] officials have made clear their intent to prevent any scientist publicly skeptical of Darwinian theory from ever being appointed as a Research Associate, no matter how sterling his or her professional credentials or research.[295] In my opinion, she should remain *incognito* at least until she has tenure."

A young man stood up, "Personally, I've decided not to study science at all. It's just too fraught with difficulties."

I nodded sympathetically, "Unfortunately, yours is a common attitude among young people of faith and it is of great concern to me. Science has immense potential for good or evil—I do not like the idea of giving over all scientific decisions to those who do not believe in academic freedom or scientific objectivity, let alone those who believe there is no ultimate basis for determining what is right or wrong. This is why the soon-to-be-incorporated organization I am starting, American Institute for Technology and Science Education

---

292   www.probe.org
293   www.idea.org
294   Meyer et al., 2005.
295   United States House of Representatives Subcommittee Report, 2006.

(AITSE),[296] will have preparation of young people for college and mentorship of those interested in science careers as specific goals."

Another person waved their hand and I indicated that they should approach the microphone.

"Dr. Crocker, I've been reading about you on the Internet. It says that *Expelled* is full of lies and you didn't really get fired, but your contract was over. You weren't disciplined and, if so, your discipline had nothing to do with evolution." The young man then folded his arms belligerently.

This was a fair question. I would much rather have people ask me than just believe everything they read.

"Well, that is partially true. The last contract I had was over, but the story behind it is much more complicated than that.[297] I won't explain here, but you can always buy my book, where I go into detail about what really happened," I answered with a twinkle in my eye. "However, about the suggestion that the discipline I received was not due to my questioning Darwinism, both the departmental administrator and a long-term professor told me that this was the *only* reason for my being removed from lecturing. Actually, I do not see why GMU would refuse to give the standard waiver to the law firm, forcing the firm to fire me, if my case was groundless.[298] But, in fact, they knew that had engaged in religious discrimination when they removed me from lecturing. This is why in *Expelled* the representative speaking on behalf of GMU carefully removed all references to evolution, instead just repeating that my contract was over."[299]

The young man looked thoughtful. "They also wrote that you really were teaching creationism."

I smiled, "Well, if I was, the students did not know it. Take a look at their letters on my website under "letters."[300] Only if one equates giving scientific evidence on both sides of the evolution issue to teaching creationism would I be guilty."

He had one last burning question and bravely blurted it out, "Dr. Crocker, I also read that you think dogs evolve into cats!"

I shook my head and smiled, "Surely after hearing the talk today you must know that I'm not a total idiot. Teachers do sometimes say extreme things to illustrate their lectures but most educated people recognize hyperbole when they encounter it. I recently heard that the introductory biology teacher (who is a statistician) at GMU told his students that spray painting a flower would change

296 www.aitse.org
297 Letter from Edward Sisson to Alan Merton, August 15, 2005. A copy can be found in Appendix VI.
298 http://www.youtube.com/watch?v=61Ce51CSK10
299 *Expelled: No Intelligence Allowed.*
300 www.intellectualhonesty.info

its phenotype (physical expression of the genetic makeup).[301] This is obviously grossly inaccurate, but he felt it would help the students grasp the concept. Personally, I told the student who was complaining to cut his prof some slack—he was obviously teaching outside his realm of expertise."

"In retrospect, I probably should have been much more careful about what I said. There are some slides I would not use again, but I wasn't politically astute yet and did leave myself open to cheap shots…and many Darwinists have not hesitated to take aim and fire. In the future I will take care not to give them so much ammunition."

The audience laughed and the moderator of the Hawaii event stepped forward to try to close the question time, but there were still more questions.

"Dr. Crocker, why do you think people are so opposed to the questioning of Darwinism?" asked a father balancing his toddler on his hip.

"My suspicion is that it is, at heart, because religion (humanism and atheism) is being challenged. As Gould said, 'Before Darwin, we thought that a benevolent God had created us.'[302] Will Provine, who is also featured in *Expelled*, crows, 'Evolution is the greatest engine of atheism ever invented.'[303] I would suspect that the dogmatic teaching of neo-Darwinian evolution may be just as religiously motivated as the teaching of creationism. According to Dr. Michael Walker, 'One is forced to conclude that many scientists and technologists pay lip-service to Darwinian Theory only because it supposedly excludes a Creator from yet another area of material phenomena, and not because it has been paradigmatic in establishing the canons of research in the life sciences and the earth sciences.'[304] In comparison, I tried not to indoctrinate, but merely to fulfill a basic duty of honesty and objectivity that arises due to the open-minded nature of science and the need for religious neutrality."

Campbell's *Biology* is a leading biology textbook in public high schools and colleges, but the test bank contains a question about natural theology and god.[305] This is evidence that the authors and/or publishers, and those who insist on the use of this book, may be at least somewhat religiously motivated. In fact, the text itself admits that evolution is a challenge to a previous worldview.[306]

An older man dressed in a suit stepped up to the microphone, "So, if Darwinism is partially religion, why do you think that ID isn't? I've heard its just creationism in disguise."

---

301 Interview by Caroline Crocker of GMU student, November, 2008.
302 Gould, 1978.
303 Provine, 1998.
304 Walker, 1981, p. 45.
305 Campbell Biology Testbank v. 6.0
306 Campbell and Reece, 2002. p. 439.

Since this is a common source of misunderstanding, I wanted to be clear about my answer, "Well first I want to clarify that the theory of evolution is not religion, but it is consistent with one: atheism or humanism,[307] and is frequently used to promote that religion.[308] Intelligent Design is also not religion, but is consistent with some types of religion: theistic ones. In my experience, the ID movement is all about seeking scientific, not religious, truth. Religion is defined as something based on a religious text and requires adherents to observe certain beliefs or behaviors. In contrast, ID advocates do not support or require adherence to a particular religious point of view. In fact, not everyone who is sympathetic to ID is a member of some organized theistic religion (e.g., Dr. Steven Fuller and Dr. David Berlinski for example). They merely point out that the scientific evidence for evolution is inadequate or incomplete, that intelligence is a natural phenomenon, and that we have scientific methods for detecting intelligence. Intelligent Design may be compatible with theistic faith or some other belief systems, but that does not make it religion. Like macroevolution, it is a forensic science."

Even though I had just spoken about this, the man requested clarification, so I continued.

"Well, at the moment, the scientific detection of the operation of intelligent beings is being or has been used in archeology, SETI (the Search for Extraterrestrial Intelligence) and forensics. ID science involves the application of these same tried and tested methods for the detection of intelligence to other branches of science, like astronomy and biology. By using these methods, there appears to be evidence indicating that some of the phenomena we observe in the natural world may be the result of the operation of an intelligence."

"But, what about the charge that ID will stifle scientific research because people will say that God did it?"

I shook my head, "This is just scaremongering. A bit of thought will show that even believing 'God did it' never has and therefore most likely will not stop people from investigating our world. In fact, one could likewise suggest that finding out how God did something is every bit as enticing as finding out how 'nature' did it. Many great scientists were people of faith: Copernicus, Mendel, Newton, Pasteur, and Collins. Some even wrote that their results pointed to

---

307   The 1933 Humanist Manifesto says that humanism is a religion that is meant to replace all theistic religions.
308   It is important to note that the National Center for Science Education, one of the main contenders for the one-sided teaching of evolution, endorses humanism, a U.S. Supreme Court-defined religion. http://ncseweb.org/media/voices/council-democratic-secular-humanism

Intelligent Design.[309] Even Einstein, although not a believer in a personal God, firmly believed that the physical laws governing the universe exhibited evidence of design. He used this principle to guide his work, 'When I am judging a theory, I ask myself whether, if I were God, I would have arranged the world in such a way.'" [310]

I paused to allow the audience to digest this quote and then continued, "Contrary to modern Darwinists, Einstein believed that anyone who is a serious scientist will be convinced that there is an intelligence shown in the universe that is greatly superior to man.[311] I wonder, if Einstein had lived today, would he have found himself banned from publishing his ideas as are so many scientists today?"

A gray-haired genteel lady stepped forward, speaking urgently, "Dr. Crocker, what can we do about all this? It's obviously not just about science."

I was pleased to hear that this message had been received, "You're right. It's about worldview. Academia appears to be intentionally indoctrinating our young people with an antitheistic worldview. As for what to do—I would suggest finding out if your *alma mater* allows free discussion of origins issues. If not, stop donating and let them know why you are taking this action. I suspect that a lot of institutions and scientists are going along with the party line simply because they will stop receiving grants if they don't. So hit them in the wallet!

Second, if you are not a person hoping to advance in a scientific career, talk about the issue. Most adults are woefully unaware of what is happening to our students, but they need to know. Things have changed dramatically in the last ten years. Third, it is vital that laws are passed to prevent universities from depriving their professors of their right to legal help. Remember how this was done to me by hiring the law firm that was representing me. When this is done, all the university needs to do is to declare the law firm's representation of the professor as a conflict of interest. Make the current state of affairs known and campaign for the legal rights of professors. Finally, how about supporting the efforts of those on the frontlines of the battle for accurate and honest science education? Check out my website at www.intellectualhonesty.info or www.aitse. org and support American Institute for Technology and Science Education. Or how about supporting the work of Access Research Network,[312] Discovery Institute[313] or other organizations with similar goals? Help us fight this battle to encourage scientific integrity and allow objective evaluation of scientific evidence."

---

309 Meyer, 2009, p. 145.
310 Letter from Albert Einstein to Banesh Hoffman, late 1930's.
311 Letter from Albert Einstein, August 1927.
312 www.arn.org
313 www.discovery.org

On this note the moderator turned off the microphones, closing the question and answer time.

More interview requests came flooding in from magazines, newspapers, radio stations, and even CBN television. I soon had the routine down, so the interviews with radio and print reporters became old hat. But, television was another story. Here I would be visible to the audience, even though they would not be visible to me. There's so much that goes into a TV appearance, most of which is totally new territory for a scientist. In the lab one covers old clothes with a lab coat. Hair is tied back since it is definitely undesirable to have it hanging in an experiment. So, I bought a suit and paid a visit to my hairdresser. Since test tubes, microscopes, and experiments are not particularly influenced by how the researcher looks, paying attention to this kind of thing was very strange to me, but I gamely went along with it.

I recall traveling into D.C. on the metro in the spring of 2008 for my first TV appearance.

A casually dressed woman met me at the door of the studio and escorted me to the waiting room where I could watch the show and wait to be called. As the minutes passed I grew more and more nervous. Finally, I was called to the room; it was not what one sees on TV, but looked more like a huge warehouse. I was seated on a stool with a camera in front of me, and a monitor off to my right. The person interviewing me could be seen on this monitor, but I was told to look at the camera, not to move my hands, and under no circumstances to glance at my interviewer. As they began to count down the time until the start of the show, I could feel myself panic. My heart began to race, my breathing sped up, my hands grew sweaty and I seriously considered bolting for the door. But, they'd already announced me.

So, I took a deep breath and decided to go through with it. It was important for me to tell my story. The "good old boy" academic system needed transformation, and I needed to do my part to help influence that positive change. I didn't want others to suffer the same prejudice and abuse I'd experienced. Luckily, I had memorized the answer to what I suspected the first question might be and this is precisely what I was asked. Once I started, the rest of the story flowed fairly naturally and I actually enjoyed the interview.[314] Afterwards it took me hours to come down from the adrenaline high. Perhaps this is why TV personalities do it? Even so, I was not sure I would ever want to repeat the experience.

And so I became better known, even occasionally being asked for my autograph. It made me giggle, but I figured I might as well go along with it since it

---

was bound not to last. After all, I never expected to be asked to address a group of congressmen, be interviewed by a person from James Dobson's ministries, speak on live radio for 45 minutes,[315] and even win the Wedge of Truth Award after speaking at a conference in Kansas.[316] Who would want to hear an expelled scientist speak?

The highlight was being invited to and attending the black tie world premiere of *Expelled: No Intelligence Allowed* in Dallas, Texas. We were housed at a luxury hotel; many guests attended, but we were made to feel special by being taken to the movie showing by limousine and dropped off in front of the red carpet. Ben Stein arrived soon afterwards and was greeted by the producer of the movie, Walt Ruloff, and three of his sons, all dressed as Ben Stein look-alikes complete with red-striped ties and sneakers. After watching the movie (for the fifth time), my husband and I were again transported by limousine, this time to a grand reception with live music and flower arrangements made specifically in honor of each scientist. I was so besieged with people congratulating me and asking questions that I did not even get a chance to eat. It did not matter. This was the experience of a lifetime.

* * * *

When we got home, I really got to work on making the IDEA Center a success. I needed to do some fundraising, encourage students to start clubs, support those who were already involved in clubs, and more. But, difficulties arose. The main goal of the IDEA Center was to start and maintain IDEA clubs on campuses,[317] but I was receiving feedback saying that students engaged in this kind of activity were encountering all kinds of opposition. The IDEA Center was founded at a time when the debate was less politicized and students could be openly pro-ID without fearing extreme retribution. Since the first IDEA Club had formed in 1999 things had changed. In some cases students had to form IDEA Clubs under pseudonyms or the clubs had to serve as secret safe houses where pro-ID students could be "out of the closet" about their pro-ID views.

Despite the opposition, IDEA Clubs still exist on university campuses. However, for myself, I felt that the best thing I could do to help students would be to provide them with verifiable scientific evidence, clear explanations, and the intellectual tools necessary to make informed decisions about the implications of technology and science for society, rather than just helping them form clubs. When several of the leading lights in the ID movement encouraged me to

---

315 Interview of Caroline Crocker by Jan Mickelson, WHO radio, June 2008.
316 Darwin Design and Democracy conference, April 19-20, 2008.
317 www.ideacenter.org

start another work, one specifically geared to my gifts and passions and those of the group of people working with me, the IDEA Center and I decided that we would both be more effective if we simply parted ways amicably. They hired a person ideally suited for promoting and monitoring clubs and I was encouraged to follow my dreams.

After much talk, planning, brainstorming, and work, the American Institute for Technology and Scientific Education (AITSE) is now up and running.[318] The vision of the Institute is "Good Science—Based on Evidence, not Consensus," and its mission is to 1) be a consortium of scientists, engineers, physicians and professionals from other disciplines working together to improve science education and increase scientific integrity, thereby unleashing a new era of scientific discovery, 2) offer clear, reliable, and balanced education with the goal of liberating science and technology from ideology, politics and the illusion of consensus, and 3) operate programs that advance honest, ethical, and beneficial scientific progress that is responsive to the real needs of present and future generations. I am excited about the potential that this organization offers for securing America's technological and scientific future.

* * * *

The United States of America was built on the foundation of freedom: freedom of speech, press, religion, freedom not to be persecuted for one's beliefs, freedom to be considered innocent until proven guilty. But inherent within freedom is the right to be different and for this one needs to have choices and be aware of what they are. Our society today has lost many of those freedoms; those who question the prevailing opinion are denied their constitutional rights, their jobs, and in my case, even find it difficult to get legal help.

My concern is that if we sit back and watch as scientists from a variety of disciplines are not allowed to exercise scientific integrity and academic freedom, professors and teachers are forced to indoctrinate students into neo-Darwinism (or other theories that are accepted on the basis of consensus instead of evidence), and young people are not allowed to indulge in scientific objectivity, everyone in our society will suffer. We need to make this suppression of academic and religious freedom known and then we need to ensure that free discussion of ideas is allowed in our society, universities and research institutes.

It is a despicable commentary that students are afraid to be intellectually honest for fear of what their professors will do to ruin their future careers. It is deplorable that the list of scientists who question neo-Darwinian evolution, anthropogenic global warming, or other politically correct viewpoints must keep

---

318   www.aitse.org

this secret for fear of finding themselves on an academic hit list. It is a sorry state of affairs to see so many promising scientists being denied the right to work because they have already "come out" as skeptics about consensus-based science. In school we are taught this happens in other countries where freedom is not prized. But it's happening right here in America today. I was extremely surprised to learn that North American academia is so vehemently opposed to the teaching of all angles of a scientific theory. It is incomprehensible that many are fearful of even discussing it.

According to the GMU Faculty Handbook, every person "has the right to express their views responsibly without fear of censorship or penalty...the right to unrestricted exposition of subjects (including controversial questions) within one's field, both on and off the campus, in a professionally responsible manner."[319]

Most Americans believe that the scientific evidence on both sides of the evolution debate should be taught in high schools,[320] but this right to hear both sides is now even being denied to our university students. Similarly, performing the duty to teach all the scientific evidence impartially was refused to me and is currently being denied to many others. If we, as Americans, do not step up to the plate and protest, one day we will find ourselves without many of the freedoms we hold dear. Freedom must be protected right here in America. If we don't, we may become very intellectually and economically backward, simply because we will not allow our populace to think and challenge the *status quo*. And that is why scientific integrity matters!

---

319   GMU Faculty Handbook, 2004, no longer available on the Internet.
320   Zogby Poll, 2009.

REFERENCES

7th Circuit Court of Appeals. 2005. April 20 ruling. Discussion can be found at http://www.democraticunderground.com/discuss/duboard. php?az=view_all&address=263x9681 (as of 4/2/09).

Access Research Network. www.arn.org (as of 4/2/09).

Anonymous. 2001. "A Scientific Dissent from Darwinism." http://www. dissentfromdarwin.org/ (as of 03/30/09).

Anonymous. 2005. "Intelligent Design Critic Eugenie Scott to Visit Mason." *Mason Gazette*. November 30. http://gazette.gmu.edu/articles/7537/ (as of 4/2/09).

Anonymous. 2005. Interview of GMU students attending an IDEA club meeting by Caroline Crocker, November. Student's identities are withheld at their request.

Anonymous. 2006. Interview of immunologist by Caroline Crocker, January. Scientist's identity is withheld at their request.

Anonymous. 2007. Interview of National Institutes of Health postdoctoral scientist by Caroline Crocker, October. Scientist's identity is withheld at their request.

Anonymous. 2008. "Expelled Professor Talks; Movie Faces Lawsuit." April 28. http://www.cbn.com/cbnnews/365574.aspx (as of 4/2/09).

Anonymous. 2008. E-mail from former IDEA club leader to Caroline Crocker, May. Student's identity is withheld at their request.

Anonymous. 2008. E-mail from former IDEA club leader to Caroline Crocker, June. Student's identity is withheld at their request.

Anonymous. 2008. E-mail from student in California to Caroline Crocker, June. Student's identity is withheld at their request.

Anonymous. 2008. Interview of GMU non-biology major student by Caroline Crocker, November. Student's identity is withheld at their request.

Anonymous. 2008. Interview of GMU pre-medicine student by Caroline Crocker, December. Student's identity is withheld at their request.

Anonymous. 2009. Interview of GMU biology student by Caroline Crocker, July. Student's identity is withheld at their request.

Anonymous. 2009. Interview of GMU ecology student by Caroline Crocker, March. Student's identity is withheld at their request.

Anonymous. 2009. Interview of University of California biologist by Caroline Crocker, March. Scientist's identity is withheld at their request.

Avalos, Hector. 2005. E-mail from Hector Avalos to colleagues. August 2.

Bergin, Mark. 2005. "Mad Scientists." *World*, August 20, p. 23.

Bergman, Jerry. 2008. *Slaughter of the Dissidents*. Port Orchard, WA: Leafcutter Press.

Bhattacharjee, Yudhijit. 2003. "Evolution Battle on Campus." *Science*, 300:247.

Birx, H. James. 1994. Council for Democratic and Secular Humanism. *National Center for Science Education*. http://ncseweb.org/media/voices/council-democratic-secular-humanism (as of 5/2/09).

Bradley-Hagerty, Barbara. 2005. "Intelligent Design and Academic Freedom." All Things Considered. *National Public Radio*, November 10.

"Buckley", Robert. 2005. Faculty website. http://www.nvcc.edu/home/rgorham/Sites/Home/Documents/Intelligent%20Design.html (as of 4/1/09).

Campbell, Joseph. "Joseph Campbell's Loss of Faith." http://www.youtube.com/watch?v=vJmNBxbExuA (as of 6/10/09).

Campbell, Neil A., Jane B. Reece. 2002. *Biology* 6th edition. San Francisco, CA: Benjamin Cummings.

Campbell, Neil A., Jane B. Reece. 2002. *Biology* Testbank Version 6.0.

Chapman, Michael. 2007. "Vast Majority Support Teaching Evidence for and against Darwin's Evolution Theory." *CNS News*, February 12. http://www.cnsnews.com/public/content/article.aspx?RsrcID=43417 (as of 4/2/09).

Cordova, Salvador. 2009. "GMU's Lesbian, Gay, Queer Professor Feels Comfortable Offending Christian and pro-ID Students. *Young Cosmos*. March 26. http://www.youngcosmos.com/blog/archives/362 (as of 4/2/09).

Crichton, Michael. 2008. "'Aliens Cause Global Warming'," reprinted in *Wall Street Journal*, November 7.

Crocker, Caroline. 2007. Personal website. www.intellectualhonesty.info (as of 4/2/09).

Crocker, Caroline. 2008. Interview of Caroline Crocker by Matt Barber. "Biology Professor 'Expelled' for Questioning Darwinism." *Concerned Women for America*, Radio broadcast April 18.

Cushmann, Candy. 2001. "Heresy Trials: Is a Vocal Christian Inherently Unqualified to Teach Biology?" *World*, 16(31):18-21. August 18.

Darwin Design and Democracy VII. 2008. Intelligent Design Network, April 19-20.

Dawkins, Richard. 1989. "Dawkins Review of Blueprints: Solving the Mystery of Evolution." *New York Times*, April 9.

Dawkins, Richard. 1997. "Is Science a Religion?" *The Humanist* 57(1), January/February. http://humanist.net/publications/humanist/dawkins. html (as of 3/2/09).

Dawkins, Richard. 2006. *The God Delusion*. Boston, MA: Houghton Mifflin.

Discovery Institute. www.discovery.org (as of 4/2/09).

Dodgen, G. 2008. "*Expelled* at Biola— Ben Stein Receives the Phillip Johnson Award." March 28, http://www.uncommondescent.com/expelled/ expelled-at-biola-ben-stein-receives-the-phillip-johnson-award/ (as of 4/2/09).

Einstein letters in Alice Calaprice. 2000. *The Expanded Quotable Einstein*, Princeton, NJ: Princeton University Press.

George Mason University Faculty Handbook 2004. No longer available on the Internet.

Gonzalez, Guillermo and Jay W. Richards. 2004. *The Privileged Planet: How Our Place in the Cosmos is Designed for Discovery*. Washington D.C.: Regnery Publishing.

Good, Ron, 2003. "Evolution and Creationism: One Long Argument." *The American Biology Teacher* 65(7):512-516.

Gould, S.J. 1978. "So Cleverly Kind an Animal," *In Ever Since Darwin: Reflections in Natural History*, 1991, reprint, p. 267. London, UK: Penguin.

Grant P.R., B.R. Grant. 2002. "Unpredictable Evolution in a 30-year Study of Darwin's Finches." *Science* 296:707-11.

Hauptman, John. 2007. "Rights are Intact; Vote Turns on Question, 'What is Science?'" *Des Moines Register*, June 2.

Humanist Manifesto. 1933. Copy may be found at http://www.garymcleod. org/humanist.htm (as of 6/2/09).

Laskowski, Tara. 2005. "What George Mason Experts are Saying about Intelligent Design Theory." *Mason Gazette*. September 19. http://gazette. gmu.edu/articles/7155/ (as of 4/2/09).

Luskin, Casey. 2008. "How to Rebut Barbara Forrest in Two Words." June 2. http://www.evolutionnews.org/2008/06/how_to_rebut_barbara_ forrest_e.html (as of 6/5/09).

Luskin, Casey. Undated. "Intelligent Design and Evolution Awareness Center." www.ideacenter.org (as of 4/2/09).

Michelson, Jan. 2008. Interview of Caroline Crocker by Jan Michelson on WHO radio. June.

Meyer, S.C., S. Minnich, J. Moneymaker, P.A. Nelson, R. Seelke. 2005. *Explore Evolution*. London, UK: Hill House Publishers.

Meyer, Stephen C. 2009. *Signature in the Cell. DNA and the Evidence for Intelligent Design*. New York, NY: HarperCollins.

American Institute for Technology and Science Education. www.AITSE.org.

Nowicki, Sue. 2008. "Many Students Lose Faith at College." *Anniston Star.* http:// www.annistonstar.com/religion/2008/as-churchnews-0614-0-8f13s3222.htm (as of 4/2/09).

Provine, William B. 1998. "Evolution: Free Will and Punishment and Meaning in Life." Abstract of Prof. William B. Provine's Darwin Day address, University of Tennessee, Knoxville, TN. http://fp.bio.utk.edu/darwin/1998/provine_abstract.html (as of 2/23/09).

Ruse, Michael. 1983. *Darwinism Defended: A Guide to Evolution Controversies*. 3rd edition. Boston, MA: Addison-Wesley, p. 58.

Sager, C., A. Bottaro. 2008. "The Expelled Case of Caroline Crocker. Academic Freedom Martyr or Pseudoscience Hack." *Skeptic* 14(2):59. http://www.skeptic.com/eskeptic/08-04-23.html#part3 (as of 4/2/09).

Sentell, Will. 2008. "House Gets Legislation on Teaching Evolution." *The Advocate*, May 22. http://www.2theadvocate.com/news/1916529.html (as of 2/4/09).

Sisson, Edward. 2005. Letter from Edward Sisson to Alan Merton. August 15.

Sisson, Edward. 2006. Podcasts at http://www.youtube.com/watch?v=6lCe5ICSKI0 (as of 4/2/09).

Skell, Philip. 2005. "Why do we Invoke Darwin?" *The Scientist* 19(6):10.

Stein, Ben. 2008. *Expelled: No Intelligence Allowed*. Documentary released in April.

Steinberg, Arnold and Associates. 2004. "Californians say Teach Scientific Evidence Both For and Against Darwinian Evolution, Show New Polls." May 3. http://www.discovery.org/scripts/viewDB/index. php?command=view&id=2024 (as of 4/2/09).

Sternberg, Richard. 2008. "Smithsonian Controversy." http://rsternberg.net/smithsonian.php (as of 4/2/09).

United States House of Representatives Subcommittee Report. 2006. "Intolerance and the Politicization of Science at the Smithsonian." December. http://www.kolbecenter.org/Intolerance.pdf (as of 4/2/09).

Walker, Dr. Michael. 1981. "Evolved or Not: That's the Question." *Quadrant*, October. p. 45.

Wells, Jonathan. 2000. *Icons of Evolution: Science or Myth?* Washington, D.C.: Regnery Publishing Inc.

Wells, Jonathan. 2006. *The Politically Incorrect Guide to Darwinism and Intelligent Design*. Washington D.C.: Regnery Publishing.

Zogby Poll. 2009. http://www.evolutionnews.org/2009/02/americans_agree_with_darwin_th.html

Call to Action

Shocked that such a loss of freedom is not only possible but is occurring with increasing regularity here in the United States of America, people often ask me, "What can I do to help?" They realize that, as Edmund Burke so concisely stated, "The only thing necessary for the triumph of evil is for good men to do nothing." It is obvious that we need to take action. Ignoring this important issue will have wide-ranging and extremely negative consequences for our society in terms of the health of our population, the vigor of our economy, and our competitive edge in the global marketplace.

Our first step in this action plan is to understand, not just the rhetoric of those who stifle academic freedom and scientific objectivity, but also the basis of their opposition: their fears and motivations. A pragmatic scientist may be resistant to change due to trepidation that their study, research and teaching, their entire life's work, has been based on a flawed theory. Or, a scholar or scientist may resist change because they are using neo-Darwinism as the foundation for their religious beliefs (atheism or humanism). Still others object to what they perceive as an untenable "religious" approach to this issue. It is critically important that we exhibit patience both with those who oppose new discoveries in science and with those who dare to offer dissent about "orthodox" views, demonstrating wisdom and discernment in how we proceed, shrewdness in our actions, and winsomeness in our demeanor. But we must act.

This is one of the purposes of the American Institute for Technology and Science Education (AITSE), not to be confused with Eugenie Scott's organization known as the National Center for Science Education (NCSE), which does not promote unbiased science and opposes many efforts of those who do.[321] In direct contrast to the NCSE, AITSE works to bring about a healthy change in our universities and science organizations by fostering an environment that is conducive to the pursuit of scientific discovery. AITSE is working to usher in a new era in which we can fully embrace modern science and respect differences while insisting on sound scholarship. It does this by educating to increase scientific understanding and integrity at every stage of the scientific process by:

1. Assisting those who are seeking scientific truth by providing information contributed by highly qualified scientists, engineers, and physicians,

---

321 The stated purpose of Eugenie Scott's organization, the National Center for Science Education, is to keep "evolution in the science classroom and creationism out." Unfortunately, in its zeal to promote naturalistic neo-Darwinism, the NCSE also works to ban intelligent design (which is not religion) and even objects to teaching science that casts doubt on any aspect of evolutionary theory.

2. Encouraging and facilitating the even-handed assessment of scientific information by students, professionals, and the public

3. Promoting sound and beneficial scientific discovery and technological implementation, and

4. Modeling and offering clear and balanced teaching of theoretical and applied science.

If we work together, we can bring reform to the scientific establishment by encouraging scientific integrity and opposing enforcement of consensus science, thereby allowing the work of unconventional innovators so that new advances in medicine and technology are achieved. After all, it is this freedom to be inventive and think outside the box that has made the USA competitive in the global marketplace. We can expose and neutralize those who operate as obstacles to scientific collegiality, misuse science for political or personal gain, and breach ethics, thereby damaging society and culture through the application of misdirected constraints against scientific advancements.

The first step in our proposed Action Plan is for each of us become aware of which organizations do not respect scientific inquiry, muzzling honest inquiry in the quest for scientific accuracy. Does your alma mater support or hinder the work of scientists who challenge archaic theories such as macro-evolution via mutation and natural selection? Frankly, it may be difficult to uncover the truth. It is common even for private and/or religious universities, such as Baylor University,[322] to be among the worst offenders. Universities require funding and scholars are often so concerned about being accepted by their peers and fearful of being denied institutional advancement or grants, that they become intolerant of those who wish to objectively evaluate scientific evidence. This is particularly true regarding new discoveries that challenge Darwin's theory, but is by no means the only area in which new scientific discovery is being throttled.[323, 324, 325]

If you are unable to obtain clear position statements from a university or organization on an issue, consider this to be a "red flag" warning. They are likely offenders hoping to keep their donors in the dark on the theories or viewpoints they are promoting. Let them know that you will withhold your financial support until they make their position clear. If it is a university, make sure that you

---

322 Bergin, Mark. 2007. "Not So Fast." *World Magazine*, September 15.
323 Duffy, Ed. 2009. "EPA Global Warming Report Nixed." *Denver News Examiner*, June 29.
324 http://www.yourlawyer.com/topics/overview/lexapro, This website gives links to FDA warnings about the connection between use of anti-depressants and increased suicide risk; links have been removed.
325 Holguin, Jaime. 2004. "Statins' Side Effects Under Fire." *CBS News.com*, October 11. http://www. cbsnews.com/stories/2004/10/11/eveningnews/main648685.shtml

also let them know that you will not be sending them students unless they demonstrate by their policies that they are worthy of your endorsement. At the very least, we need to make sure that our organizations are signatories to a statement that protects science professors from those who enforce consensus science. On the website for American Institute for Technology and Science Education (www. AITSE.org) you will find a model statement we suggest academic institutions adopt.

Second, we need to support those organizations that are willing to buck the mainstream and seek the truth on controversial issues. If your alma mater does not support true academic freedom and objectivity in teaching, consider transferring your financial support to the AITSE or another worthy organization. There are a number of organizations that abide by Plato's advice to follow the scientific evidence wherever it leads. Beware of organizations that will not even speak to those with a point of view different from their own. Unfortunately, these include religious as well as secular organizations, so be sure to investigate whether the organizations you support are thoughtful and respectful of others. We as people must be free enough to explore all the options, humble enough to listen to others, and courageous enough to search for the truth in an intellectually honest manner. The organizations that we support need to do likewise.

Next, if you are a scientist, whether a Ph.D. teaching in a university, a professional researcher or engineer working in an applied science field, I strongly encourage you to go to the AITSE website and sign the *Scientist's Pledge* which advocates and pledges a personal quest for truth and respect for others who are similarly engaged. This non-political and non-religious statement, anonymous but externally audited to validate the credentials of each signer, can help set the tone for a new era of civility that will encourage discovery and hone scholarship. Although it is not required, I encourage you to post this statement on your personal website as an indication of your commitment. A similar statement, specifically for students, is also available, but should not be posted.

Finally, if you are a concerned citizen, whether student, parent, or other interested party, wishing to protect objective science, competitive technology, economic stability, and intellectual freedom, go to the AITSE website and sign the citizen's pledge. Again, your name will not be released, but your demonstration of commitment has great value. These Constitutional and commonsense freedoms are not only for the elite, but for us all.

The intent of these actions is not simply to protect dissenting scientists who might in the future become victims of the intellectual elitism, snobbery and prejudice that I experienced, but also the future of science in our society. If we are to promote and enjoy the fruits of discovery and innovation and attract students to careers in the sciences, we need to be willing to articulate that we are engaged in an honest quest for the truth, unbridled by all who seek to control the scientific establishment based on politics, financial considerations, or their personal religious beliefs and philosophies, instead of sound science.

To be apprised of developments in this quest and to be connected with cutting-edge resources, please go to the American Institute for Technology and Science Education website (www.AITSE.org) right now, and sign up for the free newsletter. Also, feel free to contact us at info@AITSE.org. Thank you for joining us in making a difference in our society.

Appendix I: Vocabulary
Simple Definitions of Difficult Words

The definitions listed below are for the use of non-science readers. In the interest of clarity I have simplified them so that they are easily understood. For scientifically rigorous definitions, please refer to another source. However, if clarity and simplicity are what you want, then you are in the right place.

Accommodation	Disabled students have the right to request that teachers make minor alterations in their courses and teaching that will enable the disabled student to have the same chance of success as a student without a disability. These alterations are called "accommodations."
Activated T-cells	A type of white blood cell (the director of the immune response) that has been exposed to a perceived "enemy" of the body like a bacterium or virus.
Agar	A gelatinous substance made out of seaweed that is used as a surface for growing bacteria in the laboratory.
Amino acid	The fundamental subunit of a protein. There are 20 different amino acids and these are arranged into a specific unique order for each kind of protein that is made. The sequence of the amino acids plays a major role in the function of the protein.
Amino and carboxy termini	Each amino acid contains a carboxy group (COOH), an amino group (NH2), and some other group. Carboxy and amino groups react to form links, called peptide bonds. When a long string of amino acids react in this way, the end of the string that has the amino group is called the amino terminus. The end that has the carboxy group is the carboxy terminus.
Anthropology	Investigation of past humanity.
Antibiotic resistance	Antibiotics are substances that are poison to bacteria, but not to people or animals. Sometimes a bacterium can resist the effect of the antibiotic, making it "resistant."

Antibodies	Certain white blood cells make these special proteins that stick to substances that the body recognizes as foreign, like the outside of a bacterium or a virus.
Antigens	Those parts of foreign substances that white blood cells recognize as foreign; antibodies are made in response to antigens. One foreign substance may have many antigens, just as one elephant can be recognized by its trunk, its legs, or its ears.
Archaeology	The study of human cultures by investigation of what they leave behind (artifacts).
Asthma	A condition where the airways become inflamed, constrict, and fill with mucus, making it difficult for the patient to breathe. Asthma may have a number of causes, but is often connected with allergies.
ATP	Short for adenosine triphosphate, the primary molecule that the body uses for energy. The energy from food is converted into ATP and used to power body processes. ATP is the body's gasoline.
Axonemal	The inner core of a hairlike projection that the cell uses to move through liquid (flagellum) or to move liquid over itself (cilium).
Bacterium	A comparatively simple single-celled organism that measures approximately 0.0001-0.001 mm in diameter.
Biogenesis	A law of science that states that all life comes from pre-existing life. This law has been questioned many times, but has proven to be true again and again.
Botany	The study of plants.
Cascade	One way a message is passed from the surface of a cell to the nucleus (head office). One protein activates others, those activate still more, and the message is passed down in domino fashion until the destination is reached.

Cells	The smallest unit of matter than can be alive. Cells are enclosed by a membrane, contain genetic material, reproduce, use energy. They are like highly automated and complex factories.
Chaperonin or chaperone protein	A family of proteins shaped like barrels whose prime function is to fold newly-made proteins into their proper shapes. Since proteins act like machines in cells, their function is dependent on their shape, so proper folding is essential.
Chlamydia	A bacterium that is responsible for the most frequently-reported sexually transmitted disease in the USA. It is estimated that 10-20% of the population may be infected with Chlamydia, but most will not have symptoms and are not treated. Untreated Chlamydia infection is a leading cause of infertility (Centers for Disease Control).
Chloroplasts	An organelle (organ in a cell) that uses the energy of light to convert carbon dioxide and water into sugar.
Chromosome	A single string of tightly folded genetic material (DNA). Humans have 23 paired chromosomes (46 total).
Cilia	Many hairlike projections from the surface of cells that are used to move liquids over the outside of the cell.
Cleave	One protein splitting another into two or more parts. In contrast, "cleaves to" means one protein sticking to another.
Co-dominant	Humans have two versions of every gene, one from the mother and one from the father; when both versions are evident, then the genes are said to be co-dominant. For example, people with a gene for Type A blood and a gene for Type B blood will have blood type AB.
Co-option	A gene that was previously used for one purpose is now used in another. Similar to using the wheels from a lawnmower for a go-cart.

Colony	A population of bacteria that are located in one place and result from the reproduction of one bacterium. Colonies consist of clones.
Complement	Proteins found in the blood that take part in a cascade-type reaction to remove disease-causing organisms from the body.
Confocal microscope	A specialized microscope that makes it possible to view a three dimensional image of thick specimens (even the depth of a cell).
Creationism	Belief system about the origin of the universe and/or life that is derived from religious texts. There are many different flavors of creationism depending on the religious text used and the way it is interpreted. Creationism is profoundly different from ID because creationism is based on writings in holy books, while ID primarily appeals to empirical data and logic.
Culture	Growing bacteria or the results of growing bacteria.
Cumulative complexity	Complexity that increases in a step-by-step fashion. This is what neo-Darwinian evolution predicts.
Cyclic AMP (cAMP)	A molecule found in cells that carries a message from a receptor to other proteins; elevated levels cause relaxation of smooth muscle.
Cytoplasm	The region of the cell outside of the nucleus. Cytoplasm serves as the "factory floor" for protein manufacturing and other cellular activities (see also "nucleus").
Cytoskeleton	The "bones" of the cell. Consists of several types of protein constructs.
Darwinism	In this book, the term Darwinism is short for "neo-Darwinian evolution," and refers to a belief that is a mixture of 1) the scientific theory of evolution (including common descent, random mutation, and natural selection) and 2) materialistic philosophy (the belief that there is nothing outside nature—the supernatural does not exist).

Deletion	A piece of DNA code is missing; this could consist of just one "letter" up to an entire segment of a chromosome encompassing many genes. Because the letters in DNA are read as three-letter words, removing one letter results in the rest of the gene being read incorrectly (frameshift).
Designoid	Something that looks designed but, according to some neo-Darwinian evolutionists, we "know" that it could not have been intelligently designed.
DNA	Short for deoxyribonucleic acid; the "ink" in which the genetic code is written. DNA is made up of four types of nucleotides (C, G, A, T) and their sequence is what contains genetic information.
DNA construct	A DNA sequence that is created in the laboratory by fusing DNA from several sources.
Dominant	Humans have two versions of every gene; the dominant version is the one that is evident. For example, people with a gene for Type A blood and a gene for Type O blood will have Type A. A is dominant to O.
Ecology	The study of how organisms interact with their environment.
Electrophoresis	A method of separating DNA fragments by running them through a gel using an electrical current. Since DNA is negatively charged, it will move from the negative to the positive pole. Ignoring the effect of DNA folding, the smaller pieces of DNA will move more quickly than the larger.
ELISA	Short for enzyme-linked immunosorbent assay: A biochemical test that makes use of the specificity of antibodies and antigens to accurately quantify protein in a liquid.
Enantiomers	Since the atom carbon makes four bonds that are equally spaced over its surface, molecules containing carbon can have mirror images. These are termed enantiomers.
Endoplasmic reticulum	A networked membranous structure used by the cell in making and modifying some proteins.

Endosymbiosis	A theory that suggests mitochondria and chloroplasts evolved from bacteria that lived inside of larger cells.
Endothelial	Tissue that lines internal surfaces in the body; for example, blood vessels are lined by a one cell thick layer of endothelial cells.
Enzyme	A protein that acts as a catalyst in biological reactions. Catalysts speed up reactions that would have proceeded slowly in their absence.
Flagella	Whip-like projections on the surface of a cell that help it to "swim," much like a propeller on a boat.
Gamete	Egg or sperm; a sex cell.
Gel electrophoresis	See electrophoresis.
Gene	For the purposes of this book, a gene is a part of a chromosome (made of DNA) that codes for a single string of amino acids (polypeptide) called a protein. The definition of a gene has "evolved" as our understanding of molecular biology as grown and genes are now understood to be much more complex and amazing than was previously understood.
Genetic engineering	Manipulating DNA in order to alter the function of a cell. For example, insulin is now made by fusing a gene for insulin (from a human cell) into DNA that goes in a bacterium, thus tricking the bacterium into making insulin.
Genetics	The study of genes and how they are inherited.
Genome	The sum total of an organism's genes; all the DNA. Most cells in our body contain a complete copy of all the DNA in our genome made up of two sets of chromosomes, one from our mother and one from our father.

Glucocorticoid	A type of cholesterol-like hormone (steroid) that is naturally produced by our bodies, but is also used as a drug to decrease inflammation. Glucocorticoids have many other effects, as well.
Golgi apparatus	A membranous structure used by the cell as a protein processing plant.
Granulocyte	A type of white blood cell that releases chemicals; some granulocytes also engulf and "eat" invaders and other cells.
Haeckel's embryos	Falsified drawings of embryos done by Ernst Haeckel showing how similar the embryos of different species are. Used to "prove" that embryological development mirrors evolutionary history.
Herpes	A virus that can cause an incurable sexually transmitted disease. According to the Centers for Disease Control, approximately 25% of women and 12% of men have this disease; many do not have symptoms. Herpes can be transmitted during birth and is potentially fatal to newborns.
Histone	A protein that helps in packaging DNA into chromosomes.
HIV	Human Immunodeficiency Virus; the virus that causes AIDS.
Hood	A semi-enclosed space where an experiment can be conducted at minimal risk to the investigator. Airflow ensures that the person is not exposed to the chemicals or that the experiment is not contaminated by the person.
Human Papilloma Virus	Otherwise known as HPV, this incurable sexually transmitted virus is endemic in our population, infecting up to 60% of university students. Recent data shows that the body overcomes 90% of HPV infections; a vaccine that protects against 70% of the strains is now available. HPV can cause cervical cancer.
Humors	Substances that the ancients thought the body was filled with: black bile, yellow bile, blood and phlegm.

Hypothesis	Commonly called an educated guess. Must be testable.
Immuno-modulatory	Controls the immune system.
Immuno-pharmacology	The study of how drugs affect the immune system.
Incubator	A constant temperature device, much like a low-temperature oven, used to grow bacteria in the laboratory.
Insertion	A mutation where extra "letters" are mistakenly placed into DNA.
Intelligent design	The study of patterns in nature that are best explained as the product of intelligence.
Intermediate form	A group of organisms that has characteristics distinctive to two or more other groups of organisms.
Irreducible complexity	A type of complexity that results from a network of parts that work together to perform one function.
Lancet	A sharp instrument used to prick the finger and obtain a blood sample.
Law of nature	A statement of fact; observed to be true repeatedly and never shown to be wrong. Mathematical laws are the most certain. Other laws include the laws of gravity, thermodynamics, and biogenesis.
Ligation	Joining two or more DNA sequences into a single string by sticking the ends together using an enzyme called DNA ligase.
Macroevolution	Evolution resulting the formation of a new type of organism (with a new morphology or shape). Requires generation of significant amounts of new information.
Media	Nutrients for bacteria. Bacteria like to float in or grow on their food.
Meiosis	Cell division to produce sex cells or gametes (sperm and eggs).

Membrane	An ultra-thin, flexible, semi-permeable, self-repairing layer that surrounds cells.
Messenger RNA (mRNA)	RNA (ribonucleic acid) that takes copies of genes containing instructions for construction of proteins from the nucleus (head office) to the ribosome machine-complex where new protein machines are constructed.
Microbiology	The study of small living organisms; mostly bacteria.
Microevolution	Small changes in a population of organisms that do not change the fundamental nature of that organism (color, size, antibiotic resistance).
Microtubule	A kind of "bone" in the cell that is hollow and acts as railway tracks, supports cilia and flagellae, and helps with cell division.
Mitochondria	An organelle (organ in a cell) that converts sugar energy to ATP (cell energy) using oxygen.
Mitosis	Cell division in all cells except those that produce gametes (these undergo meiosis) and those without a nucleus (bacteria undergo binary fission).
Molecular biology	The study of DNA, often by manipulation of the sequences, deliberate mutations, and moving of DNA from one organism to another. Other molecules involved in life may also be studied.
Morphology	The form or structure of an organism.
Mutation	A change in the DNA sequence; only can affect evolution if the mutation is in a gamete. If mutations occur in body cells, they can lead to cancer.
Niche	The place or set of circumstances that an organism is adapted to live in.
Nucleotide	A single "letter" of DNA. DNA is made of four types of nucleotide bases (adenine, guanine, cytosine, thymine). Their order contains information, much like the order of the letters in the alphabet contains meaning.

Nucleus	A membrane-enclosed space in the cell where the DNA is found (head office). Bacteria do not have nuclei; their DNA is not enclosed.
Osmosis	Movement of water through a membrane from an area of low to an area of high solute (what is dissolved) concentration.
Oxidizing	An atmosphere that removes electrons; usually containing oxygen, which is notorious for "liking" electrons.
Paleontology	The study of ancient life through the fossil record.
Parasite	A single celled or multi-cellular organism that benefits from living on another organism. The second organism is damaged by the relationship.
Peptide bonds	Bonds between amino acids. These occur between the carboxyl group of one amino acid and the amino group of the next.
Philosophy	The systematic study of reality through logic and reasoning.
Phospho-diesterase	An enzyme that converts cyclic AMP (cAMP) into AMP. Since cAMP tends to activate cells, this limits the length of time that a cell is active.
Phylogeny	The hypothetical evolutionary history of ancestors and descendents leading to a specific organism or group of organisms.
Pipette	A dropper used to transfer liquids in the laboratory.
Point mutation	A small change in the DNA sequence. Examples would be deletion, insertion, substitutions, or translocation of one to a few nucleotides (letters in the DNA language).
Protein	Molecules made of amino acids and coded for by DNA that do most of the work inside cells. Proteins function in structure (they make up the bones of the cell), function (they act as machines), transport (they are like immigration officials for the cell), and more.

Proteosome	An organelle (organ in a cell) that destroys misfolded, mutant, or unwanted proteins.
Punctuated equilibrium	Evolution that occurs in fits and starts, rather than as a slow gradual process. Proposed by some evolutionists as an explanation for gaps in the fossil record.
Racemic	A mixture of left-handed and right-handed molecules.
Reagent	A chemical that is used up during a reaction.
Recapitulates	Repeats or copies.
Receptor	A molecule that is usually located on the surface of a cell that responds to and relays messages from the cell's surroundings. Analogous to an intercom.
Recessive	Humans have two copies of every gene; if they are different, the recessive version is the one that is not evident in the organism's phenotype. For example, people with a gene for Type A blood and a gene for Type O blood will have blood type A. O is recessive to A.
Reducing	In the Miller-Urey experiment, this refers to an atmosphere that donates electrons; usually containing hydrogen.
Replicate	Copy. DNA is copied by taking the two complementary strands apart, matching each nucleotide base up to its complement and sticking them together. Each old strand ends up paired to a new one.
Restriction digest	DNA that has been cut in specific places by special restriction enzymes. Restriction enzymes are much like precision scissors that can only cut at specific nucleotide sequences in the DNA.
Ribosome	Organelle (organ in a cell) where proteins are made according to instructions encoded in DNA that are relayed by mRNA.

RNA	Ribonucleic acid. Used in the process of making proteins according to the instructions found in DNA. Chemically, RNA is very similar to DNA.
Scantron	An exam answer sheet that allows automated grading. A soft-lead pencil is used to fill in ovals for each multiple choice answer (a-e).
Science	From the Greek word meaning "to know;" the study of the natural world.
Secretion	Release of a chemical from a cell.
Sex-linked	Genetic traits that are carried on the sex chromosomes and are differentially inherited between the genders. For example, color blindness is on the X chromosome and tends to occur more in men.
Signal	A chemical message.
Smooth muscle	Muscle that is not under voluntary control. For example, the muscles regulating the width of the bronchi cannot be controlled by an act of will.
Somatic	"Of the body." In humans, all chromosomes except the X and Y sex chromosomes are called somatic chromosomes.
Speciation	Formation of a new inter-breeding population of organisms that is isolated from breeding with other populations.
Specified complexity	This concept is best explained by an example given by Dembski, "A single letter of the alphabet is specified without being complex (i.e., it conforms to an independently given pattern but is simple). A long sequence of random letters is complex without being specified (i.e., it requires a complicated instruction-set to characterize but conforms to no independently given pattern). A Shakespearean sonnet is both complex and specified." http://www.leaderu.com/offices/dembski/docs/bd-specified.html
Substitution	A DNA mutation where one type of nucleotide is replaced by another.

T-cell	The white blood cell that directs the specific immune response.
Testbank	A list of suggested questions for exams relating to a specific textbook.
Tetrahedral	A three dimensional shape with exactly four triangular sides, like a triangular pyramid.
Theory	An explanation based on thought and the results of observations and experiments; has been tested. For example, the theory of relativity.
Tissue	A group of cells of the same type.
Transcription factor	A protein or other molecule that helps the cell know which gene to copy into mRNA in order to make a protein. Usually many transcription factors are needed to activate one gene, much as there are many numbers in a telephone number to phone one person.
Transcription	Copying the code from DNA into mRNA.
Transfection	Infection of a cell with viral DNA so that the cell then produces virus.
Transfer RNA (tRNA)	RNA that is complementary to mRNA "words" on one side and carries the corresponding amino acid on the other. Transfer RNA acts in translation of the DNA message into protein "language."
Transformation	Uptake of DNA by bacteria. Used in molecular biology because the bacteria then make more of the DNA of interest as they grow.
Transitional form	A group of organisms that has characteristics distinctive to two or more other groups of organisms. In evolutionary theory, transitional forms should be between ancestors and descendents in time and thus in the fossil record. In general the fossil record shows few possible transitional forms, while neo-Darwinism predicts that they should be abundant.

Translation	Making protein using the instructions that have been relayed to the ribosome by mRNA.
Translocation mutation	Change in the DNA where sequences from two different chromosomes are exchanged.
Transposition	Change in the DNA where a sequence gets moved to a different location on its chromosome, or even a different chromosome.
Unicellular	One-celled; bacteria are unicellular.
Vesicle	A membranous sac inside a cell; can be used for transport or storage.
Virology	The study of viruses.
Virus	Tiny particles (0.000005-0.0003 mm) made mostly of DNA (or RNA) and protein that hijack cells and force them to make more virus. Because these particles do not exhibit most of the features of life, viruses traditionally are not considered to be alive.
Western blot	A method used to isolate and identify proteins.
Wire loop	A thin piece of wire attached to a heatproof wand. The wire is shaped into a loop. This loop is heated to red hot to sterilize it, cooled, and then used to pick up a bacterial colony and transfer it elsewhere.

Appendix II: Letters and E-mails from Students

a. Miscellaneous Relevant Correspondence (2009, 2004, 2004, and 2010)
(referenced in Chapters 7 and 10)

You were always and still are the greatest teacher I've ever met, you're so kind and generous and I would never forget the help and care you've given me.

This was a challenging class and I always like the challenge. Keep your teaching style the same because even though grades are not high, it really makes you understand and learn the material.

Thank you Dr. Crocker for a great semester.! Though your multiple choice questions tricked me a lot, I feel like I know everything in that book from Chapters 1-20! (except those two exam questions X-X)

I've missed seeing you and speaking with you. I see that you are in sunny California, and am admittedly jealous! It looks like life after Mason has been awesome for you. I must admit, Mason felt like a thwarting force on independent thinking.

I hope that we can keep in touch.

Also, I want to thank you for having been there for me through one of the toughest times of my life. I truly will never forget the impact you had on my life.

---

b. Copy of Rate-My-Professor (Printed on 5/31/05)

(referenced in Chapter 8)

RATE THIS PROFESSOR

2.65% APY

Date	Class				Comments
4/28/05	Biol 213	3	5	5	3	Dr. Crocker is the best science teacher I have ever had. True, there are vocab quizzes just about every week, but she gives out word lists ahead of time. She assigns worksheets which are very helpful in learning and, if you go to her study sessions, she is happy to help.

Registered users can respond to this rating

| 1/28/05 | Cell Bio 213 | 3 | 3 | 4 | 5 | Her lectures and slides were extremely comprehensive...that would have been great if they were even remotely related to the tests! At least she gives you the final essays ahead of time so you can prepare (and you better!) She is a better lab instructer than lecture professor |

Registered users can respond to this rating

| 1/24/05 | Bio 213 | 2 | 3 | 5 | 5 | very hard, but easy to learn in her class because she gives you notes, you just have to follow them in lecture and study. |

Registered users can respond to this rating

| 1/10/05 | Bio 213 | 2 | 5 | 4 | 4 | Class is challenging but not that difficult. Considering all of the extra credit available and the opportunity to drop one test, any reasonably adept student can get an A. This course takes less prep time than gen chem or physics. Remember, don't underestimate the Bio 213 lab! |

Registered users can respond to this rating

| 1/8/05 | BIO 218 | 1 | 3 | 3 | 1 | Ah, cell bio. Well, let's see: I read 5 chapters out of the book, BUT I went to the review sessions, e-mailed her for help, and had her a lab instructor. I got a B in the class. SO! There is hope for you my young ones. Don't give up on Doc Crock. |

Registered users can respond to this rating

| 1/2/05 | Bio 213 | 3 | 4 | 3 | 4 | Bio 213 is a weed out class meaning its supposed to separate all the kids whose parents want them to b doctors and those who are actually interested. Overall her class is difficult but not impossible just read the material, seriously all these people who are complaining dont read. She gives few e.c. |

Registered users can respond to this rating

| 12/31/04 | Bio 213 Cell | 3 | 2 | 4 | 4 | Not as bad as everyone says. I hardly ever came to class, skimmed the book, and even bombed a test and still came out with an A-. Do all the worksheets and extra credit, and take her for lab so she'll be merciful in lecture. |

Registered users can respond to this rating

✉ - Rating left by a registered user. (**Gold members** can contact registered users; all

c. From a Pre-dental Student (April, 2004)

(referenced in Chapter 6)

Dear █████████

I'm a senior student in Biology from VCU and will be receiving my degree in honors in fall 2005. I had the honor to be in two of Dr. Crocker's classes(Biology 101 and Cell Biology) on my freshman year in Northern Virginia Community College. There are many reasons that I would value Dr. Crocker as one of the most outstanding professors I've had throughout my undergraduate but I'll narrow it to couple of reasons. Most of the students find cell Biology as a very hard and challenging course, but Dr. Crocker's lectures was always excellent and very clear that I never found myself not liking this course. She was always willing to help me with my questions. The way she explains the material is one of the reasons I enjoyed being a part of her class. She is very responsible towards her students, very helpful and encouraging. The exams were always fare and I can say any student who is putting effort for her class and is attending all of her lectures can earn a perfect grade in Dr. Crocker's class.

At the end I would like to use this chance to show my appreciation to Dr. Crocker and wish her the best.

Sincerely,

d. From a GMU Student (12/19/04)

(referenced in Chapter 5)

To Whom it May Concern,

I am very disturbed to hear that Dr. Crocker may not be a lecture professor any longer at George Mason University. I took Dr. Crocker's Biology 213 class this fall 2004 semester, and would like to address the idea of her teaching creationism in her lectures. I am unbiased about the subject of creationism, and am shocked to hear that she is being falsely accused. I have attended all of her lectures and I have followed along all the lecture notes that she provided. She does not cover any other material in her lectures other than what is outlined in her lecture notes. In addition not only has she not taught creationism in particular, she even skipped the section of evolution, the closest topic to creationism from the entire course. If needed I currently have a complete set of all of her lecture notes, and the two supplementary packets that were available from the reserve collection. I am so upset to hear of this misfortune because I have never learned such an extravagant amount of biology in one semester. I have previously taken this course and received a C because I did not pick up any of the material in class. When I attended her lectures she already had her lecture notes typed up and posted on her website - all that I had to do was to listen and take any additional notes needed to help me remember when studying for the exams. Besides making the lectures very easy to follow, she is also the most accessible professor in the science department at George Mason. In addition to having two office hour sessions weekly (each one hour) she also conducts study sessions about 4-5 times a week – where small groups of students can interact with the professor and ask specific questions. Over the weekend before the exams she has a thorough study session on that Saturday outlining and going over all the material that will be on the exam. She leaves no room for anyone's questions to be unanswered. Usually after taking exams it is hard to retain the majority of the material since biology consists of detailed memorization – but with this said I can recite almost everything I have learned in her class. As you can see she surpasses all the expectations of a professor, I feel it is a major loss to the Biology department and to George Mason University if Dr. Crocker does not lecture biology. I was looking forward to maybe taking another class with her in the near future. There is so much I can explain and discuss about her exquisite means of teaching – if needed I would appreciate a call or if needed I would like to meet with the person responsible for this decision.

Sincerely,

e. From a Pre-med Student (12/22/04)

(referenced in Chapters 2 and 4)

December 22, 2004
Dr. I C Crocker
Visiting Professor
Department of Molecular and Microbiology
George Mason University

Dear Dr. Crocker,

As a student in your BIOL 213 Cell Structure and Function course, Fall 2004, I want you to know that I appreciate, admire, and respect you as a professor – your fairness, your organization, your intellect, your enthusiasm for teaching and helping students. I am only a college freshman, and although you are my first biology professor, I believe you are the epitome of what one should be. I can only hope that all my professors after you will be as wonderful. From what I have heard from my peers, cell biology is supposed to be a difficult and tedious subject. Yet, I can truly say that I enjoyed coming to class, learning from you, and understanding the topics, however detailed they may have been.

On the subject of evolution, you taught what was necessary for cell biology students to learn. You did not teach creationism. During the first lecture, you said outright that this biology course could not answer the 'who' or 'why' questions pertaining to the operation of physical life, that these questions were for philosophy or theology courses. When you did mention evolution in your lectures, you did not assert your opinion above any other. In actuality, I found it difficult to ascertain your opinion in most cases. Even when some students asked if you were suggesting the existence of God, you did not declare your opinion as fact. You only taught what you should have, that there are different theories. For each theory, you even gave the scientific facts to support or refute each claim. You provided your students with critical thinking skills and the knowledge, the known facts, to make up their own mind on the subject of evolution versus intelligent design.

I feel it is imperative for you to understand that your teaching, your course, has improved my awareness of science and self. Not only did you teach the details of the cell, you also taught of the 'bigger picture.' You always returned to the application of our newfound knowledge, supported by your experiences in research. Because of your passion for the subjects, I found interest in your lectures, and you made me realize my love for biology and science. You have helped me decide to major in biology and pursue medical school. Through both your lectures and numerous weekly study groups, your enthusiasm for biology and helping students has shone all semester, making you a truly remarkable and impressive professor. George Mason University is lucky to have you.

███████████████

f. From a Chemistry Student (01/31/05)

(referenced in Chapter 6)

January 31, 2005

To Whom It May Concern:

I am ███████████████ a sophomore at George Mason University. As a part of my B.S. degree in Chemistry, I had the fortune to have had Dr. Crocker as my Cell Biology professor for the fall 2004 semester. The purpose of this letter is to inform you that Dr. Crocker's class is one of the most unforgettable college courses I have ever taken, and that the subjects in the class were covered in a such a way that even a non-biology major, who has never taken any courses in biology, could succeed. Her teaching of the subjects were so interesting and relevant that her lectures are still with me, and using her terminology, techniques of pedagogy, and even humor, I have been able to tweak interest in biology in quite a few of my friends.

On the first day of class, a fear hung over the lecture hall. Dr. Crocker admitted that Cell Biology is a hard course; but she also told us that if we were willing to do the work, come to class, and even take advantage of the extra-credit options, then we would be able to succeed. She did not say that this would be an easy course, but the syllabus seemed manageable. What scared me, however, was the whisper around the lecture hall: "How many times have you taken her class? Really? Me, too!" I awaited a semester of disappointment, poor teaching, and little learning.

As the semester took off, however, I decided to approach Dr. Crocker and ask about how I can do well in her class. She smiled and said the same things that she had said the first day of class. I followed her advice, and succeeded in the course.

Her teaching style was great, and her pace of teaching was as was necessary to cover the materials in the course. She was always helpful, and willing to arrange times for extra help. Extra credit opportunities throughout the semester gave people an opportunity to make up for a time when they did poorly for some reason or other. All in all, Dr. Crocker did all she could to help her students succeed in the difficult course.

g. From Teacher's Aide Donald Willcox (04/29/05)

(referenced in Chapter 4

April 29, 2005

Dear ████████

I am writing to you at the request of Dr. Caroline Crocker. We had a chance meeting at the Histology lab last Tuesday, and she mentioned to me that the Biology department was reviewing her teaching methods and effectiveness.

Dr. Crocker asked me if I would send an email to you describing my experience with her as a student in Cell Biology 213 in the spring term of 2003 and working with her as a teacher's aide under a grant from the Center For Teaching Excellence in the fall term of 2003.

I am an older student returning to school to meet science requirements I need to be considered for admittance to various graduate physical therapy programs. My previous undergrad training was in literature and philosophy, so my return to school has been really exciting – I never really took chemistry and biology before, and it turns out I really love bio!

I loved the challenge presented by Biol 213 and felt that Dr. Crocker was very demanding as a teacher. I knew that she wanted me (and the other students) to have a command over as much material as possible. Her high expectations were companioned by what I perceived to be a genuine commitment to help us accomplish same.

The amount of extra work that Dr. Crocker put into the course provided the kind of example that, to me, communicated a partnership – she would push us, but she was determined to provide us with the tools to succeed. This presented a compelling and motivating model for me.

Specifically, Dr. Crocker provided regular study sessions twice a week open to all students to review that week's material. For students unable to attend these regular study groups, she had a standing invitation to arrange alternate study meetings. This is all in addition to her regular office hours.

That represents only a portion of her time commitment. In addition to the study groups, Dr. Crocker assigned comprehensive worksheets and gave weekly written quizzes – all graded by hand for each of the 120+ students per section (in addition to her Lab instruction duties). I would not have learned all the material had I not been pushed along by these assignments.

After completing her course as a student, I was lucky to apply for and get a grant to be a teacher's aide. I did this both to bolster my vita and to reinforce my command of what I deemed to be really important material. I held study groups on weekends, proctored exams and, most importantly, worked under Dr. Crocker's direction to vet out better ways to teach the material. Under her guidance we created and distributed an anonymous mid-term survey. In the survey we asked students to openly critique/praise course instruction through a mix of short response and ranked response queries. I then processed the results, and we worked to modify some aspects of the course instruction according to the data. While my assignment as an aide was a first and temporary position, it is my hope that these efforts and Dr. Crocker's efforts may have contributed to the ongoing participation of TA's in Cell Biology at GMU today.

If this sounds like a 'rave review' of Dr. Crocker, I suppose it is. However, I am not qualified as an expert on teaching, and it is really not fair at all considering I love the material as I do. I have come to feel that students are largely responsible for learning and that the only seminal thing professors are truly able to 'teach' or pass along is their own passion for a body of knowledge. In my case, and I believe is the case with many other students, Dr. Crocker vested us with an abundance of this.

Sincerely,

Donald A. Willcox
Extended Studies Student
George Mason University

h. From a Lawyer and Student (05/04/05)

(referenced in Chapters 2 and 4)

May 4, 2005

██████████████████████████

George Mason University

Re: Dr. L Caroline Crocker, Grievance Committee

Dear ████████

It has come to my attention (yesterday) that Dr. Crocker is apparently under some kind of investigation or review by the Grievance Committee. It is my understanding that certain allegations have been made against Dr. Crocker arising from her teaching of Biology 213 (Cell Structure and Function) - namely, Dr. Crocker's "teaching" of creationism and/or "poor teaching" by Dr. Crocker. As a former student of Dr. Crocker (as well as being an attorney), I cannot stand idly by and permit these specious and patently false claims to smear an otherwise outstanding professor. I write to you as you may be the head of said committee. (If not, kindly forward this letter to the appropriate person.)

By way of background, I took Dr. Crocker's Biology 213 class last spring (2004 spring semester) as a post-baccalaureate student having been graduated from Dartmouth College (Hanover, NH) in 1991 and Fordham University School of Law (New York City) in 1996. In addition to Dr. Crocker's class, I have also taken the other prerequisite pre-med science courses at GMU (as I am a Virginia resident) in hopes of attending medical school next year after having practiced law in Virginia, Maryland, and the District of Columbia for nearly seven and a half years. Therefore, I believe I can provide some perspective that a typical college student may not have. For full disclosure, I received a grade of "A+" from Dr. Crocker in Biology 213. I have also received grades of "A+" in Chemistry 211 and 212 (General Chemistry), Biology 303 (Animal Biology), Physics 243 (College Physics I), Chemistry 313 and 315 (Organic Chemistry and Lab I), and a grade of "A" in Physics 244 (College of Physics Lab I); furthermore, I anticipate receiving grades of "A" or "A+" in Chemistry 314 and 318 (Organic Chemistry and Lab II) and Physics 245 and 246 (College of Physics and Lab II) at the end of the semester.

In regards to the above mentioned allegations against Dr. Crocker, any and all claims of Dr. Crocker teaching creationism in class or Dr. Crocker being a poor teacher are absolutely false. In fact, any negative or derogatory claim against Dr. Crocker cannot have any merit whatsoever. Obviously, my comments are based on my experiences from the 2004 spring semester and while I cannot directly comment about anything that may or may not have happened in the 2004 fall semester, I believe my comments would still generally apply.

As to the spurious claim of Dr. Crocker teaching creationism in class, this must be summarily dismissed. At no time did Dr. Crocker ever teach creationism or any "theory that humankind was created by a divine being" as defined by the United States Supreme Court. At no time did Dr. Crocker utter the word "God" or any other word referring to any "divine being." From my recollection (as I never missed a class) and my review of my Biology 213 notes, Dr. Crocker did give one lecture regarding evolution and discussed the theories of microevolution (natural selection), macroevolution, and intelligent design; moreover, Dr. Crocker presented "only scientific explanations for life on earth" and, if any, only "scientific critiques of evolution" as outlined by the United States Supreme Court. I find it incredible how any reasonable and prudent student could honestly believe or state that creationism was being directly or even obliquely taught by Dr. Crocker. This claim is absurd. Furthermore, even after that lecture on evolution and having sat through every lecture, I have absolutely no idea what Dr. Crocker believes religiously or scientifically or realistically as to the origins of life.

2   May 4, 2005

As to the ridiculous claim of Dr. Crocker being a "poor teacher," I take great offense and umbrage at any one who has the temerity to make such a brazenly false statement. Frankly, the only kind of person who could make such an allegation with a straight face is an idiot (for lack of a better word) who obviously did poorly in class and now seeks malicious retribution against Dr. Crocker. There can be no other reasonable explanation (perhaps some other malicious hidden agenda). I believe Dr. Crocker did an excellent job teaching an otherwise complex subject to a large class. She presented the material in an organized, logical, and interesting fashion. (For example, during the semester, Dr. Crocker made a point of emphasis for students to learn the vocabulary of cell biology and even gave "pop" vocabulary quizzes and emphasized vocabulary on the final exam. While I may not have been very appreciative during the semester, I am now very grateful to Dr. Crocker for having drilled the vocabulary into my head after having recently taken the MCAT exam.) We (the students) were all warned at the beginning of the semester in class and again in lab that the fail rate in the class was 40%! Not withstanding the grim outlook, Dr. Crocker gave every student every opportunity to obtain a good grade in the class. To this date, I have yet to encounter any professor anywhere who made herself patiently available to students not only for regular office hours but also for regular review sessions - even on weekends before a Monday exam! When I heard the allegation of "poor teacher," my immediate thought was "is this some kind of sick joke?"

I have been quite fortunate and am very appreciative to have had excellent and competent professors here during my limited experience at George Mason, and Dr. Crocker is no exception. I am disappointed that there is even one student who does not appreciate the job and effort Dr. Crocker has provided in her teachings. I can only assume such students would only be satisfied by a professor who simply provides all of the answers to an exam or curves rather liberally. (I can imagine myself being quite satisfied with such a professor if I was an unmotivated undergraduate college student, again.) Interestingly, I was recently introduced to a website called "ratemyprofessor.com" by a fellow classmate. Judging from some of the comments posted at their website, one could wonder if there is a good professor anywhere or if "good professor" is simply an oxymoron. Nevertheless, I believe it would be a tragic loss to George Mason and to future students attending George Mason if Dr. Crocker did not teach at George Mason, for whatever reason. I can only hope that strong efforts are being made to retain Dr. Crocker.

My only regret is that I am unable to devote more time and effort to this letter due to my desire to get my comments to you (and any other appropriate person) with all due speed (not to mention having to prepare for four final exams - two tomorrow). If necessary, I am ready, willing, and able to discuss this matter with you or any other appropriate person at a mutually agreeable time. I can be contacted at ███████████ or at ███████ or at the address listed below. It is a sad commentary that a fine professor such as Dr. Crocker has to be caught up in the politicking that is so pervasive in the work environment due to the disgruntled few.

Lastly, as you can see, I am providing a carbon copy of this letter to Dr. Crocker so that she is aware that there is at least one appreciative former student and so that she can do whatever with this letter as she sees fit.

I look forward to hearing from you soon, even if it is only an acknowledgement of receipt of this letter. I trust the right thing will be done.

cc: Dr. L Caroline Crocker

i. From a Former Student (05/17/05)

(referenced in Chapter 5)

Sent Tuesday, May 17, 2005 1:34 am
  To icrocker@gmu.edu
  Cc
  Bcc
Subject Microbiology/other bio classes

Hi, my name is ▓▓▓▓▓▓▓ I was in your 213 class last semester and I have a question about upper level bio classes. I was wondering if you might ever teach a class other than 213, like micro or genetics?? I know I'm not the only one wondering this, several of my classmates this semester, as we study for our tests in our current class were wondering if you might teach other classes. We feel like benefited and learned a lot from your class and are worried about having an unorganized, unclear teacher for a really challenging class such as micro. This is probably a very odd sounding e-mail, I don't think any of the other kids I know who are wondering this actually have e-mailed you, but I am very curious.

Thank you for you time and sorry for any inconvenience,

j. From Teacher's Aide Donald Willcox (February, 2009)

(referenced in Chapter 4)

...On your teaching it was obviously your sections on Evolution that were the problem.

What you did is quite accurately outlined in your notes, quizzes and tests. What you did not do was ever mention God, church or religion. My previous University training was Literature and Philosophy so I found your approach quite interesting. At the time I will admit to thinking you were being pretty gutsy by pressing the issue and diverting from the standard dogma. I feel a little guilty in thinking it somewhat amusing that you did this for several semesters before they objected. Something happened. Either they were not paying attention to what you were doing all that time (not good considering you were a new teacher) or a person or persons of power lowered the boom on the department. I would love to find out what really did happen there.

Yes I know some student complained, and given it was Fairfax, they may have had an attorney to threaten the school (e.g. 'If you want to keep getting state funding, you better establish that you are non-sectarian...) but that still does not explain the fact that, from what I know, they never cited your teaching of Evolution as the problem. The notion that your teaching was sub-par is simply not defensible - that argument would fail unless they felt that you did not teach the Evolution section properly. You certainly did not teach the majority of the dogma (as covered in the 100 level Biol I took). I remember you working very hard to the end of getting a longer term contract. I recall you came from NOVA on a year-to-year contract. Starting your second year at GMU, when I was working with you as a student aide under a grant, I remember you mentioning that you were really excited to get a longer term contract. I recall discussing this with you in person at your home and at school. You and your family were in need of the money with your son in College (abroad I believe) and of course the expense of living in Northern VA. In my opinion the longer term was well deserved.

The transformation from single year contract to multi-year contract raised my hopes you would be someday tenured. Not only did I think you were (are) one of the best teachers I have had in my many, many years of university study I selfishly hoped you would be around as a reference and mentor as I approached Grad school.

Finally, I recall how confused and surprised (the fall following my work as student aide) I was when you told me they might not renew your contract for the next year. I was surprised because I though you were there for a longer term. I recall you explaining a rather devious bait-and-switch 're-execution' of your contract under a premise of adding a section (rather than changing the term). It seemed quite insidious.

Just recalling how they treated you makes me quite sad - you worked so hard for the students and school.

don

Appendix III: Letters and E-mails from Faculty

a. From GMU Provost Peter Stearns (03/22/04)

(referenced in Chapter 5)

George Mason University

Office of the Provost
4400 University Drive
Fairfax, Virginia 22030

Phone:
Fax:

MEMO

Date: 22 March 04

To: Professor I. Caroline Crocker, MMB, 3E1

From: Dr. Peter Stearns, Provost
           Dr. Marilyn M. McKenzie, Associate Provost for Educational Programs

Re: Review of Student Evaluations of Fall 2003 General Education Courses

Dear Professor I. Caroline Crocker:

We write to congratulate you and thank you for an outstanding performance in the general education course you taught last fall term, as evidenced by unusually high student rankings. This kind of teaching quality is essential for this vital educational program, and we're very grateful for your successful efforts.

Our review of student rankings represents a first level of analysis given the fact that the data are ordinal (ranked) data. As you know, it is our goal to review the general education curriculum and recommend possible adjustments after the first few years of implementation. As a part of our review, we have identified outstanding student rankings of courses (equal to or >4.75, Question 6 "The Overall Rating of this Course"), and your course was included in this noteworthy group.

Thank you for your outstanding contribution to the success of the University General Education Program, and thank you for your program's support of and contributions to the General Education Program. Best wishes in your future teaching!

CC: Department Chair
           Dean

b. Letter from GMU Professor in the School of Computer Science David Rine (05/05/04)
(referenced in Chapter 6)

Dear Grievance Committee,

I wish to lend my professional support for Dr. I. Caroline Crocker and her 'Reinstatement of Dr. Crocker's Current Term Teaching Position in the Department of Molecular and Microbiology.' In a professional capacity at GMU I have known Caroline for several years. I am also knowledgeable of the general facts surrounding this particular case. I also have been both an administrator and a professor at GMU for twenty years, and in that capacity I have both defended and cherished the vision of our wonderful university as a community of scholars dedicated to preserving and 'evolving' the emergent concept of a great and diversified place of learning and sharing ideas and lives. I am also both aware of and a defender of our Provost's and President's stands on both diversity and academic freedom for faculty and students. Moreover I am highly respectful of the important responsibility your committee maintains, and I am a supporter of the due processes for GMU faculty as defined in the GMU Faculty Handbook. Thank you for allowing me to submit this letter of support for the current case.

I have first hand knowledge of Dr. Crocker's academic speaking and lecturing characteristics. I have attended lectures by her and have witnessed the following characteristics of her presentation style:

1. Excellent audience eye personal contact,
2. Friendly and supportive audience manners,
3. Enthusiasm in entertaining of audience questions,
4. Excellent preparation of lecture materials,
5. Openness to alternative ideas and opinions from the audience,
6. Excellent pre-preparation of visual aids,
7. Focus and reinforcement of the topic of the presentation,
8. Deep knowledge of the material.

As is Caroline, I am a scientist, as well as an engineer who applies science, and I am keenly aware of the practices of the scientific methods as a broad spectrum of possibilities, depending upon the investigative setting. I have written and published about 300 papers, along with a number of books. I have directed a large number of PhD dissertations here at GMU. I have a good understanding of the general differences between science, philosophy and religion. I am just offering this to indicate that I am not naïve of the scholarly context in which this case is generally presented. Moreover, in my classroom sessions I try to offer my students a broad understanding of the various alternatives in the topics I present. I also have applied the general concepts of 'evolution' but applied more to the context of applied science, engineering and ethnography, instead of cell biology. Moreover, the ideas behind 'evolution' take on an enormous spectrum of alternatives, not just one. I also teach courses in the foundations of design theories and practice.

It is unimaginable to me, personally, to conceive of Dr. Crocker engaging in this kind of behavior in which she was wrongfully charged by an anonymous student. This would be completely uncharacteristic of Dr. Crocker as I know her style.

I, therefore, support an outcome of this case so as to 'Reinstate Dr. Crocker to her Current Term Teaching Position in the Department of Molecular and Microbiology.' I offer this out of respect to your committee and the procedure you are following.

Respectfully yours,

David C. Rine
Professor
School of Information Technology and Engineering
George Mason University

[original document]

Dr. I. Caroline Crocker GMU Grievance Case

		)	Case No.: No. -1
		)	
	Plaintiff,	)	PLEADING 'Reinstatement of Dr. Crocker's
vs.		)	Current Term Teaching Position in the Department|
		)	of Molecular and Microbiology'
		)	
	Defendant	)	·

Plaintiff,

Dr. I C Crocker

Visiting Professor

Department of Molecular and Microbiology

George Mason University

Dear Grievance Committee,

I wish to lend my professional support for Dr. I. Caroline Crocker and her 'Reinstatement of Dr. Crocker's Current Term Teaching Position in the Department of Molecular and Microbiology.' In a professional capacity at GMU I have known Caroline for several years. I am also knowledgeable of the general facts surrounding this particular case. I also have been both an administrator and a professor at GMU for twenty years, and in that capacity I have both defended and cherished the vision of our wonderful university as a community of scholars dedicated to preserving and 'evolving' the emergent concept of a great and highly diversified place of learning and sharing ideas and lives. I am also both aware of and a defender of our Provost's and President's stands on both diversity and academic freedom for faculty and students. Moreover I am highly respectful of the important responsibility your committee maintains, and I am a supporter of the due processes for GMU faculty as defined in the GMU Faculty Handbook. Thank you for allowing me to submit this letter of support for the current case.

I have first hand knowledge of Dr. Crocker's academic speaking and lecturing characteristics. I have attended lectures by her and have witnessed the following characteristics of her presentation style:

1. Excellent audience eye personal contact,

2. Friendly and supportive audience manners,

3. Enthusiasm in the entertaining of audience questions,

4. Excellent preparation of lecture materials,

5. Openness to alternative ideas and opinions from the audience,

6. Excellent pre-preparation of visual aids,

7. Focus and reinforcement of the topic of the presentation,

8. Deep knowledge of the material.

As is Caroline, I am a scientist, as well as an engineer who applies science, and I am keenly aware of the practices of the scientific methods as a broad spectrum of possibilities, depending upon the investigative setting. I have written and published about 300 papers, along with a number of books. I have directed a large number of PhD dissertations here at GMU. I have a good understanding of the general differences between science, philosophy and religion. I am just offering this to indicate that I am not naïve of the scholarly context in which this case is generally presented. Moreover, in my classroom sessions I try to offer my students a broad understanding of the various alternatives in the topics I present. I also have applied the general concepts of 'evolution' but applied more to the context of applied science, engineering and ethnography, instead of cell biology. Moreover, the ideas behind 'evolution' take on an enormous spectrum of alternatives, not just one. I also teach courses in the foundations of design theories and practice.

It is unimaginable to me, personally, to conceive of Dr. Crocker engaging in the kind of behavior in which she was wrongfully charged by an anonymous student. This would be completely uncharacteristic of Dr. Crocker as I know of her style.

I, therefore, support an outcome of this case so as to 'Reinstate Dr. Crocker to her Current Term Teaching Position in the Department of Molecular and Microbiology.' I offer this out of respect to your committee and the procedure you are following.

Respectfully yours,

David C. Rine

c. From GMU Provost Peter Stearns (12/23/04)

(referenced in Chapter 5)

Dear Professor I. Caroline Crocker:

We write to congratulate you and thank you for an outstanding performance in the general education course you taught last _____ term, as evidenced by unusually high student ratings. This kind of teaching quality is essential for this vital educational program, and we're very grateful for your successful efforts.

Our review of student rankings represents a first level of analysis given the fact that the data are ordinal (ranked) data. As you know, it is our goal to review the general education curriculum and recommend possible adjustments after the first few years of implementation. As part of our review, we have identified outstanding student rankings of courses (equal to or >4.75), Question 6 "The Overall Rating of this Course"), and your course was included in this noteworthy group.

Thank you for your outstanding contribution to the success of the University General Education Program, and thank you for your program's support of and contributions to the General Education Program. Best wishes in your future teaching!

[original document]

George Mason University

Office of the Provost
4400 University Drive
Fairfax, Virginia 22030

Phone: 703-993-8770
Fax: 703-993-8645

MEMO

Date ▮▮▮▮▮▮ber 23, 2004

To: Professor I. Caroline Crocker, Molecular and Microbiology, 3E1

From: Dr. Peter Stearns, Provost
               Dr. Marilyn M. McKenzie, Associate Provost for Educational Programs

Re: Review of Student Evaluations of semester General Education Courses

Dear Professor I. Caroline Crocker:

We write to congratulate you and thank you for an outstanding performance in the general education course you taught last spring term, as evidenced by unusually high student rankings. This kind of teaching quality is essential for this vital educational program, and we're very grateful for your successful efforts.

Our review of student rankings represents a first level of analysis given the fact that the data are ordinal (ranked) data. As you know, it is our goal to review the general education curriculum and recommend possible adjustments after the first few years of implementation As a part of our review, we have identified outstanding student rankings of courses (equal to or >4.75, Question 6 "The Overall Rating of this Course"), and your course was included in this noteworthy group.

Thank you for your outstanding contribution to the success of the University General Education Program, and thank you for your program's support of and contributions to the General Education Program. Best wishes in your future teaching!

CC: Department Chair
               Dean

d. From My Departmental Administrator (02/28/05 and 05/12/05)

(referenced in Chapter 6)

> **Date: Monday, February 28, 2005 3:19 pm**
> **Subject: Fall 2005 schedule**
>
> > Please review the attached Fall 2005 schedule. Final revisions
> > must be
> > received by Wednesday March 2nd. Please let me know of problems
> > by
> > close of business tomorrow.
> > Thanks,
> >

> **Date: Thursday, May 12, 2005 11:28 am**
> **Subject: Spring 2006 schedule**
>
> > The preliminary Spring 2006 schedule is due June 3rd. If you are
> > requesting an electronic classroom, you will need to complete a
> > Technology Classroom request form which can be found at:
> > http://registrar.gmu.edu/scheduling/TechClassroomForm.pdf. As you
> > are
> > aware, these classrooms are in high demand so we need to get
> > requests in
> > even before they are due - so please return the form to me ASAP.
> > If you
> > are planning any changes to your teaching schedule - the usual
> > time that
> > your class is offered - please let me know of your plans.
> >

e. From GMU Dean of the School of Computational Sciences Murray Black (05/03/05)

(referenced in Chapter 6)

May 3, 2005

Dear ████

As just one member of the faculty, I wish to express my gratitude to you and your committee members for the valuable time and service that you provide in listening to faculty members who have a grievance or concern. Like you, I deeply am concerned about the integrity of the university and the way that we treat our professional colleagues and students. Having said that I also sympathize with the roll of administrators, particularly department chairs and academic deans, since I have been in those ranks for approximately 19 of my 34 years at GMU.

Dr. I. Caroline Crocker as a relatively new Visiting Professor recently approached me as a friend and colleague. She asked me to look at the facts with respect to her being released from teaching Cell Biology. I certainly support the requirement that the Chair of an academic department has the responsibility of staffing the courses in his or her department. In cases where there are any questions raised regarding an instructor in a course, then the Chair must carefully investigate the facts and allegations (preferably with the assistance of colleagues) and then take action to rectify the situation.

My concern in this case is the manner in which the change was handled. I believe that the rights of Dr. Crocker were violated and due process was not followed. At the very minimum, the process was not handled in a professional manner that I would expect of any chair at our university. Apparently, Dr. Crocker was told of "students and faculty" complaining that she was "teaching creationism" (nothing about her technical competence in teaching). The issue of the appropriateness of creationism is one I shall not deal with at this point. Rather, I am concerned that apparently none of the faculty ever heard her teach at all and none ever approached her about what or how she was teaching her class. In fact, from what I observe, Dr. Crocker is a very thorough teacher and relatively strict with her students, as more of us should be. In addition, she strictly enforces the honor code, again as more of us should do. As a result, students who are accused of an honor violation and/or dislike a "strict" teacher will be prone to complain to whomever will listen, particularly those in authority such as department chairs (many of us have been there!).

As a part of due process, when students complain, it is important that they put their complaints down in writing and all parties involved should receive a copy. The chair should then have a consultation with the faculty and accusing parties, or better, the chair should have the department grievance committee hear the case in an unbiased manner. In so far as I can ascertain, none of this was done at all. Incidentally, I understand that the Chair even stated that this visiting professor was pointing to sections of the handbook that are not relevant to the term faculty under a revised addendum to the Faculty Handbook.

The addendum was just that, a supplement, and certainly not a replacement of the handbook for term faculty. The addendum covers only the appointment and reappointment of term faculty, nothing more. This addendum is not even relevant in this case. The portions of the handbook that Dr. Crocker referred to in section 2.12 on Faculty Rights and Privileges must apply to all faculty members regardless of their type of appointment. I believe that the same might be said of section 2.10.3.

Did Dr. Crocker mention creationism or intelligent design in her class? I do not know, but she says that she did *not* teach it, and whenever the subject came up, she tried to be very objective in her approach, and I believe that to be the case. Certainly, all the letters I have seen on her behalf from students who were after all in the classroom with her, point very strongly to that being correct. Should it never be mentioned? I leave that to our Biology colleagues, whom I trust will be open to the fundamental right of any faculty member to the unrestricted exposition of subjects including controversial questions within one's field as clearly spelled out in our faculty handbook (7/1/94).

May I please be so bold as to suggest a solution? I believe that the communications here have been sorely lacking. Consequently, I think that there must be a clear understanding between the faculty, chair, and Dr. Crocker as to what is to be taught in the Cell Biology course in question. Perhaps this has been done, but the instructor of the course needs to have the right to openly face the issue of evolution when it is mentioned in the text, even if it is not a specific topic in the syllabus. No faculty member should ever be restricted from mentioning that there are other ideas on a topic including one like evolution. Certainly, this can be done relatively quickly in an even-handed manner.

In addition, I believe that it is important that any negative documentation associated with this case should be removed from her file. Furthermore, until any inappropriate action has been proven following the guidelines of the faculty handbook, Dr. Crocker should be reinstated to teaching the lecture in Cell Biology and like all faculty her syllabus should be approved by the Chair or his designee. Furthermore, all visiting professors should have their performance reviewed by a small group of faculty members to provide a recommendation to the chair regarding raises or renewal issues. Again, this is consistent with the faculty handbook.

I apologize for such a lengthy letter, but I do feel strongly that justice needs to be served in this case. At the university, we are to seek truth and anything that hinders a person from that pursuit defeats the purpose of our goal of having an open classroom to develop ideas and graduates who are able to think deeply for themselves.

Very respectfully,

W. Murray Black
Professor, Electrical and Computer Engineering

f. From GMU Professor in School of Computer Science David Rine (03/04/09)
(referenced in Chapter 6)

Wednesday, March 04, 2009

To Whom it May Concern,

I was a professor in the Volgeman School of Information Technology and Engineering, George Mason University (GMU), during the time Dr. Caroline Crocker was on the faculty at George Mason University. During the time frame under discussion, I had had a number of cordial conversations with Dr. Crocker in areas related to academics, teaching and design, as well as Christian education.

As best I can generally recall, I think that she started at GMU as adjunct faculty in the 2002 time frame. And she taught material generally related to biology and cell biology in her first semester. As best I can recall she continued later in the second semester (January 2003) with a regular renewable faculty contract. And I recall that the following 2003-2004 semesters she continued with these teaching assignments.

I recall that Dr. Crocker was very excited about a discussion with GMU about a further extended multi-year, renewable contract. I believe that we had assumed that this would all turn out to be the case, based on the conversations we had at the time.

I recall that Dr. Crocker was, and still is, a very good scholar in her research area of cell biology. Our academic areas generally overlapped in that both of us are interested in design sciences. Crocker's from a biology perspective and mine from an engineering and applied science perspective. This was a basis for interesting conversations while we were at GMU.

I have heard Dr. Crocker give lectures and public presentations. Based upon observation I view her as an excellent teacher and communicator.

It is my hope that Dr. Crocker will continue to be successful in her writing, teaching and research in the areas of design and cell biology.

Respectfully submitted,

David C. Rine, Ph.D.

[original document]

Wednesday, March 04, 2009

To Whom It May Concern.

I was a Professor in the Volgenau School of Information Technology and Engineering, George Mason University (GMU), during the time Dr. Caroline Crocker was on the faculty at George Mason University. During the time frame under discussion, I had had a number of cordial conversations with Dr. Crocker in areas related to academics, teaching and design, as well as Christian education.

As best I can generally recall, I think that she started at GMU as adjunct faculty in the 2002 time frame. And she taught material generally related to biology and cell biology in her first semester. As best I can recall she continued later in the second semester (January 2003) with a regular renewable faculty contract. And I recall that the following 2003-2004 semesters she continued with these teaching assignments.

I recall that Dr. Crocker was very excited about a discussion with GMU about a further extended multi-year, renewable contract. I believe that we had assumed that this would all turn out to be the case, based upon the conversations we had at the time.

I recall that Dr. Crocker was, and still is, a very good scholar in her research area of cell biology. Our academic areas generally overlapped in that both of us are interested in design issues, Crocker's from a biology perspective and mine from an engineering and applied sciences perspective. This was a basis for interesting conversations while we were at GMU.

I have heard Dr. Crocker give lectures and public presentations. Based upon this observation I view her as an excellent teacher and communicator.

It is my hope that Dr. Crocker will continue to be successful in her writing, teaching and research in the areas of design and cell biology.

Respectfully submitted,

David C. Rine, Ph.D.

Appendix IV: Documents Pertaining to the Grievance

a. E-mail from Caroline Crocker Acknowledging Discipline (12/17/04)

(referenced in Chapter 5)

12/17/04

Dr. ███

I would like to confirm what occurred at our meeting yesterday (12/16/04) at 10:30 am, in case I misunderstood the proceedings in any way. I also would like to take this opportunity to respond to it.

First, you indicated that the report I E-mailed you about the TAC project was acceptable and requested that I forward it to the TAC director. You also indicated that I should request a meeting in January and that this project may be more suitable for another course.

Second, you informed me that I am to be disciplined for allegedly teaching creationism in my Cell Bio lectures. I will not be allowed to teach the lecture course next semester and will be assigned four labs, with no assurance for Fall, 2005. You stated that you have had complaints from several faculty members and students. I would also like to confirm that you stated that you have never attended one of my lectures, despite my request mid-semester that you would. It is also a fact that no other faculty members have attended a lecture either. I would like to note that I have not been allowed to face my accusers, and indeed, do not know who they are.

Next, I would like to confirm that I told you yesterday that I have never taught creationism and, if I do the lecture on evolution, I only teach the scientific evidence for and against it. This is my right under the "academic freedom" that GMU endorses. I also told you I did not do the evolution lecture during the Fall 2004 semester. You responded that you have told me in the past that I should not teach about evolution, because it is not in the course description. However, I do not remember that conversation and there is no paper documentation.

I would like to point out that the textbook I was assigned discusses aspects of evolution in every chapter and, thus, it is not obvious that it would be out of line to teach about evolution in one lecture. In fact, the notes I got from ███ when I started at GMU, do include several mentions of evolution. Finally, I would like to confirm that you stated that you have, in fact, approved my syllabus every semester, before the semester starts. You have also had full access to my website, which includes all of the lecture Powerpoint slides, worksheets, etc. However, at our meeting, I did say that I would be happy to teach the course without the evolution lecture in the future.

I would like it documented that I feel my rights to due process and academic freedom have been violated. The accusations against me are groundless and I have not had opportunity to demonstrate this. I have not taught anything but science and have had many students expressing gratitude for the care I take to make sure they learn the material. I would like to add this document to my file, as is my right under

GMU guidelines, responding to this disciplinary procedure. At that time, I will also add a response to my annual evaluation. I am sure you understand.

Meanwhile, I would like to assure you that I will continue to teach to the best of my ability and to contribute to the department. Teaching is important to me, so much so that I gave up research so that I could spend more time on it. I take pride in the many kind notes of appreciation I have received from my students this semester. Best wishes,   Dr. Caroline Crocker

b. E-mails between GMU Dean of College of Arts and Sciences Daniele Struppa and Caroline Crocker (February 7-9, 2005)

(referenced in Chapter 5)

From ███████████████   ▶
Sent Wednesday, February 9, 2005 10:45 am
  To icrocker@gmu.edu
  Cc
 Bcc
Subject Re: Request for a meeting

Dear Dr. Crocker:

I have given some more thought to your original request, and your latest email. You point out that you feel you have been denied due process, and you indicated that you felt your academic freedom was being violated.

Under these conditions, I believe that the best course of action would be for you to file a grievance as discussed in section 2.12.2 of the Faculty Handbook.

Section 2.12.2.1 describes the policies concerning grievances, and specifically indicates that the College Grievance Committee is charged to hear grievances concerning, among other things, alleged violations of academic freedom, and work assignments.

Section 2.12.2.2, on the other hands, details the specific process which will occur, and notes that the recommendation from the Committee will be forwarded to me, for a final decision. Given my specific role in the process, I think it would be inappropriate for us to meet at this time.

I would advise you to consult the Handbook for more details and, if you decide, to file the grievance with the CAS Grievance Committee.

As of now, the members of the CAS Grievance Committee are Professors ███████████████
███████████████████████████████████████ and ███████████████. I believe you can initiate the process by contacting any one of them.

Best wishes

Daniele C. Struppa

PS. You may access both the charge and the composition of our Grievance Committee through the web page of the College, under faculty and then governance.
----- Original Message -----
From: icrocker@gmu.edu
Date: Tuesday, February 8, 2005 8:38 pm
Subject: Re: Request for a meeting

> Dear Dean Struppa,
> I understand your wish to save time, but, to be honest, I would
> find that very difficult. Dr. C has not spoken with me since the
> incident, except in mass E-mails to all the TA's. I feel
> humiliated because my integrity has been questioned (it would be
> absolutely wrong to teach religion in a science class) and I am
> being punished without having the right to due process. In
> addition, I am a woman. Although it might not seem a threatening
> situation to you, facing two men who are in positions of authority
> over me would be most uncomfortable. However, if it would be okay
> with you, I would be happy to meet with both of you in the
> presence of Murray Black, if he is available then. Otherwise, we

> may need to reschedule. Thank you for your patience and understanding.
>   Caroline Crocker
>
> Dr. I C Crocker
> Visiting Professor
> Department of Molecular and Microbiology
> George Mason University
>
> ----- Original Message -----
> From: ██████████████
> Date: Tuesday, February 8, 2005 4:46 pm
> Subject: Re: Request for a meeting
>
> > Would you mind if I were to invite Dr. ████████ as well?
> Rather
> > than listening to the two sides of the story separately, I would
> > like to have both at the same time. Would that be agreable to you?
> >
> > Thanks
> >
> > dcs
> >
> > ----- Original Message -----
> > From: icrocker@gmu.edu
> > Date: Monday, February 7, 2005 12:08 pm
> > Subject: Request for a meeting
> >
> > > Dear Dean Struppa:
> > > I am writing at the suggestion of ████████ from the
> > Office
> > > for Equity and Diversity Services to request a meeting. At the
> > end
> > > of the semester in December, I was called into my supervisor's
> > > office ████████████ and informed that I am going to
> be
> > > disciplined for teaching creationism. I epxlained to him that
> I
> > do
> > > not do this, but I do teach about the evidence for and against
> > > evolution in one lecture, which I did not do during the Fall
> > > semester because of lack of time. The sequence of events is
> > > outlined in the attached E-mail, to which I have not received
> an
> > > answer. I am also attaching a letter from one of the best
> > > students, explaining what I do teach.
> > > Meanwhile, I have seen on the GMU web site that GMU endorses
> > > academic freedom and that the course is meant to include
> > teaching
> > > on the evolution of cells (Intro to Cell Structure and
> > Function).
> > > However, ████████ has found so far that the right to
> academic
> > > freedom and due process does not seem to apply to term
> faculty.
> > I

> > > find this hard to believe, especially since I have received
> > grants
> > > from the Center for Teaching Excellence, letters from the
> > Provost
> > > about high student ratings, and many students are complaining
> > this
> > > semester because I am not teaching a lecture. A couple have
> been
> > > affected because they were hoping to be apprenticed to me this
> > > semester and they are most unhappy that I am not teaching. I
> am
> > > hoping that we can meet and a solution can be found.
> > > Thank you for your attention.   Caroline Crocker,
> > > MSc, PhD
> > >
> > > Dr. I C Crocker
> > > Visiting Professor
> > > Department of Molecular and Microbiology
> > > George Mason University
> > >
> >
> >
>
>

c. E-mail from Head of College of Arts and Sciences Grievance Committee "Karen Anderson" (05/27/05)

(referenced in Chapter 6)

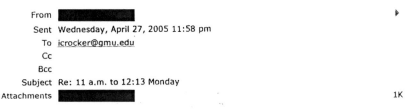

From   ██████████
Sent   Wednesday, April 27, 2005 11:58 pm
To   icrocker@gmu.edu
Cc
Bcc
Subject   Re: 11 a.m. to 12:13 Monday
Attachments   ████████████   1K

Dear Caroline:

Here are some answers to your questions.

1. First, the purpose of this INFORMAL HEARING is to get information on which the Committee can make a reasoned decision. The Committee's action exhausts the Grievant's INTERNAL Appeals so further action requires legal remedies outside the University. You should plan a prepared statement and then be ready for questions from the committee. You and ████████████ will be interviewed separately by the committee.

2. ████████████ has not yet sent the committee a response. In March, he sent a note to the committee questioning whether you were eligible for the grievance process. We concluded that you were. So, the reason you have not received his substantive response is that we don't have it yet. My understanding is that he will deliver his substantive response to you and to the committee members Friday via email and hard copy mail.

3. The committee has decided not to allow tape recording.

Thank you for your questions and your carefulness.

Best,

George Mason University
Fairfax, VA 22030-4444

https://mserver3.gmu.edu/frame.html?rtfPossible=true&lang=en   5/30/2005

d. Grievance Document (03/11/05)

(referenced in Chapter 6)

GRIEVANCE

Dr. Caroline Crocker vs. ███████████

1) Respondent: ████████████ Associate Chair, Molecular and Microbiology

2) Sections of Faculty Handbook Violated:

> 2.12.1 Academic Freedom: "the right to unrestricted expositions of subjects (including controversial questions) within one's field…in a professionally responsible manner…without fear of censorship or penalty."

> 2.10.3 The right not to be excluded from the classroom until sufficient grounds for exclusion have been found and a committee of five have approved such discipline (to be done within three days after such exclusion).

> Rights found in the Amendments to the Constitution (several of which were originated by George Mason). 1st Amendment: freedom of speech; 6th Amendment: the right to be informed of the nature of an accusation and to face one's accuser; 14th Amendment: The right to due process, innocence until proven guilty, and the right not to be punished on the basis of unsubstantiated assertions.

3) Evidence:

> A.   On December 16, 2004, I had a meeting with ██████████ where I was informed that I was going to be disciplined by not being allowed to lecture for the undefined future. The reason for this was that allegedly "faculty and students" had complained that I "taught creationism" during the fall semester. I was instructed to immediately go to ██████████ office and sign up for teaching a fourth lab, which I did. This semester I have duly been teaching four labs and no lectures. I have also received a plan for Fall 2005, which does not show anyone teaching the Cell Biology lectures.

> B.   A copy of the e-mail dated 12/17/04, written to ██████████ immediately after the incident, where I confirmed the proceedings at the meeting and gave particulars that are not included here. This was given to him twice, but I have not received an answer.

> C.   Copies of the two sections of the faculty handbook that were violated: Academic freedom and the right of not being excluded from the classroom without the decision of a committee. I have been disciplined on the basis of unsubstantiated assertions from anony-

mous persons. I was originally told that both faculty and students had complained, but this assertion was altered when I pointed out that no faculty member has attended one of my lectures. Therefore, I understand that the accusation came from a student.

D.   Two letters from students (two from Fall, 2004 and an E-mail from a student who took the class in Spring, 2003 and was my TA with a grant from the Center for Teaching Excellence in Fall, 2003). These show that I did not teach creationism, neither in previous semesters, when I taught a lecture on evolution, nor during the Fall 2004 semester when time considerations meant that lecture was omitted. The allegations are false.

E.   Excerpt from the University Catalog showing that mentioning evolution is entirely appropriate in Cell Structure and Function. The textbooks include it and ███████████ whose lecture outline I initially followed, spoke of it.

4) Remedy Sought:

A.   Reinstatement to teaching the lecture, starting Fall, 2005.

B.   Removal of negative documentation from my record.

C.   Assurance that a group of faculty members will be involved in decisions about the renewal of my contract.

D.   Annual evaluation of my teaching performance done by a person other than ██████████

e. GMU Associate Professor "Peter Carter's" Response to Grievance (04/29/05)

(referenced in Chapter 6)

(Dr. Crocker's comments are inserted in bold italicized text)

Response to Grievance filed by Dr. I. Caroline Crocker

Dr. Crocker has not made a prima facie case to the grievance committee, because it is the right of the chair or the chair's designee to set faculty teaching loads, and the Faculty Handbook sections cited by Dr. Crocker are for Tenure-line faculty and don't apply to Term Faculty. *The Grievance committee had established that the faculty handbook applies to both tenure-line and term faculty at least a month prior to this communication being sent.* Dr. Crocker's employment contract is covered under the George Mason University *Procedures for Appointment and Reappointment of Term Faculty*, an addendum to the Faculty Handbook (approved jointly by the Provost and the Executive Committee of the Faculty Senate in 2003). Also, Dr. Crocker was not excluded from the classroom. Her teaching assignment was shifted to four laboratory sections from one lecture section and three laboratory sections (all in the same course: Biol 213 Cell Structure and Function). *The printed Course Catalog had me down as a lecture teacher, my contract specified that I would be teaching a lecture, and students had signed up specifically for my class.* Although her teaching responsibilities were modified, her compensation remained constant. Dr. Crocker mentioned that she had received congratulatory letters from the Provost in July 2004 and January 2005 for receiving high student evaluations. However, she did not say that these were for laboratory sections. *These letters do not say this; a copy is included.* Her student evaluations for the five lecture sections she has taught have been below average and in her yearly evaluations she has been cautioned regarding this. *On the contrary, I pointed this out to Dr.* ▮▮▮▮▮▮ *and explained the reason for it (I reported cheating and did not tolerate tardiness). He told me to carry on as I had been.* Her student evaluations (overall rating for the course) for the lecture sections have averaged 3.63, while the average for the course (since Fall 1998) is 4.15. The departmental mean for overall rating for a course is 4.42. *I could not find these numbers on my evaluation forms. However, I do have student and faculty letters affirming that I was an exemplary teacher.*

Dr. Crocker is a Term Faculty member whose term expires on May 24, 2005. She has a 9-month contract, not a multi-year contract as she incorrectly stated in her March 18 cover letter to the Grievance Committee members. Her contract states that "There is no guarantee or right to reappointment from one contract to the next, whether multi-year or single-year." *When I received this letter, I had no knowledge of this, reason being that* ▮▮▮▮▮▮▮▮ *had switched the term of my contract without my knowledge. Added evidence for this switch was my contract for a course workbook with Kendall-Hunt, the communication from human resources about whether I would like my pay to be divided over nine or 12 months, the e-mails enquiring about the upcoming semester from the departmental administrator, and the people who saw the three-year contract.*

In the spring of 2003, shortly after becoming Acting Chair of the then Biology Department,

I received complaints from two groups of students regarding Dr. Crocker teaching intelligent design/creationism. These students would not provide a written complaint, and declined to press the complaint. *There was no written complaint—possibly because the students knew that the allegation was false.* Prior to the start of the Fall 2003 semester, I requested that she remove evolution as a lecture topic and to spend more time on Cell Biology topics, since evolution was taught in two other Biology courses required for Biology majors. Dr. Crocker agreed and modified her syllabus. *This is not true. Syllabi from all semesters can be produced. I was never asked to remove the topic and never did.* However, in the Fall 04 semester, evolution (and creationism/intelligent design) was back on the syllabus. See attached powerpoint slides set from Fall 2004 (attachment A). *Powerpoint slides were available on line, but I did not teach the evolution lecture during the Fall of 2004 because the TAC grant took up too much class time to make it possible. Student letters confirm this fact.* These slides clearly show that Dr. Crocker is presenting a lecture on evolution far outside the scope of a Cell Biology course. *Again, I did not present that lecture. However, in other semesters when I did, I ALWAYS covered all the set course material.*

In regards to course content, in the 13 years (39 semesters) that Biol 213 has been taught, only Dr. Crocker has listed Evolution as a topic on her syllabus. The other five instructors ▉▉▉▉▉▉▉▉▉▉▉▉▉▉▉▉▉▉▉▉▉▉▉▉▉▉ did not have evolution as a lecture topic on their syllabi. These syllabi are available (attachment B). This course had been taught for about 10 years prior to Dr. Crocker teaching it, and the lecture content was well-established. *True, the other lecturers did not list evolution on their syllabi, but the course description in the catalog specifies that evolution will be taught. In addition, the notes I obtained from* ▉▉▉▉▉▉▉ *integrated evolution into almost very lecture and the textbook included it in most chapters. I chose to cover the material in a different order and put all mentions of evolution into one lecture.* Additionally this well-established content was developed in relation to the content of the other required courses for the Biology major. Specifically, evolution is a lecture topic in Biol 303 Animal Biology and Biol 307 Ecology. Also, the catalog course description for Biol 213 that Dr. Crocker referenced in her point 3) E. in her Grievance specifically mentions "evolution of cells", not evolution of organisms. *When I did this lecture it was only one of about 25 lectures total. A couple of slides did go beyond cells. This is the nature of the topic. Much of the evidence about evolution is found in organisms not cells. This is extreme nitpicking.*

The letter (dated December 22, 2004) from ▉▉▉▉▉▉▉▉▉▉▉(attachment C) which Dr. Crocker included in her Grievance as either attachment C or D (I have two copies, labeled differently) also supports that she was teaching evolution and intelligent design/creationism in her class. I am referring to the last sentence of the second paragraph. *This letter confirmed that I taught completely objectively. A review of the letters I received from students will reveal that I achieved that goal (see especially the letter from my lawyer student).*

In summary,

• Dr. Crocker modified the course content to include evolution and intelligent design/creationism which is not pertinent to the Cell Biology course, even after the course coordinator directed her to remove that topic. *Not true, see above.*

• Her teaching evaluations for the lecture sections of Cell Biology have been consistently low. *Not true, see provost letters.*

- The Chair (or the Chair's designee) has the descretion to modify teaching assignments of term and tenure-line faculty as deemed necessary. *But NOT the right to force one-sided teaching of topics that have religious implications.*

- Dr. Crocker was not excluded from the classroom as she asserts, rather her teaching assignment was modified to reflect her consistendly high teaching performance in the Cell Biology laboratories. *But I was TOLD that I was removed as a "disciplinary measure" and two faculty members confirmed that this was the case.*

Regards,

Peter Carter
Assoc. Chair
Biology Program
███████████ Microbiology Department

f. Caroline Crocker's Response to "Dr. Carter" and Committee (04/29/05)

(referenced in Chapter 6)

Response to ██████████ Response to Grievance by Dr. Crocker

1. ██████████is incorrect about the cited sections of the handbook not applying to me; the handbook does not say this. Term faculty are included, except where specifically excluded (the right to have service counted towards tenure, etc). The Grievance committee has already considered and replied to his objection.

2. It is not clear what being excluded from the classroom means. I was listed in the university catalog for this semester as teaching a Cell Biology lecture section and was pulled after the December 16 meeting with ██████████

3. Although ██████████asserts in the summary that I was pulled out of teaching a lecture because of student evaluations, this is not true because, *immediately after my evaluation* (August 2004), I was given two lecture sections and only one lab to teach. Pulling me out of teaching a lecture section was done on December 16 when ██████████told me that I must be disciplined for "teaching creationism." At this time he also told me that my teaching in the Fall of 2005 was not guaranteed for the same reason. I sent him an E-mail December 17, 2005, confirming that I was being disciplined for teaching creationism and he did not disagree.

4. I wish to state clearly that I am innocent of the charges against me and for which I am being disciplined. I have never taught creationism. I have, however, sought to introduce students to the complex questions surrounding evolution with clarity and with an eye to the scientific arguments that bear upon the current debate, which entails mentioning the intelligent design proposal (as in Biology by Raven and Johnson, a commonly used textbook). However, *I did not give that lecture* in the fall of 2004, the semester for which I am being disciplined (see below for an explanation of Ms. ██████ letter).

5. ██████████says that my evaluations for lecture sections are low, but not that the standard deviation brings me to within the average for the department. That I have been cautioned for this in yearly evaluations is simply not true. He did not discuss any evaluation with me prior to sending it, nor has he ever been to one of my lectures, despite my asking him to come. ██████████ sent me a copy of the evaluation and on October 1, immediately after receiving it, *I* asked to see *him* because of what he had written, basically evaluating my performance on student response only. I explained that reporting students for cheating, not accepting late work, and maintaining high standards might upset some students. I also reminded him that exam scores improved, even though I do not curve. I want to help students to be the best they can be and asked him what I should do. *He told me to keep on as I had been.* I put a document in my file with regard to this (attached).

6. It is worth noting that ██████████now uses the methods I developed while working on a grant from the Center for Teaching Excellence on communicating effectively with large classes. Grades went up significantly; Don Willcox published this in a poster at the CTE presentation in May 2004, which I can produce, if

needed. Mr. Willcox, a former student and then a TA, has written to Dr. ███ ███ in my support.

7. I do not know why ████████ thinks I am on a 9 month contract. I am on a contract specifying that I teach 9 months/year, but it was renewed last September to 3 years (9 months per year). My contract does say that I may not be reappointed, but it ends in 2007.

8. It is not true that ████████ asked for me to remove evolution as a lecture topic in the Spring of 2003, nor is it true that I responded by doing it. The syllabus was not modified because he did not ask me to do so. I can produce all the old syllabi. If he had, I would have pressed a grievance before now. In addition, although the other lecturers do not specify evolution in their syllabi, it certainly was in ████████ notes, which I used to find the topics to cover when I started teaching the lecture section of Cell Biology. I merely put all the references to evolution in one lecture. In addition, although the lecture on evolution was on the syllabus in the Fall of 2004, *I did not teach that lecture* that semester because I had received a grant from TAC to develop a research paper assignment in the class. Therefore, there was no time and the offending lecture *was never given*. However, there are two or three slides *total* in the rest of the course that mention evolution and intelligent design. This is where ████████ comment originates. I would also like to note that I *did* cover everything else on the syllabus.

9. With regard to the paragraph on what is and is not in the course, I am happy not to teach evolution of organisms and remove those few slides from my presentation, but it will only save 5 minutes at most! Again, I must emphasize that I cover the *entire* prescribed course content. In addition, the students come and tell me they are well-prepared for future classes. I have many willing to come testify, if need be.

10. In conclusion, from ████████ response, I understand that there was no written complaint by a student. However, ████████ removed me from teaching, even though I was listed in the course catalog. This was done as a disciplinary action on the same day that he spoke to me about teaching "creationism." ████████ did not afford me due process, not even investigating to find out if, indeed, I had done it (I had not), not coming to a lecture, and not allowing me to face my accuser. The change in teaching assignment was not done as a result of student evaluations because, right after that assessment, I was told to keep on as I had been and given TWO lecture sections to teach. The change in teaching assignment was done as an unwarranted disciplinary measure.

11. My desire is to return to the original status. I was fulfilled and, I believe, making a useful contribution to the department through my teaching, which I find very stimulating and take very seriously. To be removed in this manner has been humiliating, frustrating and undeserved, not to mention harmful to my future career.

g. E-mail to Grievance Committee from Caroline Crocker (05/02/05)

(referenced in Chapter 6)

Page 1 of 2

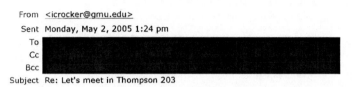

From   <icrocker@gmu.edu>

Sent   Monday, May 2, 2005 1:24 pm

To

Cc

Bcc

Subject   Re: Let's meet in Thompson 203

It was good to finally meet you all today. Please accept my apologies for not checking about bringing Murray Black as a support, but it was a last minute idea and I was not sure he would make it. I was a little scared, but found that you are all quite human! Thank you again for your time and efforts on my behalf.

Anyway, I was challenged by your question about which peer-reviewed journal have published intelligent design. I found it in several biology textbooks and in other books, but had not done a survey of the literature. What I found after a brief time is very interesting. There have been over 40 peer-reviewed articles that question aspects or key tenants of Darwinian theory, which is what I do in my lecture. The journals include Journal of Molecular Evolution, Cell, Scientific American, Science, Trends in Ecology and Evolution, PNAS, Genome Research, Evolution and Development, to name just a few.

There are also over 300 scientists, from all faiths and from no faith, who have signed on as questioning aspects of Darwinian evolution and considering the claims of Intelligent Design theory. These include a biochemist from Lehigh University, a microbiologist from Univeristy of Idaho, a biologist from University of San Francisco, an emeritis biologist from San Fransisco State, a mathematician from Baylor, and a quantum chemist from University of Georgia. There are also several scientists from GMU who are questioning neo-Darwinism.

Finally, I found several peer-reviewed sources that specifically support intelligent design. The peer-reviewed books include The Design Inference by Dembski published by Cambridge University Press and Darwin's Black Box by Behe published by the Free Press. There are also other books published by Michigan State University Press and Cambridge University Press. The peer-reviewed Journal of Philosophy of Science has published an article on irreducible complexity, a central tenant of intelligent design.There is even a peer-reviewed journal that focuses on design theory called Progress in Complexity, Information and Design. Finally, the work on intellgient design has been cited in other journals, ike the Annual Review of Genetics.

Dr. I C Crocker
Visiting Professor
Department of Molecular and Microbiology
George Mason University

h. Grievance Committee Recommendation (05/09/05)
(referenced in Chapter 6)

TO: Dean _____, College of Arts and Sciences
CC: Professors Caroline Crocker and _____, Department of
           Molecular and Microbiology
FROM: CAS Grievance Committee, 2004-2005: Professors _____
           _____(chair)_____
SUBJECT: Findings of the Committee from a Grievance Hearing May 2, 2005
           Professor Crocker, grievant; Professor _____, respondent
DATE: May 9, 2005

This memo reports our findings in the grievance of Professor Caroline Crocker against Professor _____. Both individuals are members of the biology program in the Department of Molecular and Microbiology. Professor _____ is associate department chair. We write to report our findings to you from a grievance hearing held May 2, 2005. We understand from the Faculty Handbook that your decision in this matter is final (see section 2.12.2.2.d).

Background
This matter was first presented to the committee in emails from Dean _____ and Professor Crocker to Professor _____ in February of 2005. During February and March, there was discussion by email among the committee members about how to proceed and whether the committee had jurisdiction in this case. The jurisdictional matter was resolved. We decided that when CAS faculty members have grievances, the CAS grievance committee is the body that should hear such cases. As committee member _____ wrote, "The action of the Faculty Senate on Feb. 12, 2003, in modifying the charge of the University Grievance Committee explicitly extended this process to faculty not on tenured or tenure-track lines, and who met other conditions that were not satisfied by local academic units. Indeed, the Grievant [in this case] does not fit into the guidelines for using the university committee, because (as I read it) the local academic unit that has a grievance committee should handle this."

In mid-March, a question arose from the respondent via email about whether the grievant had a right to have a grievance heard. We decided that she did. According to the George Mason University Faculty Handbook, all tenure-track and contract faculty have a right to have grievances heard by a group of faculty peers. Again, as committee member _____ wrote, "I have reviewed sections 2.1, 2.9, and 2.12 of the Handbook, and I cannot see anything that suggests that grievance procedures are limited to tenured or tenure-line faculty. Indeed, where a process, right, or responsibility is limited to such faculty, the exclusion is made specifically (see section 2.1.6). I interpret the other references to faculty in various sections of the Handbook that refer to rights and responsibilities to refer to ALL types of faculty.

On May 2, 2005, the members of the Committee met for a grievance hearing. The committee reviewed written statements with accompanying documentation developed by both parties. At the grievance committee hearing, the committee listened to presentations and then questioned both parties individually. The committee then met to discuss all information it had been given and came to the following conclusions.

1. Professor Crocker believes that she has a three-year contract with George Mason University that expires in 2007. Professor _____ believes that Professor Crocker is on a one-year contract that expires in May, 2005. Ms. _____, Human Resources Coordinator for the College of Arts and Sciences, has told the committee chair by email that Professor _____ understanding is the correct one. Professor Crocker is currently on a one-year contract that expires in May 2005.

2. Prior to Spring 2005, Professor Crocker has been teaching a lecture section of Biology 213: Cell Structure and Function. For Spring 2005, Professor Crocker was re-assigned to teach lab sections of Biology 213, rather than lecture sections of this course. We find that Associate Department Chair _____ was justified in making this re-assignment for the following reasons:

   a. Professor Crocker's quantitative student evaluations for the lecture course, which she taught in semesters prior to fall 2004, were not as high as those of other faculty teaching the same lecture course. As Professor _____ notes in his written statement to the committee, Professor Crocker's student evaluations were below average for her lecture sections and above-average for her laboratory sections. Specifically, as he writes, "Her student evaluations for the five lecture series she has taught have been below average and in her yearly evaluations, she has been cautioned about this. Her student evaluations (overall for the course) for the lecture sections have averaged 3.63, while the average for the course (since Fall 1998) is 4.15. The departmental mean for overall rating for a course is 4.42."

   b. For the lecture sections, Professor Crocker chose to lecture on material that fell beyond the purview of Biology 213. Specifically, the Biology 213 course concerns cell evolution and micro-evolutionary processes relevant to cell structure and function. Unlike the other five instructors teaching Biology 213, Professor Crocker covered macro-evolution (i.e. the formation of new species). According to Professor _____ written statement to the Committee, he asked Professor Crocker to remove macro-evolution as a topic and spend more time on cell biology and micro-evolution in fall 2003. However, when Professor Crocker's lecture material for this course was accessed in fall 2004 on the course website, the macro-evolution lecture on Power Point slides was still present.

   c. The committee finds that Professor _____ and other academic administrators have the right to make decisions about the topics a course should cover and about instructional competence. In light of the student evaluations data and concerns about the topics covered by Professor Crocker, Professor _____ had the right to re-assign Professor Crocker to lab section teaching, where her student course evaluations were higher.

4. We also find that Professor _____ and the department should use both evaluations conducted by multiple peers (i.e. faculty) as well as evaluations by students in making judgments about the quality of an instructor's teaching.

5. Professor Crocker seeks four remedies to her situation. We have a brief response to each.

a. First, she wishes reinstatement to teaching the lecture for Biology 213 for Fall 2005. We find that it is the prerogative of a department to determine which faculty members are assigned to teach lecture or lab sections of a class.

b. She seeks removal of negative documentation from her record. The Grievance Committee members have no access to Professor Crocker's personnel file. Consequently, we have no way to grant this remedy.

c. She seeks assurance that a group of faculty members will be involved in the decisions about renewal of her contract. As a Grievance Committee, we are not empowered to tell a department how to handle renewal contracts. We do recommend that both student evaluations and multiple peer reviews be used to assess teaching competence.

d. She seeks annual evaluation of her teaching performance by a person other than Professor _____. We do not see merit in over-turning Professor _____ decisions. Again, however, we recommend that student evaluations be accompanied by multiple peer evaluations when any department assesses an individual's teaching competence.

We understand from the Faculty Handbook that the dean of the relevant unit makes the final decisions in matters such as this (handbook sections 2.12.2.2.d). Consequently, we are sending this memo in hard copy to Dean _____ and distributing hard copies of the memo to the grievant and respondent.

[original document]

Grievance Committee Findings May 2005
-1-

TO:	Dean███████████, College of Arts and Sciences
CC:	Professors Caroline Crocker and ███████████, Department of Molecular and Microbiology
FROM:	CAS Grievance Committee, 2004-2005: Professors███████████████████ ██████████████████████████████████ (chair)███
SUBJECT:	Findings of the Committee from a Grievance Hearing May 2, 2005. Professor Crocker, grievant; Professor███████████ respondent
DATE:	May 9, 2005

This memo reports our findings in the grievance of Professor Caroline Crocker against Professor ███████████. Both individuals are members of the biology program in the Department of Molecular and Microbiology. Professor███████████ is associate department chair. We write to report our findings to you from a grievance hearing held May 2, 2005. We understand from the Faculty Handbook that your decision in this matter is final (see section 2.12.2.2.d).

Background
This matter was first presented to the committee in emails from Dean███████ and Professor Crocker to Professor███████ in February of 2005. During February and March, there was discussion by email among the committee members about how to proceed and whether the committee had jurisdiction in this case. The jurisdictional matter was resolved. We decided that when CAS faculty members have grievances, the CAS grievance committee is the body that should hear such cases. As committee member███████ wrote, "The action of the Faculty Senate on Feb 12, 2003, in modifying the charge of the University Grievance Committee explicitly extended this process to faculty not on tenured or tenure-track lines, and who met other conditions that were not satisfied by local academic units. Indeed, the Grievant [in this case] does not fit the guidelines for using the university committee, because (as I read it) the local academic unit that has a grievance committee should handle this."

In mid-March, a question arose from the respondent via email about whether the grievant had a right to have a grievance be heard. We decided that she did. According to the George Mason University Faculty Handbook, all tenure-track and contract faculty have a right to have grievances heard by a group of faculty peers. Again as committee member███████ wrote, "I have reviewed sections 2.1, 2.9, and 2.12 of the Handbook, and I cannot see anything that suggests that grievance procedures are limited to tenured or tenure-line faculty. Indeed, where a process, right, or responsibility is limited to such faculty, the exclusion is made specifically (see section 2.1.6). I interpret the other references to faculty in various sections of the Handbook that refer to rights and responsibilities to refer to ALL types of faculty.

Grievance Committee Findings May 2005

-2-

On May 2, 2005, the members of the Committee met for a grievance hearing. The committee reviewed written statements with accompanying documentation developed by both parties. At the grievance hearing, the committee listened to presentations and then questioned both parties individually. The committee then met to discuss all information it had been given and came to the following conclusions.

1. Professor Crocker believes that she has a three-year contract with George Mason University that expires in 2007. Professor ███████ believes Professor Crocker is on a one-year contract that expires in May 2005. Ms. ███████, Human Resources Coordinator for the College of Arts and Sciences, has told the committee chair by email that Professo███████ understanding is the correct one. Professor Crocker is currently on a one-year contract that expires in May 2005.

2. Prior to Spring 2005, Professor Crocker had been teaching a lecture section of Biology 213: Cell Structure and Function. For Spring 2005, Professor Crocker was re-assigned to teach lab sections of Biology 213, rather than lecture sections of this course. We find that Associate Department Chair ███████ was justified in making this re-assignment for the following reasons:

    a. Professor Crocker's quantitative student evaluations for the lecture course, which she taught in semesters prior to fall 2004, were not as high as those of other faculty teaching the same lecture course. As Professor ███████ noted in his written statement to the committee, Professor Crocker's student evaluations were below average for her lecture sections and above-average for her laboratory sections. Specifically, as he writes, "Her student evaluations for the five lecture sections she has taught have been below average and in her yearly evaluations, she has been cautioned about this. Her student evaluations (overall for the course) for the lecture sections have averaged 3.63, while the average for the course (since Fall 1998) is 4.15. The departmental mean for overall rating for a course is 4.42."

    b. For the lecture sections, Professor Crocker chose to lecture on material that fell beyond the purview of Biology 213. Specifically, the Biology 213 course concerns cell evolution and micro-evolutionary processes relevant to cell structure and function. Unlike the other five instructors teaching Biology 213, Professor Crocker covered macro-evolution (i.e., the formation of new species). According to Professor ███████ written statement to the Committee, he asked Professor Crocker to remove macro-evolution as a topic and spend more time on cell biology and micro-evolution in fall 2003. However, when Professor Crocker's lecture material for this course was accessed in fall 2004 on the course website, the macro-evolution lecture on Power Point slides was still present.

    c. The committee finds that Professor ███████ and other academic administrators have the right to make decisions about the topics a course should cover and about instructional competence. In light of the student evaluation data and concerns about the topics covered by Professor Crocker, Professor ███████ had the right to re-assign Professor Crocker to lab section teaching, where her student course evaluations were higher.

Grievance Committee Findings May 2005

-3-

4. We also find that Professor ███████ and the department should use both evaluations conducted by multiple peers (i.e., faculty) as well as evaluations by students in making judgments about the quality of an instructor's teaching.

5. Professor Crocker seeks four remedies to her situation. We have a brief response to each.

a. First, she wishes reinstatement to teaching the lecture for Biology 213 for Fall 2005. We find that it is the prerogative of a department to determine which faculty members are assigned to teach lecture or lab sections of a class.

b. She seeks removal of negative documentation from her record. The Grievance Committee members have no access to Professor Crocker's personnel file. Consequently, we have no way to grant this remedy.

c. She seeks assurance that a group of faculty members will be involved in decisions about renewal of her contract. As a Grievance Committee, we are not empowered to tell a department how to handle contract renewals. We do recommend that both student evaluations and multiple peer reviews be used to assess teaching competence.

d. She seeks annual evaluation of her teaching performance by a person other than Professor ███████. We do not see merit in over-turning Professor ███████ decisions. Again, however, we recommend that student evaluations be accompanied by multiple peer evaluations when any department assesses an individual's teaching competence.

We understand from the Faculty Handbook that the dean of the relevant unit makes the final decisions in matters such as this (handbook section 2.12.2.2.d). Consequently, we are sending this memo in hard copy to Dean ███████ and distributing hard copies of the memo to the grievant and respondent.

270 · Free To Think

i. Crocker Response to Grievance Committee Recommendation

(referenced in Chapter 6)

Response to College of Arts and Sciences (CAS)
Grievance Committee Recommendation

NOTE: This response was not submitted to the Grievance Committee, but was written by Caroline Crocker for inclusion in her book "Free to Think"

In the background section of the recommendation, the (CAS) Grievance Committee (GC) deals with Dr. "Carter's" persistent and repeated claims that adjunct faculty have no rights. On two occasions, despite Carter's objections (lasting through February and March of 2005), the GC decided that adjunct faculty do indeed have rights, including the right to a grievance hearing, which I was granted. Nonetheless Dr. Carter's extremely negative attitude towards this hard-working, underpaid, and dedicated group of (non-tenure track) faculty should be of concern to those working in his department.[326]

In the third paragraph of the findings document, the GC claims that they have reviewed the written documents submitted by both parties. However, no mention is made of the copious written testimony by faculty and students that I submitted to the GC demonstrating that Carter's claims were inaccurate.[327] Dr. Carter's largely unsubstantiated claims were often upheld by the GC. Support for this assertion can be found in the fact that Dr. Carter's written document,[328] which had *no* supporting evidence, is quoted and referenced many times. However, my written statements with supporting documents are not even mentioned.[329]

Section 1.

Note that the GC reports that I genuinely believed that I had a three-year contract. That is because I did indeed have one. There is much evidence to support this claim. First, my husband and our house guest at the time (with whom I am still in touch) both saw it. Second, I also showed the three-year contract to the departmental secretary (she retired soon afterwards). Third, the departmental administrator, "Mary Lou" also saw the three-year contract—and knew it existed because she e-mailed me twice to ask questions about my fall 2005 classroom requirements.[330] Fourth, one of the two TAC grants that I was awarded, which Dr. Carter signed, was multi-year and Carter did not object to this plan. If I had been hired for just one year, he would not have agreed to the modified plan to complete the grant.[331] Fifth, my

---

326   The GMU faculty handbook clearly specifies that faculty should have academic freedom (Section 2.12.1), the right not to be excluded from the classroom or disciplined without grounds and a hearing (Section 2.10.3), and the right to a grievance procedure (see Appendix VI).

327   See Appendix II for letters from students and Appendix III for letters from faculty.

328   See GMU Associate Professor "Peter Carter's" response to Grievance in Appendix IV.

329   See the introduction of the CAS Grievance Committee Recommendation, Appendix IV.

330   Appendix III.

331   Appendix V. The two TAC grants were to be funded consecutively. The first, on Endnote, would last for the year of 2004/2005. I began this project in September, 2004. The next grant, on Excel, was to be implemented in 2005/2006. Obviously, applications for these grants had to be completed prior to their approval.

teacher's aide, Don Willcox, came to my home to celebrate the new contract and has written a statement affirming this fact.[332] Sixth, GMU Professor David Rine,[333] GMU Graduate Dean J.C. Evans, and GMU Dean Murray Black have testified that they remember me talking about it. Finally, the former interim head of department Dr. "Sullivan" also knew about my multi-year contract since she 1) advocated for my original 18-month contract and told me these are usually renewed for longer contracts, and 2) recommended me to Kendal Hunt publishing company so that I could have my workbook published for use in the fall of 2005.[334] Why would she help me with this if I was not going to be around?

In contrast, Carter claims that I only had a one-year contract. This is because the three-year contract was switched without my knowledge, precipitating a discussion in the physics department led by Dr. John C. Evans. Details can be found in Chapter 6 of *Free to Think*.

Section 2

a. Unfortunately, here it is obvious that the GC believed Dr. Carter's misleading claims and, again, chose to ignore my statements and supporting documents. Dr. Carter did not present any evidence for his "numbers" showing my alleged low student evaluation ratings. Evidence to the contrary can be found in the Provost's letters sent during the semester of the discipline and the previous one, both showing that I had exceptionally high student ratings.[335] Dr. Carter claimed that the Provost's letters applied to lab courses only, but there is no mention of this in the letters themselves. In addition, my lab course ratings were very high when I was first hired and was teaching microbiology labs only.[336] Since I did not receive the Provost letters at that time, it seems clear that these commendations were only sent for lecture courses. Next, the GC had access to many student letters, all stating that I was an excellent teacher, going above and beyond the call of duty.[337] No mention of these letters is made, indicating not only extreme bias but perhaps even negligence by the GC.

Next, the GC quotes Dr. Carter as saying I had been cautioned at my yearly evaluations. This is not true since I only ever had one "review" with Dr. Carter— he had not been interim head long enough for it to be possible for there to have been more than one *annual* review. At my one review with Dr. Carter (Sept 2004), I discussed the problem of evaluating teachers solely on student ratings. I then specifically requested that faculty members attend my lectures in order to give me feedback on how to improve my teaching. Dr. Carter promised to

---

332 See e-mail from Willcox in Appendix II.
333 See Professor Rine's e-mail in Appendix III.
334 See e-mails between Kendall-Hunt and Crocker in Appendix V.
335 Appendix III. Note that this appendix also includes a recommendation for an Outstanding Teacher Award.
336 It was on the strength of these that Dr. "Sullivan" invited me to apply for the full time position teaching cell biology.
337 Appendix II.

send someone (or come himself) but never did so.[338] When I questioned him about whether I should continue insisting on intellectual honesty (no cheating, plagiarism, late work) from my students (thereby making myself unpopular with some) he instructed me to carry on as before. Documentation to this effect was placed in my departmental file.

b. Here again, the GC agreed with Dr. Carter's misrepresentations of the facts and, therefore, are guilty of submitting misleading and uncontested information to Dean Struppa. First, evolution was part of the course description for Bio 213, as can be seen in the course description.[339] The description does *not*, as is stated in this GC response, distinguish between micro- and macro-evolution; indeed, many expert scientists would say that these are not different processes.[340] In addition, although the GC claims that Carter distinguished between micro- and macro-evolution, one only needs to refer to Dr. Carter's document to see that this is not true.[341] Of course, it is possible that Dr. Carter provided the GC with a document different from the one I saw, but I have no knowledge of this.[342]

Second, Carter did not provide the GC with any proof of his claim that he had previously requested that I remove teaching on macro-evolution from the curriculum, nor his assertion that I was not covering all the other required material. Indeed, since we had only *one* annual review (which occurred in the September prior to my discipline), his written response to the committee that he had syllabi showing I removed and reinserted this lecture in response to an annual review was obviously untrue. In fact, he had no such syllabi (they do not exist), and the GC never required him to produce them (he couldn't have). The facts are, at no time did he ask me to remove the topic nor did he provide the GC with any documentation that he did so. Without such evidence, this claim, as well as many others he made about me, is without foundation. Dr. Carter also did not provide the committee with evidence of student complaints (in fact, in his response to the Grievance he specifically said that he was not given anything in writing).[343] It is true that a lecture on evolution (not macro-evolution as is claimed) was located on my website, but it was one out of about 25 lectures in total. I covered all set material for the course and the GC had access to numerous student letters saying this,[344] even though none of these were referenced in their

338 See letter from Dean Black, discussing precisely this issue in Appendix III.
339 Appendix VI.
340 It is clear here that the GC did not understand the difference between micro- and macro-evolution. Micro-evolution is not the evolution of small things (like cells) nor is macro-evolution only the evolution of large organisms (like animals) as they report that Dr. Carter alleged in his written statement. For definitions of these terms, see Appendix I. In addition, natural selection can only select for "fitter" organisms (I do realize that some organisms only consist of a single cell), not fitter cells within organisms, making it misleading to restrict teaching about evolution to cells only.
341 See Carter's submission to the GC in Appendix IV dated April 29, 2005.
342 When on April 7, 2005 I requested a copy of Dr. Carter's response to my grievance document, Dr. "Anderson" told me that Carter had submitted it but I did not receive an answer to my request for a copy. When I repeated the request 20 days later, Dr. Anderson said that Dr. Carter *had not* yet submitted it, but had been given a deadline of April 29, 2005 (See timeline and e-mail in Appendix IV).
343 See paragraph 4 of Carter's statement in Appendix IV.
344 See letters from my students in Appendix II.

recommendation. It is true that other professors might not have had evolution as a single lecture, but since it was part of the course description, they could have legitimately touched on evolution in almost every lecture. In fact, the lecture notes that I was given as a reference when I first started teaching did just that.

Finally, even though the GC claimed to have read all the written statements, they seem to have missed the student letter and my repeated written statements saying that I *did not present that lecture* during the fall of 2004![345] This was not mentioned in the recommendation to Dean Struppa, demonstrating that the GC was actively engaged in covering up and ignoring inconvenient facts.

  c. The GC found that Professor Carter had the right to rule on topics covered and on professional competence. However, Professor Carter submitted *no evidence* that I did not cover everything required in Bio 213, or that my lectures or teaching approach were deficient in any way. In comparison, I submitted plenty of evidence showing that I did more than what was expected of me, and did it well.[346] Once again, no mention of this fact was made in the GC report. I also submitted much evidence demonstrating that I did not give the supposedly offensive lecture (the TAC grant workload was such that I chose to skip that lecture during the fall of 2004), but as noted above, this fact was wantonly suppressed.

In addition, the *fact* remains that Dr. Carter did not remove me from lectures based on "competence," but as a matter of "discipline" for allegedly teaching creationism (which I did not do). I am quite certain that the departmental administrator, Ms. "Oakley" overheard the December 2004 conversation when Dr. Carter was informing me of the "discipline" he was going to implement against me, since the door was open and she occupied the office next door. This meeting was confirmed by e-mail on December 17, 2004.[347] In January 2004 two faculty members told me that this "discipline" was the *sole* reason for my being removed from lecturing. Indeed, Dr. Carter's own submission to the GC is strongly indicative of the same.

It was only in later communications that the GMU lawyers seem to have advised personnel not to talk about the "creationism issue," and to switch to slurs against my professional competence, as can be seen below. It is interesting, with regard to my competence to present lectures, that the letters attesting to my skill in this area from the Provost,[348] letters from Deans at GMU,[349] and letters from students[350] praising my teaching abilities were not mentioned in the GC recom-

---

345   See the 12/19/04 letter from a student specifically stating that I skipped the lecture on evolution (Appendix II).
346   Appendix II.
347   Appendix IV.
348   Appendix III.
349   See letter from Professor David Rine in Appendix III.
350   See Appendix II, which includes a letter from a lawyer in my class who was studying so that he could go to medical school.

mendation to Dean Struppa.[351] An impartial group would surely have provided the available relevant evidence on both sides of this dispute.

In summary, I submit that it is internally inconsistent to talk about my teaching macroevolution and then say the reassignment was because of incompetence. Either I was reassigned and ultimately lost my job because of the alleged teaching of creationism or because of incompetent teaching. The fact that the GC hedges their bets and uses both approaches (without so much as even mentioning the hard evidence I provided for both of these issues) shows that they were far from the impartial peer group that they were entrusted to be. Instead they clearly favored the unsubstantiated word of the tenured professor over the well-documented claims of the comparative new-comer.

Section 3

(This section was missed in their document, perhaps due to an error in numbering)

Section 4

Here the Grievance Committee acknowledges that the manner in which Dr. Carter evaluated my teaching was insufficient and recommended that it should be changed. However, neither the breaking of the contract that said I would teach a lecture section nor the resultant embarrassment that I suffered when students enquired as to why I was not lecturing (both allegedly resulting from improper evaluation) were ever satisfactorily addressed or resolved.

Section 5

a. The GC finds that Dr. Carter has a right to decide which faculty members are assigned to teach lab or lecture. They do not mention that my contract specified that I would teach one lecture and three labs in the spring and that to change this would be a breach of contract. This is supported by Dr. Carter's insistence that I sign a new contract because I would be teaching two lectures in the fall of 2004. The GC also did not address the fact that I was removed as a "disciplinary" measure in response to an unsubstantiated allegation and that this resulted in many disappointed students and much embarrassment to me.

b. Here, the GC says that they do not have access to my personnel file, so cannot assess if negative documentation has been added. Of course, by that time my personnel file was empty of all documents except for the one-year contract, so it was a moot point.[352]

---

351 As is documented in Appendix IV (Crocker Response to Dr. Carter) point 6 and Chapter 6 of *Free to Think*, Carter used methods that my TA and I developed while working on a project improving comprehension of cell biology in large class settings (Appendix V). *This is a strange response to work accomplished by a professor he claims to be incompetent!*
352 Chapter 6, *Free to Think*.

c. The GC does recommend that Professor Carter conduct proper evaluations in the future, since no peers had ever attended any of my GMU lectures.[353] Nonetheless, they did not act to help me to receive justice. Indeed, in submission of this obviously slanted and very incomplete report, the GC had, hopefully unwittingly, acted in a manner which deprived me of my right to due process and, of course, my job.

---

353   See letter from Dean Murray Black in Appendix III.

j. Dean Daniele Struppa's Ruling (05/17/05)

(referenced in Chapter 6)

College of Arts and Sciences

4400 University Drive, MS 3A3, Fairfax, Virginia 22030
Phone: 703-993-8720; Fax: 703-993-8714

MEMORANDUM

To: Dr. Caroline Crocker, Department of Molecular and Microbiology
        Dr. ▮▮▮▮▮▮▮▮ Department of Molecular and Microbiology

From: Daniele C. Struppa, Dean

Subject: Resolution of Grievance - Crocker-▮▮▮▮▮▮

Date: May 17, 2005

I have received the report from the CAS Grievance Committee, dated May 9, 2005, and have reviewed all the documents presented in the course of the grievance process. Further, I have reviewed the contract, dated April 20, 2004, which offers Dr. Crocker the position of Term Assistant Professor in the Molecular and Microbiology Department for the academic year 2004-2005.

On the basis of everything I have examined, I concur with the substance of the findings of the CAS Grievance Committee.

On the procedure, I find that the grievant had the right to grieve through the CAS Grievance Committee, and I find that the CAS Grievance Committee has jurisdiction in this case.

On the substance, I find that:

1. Professor Crocker is on a one-year contract which expires in May 2005.

2. It is within the purview of Dr. ▮▮▮▮▮▮▮▮ as Associate Chair of the Department, to assign the teaching load to Dr. Crocker. I do not believe that he violated any procedures or rules in doing so.

3. I cannot provide any of the remedies sought by Dr. Crocker.

Specifically:

3.1. She asks to be assigned to Biology 213 for Fall 2005. Even if she were to be offered a contract for academic year 2004-2005, it would be up to Dr. ▮▮▮▮▮▮ to decide her teaching load and assignments.

3.2. There is no negative documentation included in Dr. Crocker's personnel file.

3.3. I have no evidence that term renewals are inappropriately managed within the Department of Molecular and Microbiology. Consequently, I see no reason to ask the department to modify the process.

3.4. Dr. ███████ evaluates the teaching performance of every faculty member in the department. I see no reason to mandate that a different person should evaluate Dr. Crocker's teaching.

According to the Faculty Handbook (section 2.12.2.2.d), this decision is final and not subject to appeal.

cc: Dr. ███████, Chair CAS Grievance Committee, Department of Communication

Appendix V: Awards, Poster, and Grants

a. Center for Teaching Excellence Grant Application (Fall, 2003)

(referenced in Chapter 4)

APPLICATION
Faculty-Student Apprenticeship for Undergraduates

Student:__Donald Willcox_____   Faculty Member:_Caroline Crocker, PhD
Department:_Molecular and Microbiology_____   For: Fall   2003
Student E-mail ████████████ Faculty E-mail jcrocker@gmu.edu_____
Student Phone ███████ █Faculty Phone███████████
Student Mailing Address████████████████████████
Project Title Cell Biology Comprehension and Communication – Optimizing Large Class Instruction

Description of the proposed Faculty-Student Apprenticeship, including nature of project, nature of student activities, plans for supervision, and anticipated outcome or product:

The aim of this project will be for the student and faculty member to collaboratively and actively research methods of communicating information, pertaining to biology, to large numbers of students. Previous experience has shown that, whereas 50% of students in a Cell Biology class of 20-25 students achieve an "A" grade, in a class of 150 students, only 50% pass. Since the material and teacher were the same in both cases, it is likely that this is due to insufficient student-teacher contact. The proposed faculty member has begun to remedy this situation by offering 12-person study groups several times a week where students can have their questions answered in an informal setting.

The student project will involve 1) weekly leading of one or two study groups, 2) research on other effective ways to communicate course material, including internet sites, 3) possible improvement of offered worksheets, and 4) critical analysis of lectures. The proposed student took Cell Biology last spring and showed enthusiasm and superior ability in biology. In addition, he voluntarily assisted at that time by informing the faculty member of course-relevant material available in the media. Because he is planning to continue in biology and possibly teach, it is his wish to remain current in the field and gain teaching experience.

This project will be supervised via biweekly faculty-student meetings. In addition, the student and faculty member will be in regular contact by E-mail. The success of this project will be evaluated by monitoring of overall student grades and comparison with grades achieved by those attending study groups and grades last semester. It is hoped that the outcome will be a Cell Biology course that is accessible to a greater number of students at George Mason University, one that is exemplary for an institution dedicated to teaching excellence.

Student   Faculty
Signature_____   Signature_____

※ Please attach student's resume, including relevant experience, major, GPA, and up-to-date address, phone number, and e-mail.

※ If this is a continuation, also attach a brief progress report on the prior Apprenticeship period (1/2-1 page)

b. Technology Across the Curriculum Grants

(referenced in Chapter 4)

(Note: The first grant was funded for the school year of 2004/2005. The second proposal was submitted simultaneously, but funding and accomplishment of the work was slated for 2005/2006.)

Proposal Form
Technology Across the Curriculum
EndNote Initiative
2004 – 2005

1. **Name(s):**   Caroline Crocker, ██████████████

2. **Department:** Molecular and Microbiology

3. **Category:**   ☒ **Pilot implementation**

    ☐ **Expanded implementation**

    ☐ **Departmental implementation**

4. **Project title:** Endnote Initiative and Science Writing; implemented over two semesters

5. **Course(s) involved:** Cell Biology; Bio 213; both sections

6. **Liaison Librarian Collaborating on the Proposal:** ████████████████

7. **Specific assignment(s) that will include the use of EndNote bibliographic management software, and the relationship between such assignments and library research:**

In the first semester, all Cell Biology students will write a referenced literature review of recent developments in a topic in cell biology. The paper will be about five pages long and include ten references. These papers will be due six weeks after they are assigned.

In the second semester, after the instructors have been trained, two of the lab sections will use EndNote. The others will use conventional methods to generate their review. Lab sections using EndNote will be taught by instructors who are teaching three sections; one section from each instructor will write a report without using EndNote.

For those students using EndNote, references will be searched using Medline and other databases and stored by students with EndNote. In addition, students will use one of the custom fields of EndNote to keep notes about the cited works. The paper will be referenced using the same program.

Ideas for topics will be proposed by the instructor, although students will be allowed to present their own ideas for research. Projects will be subject to approval by the teacher. For those sections doing EndNote, one lab period (18 students/ 3 hours) will be devoted to teaching use of EndNote and hands-on guidance. As a control, those lab sections not using EndNote will be taught everything, but this program, during their lab period. All students will be taught how to write a review in the context of a lecture.

(Specific assignment attached.)

8. **Learning objectives for the assignment(s):**

TAC EndNote Proposal   1
2004-05

Proposal Form
Technology Across the Curriculum
2004 – 2005

1. **Name(s):** Caroline Crocker, ████████████

2. **Department(s):** Molecular and Microbiology

3. **Category:** ☒ **New Project**

     ☐ **Continuing Project**

     ☐ **Departmental Project**

4. **Project title:** Analysis and Presentation of Data in Cell Biology Labs

5. **Course(s) involved:** Cell Biology (Bio 213)

6. **Brief (one- to two-paragraph) description of the project (for use on project profile Web site):**

   An existing assignment in the Cell Biology lab course will be modified to teach the students to analyze and present data with information technology. Currently, students submit a lab report on one of the labs, requiring the generation of three graphs. In this project, the data from the class will be pooled by entering into an Excel spreadsheet and statisical analyses will be performed. Graphs will be created and reports presented by groups of three students using PowerPoint.

7. **Specific assignment(s) involved in the project:** Students will be required to write an individual lab report on one of three data-generating labs. Information technology skills needed to complete this assignment will be taught during a lab session. Data will be obtained from the entire class and analyzed using Excel. In addition, groups of three students will be required to present the data as a PowerPoint presentation, including appropriate illustrations (tables and graphs).

8. **Learning objectives for the assignment(s):** Students will learn to create a spreadsheet, enter data, perform basic statistical analyses (mean and standard deviation), create, format, and label graphs, and design a PowerPoint presentation. As part of this, they will learn to import graphs from one program to another.

9. **Relationship to learning goals for the course or for the program of study:** Cell Biology is the first required science course for all biology majors. It is important for the students to learn how to analyze and present data, since research careers are dependent on this ability.

10. **Technology skills and level of skill fostered by the assignment(s) (refer to the set of IT goals published on the TAC Web site):** This project will teach students IT goals 3a, b, and c, 6 (basic level), 7 (basic level) and 8 (basic level).

11. **Assessment plan:**

c. Don Willcox's Poster (02/09/04)

(referenced in Chapter 4)

Cell Biology Comprehension and
Communication :
Optimizing Large Class Instruction

Donald A. Willcox

2/9/2004

Abstract

Introduction to Cellular Biology is a core requirement for science majors comprised of a large quantity of complex material presented to classes exceeding 100 students. The purpose of this study is to explore and implement methods of teaching that increase student success and decrease the typically high percentage of students with unsatisfactory grades. An instructor and teacher's aide applied a combination of student surveys, study groups, and various didactic exercises to improve student grade outcome. The results after one semester show an overall improvement in grades and an eleven percent reduction in students receiving unsatisfactory grades.

Comparison of Teaching Approaches

Previous Teaching Approach (Spring 2003)
- 2 weekly study groups
- Lecture
- 10 quizzes, 3 worksheets
- 3 exams and Final Exam

Plan for Improvement of Large Class Performance (Fall 2003)
- Add a Teacher's Aide
- Confidential midterm student survey of teaching effectiveness
- Add TA Sat. study group and pre-test reviews
- Make lecture diagrams available to students
- Reduce grading workload with TA assistance
- TA evaluation of lectures
- Increased invigilation

Summary of Research Results

Students dropping out or receiving unsatisfactory grades:
- improved from 54% (Spring 2003) to 32% (Fall 2003) (Figure 1)

Students completing course:
- Overall increase in grades (Figure 2)
- 11% decrease in unsatisfactory grades (Figure 3)

Increased student demand:
- Most popular section of Cell Biology for Spring 2004

Conclusion

The results of the study show a 22% reduction in dropouts and unsatisfactory final grades. This strongly supports a positive correlation between teaching methods used and improved student performance outcome.

The study succeeded in giving me experience in grading, course evaluation, study group instruction, grant application procedure, scholarly presentation and time management.

Future Directions

Changes for the Spring semester 2004 based on observations from this study:

- Three midterm worksheets broken down into smaller assignments with weekly due dates.

- Students responsible for correcting worksheets.

- Vocabulary quizzes given on material before it is presented in lecture.

d. Recommendation for Crocker to Receive Outstanding Teacher Award (06/17/04)

(referenced in Chapter 10)

Honoring Our Nation's
Most Respected Teachers ™

RESPONSE NEEDED BY:

June 17, 2004

URGENT MESSAGE FOR:

NOMINATED BY:

Dr. Caroline Crocker
George Mason University
4400 University Drive
Fairfax, VA 22030-4422

ld.ldd.lll....lldll....l.ddl.l.l.d.lll..ll.....lll

Dear Dr. Caroline Crocker:

"You made a difference in my life."

I know of nothing that makes a teacher feel as good as words like these, spoken by a student.

And by nominating you to be honored in the 8th edition of *Who's Who Among America's Teachers*, that's just what one of your former students has said about you.

I know. You work hard to be a good teacher. You make sacrifices above and beyond the call of duty. But you don't do it for recognition. You do it because you truly care about your students' hopes, dreams and futures.

Now one of them wants to give you something in return . . . and it makes them feel good to do it.

As of April 21, 2004, however, we haven't received your completed Data Form. It's needed so we can include it in this year's publication. I know your students come first, and this process is probably the last thing on your mind. So I've enclosed another form for your convenience.

Please, while you have it in front of you, take a few minutes to fill it out and send it in. You will be glad you did. Remember only 5% of our nation's teachers are honored in this prestigious publication.

You see, while paying tribute to our country's best teachers is the primary objective of *Who's Who*, it's not our only purpose. Just as important, we believe the biographies of the educators included in this publication serve as examples for all teachers who are committed to their students, just as you are.

(over, please)

Who's Who Among America's Teachers
1701 Directors'Blvd., Suite 920 PO Box 149314 Austin, TX 78714-9314
(512) 440-2300 FAX (512) 447-1687 www.whoswho-teachers.com

e. E-mails with Curtis Ross of Kendall Hunt Publishing (05/25/05)

(referenced in Chapter 6)

Page 1 of 3

From Curtis Ross ███████████████████

Sent Wednesday, May 25, 2005 9:05 pm

To icrocker@gmu.edu

Cc

Bcc

Subject Re: Teaching assignments

Unfortunately, we cannot publish it without sufficient annual enrollment. I'll be getting the manuscript in a week or so. I'll send it to you. curtis

Curtis L. Ross
Acquisitions Editor
Kendall/Hunt Publishing Company
████████████████

>>> <icrocker@gmu.edu> 05/25/05 19:05 PM >>>
The mail sent before I meant to do it. Anyway, I have a question. Are you going to publish it anyway? If not, I need to photocopy and bind it myself for this summer. That is why I ask.   Caroline

Dr. I C Crocker
Visiting Professor
Department of Molecular and Microbiology
George Mason University

----- Original Message -----
From: Curtis Ross ███████████████████
Date: Wednesday, May 25, 2005 5:00 pm
Subject: Re: Teaching assignments

> That sounds pretty crazy! As far as the book goes, we'd likely
> need to
> find a lot more usage than at NVCC, right? What are the potential
> enrollment numbers?
>
> Curtis L. Ross
> Acquisitions Editor
> Kendall/Hunt Publishing Company
> ████████████
> >>> <icrocker@gmu.edu> 05/23/05 16:13 PM >>>
> Curtis,
> I lost my job because I said that there is evidence both for and
> against evolution. The book also says this. I was hoping that the
> faculty grievance committee would see that my academic freedom has
> beenviolated, but there are over 800 professors nationwide who
> have lost
> their jobs for saying this and I have joined the ranks. NPR will be
> doing a story in August.
>   I am sure that no one at GMU will want to use anything to do
> with me
> because their jobs would also be at risk. However, the head at
> NOVA is
> much more able to see both sides of the debate and is very willing for
> the book to be used. I am also sure████████████████████████

> ███████████████
>
> So, what now?   Caroline
>
> Dr. I C Crocker
> Visiting Professor
> Department of Molecular and Microbiology
> George Mason University
>
> ----- Original Message -----
> From: Curtis Ross ██████████████████
> Date: Monday, May 23, 2005 3:23 pm
> Subject: Re: Teaching assignments
>
> > Caroline,
> > This comes as a complete surprise to me; I hope you are doing
> > okay.
> > Since you've done all of this work, do you think that it is
> > possible for
> > the instructors to use it so you can get renumerated for your
> efforts?> Please give me a call if I can assist you. Curtis
> >
> > Curtis L. Ross
> > Acquisitions Editor
> > Kendall/Hunt Publishing Company
> > ██████████████
> > >>> <icrocker@gmu.edu> 05/23/05 11:20 AM >>>
> > Dear Charmayne, Curtis, Costie:
> > I have just been informed that I have not been assigned
> teaching at
> > GMU in the Fall. I will still be teaching Cell Bio at NOVA in a
> > month,> and have applied for a job there, but have not yet heard.
> I am not
> > surewhat this will do to your plans, but thought you should be
> > informed.
> > Best wishes, Caroline
> >
> > Dr. I C Crocker
> > Visiting Professor
> > Department of Molecular and Microbiology
> > George Mason University
> >

Appendix VI: Letters and Legal Documents

a. Cell Biology Course Description (2004)

(referenced in Chapter 5)

213 Cell Structure and Function (4:3:3). *For science majors and preprofessionals in the life sciences.* Introduction to the chemistry, metabolism, genetics, and evolution of cells. f, s, sum

b. GMU Faculty Handbook 2004, Excerpt

(referenced in Chapter 5)

2.12 Faculty Rights and Privileges

2.12.1 Academic Freedom and Civil Liberties

One of the vital activities of a university is the critical examination of ideologies and institutions. It is essential that faculty members have the right to express their views responsibly without fear of censorship or penalty. The University defines academic freedom as:

1. the right to unrestricted exposition of subjects (including controversial questions) within one's field, both on and off the campus, in a professionally responsible manner; and

2. the right to unrestricted scholarly research and publication in a professionally responsible manner within the limits imposed by the acknowledgment of teaching as a faculty member's obligation and the limits imposed by the resources of the institution.

The University is fully aware that faculty members must enjoy, in addition to academic freedom, the same civil liberties as other citizens. In the exercise of their civil liberties, faculty have an obligation to make clear that they are not representing the institution, its Board, or the Commonwealth of Virginia. All employees have an obligation to avoid any action which appears or purports to commit the institution to a position on any issue without appropriate approval.

Decisions in such faculty personnel actions as initial appointment, reappointment, and promotion will not be affected by non-academic considerations.

2.10.3 Exclusion of Faculty from the Classroom

If at any time a faculty member's continued responsibility for a course or courses is judged by the President or a designated representative to constitute a serious threat of substantial damage to the faculty member or to his or her students, the faculty member will be excluded from the classroom and replaced by a qualified substitute. The mere initiation of dismissal proceedings or of notice of non-reappointment will never constitute by themselves sufficient grounds for such exclusion.

To guard against abuse of this authority, a committee of five faculty members will be elected from and by those of the same academic unit as the suspended person within three days after any such exclusion, and this committee will conduct a brief but careful examination of the particulars and report within three days to the President. Should the committee's findings not support the exclusions, this committee will also report its findings to the Faculty Senate at its next regular meeting, and to the suspended person's collegiate faculty.

c. Contract between Caroline Crocker and George Mason University (04/20/04)

(referenced in Chapter 4)

George Mason University

Fairfax, Virginia 22030

April 20, 2004

I. Caroline Crocker, Ph.D.

Dear Dr. Crocker:

      I am pleased to offer you the position of Term Assistant Professor in the Molecular and Microbiology Department at George Mason University.

The terms of the offer are as follows:

- Title: Term Assistant Professor

- Term: August 25, 2004 through May 24, 2005.
  (9 month appointment)

- Salary: $32,597/nine months

- Other terms: Classes begin August 30, 2004. You are expected to be available two weeks before classes begin and two weeks after classes end.

Your duties in the academic year 2004-2005 are as follows:

This position requires teaching two large sections of BIOL 213 Cell Biology in the fall semester as well as one Cell Biology labs. In the spring semester you will be responsible for teaching one large Cell Biology lecture and three Cell Biology labs. This appointment is a Term Appointment with an Instructional focus. Service in this position is not applied for consideration for tenure. This position requires regular reappointments, as stipulated in *The Procedures for Appointment and Reappointment of Term Faculty* (addendum to the *Faculty Handbook* and *George Mason University Research Personnel Policies and Procedures*), depending upon the availability of funding and mutually acceptable performance. There is no guarantee or right to reappointment from one contract to the next, whether multi-year or single-year. The total duration of repeated single-year appointments is normally five years but may be extended for additional time depending on the needs and circumstances of the University. Further, should this position be converted to a permanent full-time tenured or tenure track position, the University may conduct a national search. You are not automatically entitled to this position but may be an applicant for this permanent position.

The Southern Association of Colleges and Schools requires that all faculty, including part-time faculty, hold credentials appropriate to the level and subject matter they are teaching, and that the institution verify those credentials. Generally, the earned doctorate or terminal degree in the field is required. Instructors teaching at the undergraduate level must hold at least a master's degree in the field. An <u>original transcript</u> from the institution awarding the highest degree is acceptable and appropriate documentation to meet this requirement. Employment is contingent upon presentation of satisfactory documentation of credentials prior to employment.

This appointment is subject to approval by the appropriate University administrative officer. The appointment is also subject to the policies of the Board of Visitors and approval by the Board of Visitors, where required. As with all other employees, your appointment is contingent upon the appropriation and availability of funds. You must also satisfy all Federal employment eligibility requirements. If you accept this offer and it is your first appointment to George Mason University, you must complete tax forms and an I-9 (in person) in order to receive payment. The I-9 is the employment eligibility verification form. Please contact the department for help with this. Electronic direct deposit is mandatory for all salaried and wage employees hired (or re-employed) on or after February 1, 2002. You will receive a direct deposit form in the Welcome Packet sent to you by Human Resources.

This offer will remain open until May 14, 2004. If these terms and conditions are acceptable to you, please sign and date in the space provided below and return the original to my office. This letter, together with the administrative policies and regulations of the University, currently in force and as amended in the future, will constitute your employment agreement with George Mason University. If you do not sign and return this offer of employment before May 14, 2004, the offer will be null and void.

I look forward to your acceptance of this offer and to a rewarding professional association in the future. Should you need additional information or assistance, please do not hesitate to call me. My telephone number is ███████████.

Sincerely,

Associate Chair
Molecular and Microbiology Department

I accept the appointment described under the terms and conditions set forth above in this letter, I hereby acknowledge that this letter will constitute the entire employment agreement between myself and George Mason University. I further acknowledge that I will be governed by the administrative policies and regulations of the University, currently in force and as amended in the future. I also acknowledge that said rules do not create any vested employment rights. I further understand that this appointment is contingent upon the appropriation and availability of funds.

I. Caroline Crocker

_5/14/04_
Date

.

cc:Human Resource Department
Dean/Director
Provost

d. Letters between then Democratic Virginia House Delegate J. Chapman Petersen and GMU President Alan Merton

(referenced in Chapter 7)

Date: Mon, 27 Jun 2005 18:07:31 -0400

Mr. Alan Merton
President, George Mason University

Dear Alan:

I trust you are doing well and looking forward to an exciting fall semester. My daughters and I really enjoyed your homecoming basketball game back in February. Thank you again for inviting us.

I am writing you on behalf of a constituent, Caroline Crocker, M.Sc. and Ph.D., who has been teaching at GMU for the past five years in the field of Molecular Science and Microbiology. I know Caroline, her husband and her family quite well and am proud to call them friends.

In December 2004, Caroline had a meeting with ███████████, Associate Chair of the Biology program. Up to that time, she had been teaching for approximately five years at GMU on the evolution of cells, with no complaints and consistently strong marks from her fellow professors and students. She was teaching on a contractual basis and did not have tenure. At the December 2004 meeting, ████████ accused her of "teaching creationism" in her class and stated she would

be disciplined for doing so. The basis for this allegation, according to ████████ were anonymous complaints from students. Immediately, Caroline sent an email to ████████ asking for clarification of this discipline. A copy is attached. No response was ever made. However, the department refused to keep her on as a professor, due to this alleged indiscretion. She is currently without employment and bearing a stigma that she has been fired from GMU.

I am not aware of any state law mandating the curriculum for the evolution of cells. Therefore, I'm not aware of what's a "proper punishment" for someone who strays from such a standard. However, I am aware that GMU, and many other top universities, permit "academic freedom" where ideas are freely exchanged regarding complex and controversial subjects. From my discussions with Caroline and my review of letters written by former students, it is clear that she did hav one class a semester which broached the broader subject of evolution and offered arguments "for" and "against" it. Considering that cell evolution bears indisputable parallels with human evolution, this would seem to be an obvious discussion topic for precocious Mason students. There is no evidence that it detracted from the delivery of the remainder of the curriculum. Nor is there evidence that she attempted to impose a "right" answer on her students (I contrast that with the Marxist economics professor that I had in college).

Using an "anonymous" complaint to denigrate this lecture -- or the ability of the teacher -- is not an act worthy of respect. In contrast, I note that students and faculty have written on Caroline's behalf, with comments specifically pertaining to the allegations made. I am attaching these statements. In a court of law, their first-hand testimony would be admissible to refute any charges. On the other hand, an anonymous complaint sheds no light on the defendant, only on the accuser.

I am aware that department chairs need to have discretion in hiring and that there is no guaranty of employment here. So I will not alter the facts by stating that there is a breach of contract. That being said, I feel very strongly that a constituent and a friend has been maligned for no reason.

Alan, thanks again for seeing that some sort of justice comes out of this situation. Feel free to call me directly at my law office. (███████████) if you wish.

Sincerely, JCP

Chap Petersen

(referenced in Chapter 7)

Dear Chap,

Thank you for your letter of June 28, 2005 inquiring on behalf of Dr. Crocker. Contrary to what she implies, this matter has been fully reviewed by the appropriate academic committee.

As you are aware, we are very cautious about releasing personal information without the express permission of the employee or former employee. However, be assured that all University procedures were followed to review issues raised by Dr. Crocker. I have every confidence in the faculty who review matters such as this, and rely on their findings.

Finally, Dr. Crocker was not "fired" As a term instructor, her contract was simply not renewed. This is a neutral action on the part of the University and should not be construed as anything more.

I can understand your concern. Rest assured that Dr. Crocker has received both a fair hearing and appropriate due process.

Sincerely,

Alan G. Merton

[original document]

Alan G. Merten
President

4400 University Drive, MS 3A1, Fairfax, Virginia 22030
Phone: 703-993-8700; Fax: 703-993-8880; E-mail: amerten@gmu.edu

July 22, 2005

The Honorable J. Chapman Peters

Dear Chap:

Thank you for your letter of June 28, 2005 inquiring on behalf of Dr. Crocker. Contrary to what she implies, this matter has been fully reviewed by the appropriate academic committee.

As you are aware, we are very cautious about releasing personnel information without the express permission of the employee or former employee. However, be assured that all University procedures were followed to review issues raised by Dr. Crocker. I have every confidence in the faculty who review matters such as this, and rely on their findings.

Finally, Dr. Crocker was not "fired." As a term instructor, her contract was simply not renewed. This is a neutral action on the part of the University and should not be construed as anything more.

I can understand your concern. Rest assured that Dr. Crocker has received both a fair hearing and appropriate due process.

Sincerely

Alan G. Merten

(referenced in Chapter 7)

Dear Alan:

Thank you for your letter of July 22nd, responding to mine of July 28th. I understand you to state the following:

- The matter of Dr. Crocker's academic status has been properly reviewed;
- You are reluctant to release her personnel information;
- She was not "fired" but rather her contract was not renewed.

I don't dispute any of the above. The point of my letter was not to ask whether or not there is a legal basis for the University's actions. I am sure that there is. My point was to ask whether Dr. Crocker was not renewed in her employment because of an anonymous (and erroneous) complaint that she was "teaching creationism"—an allegation that is now hampering her ability to find future employment. I am sorry that we can't obtain an answer to that inquiry.

In the meantime, I will get a formal release signed by Dr. Crocker so we can request her file. Thank you.

Sincerely,

J. Chapman Petersen

[original document]

COMMONWEALTH OF VIRGINIA

HOUSE OF DELEGATES

RICHMOND

J. CHAPMAN PETERSEN
MINORITY WHIP

COMMITTEE ASSIGNMENTS:
MILITIA, POLICE AND PUBLIC SAFETY
SCIENCE AND TECHNOLOGY

THIRTY-SEVENTH DISTRICT

August 3, 2005

Mr. Alan Merten, President
George Mason University
4400 University Drive, MS 3A1
Fairfax, VA 22030

Dear Alan:

Thank you for your letter of July 22nd, responding to mine of June 28th. I understand you to state the following:

- The matter of Dr. Crocker's academic status has been properly reviewed;
- You are reluctant to release her personnel information;
- She was not "fired" but rather her contract not renewed.

I don't dispute any of the above. The point of my letter was not to ask whether or not there is a legal basis for the University's actions. I am sure that there is. My point was to ask whether Dr. Crocker was not renewed in her employment because of an anonymous (and erroneous) complaint that she was "teaching creationism" – an allegation that is now hampering her ability to find future employment. I am sorry that we can't obtain an answer to that inquiry.

In the meantime, I will get a formal release signed by Dr. Crocker so we can request her file. Thank you.

Sincerely,

J. Chapman Petersen

JCP:smh

e. Letter from Lawyer Edward Sisson to GMU President Alan Merton (08/15/05)

(referenced in Chapter 7)

ARNOLD & PORTER LLP

Edward Sisson
Edward_Sisson@aporter.com

202.942.5495
202.942.5999 Fax

555 Twelfth Street, NW
Washington, DC 20004-1206

August 15, 2005

Dr. Alan G. Merten
President
George Mason University
4400 University Drive, MS 3A1
Fairfax, VA 22030

Dear Dr. Merten:

I represent Dr. Caroline Crocker concerning matters that I understand you have already discussed with Virginia Delegate J. Chapman Peterson. I have reviewed your July 22, 2005 letter to Del. Peterson, and his response dated August 3, 2005. There are several matters that require your most immediate and prompt attention.

First, Dr. Crocker *is currently under contract* with George Mason University ("Mason") for the upcoming fall term and thereafter through the end of the Spring term 2007. *She is entitled to and expects that Mason will timely perform all of its obligations pursuant to that contract.* The term stated on the first page of the document that Mason delivered to Dr. Crocker after the hearing on her grievance does *not* reflect the agreement that she reached with Mason in April, 2004. At that time, as Dr. Crocker's then-current term contract was in its final semester, Dr. ▮▮▮▮▮▮ offered to Dr. Crocker a new contract whose term was three years, ending at the conclusion of the Spring semester 2007. Dr. Crocker received that contract offer in her Mason mailbox on a Friday morning, immediately prior to the regular 9:30 AM lab meeting. At the beginning of that meeting she informed others present at the meeting that Mason had offered her a new three-year contract. After the meeting Dr. Crocker took that contract home, and showed the document to her husband and to another person, and each of these persons independently recall that they read therein that the term was three years. Dr. Crocker signed that contract and returned the signed original to Dr. ▮▮▮▮▮▮. She did not keep a copy. By signing and delivering the contract document that Mason had given her, Dr. Crocker formed a three-year contract with Mason.

Subsequent to her signing and delivering the three-year contract, Dr. Crocker spoke to Dr. ▮▮▮▮▮▮ about assuming an additional duty not stated in the three-year contract. Specifically, she offered to teach a second "large section of BIOL 213 Cell Biology" that Dr. ▮▮▮▮▮▮ was going to teach in the fall of 2004. ▮▮▮▮▮▮ agreed. Dr. ▮▮▮▮▮▮ stated that Dr. Crocker would have to sign a modified contract that would specify the additional teaching duties. On May 14, ▮▮▮▮▮▮

ARNOLD & PORTER LLP

Dr. Alan Merten
August 15, 2005
Page 2

approached Dr. Crocker while Dr. Crocker was in the midst of meeting with several students in a seminar room. He said that she had to sign a revised contract immediately because of an administrative deadline, and handed to her a document to sign (the "May 14 Document"). Dr. Crocker, relying on ███████████ representation that the only change in the contract was the description of the workload (the teaching of the second large section) signed the last page of the three-page May 14 Document without examining the statement of the term of the contract. ███████████ promptly took the May 14 Document from Dr. Crocker and never gave her a copy. Thus she had no opportunity to review it. Nor did she believe she needed to. She justifiably relied on the representations of her departmental superior that the only change in the contract was the teaching of the additional lecture section.

Subsequently, as you are aware if you have examined the record of Dr. Crocker's grievance, at a meeting on Dec. 16, 2004, Dr. ███████ barred Dr. Crocker from teaching the lecture class for the Spring 2005 semester. Dr. Crocker filed a grievance. In that grievance, the first remedy she requested was "Reinstatement to teaching the lecture, starting Fall, 2005." Obviously, if Dr. Crocker had believed that her contract extended only through the end of the Spring 2005 semester, which would conclude shortly after the decision on the grievance, she would not have requested this remedy. Similarly, her fourth request in the grievance, that her "annual evaluation" be conducted "by a person other than ███████████," would not have been included, because she would have understood that there would be no future "annual evaluations." And she stated in her cover letter that she had a multi-year contract.

Moreover, department administrator ███████████ sent Dr. Crocker questions about classroom requirements for Fall 2005, which demonstrates that she understood that Dr. Crocker's contract extended longer than the end of the Spring 2005 semester. And ███████████ did not demur when TAC suggested that Dr. Crocker do one grant in 2004/2005 and the next in 2005/2006.

███████████'s assertion, in his response to the grievance, that her contract expired on May 24, 2005, was the first notice Dr. Crocker had that anyone associated with Mason believed that this was the date on which her contract terminated. In her written reply to ███████████'s response, she stated that "My contract ... ends in 2007."

The document delivered to Dr. Crocker after the grievance proceeding – purportedly the May 14 Document – thus does not reflect the agreement of the parties

ARNOLD & PORTER LLP

Dr. Alan Merten
August 15, 2005
Page 3

regarding the term of the contract. Since ▓▓▓▓▓▓▓ did not alert Dr. Crocker that the May 14 Document changed the term of the contract (if, in fact, the document he presented her on May 14 *did* contain a change in the term; the front page that appears on the document delivered to Dr. Crocker after the grievance hearing may have been substituted *after* May 14), and since he presented the May 14 Document to her with the statement that she must sign it immediately so that he could comply with an administrative deadline, the document presented to Dr. Crocker after the grievance proceeding incorrectly states the *agreed* term of the contract, which is that she will remain as a term professor until May, 2007.

The Resolution of Grievance issued by Dean Struppa on May 17, 2005, states that the contract "expires in May 2005." However, the term of the contract was not raised by Dr. Crocker in her grievance, and it is outside the scope of the grievance proceedings to render binding decisions concerning the contract obligations of Mason. The facts related above were never before the grievance committee, nor was there any requirement that Dr. Crocker present those facts to the grievance committee.

Dr. Crocker has never accepted any attempt by Mason whereby Mason could shorten the term of the contract or otherwise modify or escape its contract obligations. If Mason wished to shorten the term of the contract, it was incumbent upon Mason to ask Dr. Crocker to agree to shorten the term. Mason has never made such request. Instead, Mason has attempted to cause Dr. Crocker to believe, erroneously, that Mason had a unilateral authority to change the contract term. But Mason did not have, and does not have, the authority unilaterally to reduce the contract term.

Accordingly, Dean Struppa's "finding" is incorrect. In your July 22, 2005 letter, you state that you "have every confidence in the faculty who review matters such as this, and rely on their findings." Thus, because this finding is incorrect, your reliance on that finding is misplaced. Your statement that Dr. Crocker's contract "was simply not renewed" is factually incorrect. Mason renewed her contract in April, 2004, for a term extending to late May, 2007, and that contract remains in force.

Dr. Crocker is ready, willing, and able to perform all of her duties under the contract. Dr. Crocker insists on all of her rights under that contract. If Mason refuses to honor its obligations, that act of refusal will be a breach of Mason's contract with Dr. Crocker and a repudiation of that contract and will cause severe injury and harm to Dr. Crocker. I strongly urge you to cause Mason to honor its contract on time and in every particular, *and I expect you to inform me immediately that Mason will do so.*

ARNOLD & PORTER LLP

Dr. Alan Merten
August 15, 2005
Page 4

  Second, the record clearly shows that ███████████ on Dec. 16, 2004, removed Dr. Crocker from teaching the lecture course in the Spring 2005 semester for an improper and discriminatory reason, in violation of her constitutionally-protected and statutorily-protected rights and her rights to academic freedom. Moreover, regardless of the general authority ███████████ may have had to assign teaching assignments in the Department, Dr. Crocker's contract clearly stated that she was to teach the lecture course, and thus ███████████'s discretion to remove her from the lecture course was constricted by Mason's contractual promise to Dr. Crocker, such that his removal of her from the teaching of that course caused Mason to breach its contract with Dr. Crocker, again causing her injury and harm.

  Dean Struppa found that ███████████ did not "violate[] any procedures or rules" in "assign[ing] the teaching load to Dr. Crocker," *i.e.*, removing Dr. Crocker from the lecture course for the Spring 2005 semester. But this completely misses the point. Dr. Crocker's grievance alleged that ███████████'s removing Dr. Crocker from the lecture course for the Spring 2005 semester violated Dr. Crocker's "right to unrestricted expositions of subjects (including controversial questions) within one's field ... in a professionally responsible manner ... without fear of censorship or penalty." Dean Struppa did not rule on whether Dr. ███████████ action violated Dr. Crocker's *rights*. Instead, Dean Struppa merely found that Dr. ███████████ action did not violate a Mason rule or a Mason procedure. But Dr. Crocker's complaint was not that ███████████ had failed to comply with procedures or rules, it was that the substance of ███████████'s action violated Dr. Crocker's *rights*, even if we accept for purposes of argument Dean Struppa's finding that he performed the action in a manner that followed Mason's procedural rules. Thus, Dean Struppa's May 17 Resolution of Grievance does not in fact represent a resolution of the question presented by Dr. Crocker's grievance.

  The question presented by Dr. Crocker's grievance was whether evolution and intelligent design, even if considered "controversial questions," are "subjects ... within [Dr. Crocker's] field." *See* Faculty Right and Privilege 2.12.1 (1). If those subjects are within Dr. Crocker's field, then Right and Privilege 2.12.1 (1) assures Dr. Crocker "the right to unrestricted exposition" of those subjects in the lecture course that Mason contracted with her to teach.

  ███████████ in his response to the grievance appeared to focus on whether "evolution" is properly part of the subject-matter of the lecture course in question, Biol. 213. But he never said that evolution is outside *Dr. Crocker's* field – a field which is

ARNOLD & PORTER LLP

Dr. Alan Merten
August 15, 2005
Page 5

larger than just the field covered in Biol. 213. Faculty Right and Privilege 2.12.1 (1) protects Dr. Crocker's right to teach subjects within *her* field – not just subjects within the field of a particular course that she is teaching.

Moreover, even if Faculty Right and Privilege 2.12.1 (1) only applied to subjects within the field of the course in question, ▮▮▮▮▮▮▮▮ did *not* say that the subjects of evolution *or* intelligent design are outside the field of cell structure and function, which is the stated field of Biol. 213. And had he done so, he would have been rebutted by Mason's own course catalog, which states that Biol. 213 includes "evolution of cells," and by the textbooks Mason assigned for the class, Campbell's *Biology* (the assigned text for the Fall 2004 semester) and Albert's *Essential Cell Biology* (the assigned text in previous semesters). The subject of evolution also pervades other leading textbooks, such as *Molecular Biology of the Cell*, 4th ed..

Evolution is broadly claimed by many educators to be one of the fundamental facts of biology. Thus, the fact that other courses such as Biol. 303 and Biol. 307 may address evolution in the contexts, respectively, of animal biology and of ecology, cannot be taken as demonstrating that it is inappropriate to cover evolution in the context of cell structure and function. One wonders what ▮▮▮▮▮▮▮▮'s response would be if persons opposed to the teaching of evolution cited his position here as supporting a demand that evolution **not** be taught in **any** cell biology class, because, *according to* ▮▮ ▮▮▮▮▮▮▮, evolution is not part of the field of cell biology. It should be readily apparent that ▮▮▮▮▮▮▮▮ would deny that such a statement accurately presented his position concerning evolution and cell biology.

Indeed, ▮▮▮▮▮▮▮▮ did not even assert that the *other* teachers of Biol. 213 omitted evolution from their *lectures*. He said only that the other professors omitted the word "evolution" from their *syllabi* for Biol. 213. While his statement may have been intended to lead the grievance committee to conclude that evolution was never taught in *lectures* in Biol. 213 by any other teacher, there is no basis for assuming that these other professors omitted this subject from their *lectures*. To the contrary, Mason provided to Dr. Crocker the lecture notes of a prior teacher of Biol. 213, Dr. ▮▮▮▮▮▮▮, and she discovered therein that ▮▮▮▮▮▮▮▮ taught evolution in Biol. 213. And even if some of these professors omitted evolution, ▮▮▮▮▮▮▮ provides no basis for concluding that the omission of the subject stemmed from a judgment that the subject was not properly included in the course. Omission of the subject may have reflected individual professors' judgment that other topics were simply more important to cover in the limited time available. Indeed, Dr. Crocker herself omitted the lecture in the Fall 2004 due to the

ARNOLD & PORTER LLP

Dr. Alan Merten
August 15, 2005
Page 6

needs of a grant she obtained that required her to devote the class time to a different
subject.

     If Mason justifies Dr. Crocker's removal from Biol. 213 on the grounds that
evolution may not be discussed in Biol. 213 *lectures*, we must then inquire whether other
instructors of Biol. 213 – including ███████████████ himself – have been and are being
instructed that they must not discuss evolution in *lectures* in that course, and have been or
are threatened with removal from the course if they lecture on evolution. If the results of
such an inquiry demonstrate that all teachers *except* Dr. Crocker have been and are
permitted to lecture on evolution in Biol. 213 – including ███████████████ himself – then
it will be abundantly clear that ███████████████'s action singled out Dr. Crocker,
discriminated against her, and denied her right of academic freedom.

     The reason for that unique discrimination is easy to find: it is ███████████████'s
accusation that Dr. Crocker was teaching "creationism" in her lecture. According to ███
███████████, "intelligent design" is equated with "creationism." It is this assertion that is
the cause of the discrimination against her. In equating "intelligent design" with
"creationism" ███████████████ is asserting in substance that Dr. Crocker taught religion,
not science, in a science class. She denies this, and asserts that everything she taught in
Biol. 213 was science. Dean Struppa's decision makes no ruling on this question,
perhaps because Dean Struppa apparently believed – erroneously – that ███████████████
could remove Dr. Crocker from the lecture course regardless. To the contrary, being
science, all the material Dr. Crocker taught was appropriate for the class, and she had the
right to teach it under Mason's Right and Privilege 2.12.1 (1), and under the constitutions
and statutes of the Commonwealth and of the federal government – even if some persons
believe that the scientific data she taught may lead some persons to conclusions that may
affect some religious beliefs of some people. Indeed, that very argument typically is
made to justify the teaching of natural selection as the cause of evolution: that, being
science, it must be taught in science classes, even if the teaching may lead some persons
to conclusions that may affect some religious beliefs of some people.

     Ultimately, therefore, ███████████████ discriminated against Dr. Crocker
because the scientific evidence Dr. Crocker taught might cause some persons to reach
certain conclusions regarding some religious beliefs that are contrary to the conclusions
many people reach when they are taught only the scientific evidence that ███████████████
finds acceptable. His removal of Dr. Crocker from the lecture course is an act of
religious viewpoint discrimination based on the effect he perceives her *science* teaching
may have on the *religious* beliefs of some students. Since Mason is a Virginia

ARNOLD & PORTER LLP

Dr. Alan Merten
August 15, 2005
Page 7

Commonwealth institution, federal and Commonwealth statutory and constitutional provisions apply, and they bar Mason from discriminating against Dr. Crocker in this fashion.

Dr. Crocker's right to teach the lecture course continues for the remaining term of her contract, which as we have established above, continues through the end of the Spring 2007 semester. Accordingly, in insisting that Mason honor its contract with Dr. Crocker for the Fall semester that will soon begin, and for the succeeding three semesters, please understand that this demand specifically includes the demand that Mason assign Dr. Crocker to teach the lecture course, pursuant to Mason's contract promise.

However, please also understand that we expect Mason to continue Dr. Crocker's salary payments, and to treat her as a term professor, pursuant to the contract, even if Mason disputes that the contract and the law require that Mason assign her to teach Biol. 213. In other words, we do *not* agree that Mason may escape its *payment* obligations, and its obligations to accord Dr. Crocker continuing recognition as a term professor through the end of the Spring 2007 semester, if it were determined that the scope of her contract and constitutional rights did not extend so far as to mandate that Mason must assign her to Biol. 213, but would instead allow Mason to assign her to other lab or lecture classes.

I look forward to Mason's *prompt* performance of its contract obligations, including prompt salary payments to Dr. Crocker, the scheduling of her lecture class and the selection of students for that class, and all other performance by Mason called for under the contract.

Sincerely yours,

Edward Sisson

Edward Sisson

f. E-mail from Edward Sisson to Caroline Crocker, dropping the case

(referenced in Chapter 8)

Caroline, you will recall that a few weeks ago I requested and you agreed to waive any conflict that might be created by Arnold & Porter seeking to represent George Mason in a proposed matter unrelated to our representation of you, as to which the Firm alerted you that the Firm would withdraw from representing you if George Mason accepted the Firm in that matter. George Mason has accepted the Firm in that matter, so the Firm is now withdrawing from its representation of you.

The Firm has also authorized me to let you know that I will be leaving the Firm by Jan. 7, 2006, or earlier if I so choose. I will let you know when I leave the Firm, and whether I will be in a position once I have left the Firm (i.e., if I am in private practice) to represent you again.

The Firm has also authorized me to tell you that you have the right to instruct the Firm to deliver to you, to me, to other counsel of your choosing (not Arnold & Porter counsel, of course), or to any other person the file I generated while I was representing you. To do this, you need to provide the instructions in writing direct to Richard Alexander at the Firm. This can be done simply by sending Richard an e-mail ▮▮▮▮▮▮▮▮▮▮▮▮▮ stating that you want your file to be (a) delivered to you, (b) delivered to me, (c) delivered to some other counsel of your choosing. If you do not provide any instructions, the Firm will simply store the file as it does in the normal course of business with any closed matter.

Please note that if you instruct the file to be delivered to me prior to my leaving Arnold & Porter, I will hold it not as your lawyer, but only in my personal capacity as a friend, since I not be able to serve as your legal counsel while I am still with Arnold & Porter.

Please also note that for various administrative reasons unrelated to teh Firm's relationship with you, I will be going "off" of the Firm's e-mail system, effective probably Saturday afternoon or evening. I am arranging a new personal e-mail address and will let you know what it is when I have it. My phones remain teh same: I am sorry that this e-mail has a rather formal tone, but sometimes we lawyers have to sound a bit stuffy. I look forward to enjoying your kind dinner invitation, perhaps next weekend.

Best Wishes, Edward

Index

A

B

C

D

E

R

S